MW00560533

Praise for **GLORIOUS ALCHEMY**

"To me, this book is almost beyond praise. Stunning in its perfectly balanced blend of clarity, precision, concision, erudition, and accessibility, it is simply the best book on the Lalitā Sahasranāma in the English language. This book is not merely informational, however: it is designed to have maximum impact on your spiritual life, and if you take the abundant guided meditations in this sublime work into deep practice, you may experience radical opening and transformation. Especially if you are a lover of the Goddess, this book could become the primary touchstone of your spiritual life."

—Christopher Wallis (aka Hareesh), M.Phil., Ph.D., author of *Tantra Illuminated* and *The Recognition Sutras*

"This masterful illuminating book is a gift from Devi Herself as manifested through a brilliant contemporary practitioner, Yogini and householder, Dr. Kavitha Chinnaiyan. It is a timely, accessible and empowering resource that elucidates the rich, often complex and esoteric doctrine of Śrīvidyā and opens the multivalent portals of Devi Lalitā's 1000 names in intelligent, refreshing and relatable ways. Scholars, practitioners, spiritual seekers, and laypeople within and outside the non-dual Tantric and Vedic lineage streams will all delight in the wealth of knowledge and practical applications this precious work offers. Chinnaiyan offers the reader myriad opportunities to directly access and understand the Divine Mother and the infinite nuances and emanations of Her Reality through both knowledge and experience. In short, LSN is more than a book; it is a living revelation for which those who love Devi, those who wish to deepen their relationship with Her, and those who have yet to remember Her, have all been waiting."

—Laura Amazzone, author of *Goddess Durga and Sacred Female Power*

Praise for GLORIOUS ALCHEMY

"*Glorious Alchemy* provides foundational insights on Śākta Tantric practice, incorporating rituals with narratives that ground the practice of Tripurasundarī or Śrīvidya in Tantric esotericism. In so doing, the text details the essential aspects that constitute the pantheon of Lalitā. Over the course of my studies and teaching, I have always felt the need for an introductory text that engages the practitioners' perspectives, provides textual background for ritual dynamics and helps scholars to ground what the 'insiders' actually mean when they discuss practice. This text attempts to fill this lacuna. Broadly speaking, the polarity of orthodoxy and orthopraxy merges in a lived Hindu cultural experience where no text is sufficient without a teacher and no teaching is complete in isolation of texts. While Kavitha provides the manual for the Śākta vision, this keeps in mind the living aspect of Tantrism and the significance of in-person teaching. Kavitha's text is accessible while addressing some of the most esoteric domains of Śrīyantra, Śrīvidya, and the phonetic body of the Goddess, expressed in her one thousand names. Surely this does not replace the Agamas, as it underscores the central teachings of the Śākta Agamas. It nonetheless paves the path for the advanced students to directly engage in the classical texts. Written in lucid English with illustrations and charts, the text is a must-read for understanding Śākta Tantrism. I am confident that Śākta aspirants as well as scholars seeking insider perspectives on Śākta Tantrism will find this text invaluable."

—Dr. Sthaneshwar Timalsina, Professor, Religious Studies, San Diego University

"The recitation of the thousand names of the Divine Mother known as the Lalitā Sahasranāma is one of the most powerful and popular spiritual practices among devotees of the Goddess. The background for these names is the sophisticated system of non-dualistic Tantra known as Śrīvidyā. Because of its complexity and the secrecy of many of its lineages, Śrīvidyā has remained mostly an enigma to the uninitiated. In *Glorious Alchemy*, Dr. Kavitha Chinnaiyan introduces the esoteric philosophy, metaphysics, mythology, devotional sentiment, and yogic discipline of this profound tradition with elegant clarity. With the humility and respect of a devoted practitioner and the rationality of an educator, she makes the divine names come alive, showing how the Lalitā Sahasranāma reveals a path back to the Great Mother. This book is an invaluable blessing to those interested in tantra, yoga, nonduality, the divine feminine, and the Hindu worship of the Goddess. This is the book I wish I could have written."

—Rev. Dr. Swami Bhajanananda Saraswati, Head Priest and Dean of Seminary, Kali Mandir Ramakrishna Ashram, Laguna Beach, California

"Simply beautiful! I wholeheartedly recommend this monumental work on Śrīvidyā. Going over the manuscript repeatedly reminded me of the profound works by illustrious sadhakas of the past including Bhaskar Rai and Karpatri Maharaj. Particularly if you haven't been initiated into Śrīvidyā and wish to get a glimpse of its vastness, *Glorious Alchemy: Living the Lalitā Sahasranāma* by Kavitha Chinnaiyan (Saundrambika) is a read you can't afford to miss."

—Om Swami

"To prepare the reader for a meaningful experience of the thousand names of the Divine Mother, the author begins with a detailed presentation of the Tantric philosophy of the Śrīvidyā tradition. Her remarkable clarity is made all the more vivid by her enthusiasm and engaging style. All this leads to the thousand names themselves in the original Sanskrit with an excellent translation. Parallel to the text of the Lalitā Sahasranāma, a running commentary gives context and continuity to the names, bringing out the narrative power of their imagery. As a reference work *Glorious Alchemy* is a source of information to which the reader will return again and again; as a devotional manual it inspires; and as a guide to meditative practice it provides effective, step-by-step instruction to the spiritual seeker. In short, this is a work of lasting value."

—Devadatta Kali, author of *In Praise of the Goddess: The Devimahatmya and its Meaning*

Praise for GLORIOUS ALCHEMY

"For centuries, the Lalitā Sahasranāma, Śrīvidyā Tantra's exquisite thousand-name celebration of the Great Goddess, has ranked among the most powerful invocations in world religion. Yet it has also been one of the hardest to comprehensively grasp, with many of its myriad secrets, depths and revelations hovering persistently beyond the reach of even seasoned practitioners. So, in effectively bridging that gulf, Kavitha Chinnaiyan's *Glorious Alchemy* accomplishes the nearly impossible. Dr. Chinnaiyan—schooled and experienced in both traditional Śrīvidyā practice and modern Western pedagogy—expertly plumbs the cultural and philosophical concepts that underlie the Sahasranāma, while also unveiling its governing patterns and logic. The result is a fresh yet erudite, systematic yet devotionally charged revelation that brings an ancient prayer, and an intimate vision of the Goddess herself, vividly to life."

—Michael M. Bowden, author of *The Goddess and the Guru;* editor, *Gifts from the Goddess;* co-founder, *Shakti Sadhana.*

"The Śrī Lalitā Sahasranāma (LSN) contains the thousand names of Śrī Lalitā Mahātripurasundarī, beautifully sequenced to show the progress of Her worship in various forms to the formless. Although many recite the LSN with devotion, very few understand them, let alone well. Dr. Kavitha Chinnaiyan (Saundaryāmbā), a professional medical practitioner, is also an ardent practitioner of Śrīvidyā Tantra and has devoted her time to understanding the LSN in depth. Her educational background in medicine and science as well as the pursuit of Śrīvidyā makes her uniquely placed to explain many of the esoteric significances of LSN in scientific terms, and this book will surely help devotees to develop a deeper appreciation of the amazing knowledge hidden therein. May Devī's abundant grace shower upon Saundaryāmbā for many more such illuminating works that will bring joy and understanding in the hearts of those seeking the Mother."

—Sridevi Gayathri Ramesh (Amruteshwariamba) and Ramesh Natarajan (Amriteshwarananda), *GRD Iyers GuruCool*

Praise for **GLORIOUS ALCHEMY**

"There are so many reasons why this book is groundbreaking, authoritative and highly recommended. Out of all these reasons it is Dr. Kavitha Chinnaiyan's personal connection to Devi, her experience of Śrī Vidyā sadhana, and her ability to make this most esoteric subject accessible to the beginner practitioner that make this book so valuable amongst the plethora of scholarly works currently available. Besides containing one of the best overviews of the View of nondual Tantra I have ever come across, this workbook also includes many self-reflective exercises that assist in integrating the more esoteric aspects of Śrī Vidyā with moment to moment experience. With her newest book Kavitha-ji has made a fantastic contribution to the literature of spiritual practice, and I wholeheartedly recommend her new book to the beginner on the path of Tantra as well as to the seasoned practitioner.

May All Beings Benefit from this work! Jaya Mā!"

—Dharma Bodhi Tantrik Yogi, Trika Mahāsiddha Yoga

"Both a stunning love letter to the Goddess, as well as an in-depth introduction to the philosophy of the Śrīvidyā path, this is a book many of us have eagerly been waiting for. Through Kavitha's brilliant and generous guidance, we are initiated into an intimacy with the luminous Lalitā Sahasranāma, which ultimately offers us a path home to who we in our deepest essence truly are."

—Chameli Ardagh, Founder, AwakeningWomen.com

"A dynamic and accessible introduction to a foundational Śrīvidyā text, Chinnaiyan's words scintillate with the kind of lively precision and understanding that can only be forged through the fire of deep Sādhanā. In her second book, she soars to new heights of philosophical articulation and distills the esoteric significance of litany chanting with a sweetness and authenticity rarely exhibited in spiritual texts written for a popular audience. Anyone who considers themselves a 'yogi' should read this book."

—Jacob Kyle, Founder, *Embodied Philosophy*

GLORIOUS ALCHEMY

Living the Lalitā Sahasranāma

A Practical Manual of Śrīvidyā

Kavitha Chinnaiyan, MD

Foreword by Sri Chaitanyananda Natha Sarasvati

NEW SARUM PRESS

UNITED KINGDOM

GLORIOUS ALCHEMY

First edition published January 2020 by New Sarum Press

https://kavithamd.com/

Illustrations by Rashmi Thirtha Jyoti
www.shaktikalaya.com

New Sarum Press | 6 Folkestone Road | Salisbury | SP2 8JP | United Kingdom
ISBN: 978-1-9993535-8-2
www.newsarumpress.com

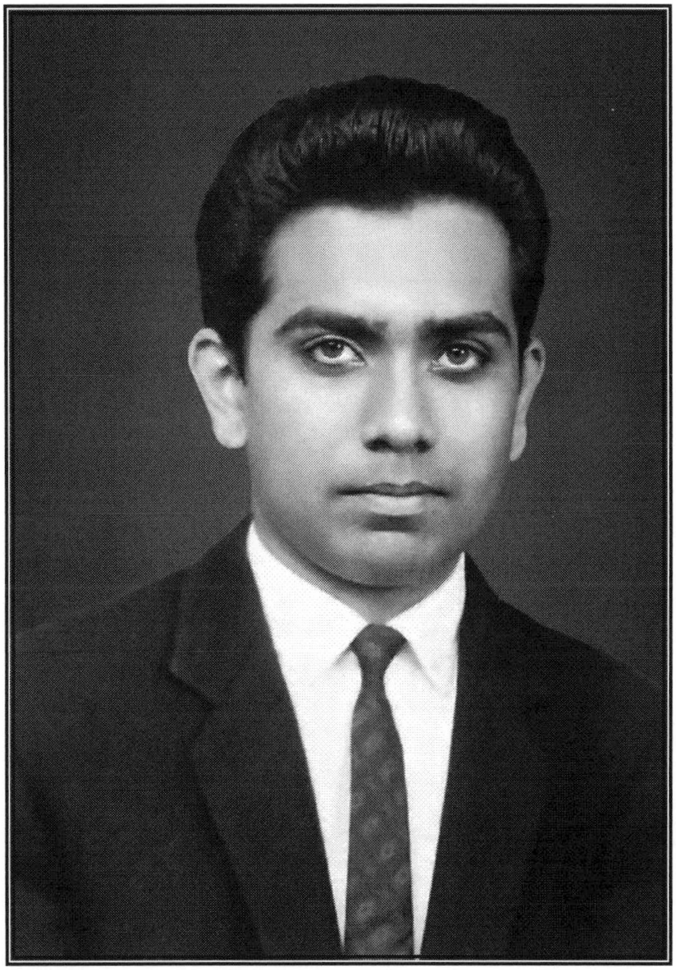

In loving memory of my father, M.S. Nataraj,
who modeled divine alchemy

Invocation

Gaṇeśa-graha-nakṣatra-yoginī-rāśi-rūpiṇīm |
Devīm mantra-mayīm naumi mātṛkāṁ pīṭha-rūpiṇīm ||

I humbly bow to that supreme Devī who is the embodiment of the gaṇeśas, planets, stellar configurations, yoginīs, constellations, mantras, the matrix of language, and sacred sites.

–Nityā Śodaṣikārṇava 1:1

gaṇeśa = the ruler of groups of beings

graha = planets

nakṣatra = stellar configurations

yoginī = goddess of perfection in yoga

rāśi = mass; also constellations

rūpiṇīm = form of

devīṁ = Devī

mantra = sacred sound

mayīṁ = composed of

naumi = I humbly bow

mātṛkaṁ = matrix of language

pīṭha = sacred sites

rūpiṇīm = form of

Dedication

This work is a humble offering of love and devotion at the lotus feet of my beloved guru, Śrī Jñānāmbika Sahita Śrī Caitanyānanda Nātha Sarasvatī (affectionately known as Haran Aiya), the pīṭhādhipatī of the Rājarājeśvarī Pīṭham in Rush, NY.

Śrī Gurubhyo Namah!

Foreword

The Lalitā Sahasranāma (LSN) is one of the most important texts for lovers of the Goddess on the path of Srividya. It has been said* that the mere desire to chant LSN, is the result of many meritorious and devoted actions in thousands of previous births. Saundaryāmba, (Dr. Kavitha Chinnaiyan) is blessed to have undertaken the monumental task of writing this book while skilfully balancing her professional and family responsibilities as well as engaging in deep sādhanā and teaching.

This book sets forth a road map of unparalleled clarity to negotiate this esoteric and highly uplifting spiritual knowledge. Until now, this knowledge has not been available to all because ancient seers have chosen to keep it hidden in coded language, whereby it unfolds in a gradual, steady sequence. In the case of the LSN, the Vāgdevatās [the goddesses of language] have couched the chant in levels of meaning that must be decoded in a particular sequence as the aspirant continues his or her sādhanā on the path. This unfolding occurs as the primordial power rises up from the lower cakras, absorbing the various tattvas and dissolving the karmic impressions associated with each. This process is followed in this book, where the aspirant is blessed with new insights and meanings of the nāmas in the LSN that were previously unknown.

* By Nedumindi Subrahmanya Iyer, a giant in Sri Vidya,

The section on the darśana, including the kośas, Kuṇḍalinī, and the associated concepts, is organized and explained in a language that is accessible to young and old and to sādhakas across generations. The author has successfully dissected and explained complex issues like the granthis—a normally difficult subject to navigate in a work of this nature. With the help of her intimate and intuitive knowledge of human anatomy as well as the vidyā, she has bridged the often hazy philosophical and scientific gap that is missing in traditional commentaries.

My sincere prayers to the Parā Devatā that Saundaryāmba will produce more and more extremely useful works of this nature.

Caitanyānanda
Sri Rajarajeswari Pitham
Rush, NY

Table of Contents

In Memoriam, M.S. Nataraj ix
Invocation x
Dedication x
Foreword xi
Preface xxv
Acknowledgements xxvii
Introduction xxix
- Is formal initiation (dīkṣa) necessary to chant the LSN? xxx
- Who is this book for? xxx
- How to use this book xxxii
- Layout of the book xxxiii
- Invoking Devī xxxiv
- Chanting the LSN xxxiv

Sanskrit Pronunciation Guide xxxvi
- The ṣadanga xxxvi

Part I: The Darśana (View) 1

Chapter 1 3

How the Lalitā Sahasranāma Came to Be 3
Lalitopākhyāna 3
The Vanity of Indra 4
The Rise of Bhaṇḍāsura 5
Devī's Conquest of Bhaṇḍāsura 7
The Magic of the Lalitā Sahasranāma 8

Chapter 2 11

What is Srīvidyā, Really? 11
The Many Facets of Worship 11
The Śrīvidyā Mantra 12
Devī's Forms 12
History of Śrīvidyā 13

Chapter 3 15

Śiva and Śakti 15
Prakāśa and Vimarśa 17
Non-duality 19
Suffering and Freedom 20

Chapter 4 23

The Descent of Creation 23
Kañcukas and Malas 26
Saṃskāra 28
Karma 29
Bhaṇḍāsura and the Āṇava Mala 31

Chapter 5 32

The Ascent of Sādhanā 32
The Impure Path 32
The Pure Path 33
Paths and Means 34
Śuddha Vidyā and the Bindu 34

Chapter 6 36

Śarīrās, Prāṇa and kośas 36
Śarīrās 36
Prāṇa 37
Koṣas 40

Chapter 7 43

Cakras and Kuṇḍalinī 43
Kuṇḍalinī 45
Granthis 47
Puruṣārtha 49
Ānanda 50

Chapter 8 52

Vāk 52
Mātṛkā and Mālinī 54
States of Consciousness 57
Jāgrat 57
Svapna 57
Suṣupti 58
Turya 58
Turyatītā 58
Language in Sādhanā 59

Chapter 9 60

The Śrīcakra in Manifestation 60
Bindu, the Stateless State 60

The Deities of the Śrīcakra 63
Trikoṇa 63
Vasukoṇa 65
Antardaśara, Bahirdaśara, Manvaśra 66
Aṣṭadaḷapadma, Ṣodaśadaḷapadma, and Bhūpura 67

Chapter 10 68

The Śrīcakra in Practice 68
Bhūpura 68
Trivṛtta 70
Ṣodaśadaḷapadma 71
Aṣṭadaḷapadma 71
Manvaśra 71
Bahirdaśara 73
Antardaśara 74
Vasukoṇa 75
Devī's Implements 76
Trikoṇa 76
Bindu 77
Kāmakalā 78

Chapter 11 80

Ācāras 80
Ācāra Prescription 81

Chapter 12 83

The Sādhanā in Śrīvidyā 83
Sthūla 83

Sūkṣma 83
Parā or Vāsanā 83
Bhāvanā 84
Mantra Sādhanā (Japa) 84
Dīkṣa (Initiation) 86
Bhakti (Devotion) 88
Discernment 89
Tarka 90
Rasa 91
Transmutation of Desire 92

Part II: Living the Lalitā Sahasranāma 95

Śrīṃ Meditation 96
Dhyāna Mantras of Devī 97

Section 1

Devī's Sthūla (Gross) Form 100
Bhāvanā on Devī's Sthūla Form 113

Section 2

Devī and Bhaṇḍāsura 114
Bhāvanā on the Internal War 119

Section 3

Devī in the Kulas 120
Bhāvanā on the Kula 124

Section 4

Devī's Auspiciousness 125
Bhāvanā on Auspiciousness 127

Section 5

Devī as Nirguṇa (Formless) 128
Bhāvanā on Nirguṇa and Saguṇa 132

Section 6

Devī's Powers 133
Bhāvanā on Time 136

Section 7

Devī's Omnipresence 137
Bhāvanā on Devī's Presence 141

Section 8

Devī as the Bīja Mantra 142
Bhāvanā on Beauty 145

Section 9

Devī as Kṣetra and Kṣetrajña 146
Bhāvanā on Kleśas 150

Section 10

Devī as Vāk 151
Bhāvanā on Vāk 154

Section 11

Devī in the Bindu 155
Bhāvanā on Śṛṅgāra 161

Section 12

Devī in the Cakras 162
Bhāvanā on Tapas 167

Section 13

Devī as the Sahasrāra 168
Bhāvanā on Equanimity 172

Section 14

Devī in Yoga 173
Bhāvanā on Karma 178

Section 15

Devī's Esoteric Forms 179
Bhāvanā on Space 182

Section 16

Devī as Transformation 183
Bhāvanā on Entrapment and Freedom 187

Section 17

Devī's Great Forms 188
Bhāvanā on Prāṇa 192

Section 18

Devī as Transcendence and Immanence 193
Bhāvanā on Offering the Perishable 196

Section 19

Devī's Omnipresence 197
Bhāvanā on Dhana (Wealth) 200

Section 20

Devī's Supremacy in the Bindu 201
Bhāvanā on śṛṅgāra 207

Part III: The Lalitā Sahasranāma 209

Resources 248

List of Illustrations and Figures

1. Lord Hayagrīva 4
2. Śrīcakra 7
3. Ardhanarīśvara 16
4. The One Reality Becoming Three 18
5. Tattva Map 24
6. The Cycle of Karma 29
7. The Ascent of Sādhanā 33
8. Malas, Śarīras and Karma 37
9. Prāṇa Vāyūs 39
10. Mahāśakti, Prāṇaśakti, Prāṇa Vāyū 40
11. Kośas (Vedāntik) 40
12. Kośas (Tāntrik) 42
13. Kuṇḍalinī 45
14. Granthis 48
15. Descent of Vāk 52
16. Mātṛkā 55
17. Vāk, Mātṛkā and Mālini 55
18. Bindu 62
19. Trikoṇa 63
20. Vasukoṇa 66
21. Antardaśara, Bahirdaśara, Manvaśra 67
22. Aṣṭadaḷapadma, Śodaṣadaḷapadma, Bhūpura 67
23. Śrīcakra in Samhāra Krama 69
24. Kāmakalā 79
25. Ācārās 81
26. Mantra Sādhanā 85
27. Stations in Japa 86
28. Śrīṃ Meditation 96
29. Vimarśa Triad 101

30. AHAM-MAHA ... 101
31. Kūṭas of the Pañcadaśi ... 120
32. Kleśas ... 149

List of Meditations and Bhāvana

1. Śrīṃ Meditation ... 96
2. Devī's Sthūla Form ... 113
3. Internal War ... 119
4. Kula ... 124
5. Auspiciousness ... 127
6. Nirguṇa and Saguṇa ... 132
7. Time ... 136
8. Devī's Presence ... 141
9. Beauty ... 145
10. Kleśas ... 150
11. Vāk ... 154
12. Śṛṅgāra ... 161
13. Tapas ... 167
14. Equanimity ... 172
15. Karma ... 178
16. Space ... 182
17. Entrapment and Freedom ... 187
18. Prāṇa ... 192
19. Offering the Perishable ... 196
20. Dhana (Wealth) ... 200
21. Śṛṅgāra ... 207

Preface

What's New About This Work?

What you hold in your hands is an experiment, and a bold one. Since the *Lalitā Sahasranāma* (referred to as LSN in this work) first appeared in written form, prolific scholars and lovers of God have offered valuable commentaries on it. What can I, an ordinary practitioner, add to this body of work? In terms of interpretation or groundbreaking new insights, the answer is… nothing!

You may wonder what my qualifications are to even attempt this book. I've wondered that too. Unlike many devotees of the LSN, I didn't grow up listening to it. It was taught at the local Chinmaya Mission center where I studied Advaita Vedānta as an adult, but even then I focused steadfastly on the main texts of that tradition such as the *Bhagavad Gītā* and Ādi Śaṅkarācārya's *Vivekacūḍāmaṇī*. The LSN never stuck in my mind, and I made no effort to memorize or learn it.

It was years later that I met my guru and became a Śrīvidyā upāsaka (practitioner). A few weeks after he gave me dīkṣa (initiation, see below), I boarded a cross-country flight and promptly fell asleep.

A Gift of Grace

Mid-flight, I woke up hearing the LSN being recited in the spaces of my mind. It flowed flawlessly from start to finish, each verse clearly and melodiously articulated by a sweet female voice. Every nāma (name) was as if encased in a ray of light, and its meaning arose spontaneously with it. What had been an esoteric chant until then became tangible, personal, and immediately relevant to my life and sādhanā (spiritual practice). The goddess wasn't a distant ideal; she was the ecstatic pulse of life in the here-and-now.

Devī as Rājarājeśvarī at the Śrīvidyā temple in Rush, NY

This miraculous incident was clearly a gift of grace, and it marked a significant turn of events. I was as if possessed by the LSN and it became a treasured daily practice. The automatic chanting didn't happen again but I was able to memorize it fairly easily after this spiritual kick-start. It stirred up a deep curiosity and longing to learn more. Why are the nāmas arranged in this particular order? How is this nāma relevant to my life at the moment? What does this verse mean, really, beyond the mythological context? The more I chanted, the greater was the longing to know. I'd scour books, manuscripts and texts to dig into the meaning of just one nāma.

Often, a nāma would reveal itself in a dream or an ordinary conversation with a patient or a colleague. Sometimes, an entire set of nāmas would suddenly rearrange itself in my mind's eye, as if unlocking a series of doors of deeper understanding. At times, a particular nāma would hold on to its secrets for days, becoming the focus of my meditations and reveries. At other times, another nāma would nudge me out of deep sleep. Whether cooking, bathing, or driving, the LSN became my constant companion and a gateway to ecstasy, deep peace, and increasing joy. It continues to be the springboard for deepening bhāvanā and inquiry.

This book is not an attempt to reinterpret this magnificent chant. Instead, what I hope to present here is an understanding of this great text in a simple, practical, and systematic way that may be useful for other practitioners.

Acknowledgements

This work is a distillation of teachings and transmissions which I've had the great good fortune of receiving in my journey to Devī from my guru, Sri Chaitanyananda Natha Sarasvati (Haran Aiya). The personification of Devī's infinite compassion (avyāja karuṇāmūrtih, N992), Aiya's love, grace, and generosity have shaped my sādhanā and life in remarkable ways. This book is entirely the product of his love and encouragement. While any of its virtue is due entirely to Aiya's profound transmission, the faults of this work are mine alone.

My deep bows to my entire guru maṇḍala and the teachers and role-models who have graced my life and sādhanā, including Swami Chinmayananda whose writings on Advaita Vedānta readjusted my thinking, Greg Goode, whose teachings on the Direct Path resulted in a deep and permanent shift, Dr. Sumit Kesarkar, whose teachings on Ayurveda and Tantra changed the way I perceive medicine, the world and myself, Śrī Śivapremānandaji who introduced me to Śrīvidyā, and Paul Muller-Ortega, whose teachings on Non-Dual Śaiva Tantra have resulted in new levels of understanding and clarity. I continue to learn and benefit from these incredible teachers.

This work would not have been possible without the support of so many of my students, who inspire me to think of creative ways to make ancient, lineage-based wisdom applicable to daily life. My humble bows to this incredible group of dedicated practitioners whose curiosity and openness prod me to refine my writing and teaching. Their love for this text and Devī was the fuel for this work. My special thanks to Kadambari Maa, who initiated this process by painstakingly transcribing my classes on the *Lalitā Sahasranāma*.

I'm deeply grateful to my beloved friends: Rashmi Thirtha Jyoti, whose spectacular cover art and illustrations have elevated this book to a higher level, Brian Campbell, for his invaluable comments on this manuscript and encouragement throughout the writing process, and David Kuttruff, who was always willing to help refine what I wanted to convey in this work. I'm especially indebted to Hareesh (Christopher) Wallis for lovingly looking over the whole manuscript and making excellent suggestions, and Aaron Michael Ullrey for going over the IAST* in detail. Any errors that remain (as they always do!) are mine alone.

My thanks to Catherine and Julian Noyce of New Sarum Press for not only making this work possible, but for their astonishing creativity, sense of humor, and friendship.

To say I'm thankful for my family would be an understatement. My unending gratitude goes to my

* International Alphabet of Sanskrit Transliteration. IAST is most commonly used in texts and in academic work, and has been in use for more than a century in books and journals on classical Indian studies.

wonderful husband Arul, to my beautiful daughters Anya and Annika, and our adorable dog Bella Māyā—thank you for putting up with me while I was juggling a full-time job and writing this book—all of which left no time for fun. My special thanks to my daughter Annika who helped with formatting and double-checking the text for errors. I bow to my parents, Geetha and Nataraj, for their undying love and support.

Finally, my eternal deep and humble bows to Devī, who flawlessly brings everything to fruition.

Saundaryāmbikā (Kavitha Chinnaiyan)
Guru Pūrṇimā, 2019
Rochester, NY

Introduction

The Lalitā Sahasranāma isn't just a pleasant chant that strings together 1,000 names (or nāmas, as they're called) of the goddess. The nāmas contain the entire philosophy and practice of the ancient tradition of Śrīvidyā (see Chapter 2), a path to liberation. Liberation from what, you ask? From the limitations of living and dying as beings subject to time and space and the suffering inherent in these limitations (see Chapter 3).

Ordinarily, we think of ourselves as a person with a particular body-mind, coming from a specific family, culture, history, and a series of life experiences. The story of "me" is so mesmerizing that we're like actors that forget that we are not the movie character. Instead, we become subject to the storyline of the movie, with its cycles of joy and sorrow, and pleasure and pain. Liberation is freedom from taking ourselves to be a character and discovering that our true essence is the same as that of the goddess. This is the possibility that is presented to us in the Lalitā Sahasranāma (LSN). It is, first and foremost, a manual for the attainment of liberation.

Chanting or listening to the LSN is a treasured practice among lovers of the goddess (Devī*, as she will be called in this book), for its beauty and the sweetness it evokes. What we can easily miss is that it is instantly applicable to daily life. It is sweet and beautiful because it catapults us out of our ordinary way of being, which revolves around our immediate concerns related to work, family, relationships, political and social climates, and so on. For the duration of the chant, we are touched by something far greater than the humdrum of daily life. Most often, the afterglow dissipates shortly after we have finished chanting, when we go back to engage with our immediate concerns. In this way, sādhanā remains separate from life, the two walled off from each other.

If we can view the LSN through the lens of the philosophy on which it is expounded, it breaks open the barriers that keep sādhanā separate from life. The nāmas pour into the moment-to-moment unfolding of life, which becomes infused with Devī's radiant presence. Instead of being hindrances to liberation, our challenging life circumstances become the doorways to freedom, and sādhanā becomes a 24/7 activity. Each of the thousand nāmas of the LSN is a mantra. When we invite the nāmas into our inner landscape, the LSN becomes a garland of mantras, where every life experience is rendered sacred because it can be found in the velvety folds of the chant. The beautiful, the profane, the unacceptable, the terrible, the must-have, and the avoid-at-all-costs events that make up our lives become enjoyable. Yes, enjoyable! To become worthy of this garland and to radiate its exquisite fragrance as we move through life, we must approach it with reverence and curiosi-

* Devī is the word used for any goddess. In this book, Devī specifically refers to Lalitā Mahātripurasundarī (see Chapter 2).

ty that extends beyond the brief periods of time that we engage in its recitation.

Is formal initiation (dīkṣa) necessary to chant the LSN?

Dīkṣa

- Derived from two roots that mean "to give" and "to destroy."
- Initiation on the spiritual path.
- Guru imparts a mantra that is empowered by the lineage and his/her own power of sādhanā.
- The bulk of the aspirant's karma (see below) is neutralized.
- S/he attains the ability and the means to attain freedom in this very life.

One question that comes up often is whether we need to be initiated in Śrīvidyā to chant or study the LSN. The short answer is, it depends (see Chapter 12 for more on dīkṣa). Some Śrīvidyā lineages adhere to the requirement for initiation, quoting textual references that support this view.

In other Śrīvidyā lineages (including the one into which I'm initiated), the LSN is available to all. The philosophy here is that since the entire universe is Devī's body (as we will discover), how can anyone be excluded from her embrace? In this approach, the firm faith is that if and when dīkṣa is deemed necessary, Devī will facilitate it by manifesting the right guru in the sādhaka's life. This is the absolute, unwavering faith and generosity that mark the guru maṇḍala* of my lineage. In concordance with this lineage, the bottom line is that you can chant the LSN whether you are an initiate or not.

Who is this book for?

The purpose of this book is to make the LSN accessible to anyone who has an interest in it, or in Śrīvidyā, non-duality, and the goddess—it is also for you if you are a Śrīvidyā initiate, of course. Even if you're already very well-versed with the philosophy and practices of Śrīvidyā, you may find this work useful, particularly the flow of the narrative of the nāmas. If you are such a sādhaka, you already know that many aspects of the LSN are extremely esoteric and complex, and perhaps this way of reading it may open up new ways of inquiry for you.

This book is also for you if you aren't an initiate but are deeply drawn to Devī. Perhaps you've grown up listening to the LSN. Maybe you heard it somewhere and fell in love with it. Maybe you're curious. In every case, this work may help facilitate a deepening of your practice and understanding of the LSN. In fact, if this book has found its way to you, it is clearly for you!

It is the kind of book I would have liked to have read while struggling to understand the vast discipline of Śrīvidyā through the LSN. Most LSN

* Lineage of gurus.

commentaries I read did not lay out the nuances of Śrīvidyā coherently, making frequent departures into esoteric concepts or topics that aren't necessarily useful for sādhanā. Many commentaries don't explain why the nāmas appear as they do in the LSN, or how the nāma sequence is relevant to sādhanā .

Darśana

- ➢ Map of the path.
- ➢ Lays out how the path views reality, the universe, the individual and the purpose of sādhanā.

In order to understand the LSN, we must begin with the *darśana* or View (note the capital V)—what is the LSN about, really? What is the purpose of praising a deity beyond the temporary effects of feeling good? What is the esoteric significance of mythology in the context of sādhanā? Is there a deeper significance to ritual? How must we meditate or engage with mantra?

Some commentaries are replete with references to rituals that may be unfamiliar to many practitioners. While there is great value in ritual worship (which is explored at some depth in Chapter 12), it is entirely possible to become so entangled in it as to lose sight of the View and the grand purpose of the LSN, which is *svatantra.** Of course, many of the concepts in the LSN make sense from the specific perspective of Śrīvidyā, but what if one is not an

Svatantra

- ➢ Absolute freedom and independence, which is the essential nature of the Divine.
- ➢ The Divine is our essential nature. This means absolute freedom and independence is our essential nature.
- ➢ The purpose of this path is to discover this, our essential Divine nature!

initiate? Can the LSN still be useful to a non-initiate? With a deeper study of the LSN, particularly in the context of the *darśana*, we come to see that even without *dīkṣa*, it has the capacity to catapult us out of our limitations. *Dīkṣa* does supercharge the process, but this doesn't mean that the LSN can't be useful for everyone interested in liberation!

At this point, it may be reassuring to know that no sādhaka in this area has to be a Sanskrit scholar or have academic qualifications to be immersed in LSN. As with any tradition, though, we do need a scholarly side and some basic mental discipline to understand the texts and teachings. The purpose of this work is not to inundate you with scholarly references or academic viewpoints (or the nuances of Sanskrit)—if you're interested in furthering your knowledge in these areas, please turn to the Resources section at the end of the book.

* Svatantra—freedom

How to use this book

1. **Read from cover to cover or begin with Part II**
   You can read this book cover to cover, spending time with each of the foundational principles presented in Part I before moving on to the nāmas. Or, you can begin with the nāmas in Part II and refer back to the foundational principles as they arise. I highly recommend reading Chapters 3-7 at least cursorily, because comprehending the concepts presented in them will help greatly with understanding of the LSN.

2. **Practice the Śrīm meditation every day**
   A Tāntrik meditation practice is provided in Part II as it relates to the first (and most important) nāma—Śrīmātā. A guided audio meditation can be accessed when you buy this book. My suggestion is to practice this daily for 10-15 minutes.

3. **Listen to the LSN audio**
   An audio recording of the whole LSN is provided for daily listening and chanting.

   Additional audio clips are provided for each segment of nāmas as it appears in this book to facilitate memorization in smaller bits. If you choose to work with one segment, listen to the corresponding audio recording, practice the bhāvanā related to it, and read the relevant sections in Part I. The most effective way to invite in the magic of the LSN is to listen to it or chant it regularly. Effortlessly, the nāmas begin to dance in our consciousness, forming gateways to svatantra. The LSN is provided in verse format at the end of this book to facilitate your learning.

4. **Journal**
   Journaling is an incredibly useful practice, especially when combined with bhāvanā (see Chapter 12). Writing helps the mind to slow down so that we can undertake a deep examination of our mental processes.

5. **Contemplate a particular nāma that appeals to you**
   Refer to Part III if a particular nāma comes to mind (as it will) as you go about your day. Contemplate its meaning in the context in which it arose, and the nāma will reveal its distinctive meaning as it relates to *your* life. Your understanding of a nāma in this fashion is far more useful than what anyone else says about it! Devī speaks to each of us in unique ways, which becomes the basis for this intimate relationship. The garland of nāmas becomes uniquely yours, which is what makes the LSN so incredibly valuable for sādhanā.

Layout of the Book

This work is presented in three parts; Part I consists of 12 chapters that present some of the important aspects of Non-dual Tantra, which form the basis for understanding the LSN. It is richly illustrated with tables and graphs to help you comprehend these concepts, and is meant to be a primer for furthering independent study.

Part II is a commentary on the thousand nāmas laid out in 20 segments. Each segment examines a group of nāmas that pertain to a particular theme. These groupings are not set in stone, and merely reflect my understanding of them. You may choose to group them differently.

Most commentaries explore each nāma through the lens of various other texts and teachings. In this model, every nāma stands on its own with no apparent relationship to the one(s) that precede or follow it. While this kind of examination provides a multi-faceted meaning to a given nāma, its relevance in the context of the flow of understanding is lost. While the rich examination of every nāma from the perspective of other scriptural references is interesting, particularly to scholars, it tends to become tedious and confusing for an average practitioner whose primary goal is deepening personal sādhanā and its bearing on life. What is unique about this commentary is that it is a running narrative as it relates to sādhanā . Each nāma is linked to the one before and the one after, as well as to the others in the LSN. Part II repeatedly refers back to Part I where a given concept is explained in depth. Extensive citations provide additional clarity.

Most segments in Part II contain a suggested contemplative practice (bhāvanā) as it relates to the grouping of the nāmas. How is this segment relevant to sādhanā? Does it deepen understanding of the concept expounded in the segment? How does this segment relate to the one before and the one following? These are some of the questions to work with as you read the running narrative.

If you want to quickly look up a particular nāma, turn to Part III, where you'll find just the nāmas and meanings without the commentary. Part III also contains the whole LSN in Sanskrit transliteration (IAST).*

* International Alphabet of Sanskrit Transliteration. IAST is most commonly used in texts and in academic work, and has been in use for more than a century in books and journals on classical Indian studies.

Invoking Devī

As with any other sādhanā, there are two ways to approach the LSN. The first is to chant it without bothering with its deeper meaning. It's indeed possible to chant it very well without really understanding or applying it to life. In this case, it becomes a tool to feel good (usually temporarily) and can become another prop for the ego (which we'll explore at length soon!).

The more valuable way to chant it is to understand it in ever-deepening practice so that it transforms us at the most fundamental level. If the LSN is deeply studied and applied in sādhanā and in life itself, no other practice would be needed for liberation. This is the approach explored in this book.

The word Lalitā means playful. The LSN evokes lightness and playfulness when we practice with it. Lalitā Devī's primary injunction for her sahasranāma is to have fun with it! However, the uniqueness of this practice is that its fruit is directly proportional to the degree of reverence we have for it. For the sādhanā of the LSN to be successful, we must approach it as a living, breathing ideal that opens itself, nāma-by-nāma, to receive our love and adoration. What would we do if Devī appeared before us in all her glory, ready to be worshiped? Imagine that you're chanting the LSN and look up to see Devī standing in front of you, blindingly brilliant and resplendent with her implements, her rosy complexion, and benevolent smile. Would your mind be wandering to your dozens of unfinished tasks or shopping lists? What would you be willing to offer her? Wouldn't you conduct yourself with uncompromising reverence and wonder?

That is the feeling we must work towards evoking when we engage with this sādhanā. Reverence directs our attention to the task at hand, and forces us to cultivate single-pointedness, which is a crucial prerequisite for practices such as bhāvanā.

> **Bhāvanā**
>
> ➢ Meditative contemplation that leads to experiential understanding of Reality.

If you're engaged in other tasks such as cooking while chanting the LSN, take a vow of silence, where you're not also pausing to chat or check your phone. Let the chant direct the task, where attention flows steadily like oil poured continuously into a cup. When the mind wanders, bring it back to the chant, paying attention to the minute inflections in voice and rhythm. Treat the LSN as Devī's presence in the kitchen, because it is! Reverence is the supercharger of sādhanā, where we rapidly awaken to her presence in our lives and within ourselves.

Chanting the LSN

Due to its sheer length as well as the depth of knowledge hidden in it, it takes persistence to learn to chant the LSN well, and from the start, we must consider some of its nuances. In general, every mantra and chant contains six "limbs" that bestow it with unique powers and characteristics. These six limbs (known as ṣadanga, see N387) are invoked at the beginning of the chant through a practice known as ṛṣyādi (ṛṣi and other) nyāsa. Nyāsa involves touching various parts of the body while chanting or uttering certain mantras. It is the process of inviting the mantra deities and powers into our bodies to enable the interiorization of the practice (see box on ṣadanga overleaf).

Since Sanskrit is tricky, we must pay attention to pronunciation. Two (or more) words with entirely opposite meanings can sound about the same, and differ only in subtle ways. It can be something as minor as replacing a short vowel with a long one, or a plain consonant with an aspirated one (see the Sanskrit Pronunciation Guide on p.xxxvi), which changes the meaning of the nāma. This is why there is such great emphasis on pronunciation when it comes to Sanskrit chants and mantras.

On the flip side, while pronunciation is important, excessive obsession with it doesn't necessarily facilitate the opening to svatantra. If all of our attention is on pronunciation and rhythm, chanting can make us feel good, but fail to catapult us out of the sense of limitation.

Ideally, the mind is simultaneously engaged with the flow and pronunciation of the chant, attention to the presence of the deity *and* the meaning of the nāmas. Although it seems like the mind is juggling many different things at once, the result of this three-pronged focus is that it forces a deeper stillness. Superficial mind activity comes to a rest and the citta, which is composed of the mental, psychological and emotional processes (see Chapter 4), rests in stillness. Here, we pay attention to the nuances of chanting, but remain committed to the darśana, which is the all-important element of any practice. The darśana is the layout of the forest, while the details of practice are the trees. Firm fidelity to the darśana prevents us from the phenomenon of getting so caught up in trees that we miss the forest entirely!

With the right attitude and practice of the LSN, we cultivate the ability to appreciate the beauty of the composition and immerse ourselves in its sweetness—not just when we are chanting or listening to it, but in the way it radically changes our thinking, feeling, behavior, worldview, and attitude toward others (and ourselves). It is said* that chanting the LSN even once during our lifetime is enough to open us to its benefits. However, this assumes a great depth of understanding of the darśana, and not just adherence to chanting rules!

"Three-pronged" attention in chanting

- Flow and pronunciation.
- Presence of the deity.
- Meaning of the chant.

In Part I, we will explore the darśana that makes up the framework of the LSN, but first we must understand its mythological context and origins. In the next chapter, we will travel to a distant point in time when Lalitā Devī manifested herself as the red-hued, playful goddess who restored desire as the essential force of creation.

* In the Lalitopākhyāna.

Sanskrit Pronunciation Guide

The International Alphabet of Sanskrit Transliteration, IAST, is a respected and familiar method of making the Sanskrit script, known as Devanāgarī, accessible to Western scholars, enthusiasts and interested readers.

With this book comes access to audio files of the Sanskrit texts contained herein. Look for them on the New Sarum Press website.

The ṣadanga

1. **Ṛṣi, the seer.** The composition of the LSN is attributed to the goddesses of speech known as Vāgdevatās, elevating it to the level of the Vedas (see The Magic of the Lalitā Sahasranāma in Chapter 1), which are "revealed" scriptures (as in, not composed by the human mind but envisioned by ṛṣis).

2. **Chanda, the meter.** The meter sets the rhythm of the chant. There are 21 meters in the Vedas, 6 of which are most frequently used. The LSN is composed or envisioned in the meter known as Anuṣṭubh, which consists of 32 syllables. These syllables are arranged in 4 half-verses each consisting of 8 syllables.

3. **Devatā, the deity.** The mantra or chant is the subtle form of the deity (see Mantra Sādhanā , Chapter 12). Lalitā Mahātripurasundarī is the deity of the LSN.

4. **Bīja, the seed sound.** The bīja is the seed of a mantra, by way of which the chant grows, flowers and bears fruit in sādhanā. The bīja of the LSN is *aim*.

5. **Śakti, the energy.** Śakti is the dynamic energy of the chant that results in transformation at every level, denoted by another bīja or seed sound. *Klīm* is the śakti bīja of the LSN

6. **Kīlaka, the esoteric innermost syllables.** Kīlaka is the esoteric, secret aspect of the mantra, which is usually unavailable (as if locked shut) without the grace of the guru by way of initiation or dīkṣa. The kīlaka is the key to the lock and is denoted by another bīja. *Sauh* is the kīlaka bīja of the LSN.

Sanskrit Pronunciation Guide

Letter	English Example	Sanskrit Example
a	org*a*n	*a*nuttara
ā	st*a*r	*ā*nanda
i	b*i*t	*i*cchā
ī	p*i*que	*Ī*śvara
u	b*u*sh	*u*nmeṣa
ū	r*u*le	sth*ū*la
ṛ	t*r*ee	am*ṛ*ta
e	th*ey*	pram*e*ya
ai	b*i*nd, st*y*le	Bh*ai*rava
o	b*o*re	*o*jas
au	b*ow*	m*au*ktikā
am	ste*m*	s*am*sāra
ah	a*ha*	Br*ah*man
k	*k*ite	*K*uṇḍalinī
kh	E*kh*art	*Kh*aḍga
g	*g*old	*G*āyatrī
gh	*gh*oul	*gh*anāghanā
ṅ	si*ng*	śṛ*ṅ*gāra
c	*c*hair	Śrī*c*akra
ch	aspirated c	*ch*andas
j	*j*am	*j*apa
jh	he*dg*ehog	Sarva*jh*ṛmbiṇi,
ñ	o*n*ion	āj*ñ*a
ṭ	*t*ub	aṣ*ṭ*amī
ṭh	ligh*t-h*earted	kūrmapṛṣ*th*a
ḍ	*d*ove	maṇḍita

Letter	English Example	Sanskrit Example
ḍh	re*d-h*ot	Aśvārū*ḍh*a
ṇ	fu*n*d	Mantri*ṇ*i
t	pas*t*a	nirmuk*t*a
th	pa*th*	ra*th*a
d	*th*us	*D*aṇḍanātha
dh	aspirated the	sin*dh*ūra
n	ba*n*a*n*a	*n*aya*n*a
p	*p*ine	*p*ūjā
ph	u*ph*ill	*ph*alapradā
b	*b*aby	*b*āṇa
bh	a*bh*or	a*bh*aya
m	*m*other	*m*antra
y	*y*es	*y*antra
r	*r*oom	*R*ati
l	*l*ight	*l*īlā
v	*v*oid	*V*āruṇī
ś	*sh*e	Ṣoḍa*ś*i
ṣ	aspirated sh	*Ṣ*oḍaśi
s	*s*avior	*s*ahasrāra
h	*h*and	*h*asta
kṣa	ma*kesh*ift	*Kṣ*obhiṇi
jña	gnya	āj*ña*

Vowels	a ā i ī u ū ṛ ṝ ḷ ḹ e ai o au am ah

Consonants	Non-aspirated	Aspirated	Non-Aspirated	Aspirated	Nasal
Gutturals	k	kh	g	gh	ṅ
Palatals	c	ch	j	jh	ñ
Cerebrals	ṭ	ṭh	ḍ	ḍh	ṇ
Dentals	t	th	d	dh	n
Labials	p	ph	b	bh	m

Semi-vowels	y r l v

Sibilants	ś ṣ s

Aspirates	h kṣ

Part I

The Darśana (View)

Chapter 1

How the Lalitā Sahasranāma Came to Be

In most Indian traditions, the Vedas are highly revered and considered the ultimate scriptural authority. The Purāṇas were composed centuries later to present the complex and esoteric concepts of the Vedas by way of easy-to-understand mythological stories. We owe the transformative beauty and effectiveness of the LSN to these ancient writings.

Lalitopākhyāna

The story of the Lalitopākhyāna begins with Sage Agastya and the mountain range in central India known as Vindhyā. In Purāṇic stories, inanimate objects such as mountains also have personalities. Being the tallest mountain range in the region, Vindhyā is overcome with pride; wanting to show off his might and without care or consideration for the forests and the life he supports, he begins to grow at an abnormally fast pace. Agastya is a revered sage of extremely high attainments, and Lord Śiva entrusts him with the task of stopping Vindhyā from causing large-scale destruction. Agastya sets off, making his way south from his home in the north. When he reaches the Vindhyā, he requests the mountain to temporarily stop growing and allow him safe passage. Vindhyā grants his request, vowing that he wouldn't resume his growth until the sage made his way back north. Agastya decides to remain in the south, making Vindhyā wait for his return indefinitely. He continues his journey south, visiting various sacred sites and assessing the pulse of the human condition along the way.

Agastya is saddened and disillusioned to see the descent of humanity into hedonism at the cost of liberation and harmony. He finally arrives at Kānchipuram where Lalitā Devī resides as Kāmākṣī.

The Vedas

- Oldest scriptures (1500-1200 BCE).
- Direct perception into the heart of reality by ṛṣis or sages.
- Manuals on how to live life and attain liberation.
- Replete with rituals and procedures for rites of passage, for social and communal growth, and so on.
- Inaccessible to the average layperson because of their high level of composition.

The Purāṇas

- Composed to make Vedic material accessible to general public.
- Complexities of Vedic practices presented as stories.
- 18 in number.
- Brahmāṇḍa Purāṇa contains the Lalitā Sahasranāma and the **Lalitopākhyāna,** which describes the conquests of Lalitā Devī.

Here, he settles down to take up severe austerities to please Lord Viṣṇu, who eventually appears as Hayagrīva (see Figure 1), and pleased with Agastya's devotion, is prepared to grant him anything. The exceedingly compassionate Agastya asks the Lord for an easy path to freedom on behalf of all humankind. Lord Hayagrīva declares that chanting the thousand names of Lalitā Devī with devotion can fulfill all desires *and* grant liberation. Interest piqued, Agastya is filled with curiosity and begs to know more. However, Lord Hayagrīva directs him to a sage (confusingly, of the name Hayagrīva) for further instruction, and disappears into thin air. Agastya goes on to find Sage Hayagrīva, who imparts the knowledge of the LSN through the story of Lalitā Devī:

Figure 1. Lord Hayagrīva

The Vanity of Indra

Once, Indra, the Lord of the Devas, wins a war against the Asuras and is consumed with conceit. Sage Durvāsa (who, like Agastya, is a sage of supreme attainment) is called upon to teach Indra a lesson and quell his arrogance. As he is traveling to Indra's abode, he comes across a woman with a garland of fragrant, ever-fresh flowers; she happily gives it to him. Durvāsa is ecstatic to be in possession of the auspicious garland, he blesses her profusely and continues on his travels.

Meanwhile, Indra sets out on his elephant to tour his kingdom and runs into the sage. Durvāsa generously offers him the auspicious garland. The conceited Indra carelessly tosses it on the elephant's head, irritating the beast. The elephant throws down the garland and tramples it, infuriating Durvāsa, who promptly curses Indra with the deprivation of all auspiciousness from his life and kingdom. The curse comes into effect immediately and Indra's kingdom suddenly loses all its luster.

The now-repentant Indra turns to his guru Bṛhaspati for advice on how he could restore the luster to his dull kingdom. Bṛhaspati gives him a long-winded explanation of the many types of transgressions and their cause-and-effect phenomena, illustrating them with stories. One such story is Devī's victory over Bhaṇḍāsura.

Sage Hayagrīva, the narrator of this story, tries to move on after this cursory introduction but Agastya is intrigued. He interrupts him with questions, "Wait a minute! Who is Bhaṇḍāsura? Why and how is Devī invoked? Please tell me all the details and please don't skip any parts of it!" Hayagrīva complies, and goes on to narrate the story that is central to the LSN.

The Rise of Bhaṇḍāsura

In mythology, Brahma, Viṣṇu, and Śiva are known as the great trinity, responsible for creating, sustaining and destroying the universe. Among them, Śiva is an ascetic, preferring to live in seclusion. At one point, he neglects his cosmic duties and becomes so absorbed in meditation that it results in a great imbalance, since life can't be sustained without death. Brahma and Viṣṇu invoke the great Śakti (see Chapter 3) to help stir Śiva from his deep meditation. Śakti takes birth as Sati, the immaculate daughter of Dakṣa, and falls in love with the meditating Śiva. Her irresistible beauty rouses Śiva from his reverie, and in spite of Dakṣa's strong dissent, Sati marries Śiva, transforming him from a detached yogi to a loving husband. Soon after the wedding, Dakṣa performs a grand fire ritual and invites luminaries from all the worlds—except for his daughter and son-in-law.

Assuming the lack of an invitation from her father to be an oversight and against Śiva's advice, Sati arrives at the ceremony. Instead of welcoming her, Dakṣa humiliates her publicly for marrying Śiva, the rogue yogi. Overcome with sadness, Sati steps into the ritual fire and immolates herself. When Śiva hears the news, he is beside himself with rage and grief, and his enraged army descends upon Dakṣa's palace, destroying it and decapitating him (he is later revived by Śiva's compassion).

In deep mourning, Śiva wanders the universe with Sati's body flung over his shoulder. Once again, his cosmic power is withdrawn and creation is stalled. Determined to help, Viṣṇu follows him, consoling him while simultaneously slicing away parts of Sati's body to lighten Śiva's burden. A sacred Śakti pīṭha (site) arises wherever Sati's flesh drops on Earth. Relieved of his physical burden and acute grief, Śiva returns to his life of solitude and withdrawal. The already out-of-balance creation becomes even more chaotic. As it happens, this chaotic state becomes the perfect milieu for the escalation of evil—a powerful asura known as Tārakāsura rises to power. Invoking Brahma through severe austerities, he cunningly asks to be killed only by a son of Śiva, with full knowledge about his steadfast celibacy. With Śiva being uninterested in procreation, Tārakāsura becomes invincible and spreads utter disharmony throughout the universe.

To draw Śiva out of his reverie and to restore balance to the universe, Śakti takes birth again as Pārvatī, the exquisitely beautiful daughter of Himavat who personifies the Himālaya mountains. Pārvatī stumbles upon the meditating Śiva on one of her walks in the mountains and falls in love with him. However, Śiva remains unmoved by her advances, and Viṣṇu and the others charge Kāma with the task of stirring his desire. Kāma, who operates through a sugarcane bow and arrows made of flowers, representing the mind and the senses (see N10-N11) arrives at the scene with his wife Rati, and playfully shoots an arrow of desire at Śiva. The arrow finds its mark and Śiva opens his eyes to see the beautiful Pārvatī standing before him. Even as he is overcome with desire for her, he turns around looking for the source of this disturbance. Spotting Kāma, he incinerates him with one angry glance. With Kāma's death, the very desire for creation to continue comes to a total standstill while Rati is torn apart in grief at the loss of her beloved.

Pārvatī eventually wins over Śiva and marries him. A son is born to them, known as Skanda, who destroys Tārakāsura. When peace is finally restored, Citrakarma, one of Śiva's commanders, gathers Kāma's ashes and sculpts the pile into the form of a boy. Śiva affectionately glances at the form, and the ash-boy springs to life! Citrakarma cares for the boy and initiates him into a powerful Śiva mantra. The boy practices austerities with such great intensity that Śiva is pleased with him and prepares to grant him a boon. The boy says, "May my opponents in battle lose half their strength merely by my presence, and may their strength be added to my own. May I be invincible and impervious to my opponents' weapons." Śiva is amused and grants him not only these unusual boons, but generously bestows upon him invincibility and sovereignty over the universe for 60,000 years. Hearing this, the all-knowing Brahma shakes his head muttering, "Bhaṇḍa! Bhaṇḍa!"*

The boy becomes known as Bhaṇḍāsura.

Becoming all-powerful through Śiva's boons, Bhaṇḍāsura creates two brothers—Viṣaṅga and Viśukra—out of his own body. They set out on a rampage, destroying everything in their way and usurping the devas from their stations. The devas hold a meeting and decide that the best course of action would be to restore Kāma, the primary force of creation and Bhaṇḍāsura's original form. Bhaṇḍāsura gets wind of this plan and decides to render all the devas impotent by drying up their rasa (see Chapter 12). Bhaṇḍāsura and his army assume the form of wind and enter the minds of the devas, depleting them of their mental faculties and robbing them of their beauty, luster and even the will to live. In short, they rob them of auspiciousness.

The desperate devas decide to invoke Lalitā Devī

Kāma, the God of Love

- Central to the LSN.
- Also known as Kāmadeva or Manmatha.
- Confusingly, Śiva is also sometimes referred to as Kāma in some contexts.
- Not just the god of erotic love; Kāma represents the fundamental juicy desire to be alive!
- Incinerated by Śiva into ashes.
- Rises from the ashes as Bhaṇḍāsura, his distorted form that is the lack of desire or juice to live and thrive.
- Restored by Devī to his original form.

* Bhaṇḍa is shame ("Shame! Shame!").

as a last resort measure. They perform austerities for 10,000 years, creating an enormous fire pit, offering up flesh cut from their own bodies. When Devī doesn't appear, they begin jumping into the fire, sacrificing themselves in desperate abandon.

Devī's Conquest of Bhaṇḍāsura

At this point in the story, an immense Śrīcakra (see Figure 2) arises from the great sacrificial fire. The astounded devas watch as this Cakrarāja Ratha grows out of the pit that had consumed so many of their comrades. Ratha is chariot; Cakrarāja is the King of Cakras. It simultaneously emits the brilliance of a million suns and the cooling effect of a million moons. Seated in the center of the Śrīcakra is Devī herself, her brilliance surpassing that of the Śrīcakra. Mesmerizingly beautiful with the complexion of a red hibiscus flower, she is adorned with the rarest gems and personifies the Śṛṅgāra rasa (see Rasa, Chapter 12) of beauty and desire. Her eyes emit unceasing love, grace, and playfulness. She has four arms in which she holds a noose, a hook, a sugarcane bow and five arrows made of flowers (see Part II, Segment 1). The whole universe stops to take in Devī's splendor and to drink in her magnificence. When Brahma and the others hear that the creator of the universe has taken form, they rush to witness this grand event.

Figure 2. Śrīcakra

With one glance, Devī restores the devas to their original state of beauty and radiance, and marries Kāmeśvara* in a lavish ceremony. She takes her place on the throne of Śrī Nagara, her capital in the midst of a mystical ocean of nectar. Celestial beings of every realm pay homage to Devī as Rājarājeśvarī, the supreme empress of creation.

Devī then sets out to deal with Bhaṇḍāsura in an elaborate battle formation, accompanied by countless Śaktis, each one commanding her own group of forces (see Part II, Segment 2). The war is a bloody one, and the Śaktis defeat Bhaṇḍāsura's generals, brothers, and sons. We will see details of the war in Part II in the context of the LSN. Surrounded by her Śaktis, Devī storms Bhaṇḍāsura's capital known as Śūnyaka. His remaining army is overpowered and annihilated. Devī destroys him before restoring him to his original form as Kāma, much to Rati's

* An exquisitely beautiful form of Śiva, who is the consort of Lalitā Mahātripurasundarī.

delight.* The ever-grateful Kāma becomes eternally associated with Devī as her arrows of desire. With the resurrection of desire, creation finally returns to balance. Devī returns to Śrī Nagara with her Śaktis to rule over the universe with her beloved Kāmeśvara.

Agastya is deeply moved by the story. Sage Hayagrīva stops talking and silence descends upon them. Agastya recalls that Lord Hayagrīva** had lauded the collection of the thousand names of Devī as the key to liberation. The sage had not revealed the thousand names yet, and Agastya wonders why. Was he unworthy of this knowledge? He voices his self-doubt and the sage joyfully responds that the thousand names of Lalitā can be taught only if the student asks for it. Now that Agastya has asked, he would teach him, of course! Agastya receives the teaching with great reverence and goes on to share it with Devī's devotees everywhere. Permanently included in its invocation, he continues to be the great teacher of the LSN to this day.

Devī's Śaktis

- Created from her own essence.
- Sampatkarī from her goad.
- Aśvārūḍhā from her noose.
- Vārāhī (a.k.a. Daṇḍanāthā Devī) from her arrows; she is the commander-in-chief who rides the chariot known as Kiricakra.
- Mātaṅgī from her bow; she is the prime minister and rides the chariot known as Geyacakra.
- All the śaktis of the Śrīcakra.

The Magic of the Lalitā Sahasranāma

The thousand names of the LSN are not the *only* names of Lalitā Devī, and she is called by other names that are not part of this text. The LSN is not unique in being a chant that extols a deity through a thousand names. Sahasranāmas extolling other deities are widely available and routinely practiced. However, the LSN is a composition of exquisite precision and brevity. The nāmas are organized in couplets, and are so perfectly arranged in meter that there is no need for filler words or conjunctions that are commonly seen in other sahasranāmas.

Although the LSN is a part of the Purāṇas, it is considered to be equivalent to the Vedās because of its mythological origins. Its composition is attributed to the Vāgdevatās, the eight goddesses that surround the innermost triangle of the Śrīcakra (see Deities of the Śrīcakra, Chapter 9). Having given them their magnificent powers of expression, Devī entrusts them with the task of composing her Sahasranāma. The Vāgdevatās compose it on the spot, pleasing Devī with its brilliance and fluency.

There are several exemplary commentaries on the LSN, the best-known of which is by the 18th century Śrīvidyā adept, Śrī Bhāskararāya Makhin. An

* Rati is Kāma's wife, who is distraught when Śiva incinerates her husband for doing his job of inciting desire in his heart for Pārvatī!

** Recall that Lord Hayagrīva is an incarnation of Viṣṇu.

The Uniqueness of the LSN

- Sahasra = thousand, nāma = name.
- Equivalent of the Vedas.
- Composition attributed to the Vāgdevatās.
- Only sahasranāma where no nāma is repeated.
- Even when many nāmas may mean approximately the same thing, the *context* of each will reveal subtle (and often, profound) differences.
- No filler words or conjunctions.

extraordinary scholar-practitioner with unsurpassed skill, he not only wrote commentaries on various classical texts but also composed several original works. An adept in the nuances of Sanskrit grammar, he assigned unusual meanings to the nāmas, drawing from his far-ranging and in-depth textual knowledge of the Tantras, Vedas, and other sources. His commentary on the LSN is considered the final authority, and is recommended for anyone interested in delving deeper into this text.*

One of the remarkable features of the LSN is that a variety of meanings can be gleaned from each nāma depending on how we approach it. These meanings may not be evident immediately, but reveal themselves over time, with ongoing practice and bhāvanā (see Bhāvanā, Chapter 12).

The LSN consists of three parts. The first part discusses its origins, the middle contains the thousand nāmas, and the last lists the benefits of the practice, including healing from disease, avoiding premature death, obtaining children, wealth and other successes, as well as liberation. It also provides a guideline for chanting the LSN, declaring that reciting it even once over a lifetime is auspicious (provided one has a deep understanding of the darśana, see Introduction), and that no other practice is needed because it is the Mahāmantra (great mantra). It is particularly auspicious to chant the LSN on one's birthday, initiation day, Fridays, full moon days, and other days as instructed by the guru. There is no prescribed auspicious time, and it can be chanted any time during the day or night. However, it does caution against chanting it in a hurry or rushing through it for the sake of getting it done. The benefits listed above assume the prerequisites (see Introduction) of

Levels of Meaning in the LSN

- Each nāma as a stand-alone teaching.
- Context of the preceding and the following nāmas.
- Context of the whole verse.
- Context of the preceding and following verses.
- Context of the section of nāmas.
- Context of the whole chant.

* The best-known English translation of Bhāskararāya's commentary is by R. Ananthakrishna Sastry via the Adyar Library and Research Centre, Madras (first edition 1899, last edition 2010).

reverence and understanding. While there is no need for specific rituals or offerings, it is said that Devī is especially pleased when we offer flowers for every nāma. While this can be taken literally, flowers refer to our saṃskāras (see Chapter 4). Setting an intention to offer up our saṃskāras to Devī and to become aligned with her will is practically more useful than offering a thousand flowers!

Devī explicitly requests the Vāgdevatās to end the Sahasranāma with the word Lalitā, to denote her absolute independence. As we will see, the meaning of the word "Lalitā" comes alive in our direct experience when we arrive at it through the path laid out in the LSN. Unlike the fierce (Raudra) forms of Devī such as Kāli, Lalitā is playful and sweet. Like a concerned mother, she indulges our petty desires at times, and scolds us at other times for our follies, but at all times she leads us to the highest truths of the path.

What are these truths? These are the topics of the next few chapters, where we'll study the map laid out in the LSN so we can know exactly where we're going. Let's begin with a brief overview of the path known as Śrīvidyā.

Chapter 2

What is Srīvidyā, Really?

Śrīvidyā (auspicious knowledge or wisdom) is the name given to the tradition that is centered around the goddess Lalitā Mahātripurasundarī. Also known as Rājarājeśvarī (the Empress of Emperors) and Mahādevi (Great Goddess), Lalitā is depicted as the most beautiful and auspicious manifestation of the Divine. While Śrīvidyā is the name of a particular path, it also refers to the central mantra of the tradition as well as its ultimate goal—svatantra or absolute freedom through the realization of auspicious wisdom.

Three main forms of Lalitā are worshiped in the tradition—the gross (sthūla) or anthropomorphic form, the subtle (sūkṣma) form that is the central mantra, and the subtlest (parā) form that is the Śrīcakra. The LSN refers to all the three forms of Śrīvidyā. Before we go further, we must understand what we mean by worship.

The Many Facets of Worship

While worship usually brings up images of rituals and procedures, here it means many other things. Ritual worship is certainly an integral part of Śrīvidyā, but the word worship also refers to the many ways in which we pay attention to Devī's presence. Examples include chanting the LSN, mantra japa (systematic repetition), meditation, reading relevant books and texts, discussions with other sādhakas, sacred art (such as drawing or constructing a Śrīcakra), and so on. Veneration of Devī doesn't look like any *particular* thing. Adoring her presence in your family, friends, and even pets is a wonderful form of worship. Constant offering up of limitations is one of the higher forms of worship. In fact, it's far more useful to engage in such higher forms of worship than to become so stuck in rituals that the darśana and purpose of sādhanā is lost (it's the case of losing sight of the forest in favor of a particular tree).

Nevertheless, ritual worship fosters the cultivation of discipline and sweetness that is otherwise difficult to summon. With the cultivation of this bhāva (attitude), all of life can become a dance of ritual. We open our eyes in the morning and think of Devī. We brush our teeth, shower, cook, take care of your family, respond to emails, and interact with people thinking about Devī. We see her in nature, and in everyone we meet (yes, even those we can't stand!), and go about our life like it belongs to her (because it does!). This kind of worship will take us more quickly toward svatantra than becoming entrenched in the minutiae of rituals (see N32, N95). As long as we remain rooted in the darśana and keep our eyes focused on the goal of svatantra, we are worshiping Devī!

The Śrīvidyā Mantra

Traditionally, the Śrīvidyā lineages, rituals and texts were distinguished by three matas*—kādi, hādi, and sādi.** They are named so based on the root of the Pañcadaśi, where the mantra begins with the syllables *ka*, *ha*, or *sa*. Kādi Vidyā, referring to the mantra beginning with ka, is attributed to Hayagrīva and Agastya (of the Lalitopākhyāna), and is the most widely practiced form of the mantra. The LSN is therefore a kādividyā text. The Tantrarāja Tantra, Bhāskararāya's Varivasyā Rahasya, Bhāvanā Upanishad and the Paraśurāma Kalpa Sūtra are other examples of Kādividyā texts.

Hādividya was precepted by Lopāmudrā, Agastya's illustrious wife. The Yoginīhṛdaya and the Khadgamāla Stotra are examples of Hādividya texts. Sādividyā, which is no longer in popular use, was precepted by Sage Dūrvāsa (whom we met in the Lalitopākhyana), without any widely known dedicated texts or handbooks on rituals.

The practice of the Śrīvidyā (Pañcadaśi) mantra is nuanced and involves elaborate methods, some of which we will explore in Chapter 12.

* Mata refers to practice or lineage and refers to a variation of the Pañcadaśī mantra

** Traditionally, there are 12 variations of the Pañcadaśi attributed to one of the following luminaries: Manu, Candra, Kubera, Lopāmudrā, Kāma, Agastya, Agni, Sūrya, Indra, Skanda, Śiva, and Durvāsa. Of these, kādi and hādi are best known. According to some scholars, there are up to 30 variations of the mantra!

Devī's Forms

Devī is known in numerous forms—sthūla, where she is the radiant goddess with four arms,*** sūkṣma, which is the Śrīvidyā mantra, parā, which is the Śrīcakra, and two other esoteric ones—Kuṇḍalinī and Kāmakalā, both of which are revealed by the guru and in progressive initiations.

In her many forms, Devī resides in the Śrīcakra, with the nine enclosures (āvaraṇas) representing nine types of borders around her palace in Śrī Nagara**** in the midst of a forest thick with Kadamba trees, which bear highly fragrant flowers that she favors (see N60). The Śrīcakra is surrounded by twenty-five other enclosures made of various types of rare gemstones and flora, and is itself made of the exceedingly rare Cintāmaṇi (see N57). Esoterically, Cintāmaṇi is the wish-fulfilling gem, and reference to this hints at the benefit of Śrīvidyā sādhanā—bhoga (enjoyment of material benefits) *and* yoga (liberation).

Devī resides in the bindu (central point) of the Śrīcakra, seated on an unusual throne. Its four legs are Brahma, Viṣṇu, Rudra, and Íśāna and the seat is Sadāśiva (see N58). Brahma is the creator, Viṣṇu the sustainer, and Rudra, who is a form of Śiva, is the destroyer. Íśāna and Sadāśiva are two other forms of Śiva. Íśāna is the concealer and Sadāśiva is the

*** Devī's most well-known form is her four-armed one bearing noose, goad, sugarcane bow and 5 flower arrows, but there are other anthropomorphic forms with varying number of arms and implements.

**** Auspicious city.

revealer (more on this in the next chapter). Devī's supremacy over these five functions of the universe are depicted by her position on the throne in the bindu of the Śrīcakra (see Chapter 8).

History of Śrīvidyā

The origins of Śrīvidyā remain mysterious, with the earliest mention of the tradition found in the Tirumandiram attributed to the 6th-7th century Tamil siddha (perfected sage) Tirumūlar.* The Vāmakeśvara Tantra originated around the same time, and is considered to be one of the oldest Sanskrit texts associated with Śrīvidyā. It consists of two parts, the Nityāṣoḍāśikārṇava and the Yoginīhṛdaya, thought to represent, respectively, the exoteric and esoteric aspects of Śrīvidyā.

By the 13th century CE, commentaries on the Vāmakeśvara Tantra by scholars of the Kashmiri non-dual Śaiva tradition emerged, establishing Śrīvidyā as a sophisticated system of practices heavily influenced by the Krama and Pratyabhijña schools.** Even as Śrīvidyā acquired its Kashmiri attributes, it became incorporated by the Śankarācāryas of South India, beginning with Ādi Śankaracārya in the 8th century. He is credited with the commentary on the Lalitā Triśatī (300 nāmas of Lalitā Devī, each beginning with consecutive letters of the 15-syllable Pañcadaśi mantra).

With the heavy influence of the Śankarācāryas, Śrīvidyā acquired a flavor of Advaita Vedānta. Advaita means non-dual and Vedanta is the end of the Vedas. Ādi Śankaracārya systematized the study of non-dual Vedanta with his extensive commentaries and original*** works. Vedanta refers to the end of transactional knowledge in favor of Self-knowledge. Transactional knowledge refers to what we learn ordinarily by way of gathering information, and through study and analysis, where we as the subject acquire knowledge as an object. By going to school to become a doctor or a lawyer, we don't *become* medicine or law. We (the subject) remain separate from the knowledge (object) in a transactional relationship. In contrast, Self-knowledge is to know who or what the subject really is without objectifying it. The initial portions of the Vedas enhance transactional knowledge whereas the end portions are about Self-knowledge.

Tantra is based on other non-Vedik texts known as the Tantras (such as the Vāmakeśvara referenced above) and the Āgamās, and differs from Vedanta in a few critical ways. Over the centuries, commentaries on various texts by scholars that differed in their interpretations (influenced by their own leanings toward particular philosophies—Tāntrik and/or Vedik) shaped Śrīvidyā into a tradition that is highly sampradāya (lineage)-specific. Depending on the sampradāya, Śrīvidyā streams can be more Vedik

* Brooks, DR, *Auspicious Wisdom: The Texts and Traditions of Śrīvidyā Śākta Tantrism in South India*, Albany 1992, Page 30.

** Golovkova, A, Śrīvidyā, in Brill's *Encyclopedia of Hinduism*.

*** Including *Upadeśasahasrī* and *Vivekacūḍāmaṇī*.

(based on the Vedas) or more Tāntrik (based on the Tantras)—even though all are centered around Lalitā Devī, the Śrīvidyā mantra and the Śrīcakra. Many Śrīvidyā adepts don't strictly identify themselves as Vedik or Tāntrik, being comfortable with seamlessly incorporating the various philosophies in their personal sādhanā. In fact, the LSN describes Devī as the embodiment of both the Vedas (see N539) and the Tantras (see N724).

Practices in Śrīvidyā differ according to sampradāya, and along with Lalitā Devī, the tradition includes the worship of other deities, particularly the elephant-headed Gaṇapatī, Bālā Tripurasundarī (the form of Devī as a young girl), Mātaṅgī, and Vārāhī.

While a detailed elaboration on all the practices and details of Śrīvidyā are beyond the scope of this book, we will explore the key aspects of the tradition as it relates to the LSN in the following chapters, beginning with the non-dual understanding of Śiva and Śakti.

Chapter 3

Śiva and Śakti

As we approach the LSN, it would help us greatly to understand the fundamental nature of Devī. Who is Devī? Is she the mother that looks after creation as idealized human mothers do? And what about Śiva? What's his role in all this?

> **Śiva (meaning auspicious)**
>
> - ➢ Transcendent.
> - ➢ Formless.
> - ➢ Ground of being.
> - ➢ Devoid of attributes.
> - ➢ Nothingness.
> - ➢ Prakāśa (illumination).

There are many ways to answer these questions (adding to a sādhaka's confusion!). The traditional way is to think of Devī as the mother-goddess who creates the universe and cares for it. This view comes from a simplistic understanding of creation as it applies to us humans. Since the process of giving birth is a uniquely female attribute in most species, we assign this property to the creative power of the Divine and call it mother. While this classification can allow for great devotion for some, we must delve deeper if we wish for a greater depth of understanding and absolute freedom.

Some other ways to understand Śiva and Śakti are through the concepts of transcendence and immanence, and formless and form. In non-dual Śākta philosophy, the Divine is the ultimate Reality (note the capital R, which is neither male nor female but is both in perfect equilibrium, as we will see a bit later) that is both form and formless, immanent and transcendent (see N90-96). Transcendent here refers to the Reality that is formless but is the very essence of form. It is the ground of being, the canvas upon which form is transcribed. The transcendent Divine is devoid of attributes such as name, form, space, and time. The immanent Divine is endowed with attributes and takes the countless forms in manifestation, from the smallest sub-atomic particle to the largest and densest cosmic body. Immanence includes subtle forms such as thoughts and emotions. Any "thing" we can possibly imagine lies in the realm

> **Śakti (meaning creative power)**
>
> - ➢ Immanent.
> - ➢ Form.
> - ➢ Being.
> - ➢ All attributes.
> - ➢ Everythingness.
> - ➢ Vimarśa (self-reflection).

of immanence. The transcendent is the *nothingness* and the immanent is the *everythingness*; both are needed for creation.

The first movement of the unmanifest toward manifestation is the one Reality becoming two complementing aspects known as Śiva and Śakti. That which is transcendent and formless is referred to as Śiva, while that which takes form and becomes immanent is Śakti. We must remember that the Śiva we are referring to here is not the same as the Śiva we have previously encountered as the yogi-god of destruction. Here, Śiva (which literally means auspiciousness) is the ground of being for creation, while Śakti is the creative energy or power. However, these two principles are not separate: they constantly flow into each other without distinct boundaries. Śiva and Śakti are inseparable like water and its wetness, and fire and its heat.

Figure 3. Ardhanarīśvara

Śiva isn't masculine and Śakti isn't feminine in the ways that we think of sex and gender. Śakti is called feminine simply because she is the creative (and every other) power of the Divine. Śiva and Śakti do not carry any specific male or female attributes. Any and all gender attributes we assign to them are products of our own human experience of being on a gender spectrum. Śakti is thought of as Śiva's creative potency; *all* his attributes are forms of Śakti. From the standpoint of non-duality, *all* attributes—including those of gender classifications—are forms of Śakti—she is maleness, femaleness, and everything in between. She is also Śiva's attribute of auspiciousness. In fact, *Śrī* in Śrīvidyā refers to auspiciousness and is the basis of this path.

It is inherently difficult for the mind to grasp the concept of attributelessness, since anything we can possibly imagine is necessarily an attribute. Therefore, even the property or attribute of "nothingness" that is assigned to Śiva is Śakti! The Saundarya Laharī, one of the central texts of Śrīvidyā, declares emphatically that without Śakti, Śiva is inert and "corpselike." In the LSN and other Śākta texts, Śakti (or Devī), because of her power over Śiva, is both transcendent and immanent.

The inseparability of Śiva and Śakti becomes evident in the iconography of Ardhanarīśvara (see Figure 3), whose right half is Śiva and the left is Śakti. He is static and she is dynamic; he is pale and she is vibrant. Śakti is Śiva in motion while Śiva is Śakti in stillness.

Prakāśa and Vimarśa

Another way to understand Śiva and Śakti is through the lens of classical Tāntrik philosophy in terms of *prakāśa* and *vimarśa*.

Śiva is prakāśa, which is pure illumination or the light of Consciousness that is eternal and unchanging. The whole universe is the light of Consciousness shining within itself—this is a crucial point. Think of prakāśa as a boundary-less, pristine mirror within which the whole universe is being reflected, but there is no object "outside" the mirror. The reflections arise spontaneously because of the many limitations that prakāśa (Śiva) imposes on himself, out of his own absolute freedom or svatantra (we will unpack these limitations in the next chapter). Just as a mirror remains unchanged regardless of what is going on with the reflections, prakāśa remains unfettered. As far as the mirror is concerned, the objects reflected in it are of its own nature—the mirror doesn't register or recognize the objects reflected in it as being different or separate from it. Similarly, as far as prakāśa is concerned, even though there is a great diversity of reflections upon its surface, they're not registered as being diverse or different from itself.

Prakāśa-Vimarśa

- Prakāśa = illumination: eternal, unchanging Consciousness.
- Vimarśa = self-awareness: consciousness of Consciousness.
- Transcendence = Śakti turned toward Śiva.
- Immanence = Śakti turned toward manifestation.

At this point, we might wonder how all these objects in the mirror are being created. And for this, we have to examine the next concept, which is vimarśa (see N548). If prakāśa is pure consciousness, vimarśa is the consciousness of Consciousness—*Reality knowing itself.* It is by this process of Reality (as Śiva) contemplating on itself (as Śakti) that creation is manifested. This power of self-reflection or vimarśa is the inherent creative potential of prakāśa. The classical analogies used in the tradition are those of a banyan tree that is contained within its seed, or the colors of a peacock's plume present in its egg yolk. The creative potential of the banyan tree or the peacock's plume is vimarśa while the seed and the egg yolk are prakāśa. As is evident in these examples, the seed/tree and yolk/plume can't be separated. Through prakāśa and vimarśa, Reality can be both transcendent and immanent at the same time. This is because of Reality's power of svatantra or absolute freedom to be nothing, anything, and everything all at once!

Prakāśa is Śiva and vimarśa is Śakti. When vimarśa is directed toward itself, Reality is transcendent and when it is directed toward manifestation, Reality is immanent. When Reality's self-awareness is directed exclusively toward Itself, it is transcendent. When Reality's self-awareness is directed toward objects, it is immanent. In other words, transcendence is Śakti turned toward Śiva, and immanence is Śakti turned toward manifestation. In her turning away from Śiva, the cosmos comes into being as the objects reflected upon him. Śakti *is* the cosmos being reflected upon the mirror that is Śiva. In her turning toward Śiva, the cosmos is reabsorbed back into her. The cosmos is continually renewed between the two polarities in this oscillation of vimarśa, which is known as *spanda*. Lovers of Devī conceptualize the universe being born and re-born with the blinking of her eyes (see N281)—when she closes her eyes (nimeṣa), Reality revels in itself. When she opens her eyes (unmeṣa), Reality manifests as creation.

The central point or bindu of the Śrīcakra is where Reality as prakāśa-vimarśa resides. As we will see in Chapter 9 (see Bindu, The Stateless State), the bindu is not a distinct or static point. It is non-localized and dynamic, the entire Śrīcakra arising from it and being reabsorbed into it in every timeless moment. The whole universe is manifested as a flash or luminous throbbing (known as *sphurattā*) from the bindu.

Through the ecstatic self-reflection of prakāśa-vimarśa, the one Reality becomes three: the experiencer (*pramātṛ*), experience (*prameya*), and the process of experiencing (*pramāṇa*), represented by the innermost triangle of the Śrīcakra (see Figure 4 and Chapter 9). Think of it this way: if we consider the bindu to be a point, it becomes two when look-

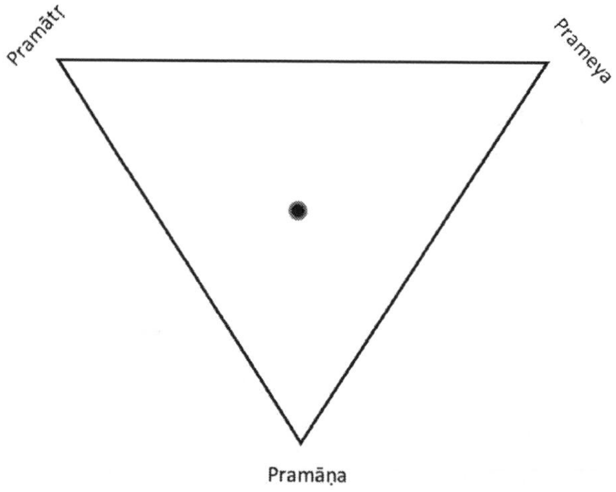

Figure 4. The One Reality Becoming Three

ing at itself. The relationship between itself as the subject (the experiencer) and the object (the experienced) is connected by the process or relationship, (the experiencing)).

In other words, Reality is always experiencing itself in every object because it is the only one that exists. The bindu is the center of every aspect of creation and every experience, exploding as the triad and collapsing back into itself. The light of consciousness (prakāśa) "folds back" upon itself (vimarśa) to enjoy *itself as itself* in every object and experience. In fact, the entire Śrīcakra is the dynamic and ecstatic arising of the cosmos as prakāśa-vimarśa, and Lalitā Devī is the union of Śiva-Śakti exploding as immanence and imploding as transcendence. We'll explore the Śrīcakra a bit later, but before we move on from the crucial understanding of Śiva-Śakti, let's examine what is meant by non-duality.

Non-duality

Ordinarily, we look at the world and see separate objects that appear to be distinct and "other" than us. In reality, however, what *is* seeing through us is the Divine and *what* it is seeing is itself. This is the purport of non-duality, which is the essential non-separation of creation from the creator. Anything we can possibly imagine—from the distant stars to our own minds and bodies—is Reality experiencing Itself.

A common question that arises here is, "If everything is Śiva-Śakti, why is there so much suffering in the world?" You may be surprised by the answer,

Non-duality

- ➢ Essential non-separation between the creator and creation.
- ➢ Oneness of the triad of experience which is the experiencer, the object of experience and the process of experiencing.
- ➢ Transcendence of dualities such as good/evil, desirable/undesirable, and so on, occurring through the collapse of the triad of experience.

which is that all of creation is a grand sport for the Divine. The One becomes many just for fun! The infinite forms of the universe and the infinite drama lines of those forms are just the One experiencing Itself in infinite ways. Śiva-Śakti is *you* living *your* life out the way *you* are. More pragmatically, it is really impossible to answer this question. As we will see in the following chapters, the very act of creation is the Divine limiting itself. Everything that exists is therefore a manifestation of this limitation. Accordingly, the very question of why suffering exists lies in the realm of limitation. When we transcend limitations in our own sādhanā, such questions stop making sense and stop arising.

Imagine a movie that you pay good money for, and it's just two hours of blandness—there are no villains and everyone is content. Would you feel entertained? What makes a movie worth the money is the whole mix of good and evil, desirable and undesirable, haves and have nots, perfect and imperfect, and so on. The good, perfect and desirable make sense only in comparison to evil, imperfect and undesirable. In other words, duality is the spice of good entertainment.

And so it is for the One. By becoming contracted into you, me, and countless other objects and forgetting Its true nature, the One can truly enjoy Itself in infinite ways. Another way of saying this is that what we call suffering or happiness is *equally* enjoyed by the One. Things appear as opposites to us because of our forgetfulness of our true nature as the One. And it is our forgetfulness and taking ourselves to be the story of "me" that keeps us bound in suffering.

Returning to the movie analogy, our predicament is like Jane who is an actor and plays the character of Kate in a movie. In the process, she totally forgets that she's Jane, and goes around thinking she's Kate. This is a bit like the issue of forgetting our true nature, except that in reality we are the screen, the producer, the characters, *and* the one watching the movie. Instead, we live out our lives as one particular character, being subject to all the dualities that come from being restricted to that storyline. From the standpoint of Reality, all storylines are the incessant interaction between Śiva and Śakti. The illusion of so many unique storylines is what makes creation so much more interesting, allowing for the experience of joy, pain, ecstasy, bondage, suffering, and freedom.

Ego

- ➢ Ideas, beliefs and habits that we associate with "me."
- ➢ Mix of stuff that clouds our ability to know our true vast and limitless nature.
- ➢ While we may think of ego as arrogance or excessive pride (as in "inflated egos"), the word ego here refers to the pervasive sense of personhood arising from being identified with whatever refers to "me."

Suffering and Freedom

We normally think of suffering as the result of things not going the way we (the character in the movie) would like. The View of this path is that suffering is not the result of the character having or not having what it wants. *Suffering is the result of being limited as the character.*

The premise of the path laid out in the LSN is that Devī as Śiva-Śakti is who we are fundamentally. Our true nature is eternal Consciousness that is always whole, blissful, encompassing all of creation while simultaneously transcending it. We don't realize it because we are ordinarily immersed in personhood or ego. Awakening is to discover our true nature, the Self.

Why bother with the grand goal of Self-discovery? Because ego-identification leads us into cycles of joy and pain, hope and fear, and other pairs of opposites known as dualities. What we take to be "me" is based on wanting some specific things to happen and other specific things to not happen so that we can be happy. In fact, *everything* that any of us does is with the intention to be happy. Some of us may engage in wonderful, creative endeavors and some of us in deceit and harming others. *What* each of us does varies according to the flavor of the "me," but the *why* is universal—we do what we do because we want to be happy—not temporarily, but permanently happy. We think that if we had everything we ever wanted, with none of the things that we abhor or fear, then our lives would be perfect. And so we live and die pursuing this ideal situation. There are two problems with this approach.

Firstly, such an ideal situation is exceedingly hard to come by. Secondly, even if it does happen by some great good fortune, it doesn't last forever. Loss is inevitable. We age and lose our youth, our physical and mental abilities, and our loved ones. We can't seem to keep the clock from ticking or the world from changing. No matter what we do, we can't have just one side of any duality. Joy will always be accompanied by pain, gain with loss, hope with fear, and so on. This never-ending cycle of dualities is known as *saṃsāra*. As long as we are identified with the story of "me," cycles of saṃsāra are inevitable. These cycles of dualities are the cause of suffering.

Saṃsāra

- ➢ Cycles of dualities such as joy and pain.
- ➢ Cycles of birth and death driven by dualities.
- ➢ Cycles of dualities arising from taking ourselves to be the "me story."

Awakening

- ➢ Self-discovery or enlightenment.
- ➢ Process of reclaiming our true identity as this eternal, unborn Self (note the capital S).
- ➢ Occurs with the shedding of the ego or the small self (note the small s).

The only way "out" is to transcend our limitations altogether, by realizing what/who we really are. What can we possibly fear or want when we transcend the constrictions of time and space? If we realize that we are always whole and nothing can or needs to be added, what can we possibly want to be happy? The teaching of the LSN is that lasting happiness is the result of awakening to our true nature, which is the very purpose of human life. Humans are uniquely gifted with the ability to choose beyond instinctual behavior that drives other life forms. We have the capacity to go against the grain of our conditioning that keeps us bound in the ego, making freedom an attainable goal.

In fact, the purpose of this (or any other) practice, is freedom, also known as *svatantra*. Svatantra is absolute freedom. Before we get too far, I want to clarify that svatantra doesn't refer to how we may ordinarily think of freedom as nonconformity or rebellion against oppression or certain ways of thinking. Svatantra is much more fundamental—it is freedom from the sense of being a limited individual.

Even though we may think we are free, we are bound by the chains of conditioning. In our everyday lives freedom means the ability to do whatever we want. However, *what* we want is heavily based on the "me story," which is a mish-mash of stuff we have learned about ourselves. For instance, we may want the freedom to dress, work, speak, or worship, in particular ways. Even when we feel that we are rebelling against certain norms by being "ourselves," the need for freedom is centered around the "me story," which is enhanced by the non-conformity. Our rebellion becomes part of the "me story." If our ideas about our "me" are accepted by others, we feel validated. If they aren't, we are enraged and indignant. We tend to hang out with those whose "me stories" are similar to ours so that the ego is continuously validated and soothed. This kind of freedom still lies squarely in the realm of saṃsāra, where our happiness is dependent on the "me story."

On the other hand, heroes like Martin Luther King Jr., Mahatma Gandhi, Nelson Mandela and Victor Frankl teach us that freedom can be attained even in the midst of oppression, slavery, imprisonment and so on. No life circumstance is a hindrance to this type of freedom, which is the purport of the LSN.

Whether we take ourselves to be good, bad, hedonistic, austere, virtuous, or spiritual is irrelevant—taking ourselves to be the *person* is the issue. As long as we take ourselves to be a discrete and separate person, we cannot know our essential non-separation from Devī, which is beyond the story of "me," including race, gender, nationality, culture, and even the history of the universe. If we really want to know Devī, we have to realize our unlimited nature and *become* her. This is the purpose of sādhanā, and the result of moving from duality to non-duality, from taking ourselves to be the limited "me story" to knowing ourselves to be non-separate from Reality. It is realizing that we are far more than the character in the movie.

While some traditions teach us that we are a part, or a spark of, the Divine, the View of this path is that we are the whole—the One Reality. The LSN is magnificent in its teaching of this path since it begins with the nāma Śrīmāta (see N1) that reveals the contraction of the limitless, non-dual Divine into limitation and duality, and ends with the nāma śrī śivā śivaśaktyaikya rūpiṇī lalitāmbikā (see N1000), that declares the unceasing auspicious union of Śiva and Śakti as the One Reality—Lalitā Devī—in every single experience in the fabric of our lives. This journey from N1 to N1000 is the path, and non-duality is the arrival at this supreme knowing of the seamless whole that is our true nature.

How does Reality as Śiva-Śakti manifest and what are its components? Let's see!

Chapter 4

The Descent of Creation

Mapping and classifying creation is a complicated business! Yet, various traditions have found a way to classify and group the "stuff" of creation in ways that foster understanding of those particular paths. The non-dual Śakta-Śaiva Tāntrik traditions describe the descent of Reality into creation by way of the thirty-six principles known as *tattvas* (see Figure 5).

> **Tattvas**
>
> ➢ Tattva = "that-ness" or "such-ness," or a principle of Reality.
>
> ➢ A way of thinking about the descent or contraction of Śiva-Śakti into matter.
>
> ➢ On the spiritual journey, they can be thought of as a map that leads us back home through a reverse process.

We'll examine the tattvas from two standpoints—the descent of creation in this chapter, where we understand how the formless becomes form, and the ascent of sādhanā in the next chapter, where we see the tattvas as the map that takes us to svatantra.

The unmanifest Divine is free of all limitations, divisions, attributes, directions, differentiation and obstructions. The process of manifestation arises from svatantra, the absolute freedom of the Divine. In other words, the Divine *chooses* to manifest the universe of its own absolute freedom.

The two aspects of the one Reality as Śiva and Śakti are the first two tattvas (see previous chapter). Śiva-Śakti's creative energy has three modes of operation, which are intention (*icchā*), knowledge (*jñāna*) and action (*kriyā*), which are the next three tattvas. Up until this point, prakāśa-vimarśa are non-separate, where objects of creation are not separate from the subject. We'll explore this further in the next chapter. For now, what this means is that at this level of the five highest tattvas, there is no separation between creator and creation. Subject and object are one.

A significant step in the descent of Śiva-Śakti into materiality is the casting of the veil of illusion known as Māyā, where the previously unlimited and expansive principle becomes contracted in time,

> **Māyā**
>
> ➢ The veil separating the subject from the object, making them distinct from each other.
>
> ➢ I (the subjective reality) and That (the objective reality) lose their unity when viewed through the veil of Māyā.
>
> ➢ As if Reality looks in the mirror but doesn't recognize the reflection as its own face.
>
> ➢ This seeming separation is brought about by Māyā through limitations known as the kañcukas.

Figure 5. Tattva Map

space, intention, knowledge and action through the kañcukas (more on this soon). The kañcukas give rise to another set of differentiation. Without the veil of Māyā, the subject-object non-differentiation is non-localized. This is to say that Reality's self-recognition is universal—at once, it is nowhere *and* everywhere. The kañcukas contract this global awareness into an individual awareness known as the Puruṣa and the objects witnessed by the Puruṣa into matter known as Prakṛti, the next two tattvas.*

The Puruṣa is the knowing subject, the one that witnesses the body, mind, and the world, all of which make up the Prakṛti. Prakṛti is the materiality, and makes up everything that is witnessed by the Puruṣa. With this step, the individual "I" or subject comes into being. This is the localization of the subject "here" while the world is "there," and the two are separate.

Puruṣa is the pure witness that has no attributes. All attributes are of the nature of Prakṛti, which is saturated with three fundamental qualities, known as *guṇas*. Guṇas are initially in perfect equilibrium,

* Note that this is where the tattva "map" of the Sānkhya system begins.

known as *mahat*. When Prakṛti is permeated by the formless Puruṣa, the guṇas go out of balance, exploding into the material universe. At the macrocosmic level, the guṇas are embedded in the structure and functioning of the cosmos, giving birth to all the subsequent tattvas. Every form becomes individuated, where it is separate and distinct from all others. This is known as *ahaṅkāra*.

At the microcosmic level, the level of the mahat is known as the buddhi or the discerning faculty through which the pure "I" of the Puruṣa is reflected as the ahaṅkāra or ego. Ahaṅkāra is the "I-maker," where the vast array of experiences and attributes (that are Prakṛti) become associated as the "I." If I were to ask you, "Who are you?," you might say you're so-and-so, with a particular culture, history, gender, race, nationality, profession, and so on. This is the function of the ahaṅkāra, where everything we take to be "me" is actually an attribute (Prakṛti), whereas who we *really* are is pure awareness (Puruṣa). The clouding of the buddhi, as we will see later, is the reason why we take ourselves to be the attributes of our stories and body-minds, rather than the Puruṣa. As with the macrocosm, the microcosm is also composed of the three guṇas. As we will see later, the clarity of the buddhi depends on the degree of sattva in it. A clear and unclouded buddhi is predominantly sattvik.

Guṇas

- ➢ The guṇas determine the structure and function of the material universe (see N77).
- ➢ Tamas gives matter its physical structure.
- ➢ Rajas is movement and dynamism, including change and evolution.
- ➢ Sattva its inherent intelligence.
- ➢ At the microcosmic level, tamas is inertia, rajas is hyperactivity, and sattva is calmness.
- ➢ Sādhanā entails moving from tamas and rajas to sattva.
- ➢ The greater the sattva, the clearer the buddhi.

The ahaṅkāra is reflected to the next tattva, which is the *manas* or mind, which is where we process and interpret the world that is taken in through the senses, and the *way* in which we interact with the world is determined. As we can see, both of these functions are strongly influenced by the content of the ahaṅkāra and the clarity of the buddhi. The buddhi, ahaṅkāra and manas together make up what is known as *citta*, the field of thinking and feeling.

We now come to the next five tattvas that are projected by the mind and also perceived by it—the five *jñānendriyās* or sense capabilities (hearing, touching, seeing, tasting, smelling). These tattvas form the gateway for us to experience the world, which can only occur through the senses. We can only *act* in the world through the next five tattvas—the *karmendriyās* or organs of action (speech, manipulation, locomotion, reproduction, excretion).

For the world to be detected by our senses, the

citta must contain subtle properties that correspond with each sense, where the sense organs pick up that property. For instance, we can have ears, but without the property of sound vibration, there is no hearing. These subtle elements make up the next five tattvas known as *tanmātras*—sound vibration, texture, form, flavor, smell. These subtle elements must correspond not only to our senses but also to the material world of the five tattvas of the five great elements or the *pañca mahābhūtas*—space, air, fire, water, and earth.

We can see from this map that from the highest to the lowest, the tattvas are nothing but Śiva-Śakti in manifestation. Each level of manifestation contains all the previous ones. At this point, you might think, "Wait a minute… If everything in creation is Śiva-Śakti in manifestation, why don't I know this? Why is this not my experience?" Well, that is the mother of all questions—why indeed?! What are these limitations imposed on us where we can't see what the tradition says is obvious? Let's see!

Kañcukas

- Rāga (limited in desire).
- Vidyā (limited in knowledge).
- Kalā (limited in action).
- Kāla (limited in time).
- Niyati (limited in space).

Kañcukas and Malas

As we've seen thus far, the manifestation of creation necessarily involves limitation of the limitless. Reality veils Itself in Māyā with her* five coverings known as *kañcukas*. Reality, out of Its own will and freedom, sheds Its unboundedness and freedom to become limited, and takes on five types of coverings of Māyā. When we look at the Tattva map, we see that Śiva-Śakti is characterized by three powers: icchā (will), jñāna (knowledge) and kriyā (action), which are the primordial creative forces. The first three kañcukas are the limitations of these three powers.

Icchā becomes limited as *rāga*, jñāna as *vidyā*, and kriyā as *kalā*. In becoming you and me, these powers contract their sphere of influence and become tied down to our individual abilities. At the macrocosmic level, even the powers of heavenly bodies such as the sun and the stars are limited in time and space. Our sun can't support life in other solar systems and galaxies. At the microcosmic level, our powers are obviously limited as well. In both cases, this limitation is because of the kañcukas.

You see, there is an inherent sense of lack associated with the unlimited Divine becoming limited. In becoming you and me, the Divine willingly becomes associated with our limited stories and identities. You ask me who I am and I tell you my story but in reality, I am (as you are) the divine Śiva-Śakti!

* Māyā is typically addressed as a feminine principle.

And even when I have no idea about Śiva, Śakti or Consciousness, I have a gnawing sense of being incomplete—because my stories don't seem to be the "full story." No matter what I do to fulfill this fundamental sense of lack, it continues to be an issue. I try to fill that gaping hole with money, fame, achievements, success, relationships, spiritual teachings… And yet, it remains unfilled, like an ulcer that just won't heal. This fundamental, universal sense of lack is known as *āṇava mala*. The word mala means impurity, and āṇava finds its root in the word aṇu, which means an atom or a miniscule entity. We feel small, unimportant and not good enough even when we are well-accomplished by common standards. It may not seem like it, but inflated egos and superiority complexes are symptoms driven by this pervasive sense of incompleteness, the āṇava mala.

Malas

- ➢ Āṇava (sense of lack).
- ➢ Māyīya (sense of being separate).
- ➢ Kārma (sense of doership).

The peculiarity of the āṇava mala is that it keeps us constantly in search of completion. What we commonly think of happiness is really the sense of *permanent* fulfillment. We think, "If only I could have this job/relationship/house/promotion/(whatever), I'd never need anything else again." Whatever it is that we're seeking, we're really seeking a state of completion, where we'll never have to seek again, but we are looking in the wrong place—in that job/relationship/house/promotion/(whatever). No matter what we gain, the sense of unfulfillment always returns. Why? Because no object gained from the "outside" can make up for the inherent sense of lack that is the result of taking ourselves to be the "me story."

If we think about it, the "me story" is created in a paradigm of time and space. It begins at birth and ends at death, accumulating experiences along the way that are also based in time and space. If I take my story of me to be me, then the story of you is you, and the story of each person is that person. We feel distinct boundaries in time and space between ourselves and others. This sense of separation keeps us on the defensive—my main concern is "me" and the world becomes "not me." When we band together in our shared stories, our concern expands to "us" versus "not us." Even though we may feel close to our loved ones, we never confuse them for ourselves. We don't mistake our loved one's face for ours. This fundamental sense of being separate and distinct is known as the *māyīya mala*.

The consequence of the "me story" is that the experiences we accumulate merely add to the story. We feel strongly that the desire, knowledge, and action we initiate "belongs" to us. "That was *my* idea," "*I* deserve the promotion because *I* work hard," "*I* failed because *I* didn't do my research," and so on. This sense of volition, where we "own" the consequences of our actions (good or bad), is known as the *kārma mala*. What we don't see, of course, is that the very premise of the "I" is faulty and fictitious! It's like the movie character taking credit and accepting blame for the movie in which she herself is being directed.

Rāga is a function of the three malas, where our desires revolve around the story of "me." What we think we are drives what we desire (rāga). We become passionate about particular things, as in wanting specific outcomes that relate to the "me," strengthening the "me story" even though it can never lead to permanent happiness. Our knowledge is limited in time and space as vidyā, which is what we gain from our experiences (which, as we've seen earlier, are objects). Limitation is the very nature of transactional knowledge - there's no way to know everything about everything in the universe!* Limited desire and knowledge give rise to kalā or limited action. No matter how influential we are, our sphere of influence will always be limited.

To understand the last two kañcukas, we need to explore another concept, known as *saṃskāra*.

Saṃskāra

When it comes to us, the microcosm, it's not that we aren't driven by the same divine powers of will, knowledge and action. We very much are! Whether we are engaged in huge creative projects or are preparing a meal, we have to have the desire, the knowledge of how to actualize the desire, and the ability to act on it. It's just that our desires don't arise in *absolute* freedom. They arise from a complex web of past influences, known as saṃskāras.

Saṃskāras

- Grooves of conditioning that determine our way of being and doing.
- All the ways we think of ourselves, such as "I am a good parent, a neat freak, a responsible adult, sucks at math, hates violence, loves nature…" are the product of saṃskāras.
- Saṃskāras are essentially the bits and pieces of the past that have become the "me" (more accurately, what we think the "me" is).

When we take ourselves to be our story, the knowledge necessary for actualizing our creative power is also limited to what we have learned in the past or within our circle of influence. We don't have complete knowledge spanning *all* spheres of influence and transcending the limitations of time. Rāga and vidyā result in limited powers of action, which is kalā. We can only act on certain things and in certain ways. Even so, we can't be assured of the outcome.

Driven by the āṇava mala, which gives rise to rāga, vidyā and kalā, we long for a specific outcome in our creative endeavor. After it is done and when we have tasted its fruit (desirable or not), we carry its traces in the "me story." The collection of stories of

* See Bhuvaneshwari in *Shakti Rising.*

the *past* that project into the *future* are the result of the next kañcuka, *kāla*—the timeless Divine becoming bound in linear time.

The ahaṅkāra is shaped by these traces of our past known as saṃskāras. As we can see, this mishmash of stuff limits us in space—all this that I think I am—is very specific to *this* mind-body. This limitation in space is the function of the fifth kañcuka known as *niyati*. It is also the limitation of causality, where we feel "I'm this way" *because* of my parents, culture, that incident, those people, and so on.

Saṃskāras bind us further in the limitations of will, knowledge, action, time, and space. They cloud the lens of the buddhi, where the ahaṅkāra accumulates objects that make up the "me story." Saṃskāras keep us entrapped in the cycles of saṃsāra, and this is known as *karma*.

Karma

Karma as the sum total of *all* our past actions that determine future outcomes. At the outset, I'd like to point out that karma is not vindictive, which is how it tends to be popularly understood! It's not a phenomenon of an unseen entity out to get us or punish us. With that out of the way, let's explore what it really means.

Another word that's used synonymously with saṃskāra is vāsanā, which literally means fragrance. There's no essential difference between the two, but one way to understand them together is that saṃskāras shape the "I," while the fragrance of the saṃskāras drive our passions as vāsanās. Think of vāsanās as the juice of our passions. In this book, we'll use these words interchangeably. Whatever we call them, these past impressions reside in the causal body (more on this later, in Chapter 6) or the subconscious mind. They are formed while an experience is taking place.

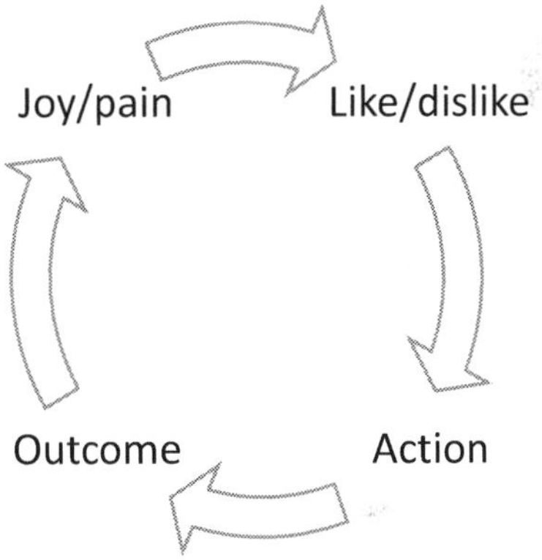

Figure 6. The Cycle of karma

Say you've never tasted a strawberry and you bite into one. In that instant, a strawberry vāsanā is created. You now know its taste through this interaction. If at some point, you become so obsessed with strawberries that the vāsanā begins to drive your action of buying them by the bushel and gorging on them, you've become a strawberry addict! When our actions are driven entirely by vāsanās without the intervention of the discerning buddhi, they become addictions. The normal functioning of the brain and the body is overpowered by the vāsanā; neural and hormonal pathways are reset by the substance that we crave. The vāsanā rules over us.

Not all vāsanās or saṃskāras are consciously formed. While some can be recalled as specific memories in the conscious mind, most of the time, we don't know *why* we like some things and dislike other things. For instance, you meet someone for the first time and there is an instant dislike. You have no idea why since you've never met this person before. Sometimes, this can be a result of a highly developed intuition, but this is an exception. Most of the time, what we think is intuition is merely a product of past impressions. To know the difference between the two takes a highly discerning buddhi. We'll explore this in some depth later (see Tarka, Chapter 12). At any given moment, our experience of life is being modified by thought forms and emotions arising out of the subconscious vāsanās. The way we interpret an experience depends on our unique vāsanās, which is why a dozen people having the same experience will register it in a dozen different ways. Even as you're reading this, various thought-forms, fragments of images, phrases and words might be arising, which determine how you'll interpret this sentence. These spontaneously arising modifications are known as *vṛttis*, and are particularly noticeable when we are trying to meditate. When people say they can't meditate because their minds are too busy, it's just that they're more aware of the vṛttis when they're sitting quietly than when they're engaged in activity. Obviously, these are the people that *need* to meditate (but we'll come to this later)!

Our past impressions bind us to the cause-and-effect phenomena of our actions (see Figure 6). We engage in certain actions because we want a certain outcome based on our likes and dislikes, which in turn arise from our past impressions. Whether the outcome is what we wanted or not, it becomes associated with the ahaṅkāra, strengthening the "me." From moment-to-moment, we create karma through our actions that are based in past impressions. It's not like the vāsanās are neatly categorized in the subconscious mind—at any given point, a whole host of related vāsanās arise to become our current thought stream, emotional state, and our behavior.

If we zoom out to look at the macrocosm for a minute, the entire universe is like a web of the karmas of all forms. Your karma is connected to everyone else's (and in fact, to every form that was ever in existence). For this particular moment to be unfolding the way it is, everything from the beginning of time had to unfold exactly as it did. Your present activity of reading this sentence is the result of your karma, which is a tiny part of this greater karma.

Saṃsāra also refers to the cycles of birth and death. Our storehouse of vāsanās is so vast that it contains impressions over a timeline that traverses countless lifetimes. We are reborn again and again as long as we continue to create karma—this is the other meaning of saṃsāra. If we were to envision our storehouse of vāsanās as a very large bank account, it's as if we withdraw some of it to live out in a particular lifetime. The cycle of saṃsāra ends when the bank balance goes to zero, but here's the rub—we keep creating more in every lifetime and so it can't ever be depleted!

A more practical way to look at reincarnation is to think of it as endless cycles of rebirth of the ahaṅkāra, which is born of desire for certain specific outcomes and fear of unwanted outcomes, driven by the three malas. The central problem is the āṇava mala, the fundamental sense of lack. We want what we want because of this sense of lack. Everything that any one of us does is to assuage this sense of lack. However, it can never be satisfied by acquiring things, degrees, relationships, emotional or psychological victories. Yet, this is exactly where we look for respite, becoming entrapped in a cycle of rāga-driven actions and their consequences. The "me story" is born again and again in our moment-to-moment interactions. The only way out of the cycles of saṃsāra is to realize our true divine nature, which is already whole and complete. With this realization, no further karma is accrued, and the bank balance is depleted. In other words, karma only applies to the "me story." As long as we take ourselves to be the movie character, we are limited to the plot of the movie. Realizing our true nature is like knowing that we are not just the character. We are that in which the entire movie is playing.

Bhaṇḍāsura and the Āṇava Mala

We have now established that the āṇava mala is the primary problem that gives rise to our limitations and keeps us bound in saṃsāra. And the āṇava mala, of course, is the symptom of having forgotten our true divine nature. In the LSN, Bhaṇḍāsura is this symptom and the unceasing itch that is the āṇava mala. In playing the character of Bhaṇḍāsura, he forgets his true nature as Kāma, the radiant god of love and desire. Even conquest and dominion over the universe for 60,000 years can't scratch his itch of wanting more.

Bhaṇḍāsura is, of course, a figment of human imagination, but he's a fine example of our ordinary state of being. Nothing we do, acquire or learn scratches the itch of wanting more. We become established in our vāsanā-driven ways, reacting in the same way to stimuli because we've lost the freedom of choosing to act otherwise. Even when we think we are free, we are slaves to our conditioning! When we call upon Devī, she arrives with her entire army of yoginīs and goddesses to destroy Bhaṇḍāsura, the malas and the kañcukas of Māyā, leading us to svatantra.

What do we need to do for svatantra? This is precisely what we'll examine next. Thus far, we've seen how the Divine descends into creation (and limitation). We'll now navigate this map in the opposite direction, which is the ascent of sādhanā.

Chapter 5

The Ascent of Sādhanā

In this chapter, we'll explore the tattvas in the reverse direction, from limitation to limitlessness. While the descent of creation was seen with respect to both the macrocosm and the microcosm, the ascent process applies to the microcosm, specifically to sādhanā.

Let's take another look at the Tattva Map (see Figure 5). As you'll see, there is an additional classification into the "pure" (*Śuddhādhvan*) and "impure" (*Aśuddhādhvan*) paths demarcated by the Māyā tattva. This is a good time to state emphatically that this classification into pure and impure has nothing whatsoever to do with conventional ideas about purity or morality. What it refers to is the sense of separation.

Remember prakāśa-vimarśa, and the aspects of the subject-object that we discussed in Chapter 4? Those aspects will be helpful for us to understand the scheme of the pure and impure paths. We've seen before that when vimarśa as Śakti turns toward manifestation, there is a split of the One into three—pramātṛ (subject), prameya (object), and the process of the subject perceiving the object (pramāṇa). (See Figure 4 in Chapter 3.) Importantly, we've seen that even though it *appears* like the subject (Ahaṃ) and object (Idam) are two different things, they are essentially the One experiencing Itself.

The Impure Path

At the level of the impure path (below Māyā tattva), all the three malas are in play, and we perceive the world entirely objectively. Things appear as solid, separate objects. This state is known as *sakala*, which is in play in the waking and dream states (see States of Consciousness, Chapter 8).* In the deep sleep or comatose states, the subject-object differentiation dissolves, but not because of Self-knowledge. It is a dissolution into the darkness of ignorance. This state is called *pralayākala*, where the kārma mala doesn't exist but the other two malas are in play.

At the level of the Māyā tattva, the state of perception is known as *vijñānakala*, which is what happens when we progress in sādhanā. Here, the dissolution of the subject-object differentiation occurs in deep meditative states. Unlike the state of deep sleep where the dissolution is into ignorance (as in, we

Pure and Impure Paths

- The pure and impure paths have to do with *seeming* differentiation between the subject or perceiver (Aham) and object or That (Idam).
- The Māyā tattva delineates the pure and impure paths.
- Below Māyā, Ahaṃ and Idam remain separate.
- Above Māyā, Ahaṃ and Idam are non-separate.

* Swami Laksmanjoo in *The Secret Supreme*, Createspace Publishing Platform, 2015.

don't wake up from deep sleep with the realization of our true nature), in the vijñānakala state, the meditative absorption is the result of wisdom or higher awareness. Here, only the āṇava mala is in play. This higher awareness, however, is not permanent.

In the impure path, there is a superimposition of Idam on Ahaṃ. This is the case where *objects* or Idam (by way of stories, experiences and attributes —remember these are all in the realm of Prakṛti) are superimposed on the *subject* or Ahaṃ because of ahaṅkāra, which, in turn, arises from the clouding of the buddhi.* We mistakenly take these superimposed objects to be who we are, the subject.

Above the Māyā tattva, there is no *essential* separation between Ahaṃ and Idam, where they are seen as a continuity of each other. The insight into this fundamental nature of reality, where there is a lack of separation between Ahaṃ and Idam is known as the pure path or *Śuddhādhvan*. Śuddha refers to purity of perception, where the veil of Māyā has been seen through. All other situations where there is a separation between Ahaṃ and Idam, are grouped together as the impure path or *Aśuddhādhvan*, referring to dualistic perception where the three malas are in play to varying degrees (see Figure 7). The pure path is that of non-dual insight where the malas have been removed.

The Pure Path

The top five tattvas of Śuddhādhvan are ways of describing the One Reality by way of phases of awareness. In both—the directions of descent and ascent —the top two tattvas remain as Śiva and Śakti. While, in the direction of descent, we have icchā, jñāna and kriyā as the next three tattvas, they are known differently in the direction of ascent. The tattva corresponding with kriyā is Śuddha Vidyā, with jñāna is Īśvara, and with icchā is Sadāśiva.

Liberation is the attainment of any of these phases. To "get" here (which is not a place!), we would have traversed the impure path to pierce the veil of Māyā. All the pure path states are associated with a sense of

Figure 7. The Ascent of Sādhanā

* Recall that ahaṅkāra means "I-maker," as in, it makes Ahaṃ out of Idam!

wonder, amazement, and joy, known as *camatkāra*. The first of the five higher tattvas in the ascent from Māyā tattva is Śuddha vidyā. At this level, Ahaṃ and Idam are one, but there is a slight dominance of Idam or That (universe) over Ahaṃ or I (perceiver). At the Śuddha Vidyā level, kriyā śakti is dominant because of emphasis on the manifested universe (That).

However, this state is not necessarily stable. With continued opening to non-dual insight, we arrive at the next state known as Īśvara.* Here, the previous state of Śuddha Vidyā is stabilized. While in the previous state the universe seemed incredulous ("What? I am THAT?"), now there is a settling into knowing that the universe is really of the nature of the I ("Yes, I am THAT. THAT I am!"). The universe (That) is felt to be in the Self (I). With the emphasis on the "I," Īśvara is at the level of jñāna śakti, the knowledge of creation. With further stabilization, we arrive at the next state called Sadāśiva, where the Self (I) is in the Universe (That). The declaration here is, "I Am That," and is at the level of icchā śakti. The next state is that of Śiva-Śakti (taken together), which is replete with all Divine powers and svatantra, absolute freedom—"I Am."

While the transition from the impure path to the pure path was a critical turnaround, progression along the five aspects of the pure path is a matter of stabilization and deepening of non-dual insight through increasing clarity of the buddhi.

Paths and Means

From the above explanation, we see that the pure and impure paths don't refer to the left- or right-handed paths known as *ācāras* (see Chapter 11), which refer to the *means* to arrive at non-dual insight.

It is again important to reiterate that these distinctions don't have conventional judgments associated with them. The use of the word impure does not refer to an individual practitioner and is not a character flaw. *Any* ācāra, be it right-handed or left-handed, can be utilized to traverse the journey from the impure to the pure path. One can tread the right-handed path with all the moral, social and cultural injunctions and continue to experience a separation between "I" and "That"—in this case, they would still be traversing the impure path despite all outer forms of conventional purity.

On the other hand, arrival at non-dual insight via the use of any of the left-handed means (which are considered morally transgressive) would be considered the pure path, despite the outer lack of purity. Impure and pure merely differentiate between dualistic and non-dualistic insight. Ignorance of our true nature is the only impurity that matters on this path!

Another way to think of the pure path is that it is the turning of vimarśa toward prakāśa, rather than toward the world of objects. It is in this "turning upon oneself" that we become privy to the secrets of Śuddhādhvan. And it is through the unclouding of the buddhi that we can turn in this direction.

Śuddha Vidyā and the Bindu

When we look at the Tattva Map, it begins with the

* Īśvara also means God.

The Supreme Teaching of the LSN:

- ➢ Devī scintillates as the bindu that explodes into every experience.
- ➢ Devī is the triad of experiencer, the infinite range of experiences in creation, as well as the process of the experiencer.
- ➢ *Devī is all that exists.*

division of Śiva and Śakti. There is a higher principle that is the very basis of the entire map, and that is Śiva-Śakti in perfect communion, where such a differentiation doesn't exist. We call this the highest or ultimate Reality, the fabric, as it were, upon which the whole map is constructed. It isn't included in the map because it is the very basis for the map, subsuming and pervading all its elements. If the words on this page represent the map, Reality is the white of the paper upon which the words appear, without which the words wouldn't exist.

The Śrīcakra is a dynamic representation of the tattvas (see Chapters 9-10). The central point or bindu is this Reality, the perfect communion of Śiva-Śakti. In the LSN and in Śrīvidyā, this Reality is represented by the bindu as Lalitā Devī. The splitting of the bindu into the innermost triangle (representing pramātṛ, prameya and pramāṇa) is the basis for the rest of the components of the Śrīcakra. However, the bindu isn't a discrete point. It pervades all the components of the Śrīcakra, Śiva-Śakti sporting with each other as prakāśa and vimarśa in all. It's just that we don't recognize it because of the limitations imposed by Māyā.

As the supreme sovereign of the cosmos, Devi controls the five actions of the Divine—creating, sustaining, destroying, concealing, and revealing (N1-5). Several nāmas in the LSN refer to these five functions and Devī's authority over the deities that are traditionally assigned to them. We visualize Devī in the bindu, sitting upon a throne whose seat is Śiva as Sadāśiva,* the revealer, and whose four legs are Brahma, Viṣṇu, Rudra and Īśāna who create, sustain, destroy, and conceal.

The cosmos expands (unmeṣa) and contracts (nimeṣa) with the blinking of her eyes. She conceals her own nature (*tirodhāna*) to become limited so that she can fully experience the range of flavors (see Rasa, Chapter 12) in her own countless forms. At her own will, she reveals herself (*anugraha*), much to her own wonder and amazement (*camatkāra*).

Śuddha Vidyā can be viewed as the path that enables the recognition of the bindu in our day-to-day experience with the resultant camatkāra. The journey to Śuddha Vidyā enables us to relinquish our habitual ways of grasping and pushing away through the cultivation of equanimity, inner silence, perfected reasoning (*sat-tarka*) and devotion to the path (*bhakti*), all of which we will delve into later (see Chapter 12). With the dawning of this recognition of Reality pulsing as the bindu in all of our dealings, ordinary experience is rendered extraordinary. This is the secret of existence.

* Note that Sadāśiva is one of the many names of Śiva, as well as one of the states of the Pure Path. In the context of the LSN, Sadāśiva as Śiva is the revealing power of Devī, and the seat of her throne!

Chapter 6

Śarīrās, Prāṇa and kośas

In this chapter, we'll explore the many ways in which we can understand the veiling of Māyā in our body-minds. Why is it so hard for us to know our Divine nature? What is the nature of our physical-emotional-psychological-psychic make-up that veils Reality? It turns out there are many different ways to explore the microcosm; they're inter-related and can seem repetitive. The microcosmic maps are presented here according to their relevance in Śrīvidyā and the LSN. We must remember again that because Śrīvidyā contains Vedik *and* Tāntrik aspects, the concepts explored here don't belong to any *one* single stream and contain concepts of both.

Śarīrās

- Sthūla śarīra is sustained by food, where everything we consume is digested and assimilated into the trillions of cells forming the various organ systems.
- Sūkṣma śarīra is the subtle body made up of prāṇa, energy, mind, and intellect.
- Kāraṇa śarīra is the causal body that is made up of vāsanās/saṃskāras or impressions.

Śarīrās

The sthūla (gross), sūkṣma (subtle) and kāraṇa (causal) śarīrās are three "bodies" that determine our particular body-mind traits. In the Tattva Map, we'd place the sthūla śarīra at the level of the pañca mahābhūtas, the five great elements in *their* gross forms. The jñānendriyās and the tanmātras are registered and karmendriyās are impelled into action in the sūkṣma śarīra. The external world is brought in through the sense organs (as seeing, smelling, hearing, touch and taste) and reaction or response to the world is sent out through organs of action (working with hands, speaking, walking, excreting, reproducing). In the Tattva Map, everything from the ahaṅkāra to the tanmātras would make up the sūkṣma śarīra.

The kāraṇa śarīra with the saṃskāras clouds the buddhi and drives the sūkṣma and sthūla śarīrās, determining how we act, choose, think, and feel from moment-to-moment. It's the kāraṇa śarīra with the clouded buddhi that prevents us from knowing our true nature. The differences in how we react to the same stimuli are a result of our vāsanā-driven personalities. My unique personality (or your equally unique personality) with its idiosyncrasies, preferences, aversions and talents is a product of vāsanās that have been collected over previous lifetimes as well as by upbringing, culture and experiences of the current one. We saw in Chapter 4 that our vāsanās are the result of the three malas. The āṇava

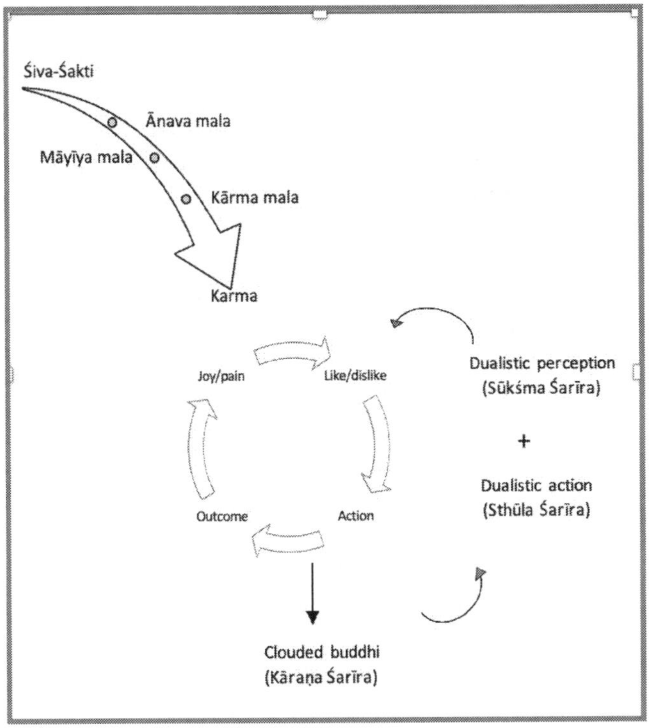

Figure 8. Malas, Śarīras and Karma

mala gives rise the māyīya and kārma malas and, together, they bind us in cycles of saṃsāra through karma and creation of more vāsanās (see Figure 8). In the process, the buddhi remains clouded, veiling our ability to know our true nature. The entire spiritual path can be viewed as the process of clearing the buddhi.

Let's pause here and consider this question. What *animates* the śarīrās to bring about clouding of the buddhi or freedom from limitations? Even more fundamentally, what animates *anything* in creation? The answer is *prāṇa*.

Prāṇa

Prāṇa is, quite simply, the energy of Consciousness. Śiva is unchanging, timeless, and static, while Śakti is dynamic and creates changes through space and time as the universe. As the primordial creator, she is known as Mahāśakti. Prāṇa śakti is a small fraction of Mahāśakti that animates *everything* in manifestation. Prāṇa is life (which is why sentient beings are called prāṇī). Without prāṇa, there's no life, no tattvas, intellect, ahaṅkāra or manas, thought, perception, feeling, breath or body. Prāṇa śakti pervades all of manifestation, and permeates every plane of existence.

In common parlance, we tend to equate prāṇa with breath or oxygen. Prāṇa is neither, but is the principle that animates both the breath and the intake of oxygen (along with every minute metabolic pathway).

The manifest universe arises from Prakṛti's three guṇas, sattva, rajas and tamas. Rajas is the principle of dynamism, whereas tamas and sattva are static. The action of rajas on tamas and sattva gives rise to the jñānendriyās, the karmendriyās, the tanmātras, and the pañca mahābhūtas (the last 20 tattvas). The pañca mahābhūtas combine in specific ways to give rise to three *doṣas*—vāta, pitta, and kapha.

Doṣas are applicable to everything in the manifest universe. The movement of the wind, planets, blood, breath, peristalsis, neural pathways, thought, and everything related to movement is a function of vāta, which is also known as vāyu (wind). Evolution, seasons, aging, metabolism, and everything related to transformation is a function of pitta. Everything related to structure is a function of kapha. The functions of pitta and kapha are dependent on vāta, which is why it is known as the king doṣa. Vāta has five subtypes known as the prāṇa vāyus, which drive the functioning of our mind-body physiology.

Doṣas

- Vāta is movement (space + air).
- Pitta is transformation (fire + water).
- Kapha is structure (water + earth).

Prāṇa and Prāṇa Vāyus

- Prāṇa śakti is the great animator of the universe.
- Vāta as prāṇa vāyus drives the functions of the body-mind.

Prāṇa Vāyus

- what is outside is taken in (prāṇa).
- what is taken in is digested (samāna).
- what is digested is assimilated (vyāna).
- what isn't processed is eliminated (apāna).
- what is assimilated is transmuted (udāna).

Prāṇa vāyu governs the other vāyus and is inward in direction as the intake of breath, food and water, sense perception, knowledge as learning, and awareness turning upon itself in sādhanā. *Apāna* governs all downward movements such as elimination, ovulation, menstruation, childbirth, and sexual activity. *Samāna* is equalizing with a churning action, governing digestion. *Vyāna* is diffusive and responsible for circulation, nerve impulse conduction, joint and muscle movements, and mental activity. *Udāna* is upward and governs expression as speech, will, effort, memory, and strength. As far as sādhanā is concerned, the strength and quality of the prāṇa vāyus determines our progress (see Figure 9). Samāna is our ability to digest experiences without creating saṃskāras/vāsanās. The strength of samāna determines whether we can see the continuity of prāṇa śakti between subject and object. The quality of samāna determines how much we can take in via prāṇa by way of teachings or sādhanā, and how much of what we take in can be transmuted to abstract thought and discernment via udāna. Samāna, prāṇa and udāna depend on apāna —if our past stuff of impressions isn't processed and eliminated, we can't possibly absorb or digest what is taken in. The greater the strength of apāna, the greater is the efficiency of vyāna with smoother flow of vāyu in the nāḍīs.

What we can gather from this brief study of the prāṇa vāyus is that *all* spiritual paths manipulate prāṇa. Everything we do in terms of sādhanā is about

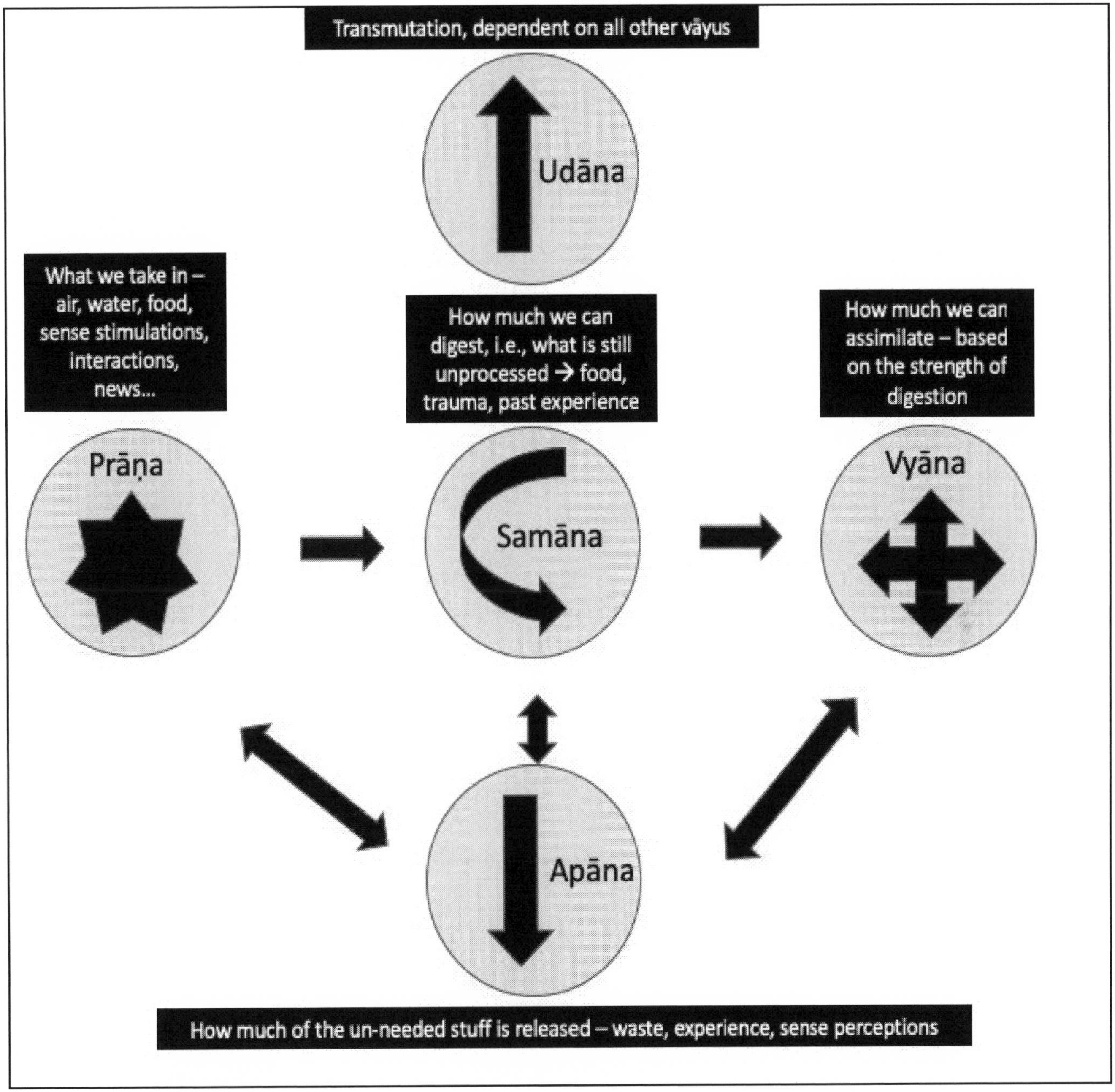

Figure 9. Prāṇa Vāyus

manipulating the prāṇa vāyus so that we may realize the essential oneness of prāṇa in all of creation.

Sometimes keeping track of these prāṇas can seem confusing and onerous, but it may help to remember that they're not separate entities. In the grand scheme of things, there's just one prāṇa. Prāṇa śakti is the primordial source of the universe, driving all classifications, including those of the prāṇa vāyus (of course, using the same name to describe two different aspects adds to the confusion!). Think of prāṇa śakti as being all the way up in the Tattva Map, driving all the other classifications, including those of the doṣas. Vāta or vāyu (along with its 5 subtypes) is itself a manifestation of prāṇa śakti, which is a portion of Mahāśakti (or simply, Śakti—see Figure 10). To further understand the all-pervasiveness of prāṇa and its role in sādhanā, let's delve into where in the microcosmic map we might be able to locate them.

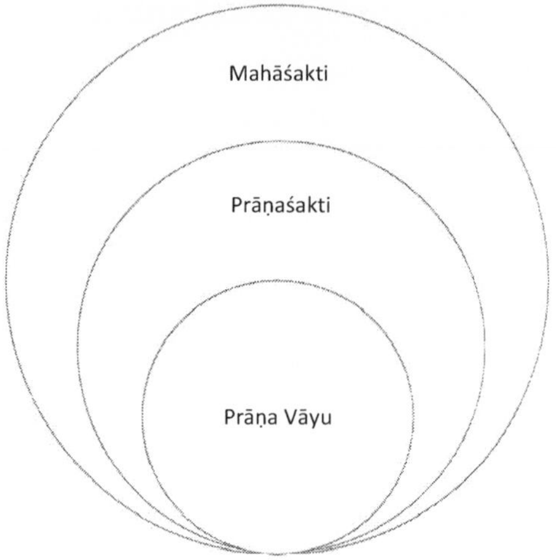

Figure 10. Mahāśakti, Prāṇaśakti, Prāṇa Vāyu

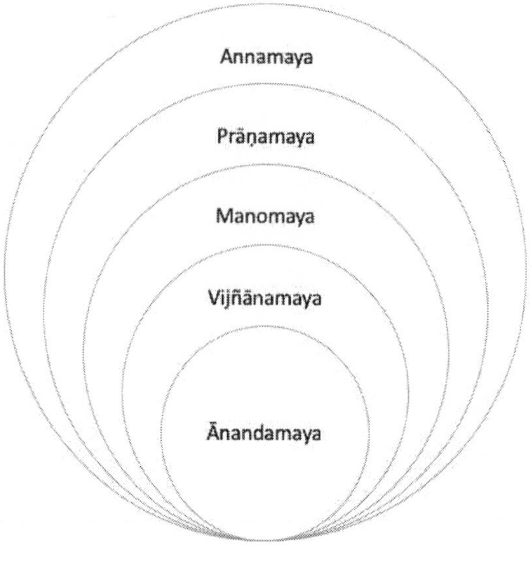

Figure 11. Kośas (Vedāntik)

Kośas

The pañca kośas or the five sheaths are another way to look at the microcosmic map. We can think of these sheaths being nestled in layers, much like the Russian nesting dolls. The kośas are described differently in Vedānta and non-dual Tantra. In Vedānta, the sheaths begin with the physical body. They influence each other and become increasingly subtle, the last being the sheath of bliss.

The annamaya kośa is animated by the prāṇamaya kośa, consisting of prāṇa. Prāṇa drives all our biological processes, from the minute sub-cellular functions to the gross movements of our body. Aging is the result of prāṇa depletion, and death of the physical body is the exhaustion of its stores.

Pañca kośa (Vedāntik)

- Annamaya kośa is the physical body made up of our cells, organs, and organ systems. The word "anna" refers to food, and the annamaya kośa is sustained by what we eat.
- Prāṇamaya kośa or the prāṇa sheath.
- Manomaya kośa consists of the thinking mind, memory, and the processing of sense impressions.
- Vijñānamaya kośa is the sheath of discernment, or the buddhi that underlies the thinking mind.
- Ānandamaya kośa is the bliss sheath.

The manomaya kośa is who we take ourselves to be, and is shaped by our early life experiences, which determine how we process our thoughts, emotions, and memories. The mind sheath is where we ordinarily "live," with the constant stream of thoughts that drive our behavior.

The vijñānamaya kośa is where we know, judge, decide, choose, and discriminate between good and bad, useful and not useful.

Kośas and Śarīras

- Annamaya kośa corresponds to the sthūla śarīra.
- Prāṇamaya, manomaya and vijñānamaya kośas together correspond to the sūkṣma śarīra.
- Ānandamaya kośa corresponds to the kāraṇa śarīra.

The ānandamaya kośa is the subtlest sheath where the seeds of vāsanās reside, obscuring our natural state of ānanda, which we will examine later.

The clouding of the ānandamaya kośa by vāsanās reflects on to the vijñānamaya kośa, creating flaws in our discernment. Flaws in discernment in this kośa are reflected on to the manomaya kośa, influencing how we think, feel, and take in the world. This is then reflected on to the prāṇamaya kośa, which is in turn reflected on to the annamaya kośa.

Conversely, the state of our body, health or disease influences the flow of prāṇa in the prāṇamaya kośas, which affects how we think, feel and interact with the world. The impressions we acquire in the process influence the vijñānamaya kośas, and are reflected on to the ānandamaya kośa as vāsanās

Pañca kośa (Tāntrik)

- Cit (pure awareness or Self).
- Śūnya (void).
- Prāṇa (life force).
- Citta (buddhi, ahaṅkāra, and manas).
- Deha (physical body).

In the non-dual Tāntrik tradition, the model of the pañca kośas is different (see Figure 12). This model is more congruent with the understanding of prāṇa śakti being the primordial energy of life, driving the body *and* the mind (more appropriately, the citta, which is the field of buddhi-ahaṅkāra-manas). Prāṇa kośa is thus more upstream, closer to the purity of the Source—beyond it are only the sheaths of void and Self. The void is the kośa of absolute stillness that is known in deep meditation states. Although Self is categorized as a kośa, it really isn't! It pervades all the other kośas and is the knower of them. It is the real "I", whereas the other kośas are "That" (see Chapter 6).* In this sense, the Self is not a kośa at all.

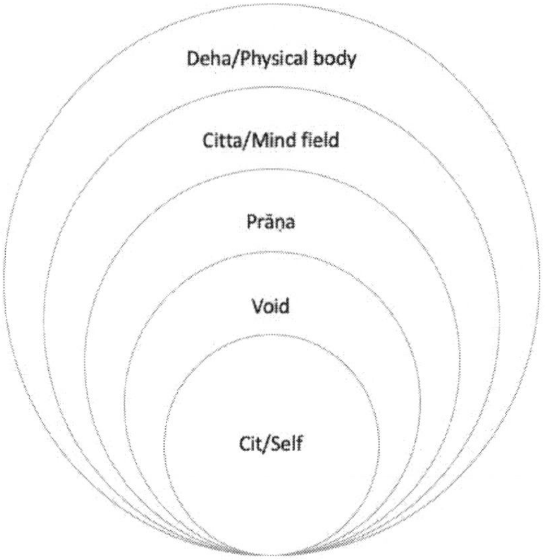

Figure 12. Kośas (Tāntrik)

We ordinarily mistake one of the outer four kośas to be the "I," and this innocent mistake is known as ignorance. Ignorance is the result of scattering of prāṇa in the kośas that maintains the (usually erratic) functioning of the deha (body) and citta. Understanding the pathways of prāṇa is a significant aspect of Tāntrik sādhanā, where prāṇa is streamlined for the purpose of awakening. One way of understanding these pathways is through a study of wheels of energy known as cakras.

* While prāṇa is placed after the void, even awareness of the void is a function of prāṇa śakti! Remember that prāṇa in the context of the kośas refers to the prāṇa *vāyus*, but prāṇa śakti is that which gives rise to the vāyus.

Chapter 7

Cakras and Kuṇḍalinī

Prāṇa is said to flow through thousands of subtle channels known as *nāḍīs*. Although they're compared to arteries and nerves, they're neither. Instead, nāḍīs are the phenomena through which prāṇa becomes limited in time and space.

Three Main Nāḍīs

- Īḍā, piṅgalā, and suṣumnā.
- Connect the perineum to the crown.*
- Reminiscent of the caduceus, the symbol of medicine.
- Suṣumnā is the central channel.
- Īḍa is on the left (cold/moon/lunar).
- Piṇgala is on the right (hot/sun/solar).
- Īḍa and piṇgala periodically wrap around to the other side.

* (Footnote: See Wallis, C in *Tantra Illuminated: The Philosophy, History, and Practice of a Timeless Tradition*. Mattamayura Press, p. 390.

Of all the nāḍīs, a dozen or so are considered important enough to be described, three of which are the īḍa, piṅgalā, and suṣumnā. For most of us, prāṇa switches between the īḍa and piṅgalā several times over the course of the day. This periodic switching is the hallmark of the dualistic tendencies of the ordinary mind, marked by our constant vacillation between our likes and dislikes, which center around "me" and result in constant mental dialogue or vṛttis. Think of it as the mechanism that maintains the illusion of the many when there is only One. As prāṇa switches between the two nāḍīs, it briefly enters the central staff, the suṣumnā, when the breath is even between the nostrils and the mind is quiet. For the most part, the suṣumnā remains closed off, except for the brief times during the switching of the nāḍīs.

Cakras

- Converging points of nāḍīs.
- There are countless cakras.
- The number of cakras that "matter" depends on the tradition, and varies greatly.
- In Śrīvidyā, six placed along the spine are important for sādhanā.
- Grounding zones of the mahābhūtas, acting as two-way gates between the microcosm and the macrocosm.
- Storehouses of particular vāsanās reflected from the kāraṇa śarīra.

Nāḍīs converge at various points forming cakras or "wheels." What is important to consider is that the

Table 1

Location	Name	Mahābhūtā	Sense	Deity	Petals	Dhātu	Food
Root	Mūlādhāra	Earth	Smell	Sākiṇī	4	Bone	Mung beans
Sacral	Svādhiṣṭāna	Water	Taste	Kākiṇī	6	Fat	Yogurt
Navel	Maṇipūra	Fire	Sight	Lākiṇī	10	Muscle	Sweets
Heart	Anāhata	Air/Wind	Touch	Rākiṇī	12	Blood	Greasy
Throat	Viśuddhi	Space	Sound	Dākiṇī	16	Skin	Pāyasā*
Eyebrow	Ājña	Mind	Mahat**	Hākiṇī	2	Marrow	Saffron

**Pāyasā is rice pudding*

***Mahat is the mind prior to sense perception*

description of cakras as we commonly think of them varies greatly according to the teacher and her/his own understanding. In Śrīvidyā, their description is more of an instruction for a procedure known as nyāsa. Each cakra is visualized as a lotus with a specific number of petals and is ruled by a particular emanation of Devī. The cakra deity resides in the center of the lotus, and within each lotus petal is a subordinate deity. Each cakra deity rules over a particular *dhātu* or body tissue, and favors certain foods (see Table 2 below and N475-534).

Each lotus petal corresponds to a Sanskrit syllable; the total number of all the petals in the six cakra lotuses add up to 50. In one nyāsa practice, we focus on the seed syllables within the lotus petals of the cakras at various bodily locations. The purpose of this practice is to direct prāṇa to each syllable through our attention, where the sound of each syllable becomes a gateway to the Self as it moves from differentiated Word (vaikharī) to the Source (parā). We'll explore this very important teaching in Chapter 8.

In Śrīvidyā, greater importance is given to the areas in the vicinity of the cakras where prāṇa becomes stuck or tangled, like knots (see granthis, below). In this tradition, we don't, for instance, "work on the anāhata" as a stand-alone practice. The visualizations and the practice of mantra are more holistic, as in, they work on *all* the cakras in any one body-mind. The sādhanā adjusts the flow of prāṇa to undo the knots of the body-mind that cloud the buddhi lens. We can understand this through another commonly-used word, which is Kuṇḍalinī.

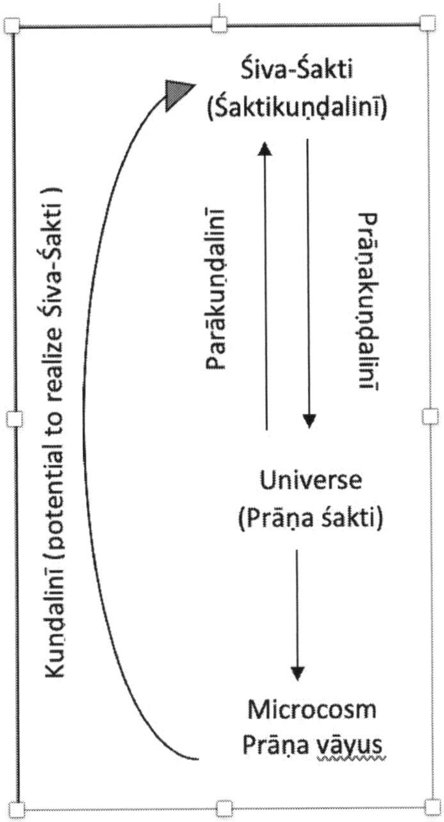

Figure 13. Kuṇḍalinī

Kuṇḍalinī

At the outset, we would be well-served to understand what the word Kuṇḍalinī even means. For this, let's retrace our steps back to Śiva and Śakti as prakāśa and vimarśa. Earlier, we saw that vimarśa when turned outward results in manifestation, and when turned upon itself returns to blissful union with prakāśa. The energy of this union that is not yet turned toward manifestation is compared to a swollen seed about to germinate.* Śakti rests as Supreme Consciousness within herself (*samvit*), and is known as *Śaktikuṇḍalinī*. Here, at the level of the ultimate Reality, there is no movement inward or outward, and the energy is perfectly balanced.

When the energy turns outward, Śiva as prakāśa becomes obscured in manifestation. This outward turning of Śaktikuṇḍalinī is known as *Prāṇakuṇḍalinī*. When it turns inward, the world as if disappears and Śiva as prakāśa shines (see Pure Path in Chapter 6). This inward turning is *Parākuṇḍalinī*. In other words, Prāṇakuṇḍalinī and Parākuṇḍalinī work in seemingly competing ways—when one is predominant, the other is obscured. It's this pulsing that is known as spanda, the world manifesting when Śakti opens her eyes, and dissolving when she closes them (see Figure 13).

Consciousness as Prāṇakuṇḍalinī emits from the One to become many, descending into manifestation as prāṇa śakti, which in turn gives rise to the prāṇa vāyus. As you may recall, the prāṇa vāyus govern the functioning of the body-mind, which is the microcosmic equivalent of the universe. The prāṇa vāyus are a fraction of the Prāṇa Śakti in the microcosm that are turned outward; ordinarily, this is where our concerns lie. We are caught up in the world of objects and the cycles of saṃsāra because

* Silburn L. Kuṇḍalinī: *Energy of the Depths*, SUNY Press, NY 1988, page 22.

> **Kuṇḍalinī**
>
> - Potential for turning inward to discover Self that lies dormant because of the outward turned prāṇa.
> - Śiva as prakāśa is said to lie at one end of the suṣumnā.
> - Kuṇḍalinī is Śakti as vimarśa at the other end of the suṣumnā.
> - Kuṇḍalinī is Devī in her subtlest form in the LSN.

of this outward turning of the prāṇa. The *potential* for turning inward lies dormant in the microcosm as what is commonly referred to as *Kuṇḍalinī*, which means the coiled one.

Kuṇḍalinī, in other words, is Śakti as vimarśa and is said to lie dormant at one end of the spine while Śiva as prakāśa resides at the other end. The two ends are connected by the suṣumnā nāḍī. Prāṇa switching back and forth in the īḍa and piṇgala is equivalent to vimarśa turned toward manifestation as Prāṇakuṇḍalinī. When prāṇa briefly enters the suṣumnā during the back-and-forth between the īḍa and piṇgala, it is as if vimarśa is turned toward prakāśa. Mostly, however, the energy is scattered in the world of objects.

Kuṇḍalinī is pictured in the center of the Mūlādhāra (see Table 1, p.44) as a snake coiled three and a half times around a point of power that represents Śiva. She is fast asleep, with her head blocking the entrance of the suṣumnā (except when she briefly and involuntarily enters it during the switching of prāṇa). When the suṣumnā opens (spontaneously or through sādhanā), the dormant Kuṇḍalinī is "awakened," and begins to flow in the suṣumnā. She uncoils and becomes erect, piercing through the knots of saṃskāras. Kuṇḍalinī in the LSN is Devī in her subtlest form. When awakened, prāṇa becomes directed inward and upward, where Kuṇḍalinī moves toward Śiva at the crown. What we must remember here is that Śiva-Śakti are never separated, even though we commonly think of Kuṇḍalinī as Śakti rushing to meet Śiva. A more accurate way of understanding the ascent of Kuṇḍalinī is that it is a progressive *awareness* of their essential non-separation.

Let's pause here to clarify what we mean by Kuṇḍalinī "awakening." While we may have heard of all kinds of symptoms associated with this, in very simplistic terms, it is the process of turning inward, from being engrossed with objects of the world (Idam) to wanting to know the subject or perceiver (Aham). To reiterate, turning inward does not mean that we lose our fascination with external objects of the world and become enamored with internal phenomena such as visions and voices. Turning inward here means to turn upon oneself, where instead of focusing on *what* we are perceiving, we are interested in that which is the *perceiver.*

Kuṇḍalinī awakening is sometimes associated with challenges and problematic symptoms, which can be related to the flow of the prāṇa vāyus before the process, and the conflict between the two. When this process begins, it tends to have a mind of its own and Śakti as Kuṇḍalinī moves according to *her* will. If these movements cause friction with our established ways of thinking and being, it can be challenging. When our attention remains on these symptoms, we remain outward-turned since symptoms are objects and not the subject. Since awakening forces the process of turning inward upon oneself, focus on symptoms creates more friction and discomfort.

Kuṇḍalinī awakening is not always a problem. In fact, it most often occurs almost unobtrusively, with progressive deepening of insight and peace as it moves through the five sheaths, integrating each into itself and opening to the vast potential of the brain. The buddhi becomes unclouded in this process, becoming progressively clear of the debris of saṃskāras because of strengthening of the apāna vāyu. Samāna vāyu becomes supercharged and balanced, and its ability to digest experience increases greatly.

Saṃskāras and the Flow of Prāṇa

- Saṃskāras direct the flow of prāṇa in specific ways, binding us in the habitual ways in which we think, feel, and act.
- Conditioning by saṃskāras restricts the flow of prāṇa to only a fraction of the nāḍīs.
- The infinite possible ways in which prāṇa can move remains only as a potential.
- Kuṇḍalinī awakening resolves saṃskāras, removing the limitations for the flow of prāṇa.

Kuṇḍalinī awakening is a massive housecleaning, where the previously unused nāḍīs open up through the strengthened vyāna vāyu. Our ability to be *other than what we are conditioned to be* increases exponentially with this housecleaning. Our perception shifts, along with our ability to choose, act, feel, think, and connect.

The root represents the area of creative energy in the body, where sexual fluids are ordinarily expelled *out* by the action of apāna vāyu. The immense potential that is encapsulated in the creative energy is thus dispersed to a large extent, with very little being available for transmutation through udāna vāyu. With Kuṇḍalinī awakening, the creative potential of the sexual fluids "turns" upward through the strengthened udāna vāyu. Instead of being discharged out, the energy is transmuted for clarification of the buddhi, cultivation of tarka and the collapse of the subject-object split. This is known as Kuṇḍalinī yoga. The whole process of awakening in Kuṇḍalinī yoga is to move from the impure to the pure path.

While we think of Kuṇḍalinī as residing in one location and moving to another, it isn't a linear process. As we see from the table of the cakra deities, Devī resides in *all* locations as *visarga*, the potential to turn inward (see Chapter 8). Thus, awakening can begin at any location and migrate to any other, to eventually move to the sahasrāra, representing the resolution of the subject-object split. For this, Kuṇḍalinī needs to undo the knots known as granthis.

Granthis

Granthis are the knots of saṃskāras that keep us bound in ignorance and saṃsāra. They are the mass of nāḍīs that are closed off due to prāṇa flowing only in particular ways. The number and locations of the granthis identified vary depending on the tradition. In Śrīvidyā, we are concerned with three of them that are named after the trinity of deities that create, preserve and destroy the cosmos (see Figure 14). Here, these three granthīs refer to the creation, preservation, and destruction of the ego or ahaṅkāra. The Brahma granthī is at the mūlādhāra and represents the lower three cakrās. This granthi is exceedingly hard to untangle because of the density of the saṃskāras related to the formation of the ahaṅkāra.

Figure 14. Granthis

Everything we hold dear, including the mass of beliefs about ourselves and the world that forms our worldview, is here in this granthi. The saṃskāras of the other two granthis are dependent on this one. As we'll see in the LSN, we create complex mental constructs (vikalpas) out of our experience beginning very early in life, and unless worked on consciously, they act as invisible puppeteers that determine how deeply we remain entrenched in saṃsāra.

The Viṣṇu granthi is at the maṇipūra*, made up of the obstructions that *preserve* the ahaṅkāra. Through ongoing creation of karma, we continue to preserve the limited sense of self, adding on more saṃskāras/vāsanās through our attractions and aversions. It is because of this preservation that the "me story" is kept alive. The Rudra granthī is at the ājña and represents the saṃskāras that prevent clarity of discernment. It is

Granthis

- Brahma granthi is just below the mūlādhāra, representing saṃskāras related to the creation of the ahaṅkāra.
- Viṣṇu granthi is just below the maṇipūra representing saṃskāras related to the preservation of the ahaṅkāra.
- Rudra granthi is just below the ājña representing saṃskāras related to the prevention of the ahaṅkāra's destruction.

* Viṣṇu granthi is described as being located at the anāhata in other sources. In the LSN, it is located at the maṇipūra.

called Rudra granthī because the ahaṅkāra is laid to rest through perfected reasoning (tarka) that brings an end to the ahaṅkāra and the three malas.

Kuṇḍalinī, in her ascent, pierces through each of these granthis, releasing the reserves of energy that were trapped in creating and preserving the ahaṅkāra, and opening previously closed off nāḍīs. However, the process of Kuṇḍalinī yoga in the Śrīvidyā path is not one where the awakening comes at the cost of a "normal" life, where we abandon the world and family, and retreat into solitude. In fact, it is a path that is deeply life-affirming, as in conducive to both bhoga (enjoyment) of the world and mokṣa (liberation) from saṃsāra. This is where we'll need to pause and understand mokṣa in the context of the puruṣārthas.

Puruṣārtha

No matter who we are or where we come from, all our desires and passions can be categorized into one of the four universal categories known as the puruṣārthas: *dharma, artha, kāma* and *mokṣa.*

Dharma is the desire to lead a purposeful life and to contribute to society. Each of us longs for a purpose, and to feel like our lives are meaningful. When our purpose is aligned with that of the family, the community or society we live in, we feel a certain degree of contentment. When misaligned with universal laws in the form of harming others or ourselves, a deep internal rift is birthed, with associated psychological, emotional, mental, and physical ailments.

Puruṣārthas

- ➢ Dharma is the desire to lead a purposeful life.
- ➢ Artha is the desire to have our material needs met.
- ➢ Kāma is the desire for fulfillment of sense pleasures.
- ➢ Mokṣa is the desire for liberation.

Artha is the universal desire to have our material needs met. While each of us needs food, shelter, clothing, and material wealth/resources, the degree to which this is sought leads to inner harmony or lack thereof. When our *wants* are greater than our *needs*, there is a web of associated issues, where we create more and more vāsanās based on attractions and aversions.

Kāma is the desire for fulfillment of sense pleasures in the form of art, music, beauty, sexual union and so on. More importantly, kāma is the biological desire for life and for the innate sense of longing for enjoyment and through connection with objects and people. Notice that Kāma is thus also the name of the deity that personifies this primordial desire.

Mokṣa is the desire for liberation, which is essentially to be free of longing and seeking. Technically, it's not in the category of the other desires, since it is the desire to be free of desire! Every other desire is merely a desire for freedom, cloaked in the particular objects we seek. Remember that *all* desires are driven by the āṇava mala. What we are really seeking is to feel whole, where nothing more is needed. Mokṣa is the actualization of this wholeness.

What each of us desires specifically is dependent upon our unique matrix of saṃskāras/vāsanās. Desire becomes rāga when it is centered around the ahaṅkāra. We may mistake this to not be the case if we are desiring something for our loved ones. However, rāga is the wanting of *specific* outcomes limited to our own little sphere of influence. It is the lack of a larger perspective or inclusion of the world in our desires. When we want a specific outcome, we fail to see that it comes at a cost to others who aren't in our sphere of influence. If I want a promotion at work and there are three others who are equally qualified, rāga is the wanting that is colored by my limited perspective. I can't see that they too are qualified, and that my getting the promotion may mean doom for one of them. I'm also unable to know whether the promotion is in my own best interests over the long-term. Rāga is the result of being stuck in the grooves of conditioning, where prāṇa is restricted to the well-traversed nāḍīs.

While all paths are based on the understanding of limited desire as rāga, they differ widely in the prescriptions to mitigate it. Some paths, like that of Patāñjali yoga, seek to cut off desire in the form of sense perception. Since the world is the source of desire, the prescription is to withdraw from the world, where it is no longer an issue. Śrīvidyā, on the other hand, is about realigning our limited desire or rāga with Devī's will or icchā. When we say it is life-affirming, we don't mean that all our limited desires are fulfilled in some magical way. It means that the path teaches us how to become aligned with Devī's icchā even while being fully engaged in the world, where we discover *ānanda* (which we'll explore next) in our moment-to-moment experience. It is a path where the buddhi is cleared in such a way that we find that our lives, bodies, minds, situations and circumstances, and the world—*everything* is perfect as is. In fact, it has always been perfect; we simply didn't know it. This attainment is known as *jīvanmukti.*

On this path, there is no need to cut ourselves off from the world. Every experience, thought, and emotion becomes a stimulus for ānanda. Every moment becomes a gateway to freedom. This is the path of bhoga, and we come to see that Devī is the bhoginī (see N293). Cloaked as "us", she is the real enjoyer of all of our experiences. After all, the purpose of creation is for the Divine to enjoy itself in countless ways. Even mokṣa can be achieved in many different ways, as far as the Divine is concerned. And so we see that, within the path of Śrīvidyā, there are various ācāras (see Chapter 11) or specific ways to go from rāga to icchā. The process of moving from rāga to icchā is like polishing an uncut diamond, where its natural radiance begins to emerge. Here, the result of the polishing is the emergence of bliss, which is also known as *ānanda.*

Ānanda

Before we move on, we should clarify what bliss really means in the context of this tradition. Unfortunately, the word in its overuse has become misconstrued to mean living and pursuing our desires (as in the famously misunderstood quote from Joseph Campbell, "Follow Your Bliss!") or being "blissed out" in what may be described as states of joy, not caring, or ecstasy, usually arising from temporarily forgetting our troubles or worries.

Ānanda

- Ānanda is the bliss arising with the coming to rest of our constant seeking.
- Ordinarily, we are driven by a restlessness because of a deep sense of not being enough (āṇava mala).
- Ānanda is the resolution of this sense of lack, where we no longer need anything to be content.
- This bliss is the overflow of our own wholeness (pūrṇatā).

One of the conundrums that we face is the mistaken notion that restless seeking is the fuel for activity and achievement. After all, this is what we are taught in modern society, where our worth is directly proportional to how much we attain in a given amount of time. Passion is a desirable quality, along with ambition and competitiveness. Of course, it's true that the restlessness of seeking is the fuel for sādhanā as well. If we didn't have the burning desire for truth and for liberation, why would we want to meditate or contemplate abstract concepts? And yet, as we peel away the layers of vāsanās, we come to rest in the core of our being and come to see that the void we were trying to fill—the āṇava mala—was merely the veiling of our always-perfect nature. Not only is our core full and perfect (*pūrṇatā*), but it flows into the other kośas, infusing them with its sweetness. The motivation for performing well shifts from *needing* to fill the void of incompleteness through greed and ambition to *wanting* to express this overflowing of ānanda.

On this path to ānanda, we are bound to come across one of the key concepts of the tradition, which is that of expression. What is the process by which the Divine comes to express Itself in the infinite objects? This is what we'll examine at some length in the next chapter.

Chapter 8

Vāk

Vāk, which means "speech" or "word," refers to the *expression* of the Divine in manifestation. In other words, the entirety of creation is the expression of the Divine as language. While this tradition isn't alone in equating Divine manifestation with language, it goes to great lengths to map out reality in terms of expression.

The highest level of the word, known as *parāvāk,* is identical to vimarśa, the power of self-awareness (see N675). As we saw earlier, vimarśa turned toward prakāśa is the state of equilibrium, where the split into the triad of experience (pramātṛ, prameya and pramāṇa) is yet to occur. Parāvāk is at the level of absolute freedom, as Parākuṇḍalinī, where all possibilities exist in the unmanifest state. Parā is the subtlest pattern of Reality, which will subsequently give rise to the triad of that which expresses (herself), that which is expressed (the universe made up of sound) and what these sounds condense into—the objects of the universe. As this great mother, she is also known as Ambikā (see N295). This is to say that from Parā flow both the objects of the universe as well as the sounds and words that refer to them. We must remember here that, in this process of contraction, parāvāk is not diminished. She remains whole and complete, subsuming all levels of expression within herself. At the level of parāvāk, there is no subject-object distinction (see Figure 15).

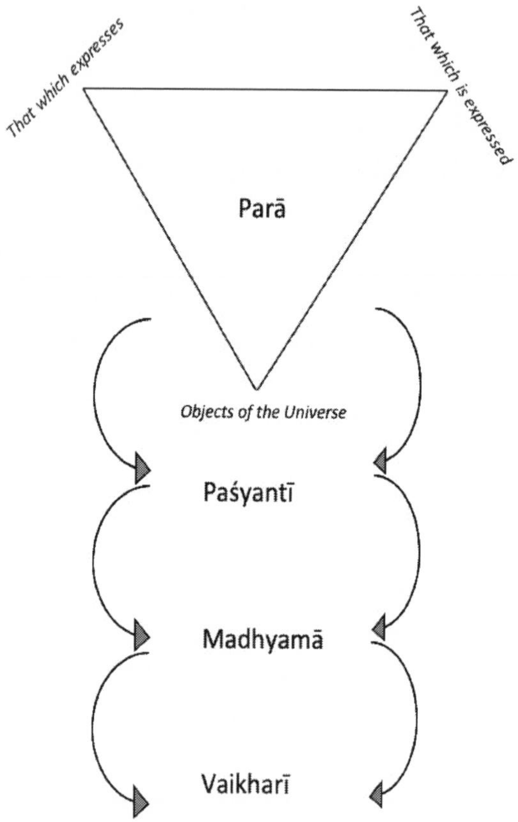

Figure 15. Descent of Vāk

With the turn toward manifestation we encounter the next level of the word known as paśyantī

Paśyantī Vāk

- ➢ Perceiving level of expression.
- ➢ The first impulse of the Divine toward manifestation.
- ➢ Language that is at the precognitive level.
- ➢ At level of Icchā Śakti.
- ➢ Vāmā.

vāk, the *perceiving* level of expression, which is a slight contraction of parāvāk. We can think of it as the stir of Divine will or icchā Shakti that precedes creation. The personification of the Devī at this level is called Vāmā, where she "vomits" out the universe that was held within her. At the microcosmic level, it is the wordless language of our vāsanās. One way to understand this is through the example of the first glimpse of on object. Before it is recognized, it is vaguely registered. There is no characterization or even an acknowledgment. It is only registered. It has been perceived, and nothing else has happened yet to differentiate it. Paśyantī is like this, operating at the level of the kāraṇa śarīra, prior to the vāsanās shaping themselves into bits of thoughts and images that make up the next level, called madhyamā.

Madhyamā Vāk

- ➢ Intermediate level of expression.
- ➢ Language that is at the citta level.
- ➢ At level of Jñāna Śakti.
- ➢ Jyeṣṭhā.

Descending from the precognitive level, expression now takes on more concrete shapes. At the macrocosmic level, madhyamā is at the level of jñāna śakti, where wordless will or icchā becomes the knowledge for actualization. Devī personified at this level is known as Jyeṣṭhā. At the microcosmic level, madhyamā is the language of the sūkṣma śarīra, including the citta with the intellect's reasoning and choosing, the mind's myriad bits of thoughts and images, and fragments of memory. Here, at this level, madhyamā reflecting the paśyantī of our vāsanās creates the "me story," and determines how it is actualized at the next level, known as vaikharī.

Vaikharī Vāk

- ➢ Articulated level of expression.
- ➢ Language that is at the gross level of objects.
- ➢ At level of Kriyā Śakti.
- ➢ Raudrī.

Vaikharī is articulated language. At the macrocosmic level, vaikharī is at the level of kriyā śakti, or the actualization of icchā and jñāna into the objects of creation. Personified at this level, Devī is known as Raudrī. At the microcosmic level, vaikharī is expression at the level of the sthūla śarīra as spoken or articulated language, which is a reflection of the sūkṣma and kāraṇa śarīras. As we have seen previously, our view of the world and ourselves is shaped entirely by our vāsanās, the primordial reason for which is the āṇava mala giving rise the māyīya and kārma malas.

At this point, we may wonder *how* the Supreme Reality manifests as the world. In the non-dual Tāntrik traditions, the actualization of the formless into form is described through the elaborate sequence of the 50 phonemes of Sanskrit.

Mātṛkā and Mālinī

Phonemes in their subtlest, as yet undifferentiated form, lie at the level of parāvāk as śabdarāśi or mass of sounds. With the movement toward differentiation, the phonemes become known as Mātṛkā, meaning "little mother" or matrix, the one that gives birth to the Universe.

Differentiated into the 50 syllables of the Sanskrit alphabet beginning with "a" and ending with "kṣa", Mātṛkā śakti is the wheel that turns the universe, permeating all levels—the subtlest to the grossest—of manifestation. The Sanskrit phonemes are dynamic representations of the explosion of Śiva-Śakti into forms with varying vibrations. Think of them as a spectrum of fifty rays of light, each with a specific vibration (nāda) and color (varṇa) (see N299 and N577).

The undifferentiated stage of parāvāk is at the highest level, where the 16 vowels *(a, ā, i, ī, u, ū, ṛ, ṝ, l, ḹ, e, ai, o, au, aṃ, aḥ*) represent states of Divine cognition (*parāmarśa*) that will then lead to manifestation. These 16 vowels and stages are also known as *tithi*, which refers to the digits of the lunar half-month. In Śrīvidyā, they are personified as the Nitya Kalā Devīs (see Deities of the Śrīcakra in Chapter 9). In the context of the śabdarāśi at the level of parāvāk, the progression from unmanifest to turning toward manifestation begins with the vowel *a*, which is known as *anuttara* (see Figure 16). This is the highest level of Reality, which will subsume all other subsequent levels.

The anuttara (*a*) splitting into two (*a* + *a*) as Śiva-Śakti gives rise to the next vowel, *ā*, which is *ānanda*, the bliss of their union. Different Divine potencies arise within Śiva-Śakti as a result of their union, becoming progressively charged from *i* to *au*.

The vowel *aṃ* is the intense focusing of this charged energy at a single point, which is the bindu. This concentrated energy of manifestation contained within Śiva-Śakti is emitted out and is represented by *aḥ*, the *visarga*. However, the visarga is not unidirectional as in only turning toward manifestation. It is symbolized by two dots, one above the other (:), representing the simultaneous turning **out** of the Divine into manifestation and **in** to revel in Its own bliss. In other words, the Divine is always experiencing Itself as manifestation. Even though there appears to be a split between that which expresses (the subject) and the objects of the universe (see Figure 15, above), they are always in perfect union.

What we need to remember here is that not only is there the perfect union of the subject-object but also of the word and the object to which it refers. For instance, the *word* tree and the *object* consisting of the trunk, leaves and roots, are, in reality, One. We tend to think that the word refers to the object when in fact they are both emanations of the One.

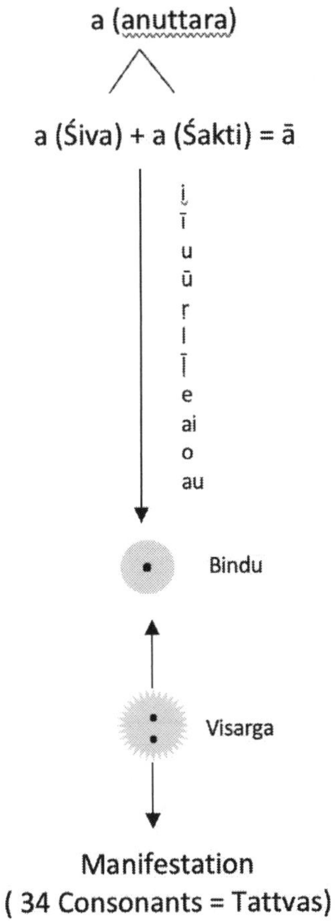

Figure 16. Mātṛkā

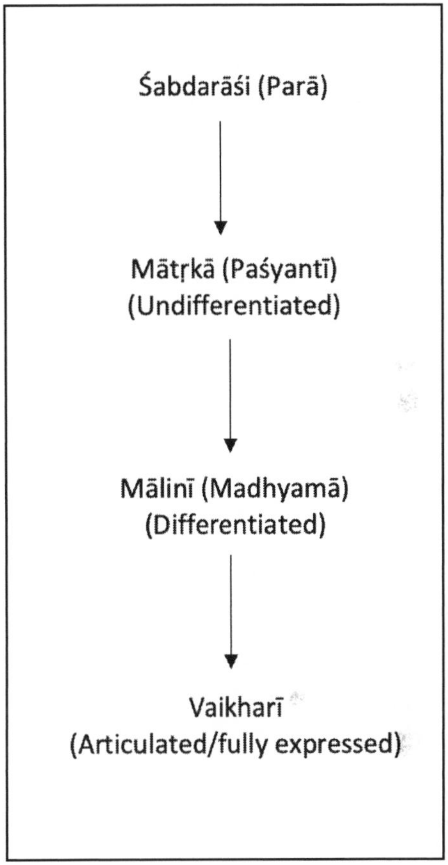

Figure 17. Vāk, Mātṛkā and Mālinī

Thus far, we are still at the level of parāvāk, and the movement from anuttara to visarga is occurring within Śiva-Śakti. Think of this as a preparatory stage before external manifestation. The turning outward of the visarga gives rise to the 34 consonants of Sanskrit, each corresponding to a tattva below the level of Śiva and Śakti (see Tattva Map, Chapter 4).

The śabdarāśi at Parā becomes reflected as Mātṛkā at Paśyantī, the tattvas being perceived in as yet an undifferentiated state. Here, the split into the subject-object and word-object has occurred, but is as yet unregistered (see Paśyantī Vāk above).

Microcosmic Stages of Vāk

- Parāvāk is at mūlādhāra as unmanifest potential or Kuṇḍalinī.
- Paśyantī is at the maṇipūra, where vāk is still undifferentiated and as yet not detected by the ordinary state of mind.
- Madhyamā is at the anāhatā as subtle thought and feeling.
- Vaikharī at the viśuddha becomes the spoken word.

Mātṛkā refers to the sequence of vowels and consonants in the order of the Sanskrit alphabet, where the vowels represent Śakti and the consonants Śiva.* The fifty phonemes with their particular varṇas also correspond to the fifty petals of the 6 cakra lotuses. As we explored earlier (see Chapter 7), each cakra is made up of a specific number of petals and is governed by a unique emanation of Devī. Each petal is ruled by a Mātṛkā whose name begins with the bīja or seed letter of that petal.

The phonemes and tattvas at paśyantī further contract and become differentiated at madhyamā, where Mātṛkā becomes reflected as Mālinī (see Figure 17). While Mātṛkā at parāvāk and paśyantī follow the sequence of vowels and consonants of Sanskrit, Mālinī is a seemingly random arrangement. The vowels and consonants are mixed together, occurring in no apparent logical order, symbolizing the inseparability of Śiva-Śakti. Here, the subject-object and word-object distinctions are almost complete—we confuse objects for the subject and words for the objects to which they refer.

Mālinī is the precursor of expression at the grossest level, which is vaikharī. At this level, differentiation between the subject-object and word-object is total, and tattvas and phonemes are "mixed up" in the material world.

What we glean from this very brief study of vāk is that at the macrocosmic level, the Sanskrit phonemes represent the actualization of creation, where Divine will and knowledge have become the objects of the universe through Divine action.

At the individual level, three of the four stages of vāk are inaudible, and only at the vaikharī stage is it expressed audibly. Even though the other three stages arise spontaneously from Parā as the stuff of the citta and spoken language, this process is shrouded in ignorance. The movement toward expression reaches paśyantī and madhyamā when we first become aware of it as the citta-stuff—thoughts, images, and fragmented bits of language—which is then articulated as vaikharī. At every level of expres-

* In the Trika system of non-dual Śaiva tantra, the vowels are Śiva (symbolizing seed) and the consonants are Śakti (symbolizing wombs), whereas in Śrīvidyā, this order is reversed. The vowels are Śakti and the consonants are Śiva, emphasizing that Śiva cannot function without Śakti—the consonants are similarly unpronounceable without vowels.

sion, all other levels are inherently present. One of the many ways we can understand the various levels of expression at the microcosmic level is through the states of consciousness.

Vāk and States of Consciousness

- ➢ Vaikharī—waking state—sthūla.
- ➢ Madhyamā—dream state— sūkṣma.
- ➢ Paśyantī—deep sleep—kāraṇa.
- ➢ Parā—turya and turyatītā—transcendence.

States of Consciousness

Our ordinary, day-to-day life can be viewed in terms of three states of consciousness—waking, dreaming, and deep sleep.

Jāgrat

The ordinary waking state known as *jāgrat* is characterized by our dynamic involvement with the gross objects of the world at the vaikharī level. The separation between me "here" and the world "there" is very apparent. Objects and the words referring to them are separate and yet become so tightly associated that we take them to mean the same. Even though the word tree refers to a particular object, we are unable to see that both the word and the object arise from the same Source! I look around at the objects of the world—nature, furniture, cars, and people, and they all appear to be concrete and discrete objects that are not "me." Here, we are operating at the sthūla level, where our attention is so much on objects that the only way we refer to ourselves is in relation to them (this is *my* house, *my* car, *my* purse, *my* partner, and so on).

Svapna

In *svapna* or the dream state, we are still experiencing objects, but they are subtle and at the madhyamā level. The dramas and storylines played out in our dreams are dredged up from the subconscious mind and play out on the screen of consciousness. Here too, they are being experienced by the subject, the "me." In my dream, the subject and the objects are of my own mind being projected onto the screen of my own consciousness. The primary difference between the waking and the dream states is how "real" the objects are; they appear to be more solid in the waking state than in the dream state.

We must remember that svapna doesn't just apply to the state into which we disappear when we are sleeping. It also includes the states of dreaming while being awake (such as daydreaming or reveries), where both I and the objects are not as solid as in jāgrat. In fact, svapna is our ordinary way of being, where we are constantly "lost in thought." These subtle mind objects take center stage and the I is defined by them. In this state, my sole concern is how I am affected by what I see, hear, feel, taste and smell, and how they "make" me think and feel. Here, the subject recedes to the background and the objects of our reverie take center place. Even though the subject and objects, as well as words and the objects to which they refer, are all arising within the same consciousness, we are unable to see that this is true. As we will see later, the waking state for a yogin (practitioner) is different, where subjectivity shines even while being engaged in the world.

Suṣupti

Suṣupti is the state of deep sleep, which is devoid of both gross and subtle objects and is at the level of paśyantī. Here, although there is a subtle differentiation between the subject-object and word-object, it is unrecognized. The subject-object relationship "hibernates," resulting in deep rest (which is why deep sleep is a necessity!). Here, we come to rest in the kāraṇa śarīra, and objects of the waking and dream state are withdrawn into their formless seeds.

Turya

Turya is the fourth state, but is technically not a state (since state refers to a temporary or changing condition). It is the witnessing awareness in which the other three states occur and is parāvāk turned toward manifestation as the visarga. The objects of the waking and dream states as well as the darkness of the deep sleep state ordinarily obscure turya, which is like the uniform white background of the pages of a novel upon which the words of the story appear. In our Tattva Map, turya is the Puruṣa that is untainted by conditioning. While in reality Puruṣa is the subject, the I, we take the *objects* that are perceived by the subject to be the I. The buddhi clouded by saṃskāras prevents us from knowing the true subject and, instead, we take the saṃskāra-driven body-mind to be who we are.

Turya is our experience in deep meditative states known as *samādhi*, where the separation between the subject (the meditator) and the object of meditation collapses. While this is also the case in deep sleep, there is a crucial difference. In both deep sleep and samādhi, time and space cease to exist because both time and space require the triad of subject-object-experience. The "me" can experience "the other" only in time-space constraints. Although there is loss of subject-object differentiation in deep sleep, it is shrouded in ignorance because when we wake up from deep sleep, nothing has changed and we continue to be identified as the "me story."

On the other hand, samādhi is suffused with Self-knowledge (where Self with a capital S is knowing our self to be the witnessing awareness). When we emerge from samādhi, things are different, at least to a certain extent. However, it is possible to have had a samādhi and still forget the Self when engrossed in the waking, dream and deep sleep states.

Turyatītā

Turyatītā is the fifth state, which is neither a state nor a hierarchical concept. It is parāvāk as the bindu, turned upon herself. Turyatītā is the lived experience of the fully awakened yogin, where witnessing awareness is stabilized and subsumes all other states. For such a one who is awake/liberated, gross and subtle objects are no different than the Self (see Chapter 5). Turyatītā is the natural condition of the awakened yogin where the Self is her experience in all other states. Distinctions between subject-object and word-object have dissolved, and all is of the same flavor (*samarasa*) of the union of Śiva-Śakti. This is the stateless state of orgasmic bliss, which pervades the other states, bubbling under the surface of every experience.

Language in Sādhanā

When it comes to sādhanā, we are often told that our outer reality is a reflection of our inner world. We must be clear that this is not a teaching about quick schemes of abundance where we learn to think in particular ways in order to gain specific results or to manipulate or "attract" certain outcomes. The purport of the teaching in this tradition is to see that how we interpret the world is entirely dependent on our inner state. In this tradition, our inner state (like the cosmos) is a matrix of language at various stages of density. When Devī as the Word rests in her undifferentiated form, Śiva looks at her in absolute amazement (camatkāra), for she contains in herself the highest Veda as well as the lowliest thought. She is the power of the Word that binds us in our saṃskāras as well as the one that frees us from them. To know this is liberation; in fact, Self-knowledge is the knowledge of Mātṛkā śakti.*

While ignorance is the path of becoming more contracted from parā to vaikharī, sādhanā is the retracing of this path, from vaikharī to parā (see Mantra Sādhanā, Chapter 12). Ordinarily, the subject-object separation that defines our experience of life also creates a paradoxical unity between an object and the language used to describe it. We innocently come to take the word for the object, even though the two are independent emanations of Reality. When we assign a particular meaning or label to an object, we lose the ability to see the object independent of the label. In this solidified word-object association, we become trapped in the limitations of Māyā, since such an association binds us in the five kañcukas. A significant leap in sādhanā is the realization that such an association doesn't inherently exist in the fabric of Reality. With the loosening of the word-object association, we begin to work directly on the āṇava mala.

The intimate understanding of language is like power-cleaning the buddhi lens. The clearer our vision, the greater is the ability to see harmony and perfection even in imperfect or undesirable circumstances. Another way to deepen our understanding of the various aspects of the microcosmic map is to examine it from the standpoint of the Śrīcakra. This is especially significant for practitioners of the LSN, since many of the esoteric names of Devī refer to her emanations in the Śrīcakra.

* Swami Lakshmanjoo in *Śiva Sutras, The Supreme Awakening,* Munshiram Manoharlal Publications, 2010.

Chapter 9

The Śrīcakra in Manifestation

While a detailed description of the Śrīcakra is beyond the scope of this book (see Resources for recommendations), a cursory understanding at least will be immensely helpful as we approach the LSN.

The entire Śrīcakra is constructed around the bindu and contains within itself the macrocosmic and microcosmic maps, formed by the intersection of nine triangles: five downward-facing of Śakti and four upward-facing of Śiva (see N71). See Table 2 below for a summary of what these triangles represent in the macrocosm and microcosm. These nine intersecting triangles give rise to 43 smaller triangles, which are surrounded by two circles of lotus petals, and an outer square. Each of these components—the square, the lotus-petal circles and the small triangles—are viewed as nine layers around the bindu, and are called āvaraṇas (coverings). They're called āvaraṇas because they cover or conceal the bindu, and each is classified as being of Śiva or Śakti.

We can think of the Śrīcakra in three ways known as *krama* (sequence). Srṣṭi krama helps us understand manifestation, from the bindu to the bhūpura. On the other hand, sādhanā is about the progressive dissolution of the āvaraṇas corresponding to the progressive unclouding of the buddhi, with untying of the granthis, transcending habitual ways of thinking and being, and the cultivation of discernment and tarka or perfected reasoning (see Chapter 12). This is the saṃhāra krama, where we move from the bhūpura to the bindu. The third is the sthiti krama, where, with the dawning of Self-knowledge, we see that life and the universe arise from and dissolve into the bindu from moment to moment. Sthiti or stability is merely the constancy of these unceasing cycles of srṣṭi and saṃhāra.

> **Kramas**
>
> - Srṣṭi is the manifestation of the bindu into subsequent āvaraṇas—to understand emanation of the universe from the bindu.
> - Saṃhāra is dissolution of the āvaraṇas into the bindu—useful for sādhanā.
> - Sthiti where creation and dissolution occur simultaneously, giving the appearance of maintenance.

We'll examine the Śrīcakra from both the srṣṭi and saṃhāra aspects, where srṣṭi (in this chapter) is the descent of the Divine into manifestation from the bindu to the bhūpura, and saṃhāra (next chapter) is the return in the opposite direction to the bindu through sādhanā.

Bindu, the Stateless State

Bindu literally means dot or point. If we view the Śrīcakra from the inside radiating out, the bindu

Table 2

Direction of Triangles	**Śakti-Śiva**	**Macrocosmic**	**Microcosmic**	**Śrīcakra Components**
Downward (5)	Śakti (Creation)	Space	Flesh	Trikoṇa
		Wind	Fat	Vasukoṇa
		Fire	Skin	Antardaśara
		Water	Blood	Bahirdaśara
		Earth	Bone	Manvaśra
Upward (4)	Śiva (Dissolution)	Māyā (one appearing as many)	Marrow	Trivṛtta
		Śuddha Vidyā (pure knowledge where mantra is the source of all)	Reproductive fluid	Aṣṭadaḷapadma
		Maheśvarā (stabilization of the explosive creative energy)	Prāṇa	Śodaṣadaḷapadma
		Sadāśivā (eternal principle that is the basis of everything else)	Jīva	Bhūpura

Figure 18. Bindu

is the starting point and the origin of creation (see Fgure 18). If we view it from the outside converging in, it is the point of dissolution, and what remains when creation ceases. Either way, it is the mysterious point that holds the Śrīcakra together. As we have seen earlier, the bindu is the ultimate Reality as a dimensionless point of concentrated energy prior to manifestation, represented by the vowel *am*. Here, prakāśa-vimarśa as Śiva-Śakti are in ecstatic union, which is about to explode as the visarga, represented by the two dots of the last vowel, *ah*. As we saw in the previous chapter, visarga is bidirectional, exploding outward into the universe and inward into the bindu. This union of visarga with the bindu is represented by the combination of the two vowels as AHAM, which, as we saw in Chapter 5, is the Supreme Reality or subject (I).

The outward turned energy of the visarga results in the split of the one into three—pramātṛ, prameya and pramāṇa (see Chapter 5)—the innermost triangle known as the trikoṇa, which then expands into the rest of the Śrīcakra. This innermost triangle represents the wondrous phenomenon of the Divine experiencing Itself as Itself in every aspect of creation.

The Śrīcakra is a dynamic representation of emanation and absorption, where the entirety of creation is constantly pulsing in and out of the bindu. At the microcosmic level, this constant contraction and expansion occurs in every moment, exploding into perception of objects via the senses, recognition of objects through language, interaction with the world through our organs of action, and resorption back into the bindu. This dynamic pulse of expansion and contraction of the bindu, known as spanda, is Devī blinking her eyes (see N281). It's just that our buddhi is too clouded to see this!

Bindu

- ➢ Although the bindu is represented by a dot in two-dimensional diagrams of the Śrīcakra, it isn't a singular point.
- ➢ The bindu is the center of everything in creation as the point from which the subject-object-experience triangle arises.
- ➢ The bindu exploding into prakāśa-vimarśa subsumes the entire structure of the Śrīcakra.

Although portrayed as such, the bindu isn't technically present *only* in the center of the Śrīcakra. One way to conceptualize this is to say that creation in every moment is the visarga of the orgasmic energy of Śiva-Śakti in perfect union as the bindu. More accurately, every moment is the visarga of the bindu since both time and space are created in this ecstatic emission. In Śrīvidyā, Devī is the bindu (see Section 20, Part II), the inner triangle, and all of the Śrīcakra. She is the orgasmic energy of the bindu and the explosive power of emission. She is the very essence of creation, ecstatically throbbing in every bit of it.

When we think about the bindu "splitting" into the innermost triangle, we must remember that it isn't one *dividing* into three. The Divine (here to mean specifically Devī) is transcendent and immanent at the same time. By becoming three, the One isn't diminished or modified or changed the way flour becomes bread when baked. The One remains undiminished, unmodified and unchanged even while taking on all forms. This is the reason for our sense of lack as the āṇava mala—we know deep down that we are so much more than what we take ourselves to be!

Bindu and Manifestation

- ➢ Bindu is the overarching supreme aspect that pervades and subsumes all the other aspects of manifestation.
- ➢ It is the Self of the kośas, the sahasrāra of the cakras, parā of vāk, and turyatītā of the stages of consciousness.
- ➢ At the cosmic level, it the tattva-less tattva that subsumes the 36 tattvas.

The Deities of the Śrīcakra

Trikoṇa

In the LSN, Devī is described as the red-hued goddess sitting in the lap of Kāmeśvara in the bindu, the universe exploding out from their union. The threefold-nature of the trikoṇa is described as the three inherent powers of icchā, jñāna and kriyā śakti, the three deities Vāmā, Jyeṣṭhā and Raudrī, the threefold-nature of vāk—Paśyantī, Madhyamā and Vaikharī, the three states of consciousness—jāgrat,

Figure 19. Trikoṇa

Table 3

Bindu	*Side 1*	*Side 2*	*Side 3*	*Attribute*
Devī (Śiva-Śakti)	Icchā	Jñāna	Kriyā	Primordial powers
Devī (Śiva-Śakti)	Mahākāmeśvarī	Mahāvajreśvarī	Mahābhagamālinī	Primordial powers
Ambika	Vāmā (creation)	Jyeṣṭhā (maintenance)	Raudrī (dissolution)	Creative powers
Parā	Paśyantī	Madhyamā	Vaikharī	Language
Turya/Turyatītā	Jāgrat	Svapna	Suṣuptī	Consciousness
Devī	Fire	Sun	Moon	Principles
Śrīṃ	*Ka E I La Hrīṃ*	*Ha Sa Ka Ha La Hrīṃ*	*Sa Ka La Hrīṃ*	Mantra
Oḍyāṇa	Kāmarūpa	Pūrṇagiri	Jālandhara	Pilgrimage sites

svapna and suṣuptī, the three kūṭas or sections of the Pañcadaśi, the energies of the sun, moon, and fire, which are the three eyes of Lalitā Devī and the three mystical seats of Kāmarūpa, Pūrṇagiri, and Jālandhara (see Table 3). In every case, Devī in the bindu subsumes the three sides as the fourth non-hierarchical principle (see Figure 19).

And so we see that all of creation occurs in triads, being pervaded by the three-fold nature of Devī—reality/truth (sat), consciousness (cit) and bliss (ānanda). Since her exquisite beauty pervades all of existence, she is known as Mahātripurasundarī (the great beauty of the three cities, where the cities are all the triads of creation).

The trikoṇa is surrounded by the Nityā Kalā Devīs, the goddesses that rule over the digits of time, as both the phases of the moon, the vowels of the Sanskrit alphabet, as well as the 15 syllables of the Pañcadaśi mantra. They reside at the trikoṇa, five to a side, while Devī herself subsumes them in the bindu as the 16th Nityā known as Mahānityā. The correspondence of the Nityās with the digits of the moon is highly significant because, ordinarily, the lunar phases give us the impression of change and of the passage of time. However, the moon itself does not change and remains as is. As far as the moon itself is concerned, it is always "full" and unchanging! The phases of the moon then are representations of the way the always-full moon *appears* to us due to various cosmic forces and conditions. Not only are the phases limited in time (only one phase is seen per day in the lunar half-month) as kāla, but it is also limited in space as kalā, *appearing* to be complete only on one day. As we've seen earlier, kalā and kāla are two of the five kañcukas. The Nityā Devīs represent these limitations that Devī as the Divine imposes upon herself when she explodes out of the bindu. She is thus Mahānityā, the principle of the

Nityā Kalā Devīs

- First 15 Nityās are modifications of Devī.
- Combinations of the three guṇas (sattva, rajas, tamas) and the five great elements.
- All 15 are said to be present in the full moon as Devī.
- On subsequent days, one Nityā is said to leave the moon until the new moon and return one at a time in the next cycle to become the full moon.
- When all the Nityās "leave," the nothingness of the new moon is Devī turning to face Śiva.
- When they return to become the full moon, it is the joyous fullness of Devī's union with Śiva turned outward.

Vāk in the Śrīcakra

- Parā in the bindu subsuming paśyantī, madhyamā and vaikharī at the three sides of the trikoṇa.
- Parā in the bindu.
- Paśyantī at trikoṇa.
- Madhyamā at vasukoṇa.
- Vaikharī at the rest of the Śrīcakra.
- Vowels (represented by the Nityā Devīs) at the trikoṇa are at the paśyantī level, as yet undifferentiated completely into subject-object and word-object distinctions
- Vowels and consonants (represented by the Vāgdevatās) at the vasukoṇa are at the madhyamā level at the stage of subtle differentiation.

unchanging, unlimited Divine that permeates and subsumes all changes and limitations. Because they appear in the unchanging sequence of the moon, these goddesses are known as Nityā (eternal).

The importance of the Nityā Devīs in Śrīvidyā becomes evident in their appearance in not just the trikoṇa but other āvaraṇas as well. Here, at the trikoṇa, they rule over the vowels of the Sanskrit alphabet at the paśyantī level.

Vasukoṇa

Immediately outside the trikoṇa are the deities of Devī's implements—noose, goad, sugarcane bow, and arrows made of flowers. The trikoṇa expands into the vasukoṇa consisting of 8 triangles, ruled by yoginīs known as Vāgdevatās, the goddesses of speech who are credited with composing the LSN (see Figure 20 and Chapter 1). Each vāgdevatā rules over a particular group of Sanskrit phonemes, known as varga (see Table 4).

Just as the central bindu and the innermost triangle subsume the rest of the Śrīcakra, the vasukoṇa forms the basis for the remaining āvaraṇas, because language is the basis for all the other powers and attributes represented in the other structures and sub-structures. The bindu, trikoṇa and vasukoṇa explode into the subsequent āvaraṇas of the Śrīcakra,

Table 4. Mātṛka and Vāgdevatās

Vāgdevatā	Phoneme Group	Phonemes
Vaśinī	Vowels	*a ā i ī u ū ṛ, ṝ ḷ, ḹ, e, o, ai, au, aṃ, aḥ*
Kāmeśvarī	Kavarga	*ka kha ga gha ṅa*
Modinī	Cavarga	*ca cha ja jha ña*
Vimalā	Ṭavarga	*ṭa ṭha ḍa ḍha ṇa*
Aruṇa	Tavarga	*ta tha da dha na*
Jayanī	Pavarga	*pa pha ba bha ma*
Sarveśvarī	Semi-vowels	*ya ra la va*
Kaulinī	Sibilants	*śa ṣa sa ha kṣa*

Figure 20. Vasukoṇa

where devolution is a process of divine sentience assuming increasingly more mundane forms. The vasukoṇa along with the trikoṇa makes up what is known as the navayonī (nava = nine, yonī = female genital organ, to mean womb here), which is the source of all the other āvaraṇas of the Śrīcakra.

Antardaśara, Bahirdaśara, Manvaśra

The navayonī explodes into the antardaśara, the inner group of ten triangles that represents the five sense organs and the five tanmātras, while the bahirdaśara is that of the ten main vāyus or winds that determine the functions of the body-mind. In yogic parlance, these are prāṇa, apāna, vyāna, udāna, samāna, nāga, kūrma, kṛkāra, devadatta, and dhanañjaya.

These vāyus have specific directions that determine whether we are caught up in the world of objects or remain centered in subjectivity (see next chapter). The manvaśra is the next āvaraṇa of fourteen trian-

Figure 21. Antardaśara, Bahirdaśara, Manvaśra

gles that are the fourteen main nāḍīs that determine the functioning of the sense organs, organs of action, mind, intellect, and ego (Figure 21).

Aṣṭadaḷapadma, Ṣodaśadaḷapadma, and Bhūpura

Surrounding the three sets of triangles is the eight-petaled lotus or the aṣṭadaḷapadma, representing the eight agitations, while the sixteen-petaled lotus or the ṣodaśadaḷapadma fulfills all wishes. The outermost āvaraṇa is the bhūpura consisting of three parallel lines representing the infatuation of the three worlds (see Figure 22).

Figure 22. Aṣṭadaḷapadma, Ṣodaśadaḷapadma, Bhūpura

Three parallel circles are included in the Śrīcakra in some lineages, the placement of which differ according to the particular tradition. Usually placed between the bhūpura and the 16-petaled lotus, these circles, known as trivṛtta, represent various triads, such as the sun, moon, and fire, representing the boundary between the gross and subtle aspects of creation.*

As sādhakas, for us the Śrīcakra becomes significant in sādhanā when examined in the reverse direction, or the saṃhāra krama.

* Brooks, DR, *Auspicious Wisdom: The Texts and Traditions of Śrīvidyā Śākta Tantrism in South India*, Albany 1992, Page 139.

Chapter 10

The Śrīcakra in Practice

In this chapter, we'll briefly explore the Śrīcakra in the saṃhāra krama, moving from the bhūpura to the bindu, as this relates to how we may progress in sādhanā. This entails moving from the gross (vaikharī) to increasingly subtle objects, and finally dissolving into the bindu (see Figure 23). The āvaraṇas of the Śrīcakra are also known as cakras, and can be placed at the locations of the traditional cakras of the subtle body in sādhanā.* However, even without such a placement, the Śrīcakra becomes internalized in sādhanā through the deepening of our understanding of its components. The most essential piece of this sādhanā is bhāvanā, which we will explore in Chapter 12.

Bhūpura

The outermost āvaraṇa is the bhūpura, which consists of three parallel lines and is shaped in the form of four doors that represent the four Vedas and the four *āmnāyas.*** This āvaraṇa is known as *trailokyamohana* (infatuation of the three worlds) cakra with

* The correspondence of the āvaraṇas with the cakras differs according to the Śrīvidyā lineage.

** Āmnāyas are the traditions associated with the four cardinal directions, each with its set of texts and practices.

Pure and Impure Paths

- The ascent from the bhūpura to the trikoṇa constitutes impure path.
- The journey from the trikoṇa to the bindu is the pure path, with progressive stabilization in its various stages

Śrīcakra Deities

- Each āvaraṇa has a presiding deity, yoginīs that denote its characteristic, a particular attainment for the practitioner that pierces into its mystery, and individual deities of its sub-structures.
- The verities that rule over the individual components play the dual roles of casting out the darkness of ignorance as well guiding the sādhaka toward the light of Self-knowledge.
- In the role of concealment, they are known as yoginī.
- In the role of revelation, they are known as cakreśvarī.

Figure 23: Śrīcakra in Saṃhāra Krama

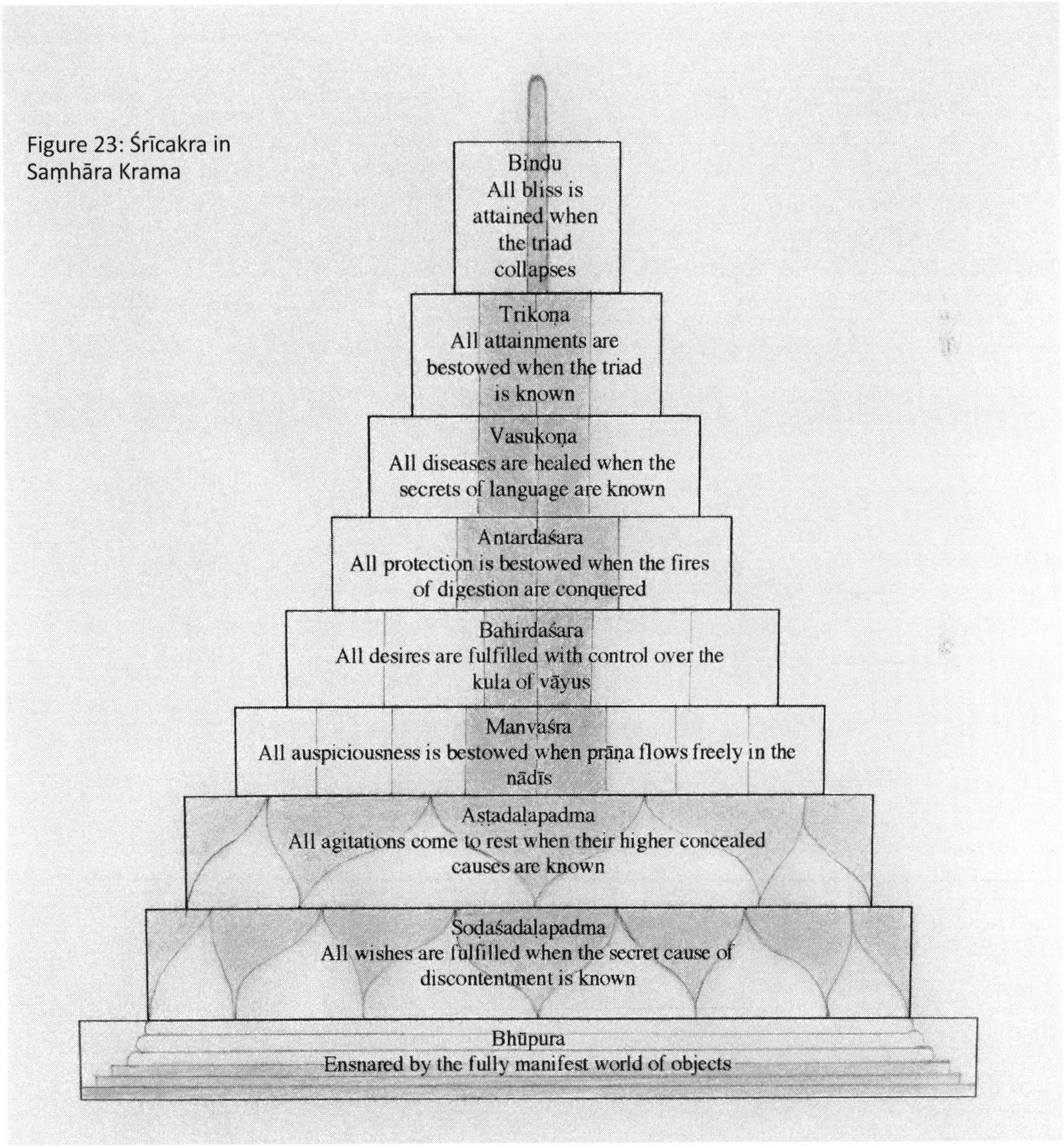
Bindu
All bliss is attained when the triad collapses
Trikoṇa
All attainments are bestowed when the triad is known
Vasukoṇa
All diseases are healed when the secrets of language are known
Antardaśara
All protection is bestowed when the fires of digestion are conquered
Bahirdaśara
All desires are fulfilled with control over the kula of vāyus
Manvaśra
All auspiciousness is bestowed when prāṇa flows freely in the nāḍīs
Aṣṭadalapadma
All agitations come to rest when their higher concealed causes are known
Ṣodaśadalapadma
All wishes are fulfilled when the secret cause of discontentment is known
Bhūpura
Ensnared by the fully manifest world of objects

Table 5

Āvaraṇa	Presiding Deity	Cakra Attainment	Yoginīs (Prakata)
Bhūpura	Tripurā	Trailokyamohanā	Outer Line: Ten siddhīs or powers - aṇimā, laghimā, garimā, mahimā, īśitva, vaśitvā, prākāmyā, bhuktī, icchā, prāpyā, sarvakāmā Middle Line: Eight Mātṛkas - Brāhmi, Māheśvarī, Kaumāri, Vaiṣṇavī, Vārāhī, Māhendrī, Cāmuṇḍā, Mahālakṣmī Inner Line: Ten mudrās - Sarvasankṣobhiṇī, Sarvavidrāviṇī, Sarvākarśiṇī, Sarvavaśankarī, Sarvonmādinī, sarvamahāṅkuśā, Sarvakhecarī, Sarvabījā, Sarvayonī, Sarvatrikhaṇḍā

28 yoginīs known as prakaṭa or fully manifest/ explicit.

The yoginīs of the outermost line represent the many ways in which the Divine becomes limited in space, and when they bestow their grace, the sādhaka attains various powers (such as becoming extraordinarily small, light, big, and so on). The yoginīs of the middle line are known as the *aṣṭa mātṛkās*, a group of eight goddesses associated with deep-rooted qualities such as anger, envy and pride that trip us up on the path of sādhanā. Their grace bestows the transmutation of these poisons to nectar, leading us to the innermost line of the bhūpura, which is governed by the ten yoginīs of *mudrās* (hand gestures) of Śrīvidyā. Not only are the mudrās used in ritual worship, but they are associated with particular flows of prāṇa that orient us to the nature of Reality.

Trivṛtta

Trivṛtta is the set of three concentric circles that are placed between the bhūpura and the ṣodaśadaḷapadma (or elsewhere in the Śrīcakra in some lineages), which can represent several triads (such as the sun, moon and fire, or the three puruṣārthas of dharma, artha and kāma). They also symbolize the Sanskrit phonemes or Mātṛkā between gross and subtle experience. Twenty-nine consonants beginning with K lie along the outermost circle and the 16 vowels along the middle circle.* The innermost circle is occupied by the Nityā Devīs that rule over time (see previous chapter).

Ṣodaśadaḷapadma

- Each of the yoginīs is an attracter (ākarṣiṇī), nsnaring the groups of the five great elements, organs of action, and sense organs, as well as the mind with all its modifications—the fundamental basis for discontent.
- The yoginīs are called gupta, because they reveal the secret of contentment, which is to tap into the very energy of longing.

Ṣodaśadaḷapadma

The next āvaraṇa is the sixteen-petaled lotus or the ṣodaśadaḷapadma and is called the wish-fulfilling (sarvāśāparipūraka) cakra (see Table 6).

The yoginīs represent the allure of the world made up of the great elements—our utter fascination with the world of objects manifests as our constant engagement with them through the sense organs and organs of action. The āṇava mala drives us to find completion in the world of objects, resulting in the mistaken notion that all our wishes (sarvāśa) will be fulfilled in the world. Since that never happens, we remain in a constant state of discontent. When attention turns upon itself, we discover that all our wishes are fulfilled—not by gaining anything from the world, but by seeing that we are already whole and need nothing for completion.

Aṣṭadaḷapadma

- The eight petals represent the five tanmātras and the three components of the citta—buddhi, ahaṅkāra and manas.
- The deeper interaction with the world of objects occurs at the level of the components of this āvaraṇa.
- The tanmātras are the interface between the citta and the sense organs; they are the subtle counterparts of the five great elements that make sensing possible.
- The yoginīs of this level are known as gupta-tara, or very secret, because this process remains so hidden that it is entirely missed.

Aṣṭadaḷapadma

The eight-petaled lotus or the aṣṭadaḷapadma, known as the sarvasaṃkṣobhaṇa cakra, is the one that agitates (see Table 7). We arrive at this āvaraṇa because the objects of the world that previously held our attention have now become the foci for restlessness.

Manvaśra

While the 8-petaled lotus represented the tanmātras and citta, we now move deeper (see Table 8). What

* SK Ramachandra Rao. *The Tantra of Śrī Chakra*. Śrī Satguru Publications, New Delhi, 2013.

Table 6

Āvaraṇa	Presiding Deity	Cakra Attainment	Yoginīs (Gupta)
Śodaṣadaḷapadma	Tripureśī	Sarvāśāparipūraka	Sixteen attractions: kāmā, buddhī, ahaṅkarā, śabdā, sparśā, rūpā, rasā, gandhā, cittā, dhairyā, smṛtī, nāmā, bijā, ātmā, amṛtā, śarīrā.

Table 7

Āvaraṇa	Presiding Deity	Cakra Attainment	Yoginīs (Guptatara)
Aṣṭadaḷapadma	Tripurasundarī	sarvasaṃkṣobhaṇa	Eight agitations: kusumā, mekhalā, madanā, madanāturā, rekhā, veginī aṅkuśā, mālinī

drives the functioning of those elements? As we've seen in Chapter 6, prāṇa is the fundamental life force that flows in particular nāḍīs, which are nothing but the flow of awareness through the citta. Conditioning is nothing but the repeated flow of awareness in certain nāḍīs as a result of which all the *other* ways of being become unavailable.

A deep awareness of our agitations in the aṣṭadaḷapadma brings us to an understanding of the flow of prāṇa in the fourteen nāḍīs that determines

Manvaśra

- The manvaśra is the next āvaraṇa of fourteen triangles that govern the fourteen main nāḍīs that determine the functioning of the sense organs, organs of action, mind, intellect, and ego.
- Called sarvasaubhāgyadāyaka cakra, the bestower of all auspiciousness, which is the result of attention turning upon itself.

Table 8

Āvaraṇa	Presiding Deity	Cakra Attainment	Yoginīs (Sampradāya)
Manvaśra	Tripuravāsinī	Sarvasaubhāgyadāyaka	Fourteen auspicious aspects: Sarvasankṣobhiṇī, Sarvavidrāviṇī, Sarvākarśiṇī, Sarvāhlādinī, Sarvasammohinī, Sarvastambhiṇī, Sarvajhṛbinī, Sarvavaśankarī, Sarvarañjanī, Sarvonmādinī, Sarvārthasādhikā, Sarvasampattipūraṇī, Sarvamantramayī, Sarvadvandvakśayaṅkarī

our way of living and being. With the clearing of the saṃskāras that had previously clogged up our buddhi, we gain access to the previously closed off nāḍīs. The yoginīs of this āvaraṇa are known as *sampradāya* because an inward turning naturally gives rise to the qualities that are traditionally lauded in most paths, such as tolerance, honesty, and non-harming. They are neither forced upon us by authority nor by pretensions about morality; they are the product of the abundant flow of prāṇa through the main nāḍīs!

Bahirdaśara

The bahirdaśara governs the aspects of prāṇa flowing in the nāḍīs represented by the manvaśra. These vāyus have specific directions that determine whether we are caught up in the world of objects or remain centered in subjectivity.

When we come to see that all our desires arises from the āṇava mala, we gain access to the root of longing. We understand the movement of energy that drives our wants. Once we see the biology of longing, we learn to harness its fundamental energy to turn back and address the āṇava mala directly. In this turning back, all our wishes are fulfilled, not because we've addressed each desire but because we have become acquainted with its root. The yoginīs

Bahirdaśara

- The bahirdaśara is that of the ten main vāyus or winds that determine the functions of the body-mind—prāṇa, apāna, vyāna, udāna, samāna, nāga, kūrma, kṛkāra, devadatta, and dhanañjaya.
- Called sarvārthasādhaka cakra, the one that aids the accomplishment of all desires.

Table 9

Āvaraṇa	Presiding Deity	Cakra Attainment	Yoginīs (Kulottīrṇa)
Bahirdaśara	Tripurāśī	Sarvārthasādhaka	Ten accomplishments: Sarvasiddhipradā, Sarvasampatpradā, Sarvapriyaṇkarī, Sarvamaṇgaḷakāriṇī, Sarvakāmapradā, Sarvadukkhavimochanī, Sarvamṛtyupraśamanī, Sarvavighnanivāriṇī, Sarvāṇgasundarī, Sarvasaubhāgyadāyinī

of this āvaraṇa are called Kulottīrṇa, which means crossing over beyond kula. Kula (see N90-96) is a word that is used for groupings of various sorts—that of the knower, known and the process of knowing, the lineage, a group of practitioners of the same tradition, or the same type of practice.

Here, kula refers to the grouping of the vāyus with functions of the body-mind. When we transcend the particular associations of the vāyus with specific ways of thinking and being, we cross over beyond the kula (see Table 9).

Antardaśara

As we've seen in Chapter 7, the world is taken in, processed, eliminated, circulated and transmuted through the five main (and the five minor) prāṇa vāyus of the bahirdaśara. Exactly *how* is the world taken in through the senses and digested to become our internal experience? This process is governed by the antardaśara. Each prāṇa vāyu contains the intelligence that drives its functioning, where it "knows" how to take in, process, eliminate, and so on.

Antardaśara

- The antardaśara is the inner group of ten triangles that represents the ten inner fires of knowledge that drives the vāyus. The attainment of this āvaraṇa is called sarvarakṣakara, the bestower of protection.

When we pierce into the understanding of the nāḍīs in the manvaśra and the prāṇa vāyus in the bahirdaśara, we arrive at this āvaraṇa where we contemplate on the nature of the dichotomy between the "world there" and a "me here." We come to see

Table 10

Āvaraṇa	**Presiding Deity**	**Cakra Attainment**	**Yoginīs (Nigarbha)**
Antardaśara	Tripuramālinī	Sarvarakṣakara	Ten Protectors: Sarvajñā, Sarvaśaktī, Sarvaiśvaryapradāyinī, Sarvajñanamayī, Sarvavyādhivināśinī, Sarvādhārasvarūpā, Sarvapāpaharā, Sarvānandamayī, Sarvarakṣasvarūpinī, Sarvepsitaphalapradā

that this is created by not only the prāṇa vāyus but by an even more fundamental force—the fire of knowledge that drives them. When this knowledge remains hidden, the flow of the prāṇa vāyus is determined largely by our conditioning, which is why the yoginīs of this āvaraṇa are called nigarbha (veiled, secret, or inner). These hidden yoginīs determine our ordinary way of operating in constant fear of being invaded, hurt, or exhausted by others. When the dichotomy between "in here" and "out there" ceases to exist, there is no "other" to fear, and no self to protect. The natural result of this contemplation is self-assurance and fearlessness. For a sādhaka who contemplates the nature of reality, the dawn of perfected reasoning results in the understanding that nothing exists "outside" of subjective experience.

When we arrive at this āvaraṇa, we finally see that our lives are always protected. The truth hidden in plain sight was that the protection we needed was not from forces outside of us, but from the correction of the previously restricted vision.

Up until now, the dichotomy between I, the subject and the objects of our experience—all the aspects of the āvaraṇas—remained distinct and separate. Moreover, words and the objects they referred to also remained distinct. We had remained in the realm of vaikharī vāk. With the attainment of fearlessness, we come to the threshold of madhyamā.

Vasukoṇa

The vasukoṇa with the Vāgdevatās is known as sarvarogahara cakra (the one that cures all ills) and the yoginīs are known as rahasya (secret). See Table 11.

The cleansing of the buddhi lens that took place until the antardaśara results in the ability to look into the very nature of bondage here at the vasu-

Table 11

Āvaraṇa	Presiding Deity	Cakra Attainment	Yoginīs (Rahasya)
Vasukoṇa	Tripurasiddhā	Sarvarogahara	Eight Vagdevatas: Vaśini, Kāmeśvarī, Modinī, Vimalā, Aruṇā, Jayinī, Sarveśvarī, Kaulinī

koṇa. When we contemplate on this fundamental nature of Reality, the very structure of language that had supported the matrix of experience begins to disintegrate. We begin to see that every aspect of experience is shaped by language representing these eight aspects. Nothing in our experience lies beyond the level of language, which evolves into the unfathomable universe of applying meanings to images, to perceptions, and all the aspects represented in the Śrīcakra! With a deepening of our understanding at this level, our entire experience of Reality begins to shift and the distinctions between subject-object and object-word begin to dissolve.

Vasukoṇa

- The eight Vāgdevatās represent heat, cold, happiness, unhappiness, desire, and the three guṇas—sattva, rajas, and tamas.
- Heat, cold, happiness, and unhappiness are dualities that drive our perception.
- Desire fuels dualistic perception.
- The three guṇas are the fundamental forces of creation that determine the quality of desire.
- In short: Guṇas make-up of our psyche → what we desire → what we like and dislike → how we digest the world of objects.

Freedom from the word-object association frees us from the limitations of time, space, and causality, which are the root causes of all "ills" that assail the human condition of suffering. The yoginīs here are known as *rahasya*, the secret of Reality, and attainment at this level frees us from all ills (sarvarogahara).

Devī's Implements

Immediately within the vasukoṇa are Devī's implements of the five flower arrows, sugarcane bow, goad and noose, surrounding the trikoṇa. With the unraveling of the power of language that forms the basis for Māyā's entrapment, we come face-to-face with the three primordial powers of the Divine (see N8-11 and Table 12). See page 79.

Trikoṇa

With the loosening of the bonds of language with the progressive unclouding of the buddhi, we now

Devī's Implements

- Bow and arrows are kriya śakti
- Goad is jñāna śakti
- Noose is icchā śakti.

Table 12

Āvaraṇa	Yoginīs
Between Vasukoṇa and Trikoṇa	Bāṇinī, Cāpinī, Pāśinī, Aṅkuśinī

Table 13

Āvaraṇa	Presiding Deity	Cakra Attainment	Yoginīs (Atirahasya)
Trikoṇa	Tripurāmbā	Sarvasiddhipradā	Three corners: Mahākāmeśvarī, Mahāvajreśvarī, Mahābhagamālinī Fifteen nityās: Kāmeśvarī, Bhagamālinī, Nityaklinnā, Bheruṇḍā, Vahnivāsinī, Mahāvajreśvarī, Śivadūtī, Tvaritā, Kulasundarī, Nityā, Nīlapatākā, Vijayā, Sarvamaṇgaḷā, Jvālāmālinī, Chitrā

arrive at the trikoṇa (see previous chapter), where we realize the fundamental triad of Reality—pramātṛ, prameya, and pramāṇa—the extreme secret (atirahasya). The grace of the deities of the trikoṇa bestows all attainments (sarvasiddhipradā) arising from the permanent and lasting resolution of the āṇava mala (see Table 13).

Bindu

The trikoṇa opens to the bindu with the collapse of the triad of experience. Here—the subject and object, as well as the word and the object to which the word refers—collapse. The pure path begins, with levels of stabilization, as we've seen in Chapter 6. At every level of stabilization, there is a deepening of the relationship between the bindu and visarga as MAHA-AHAṂ of the Kāmakalā (see below). The orgasmic bliss of Self-knowledge pours into every experience represented in the Śrīcakra. Devī's grace bestows the supreme attainment of permanent ānanda (sarvānandamaya). See Table 14.

Table 14

Āvaraṇa	Presiding Deity	Cakra Attainment	Yoginī (Parāpararahasya)
Bindu	Lalitā Mahātripurasundarī	Sarvānandamaya	Mahātripurasundarī Mahānityā (16th digit)

Kāmakalā

- Sexual union of Śiva-Śakti in the bindu.
- The upward-facing triangle of Śiva has three bindus at each angle.
- The upper bindu is kāma (desire) → condensation of the entire Sanskrit alphabet from A to HA, representing the sun.
- The lower two bindus → ecstatic emission of desire as visarga (:).
- The two bindus are the "emission" of the sun into fire and the moon → kalā, the dynamic power of Śiva-Śakti.
- The top bindu is A, the lower triangle is HA and the apex of the downward-pointing Śakti triangle is M.
- The union of A and HA becomes AHAM, the Supreme "I," the ultimate Reality, consisting of Śiva-Śakti in perfectly balanced union.
- Stretching from kāma to kalā is Kuṇḍalinī as the sacred Sanskrit syllable Īm

Kāmakalā

The supreme goddess of Śrīvidyā, Lalitā Mahātripurasundarī, is known as Parā Śakti, the Supreme Śakti, and is the union of Śiva and Śakti in the bindu (see Figure 24). The bindu is known as the Mahābindu, consisting of the union of two bindus—a white one of Śiva and a red one of Śakti. The Śrīcakra and its deities—and therefore, the cosmos—arise from her. As we've seen in Chapter 9, the cosmos is represented in Vāk as Mātṛkā Śakti.

The Kāmakalā (see N322) represents the totality of creation from A to HA, and also of Śakti in sexual union with Śiva. The apex of the upward-facing triangle is her face and that of the downward-facing triangle is her yoni, while the two bindus representing fire and the moon are her breasts. Devī as this Kuṇḍalinī flashes forth as spanda, pulsing as the

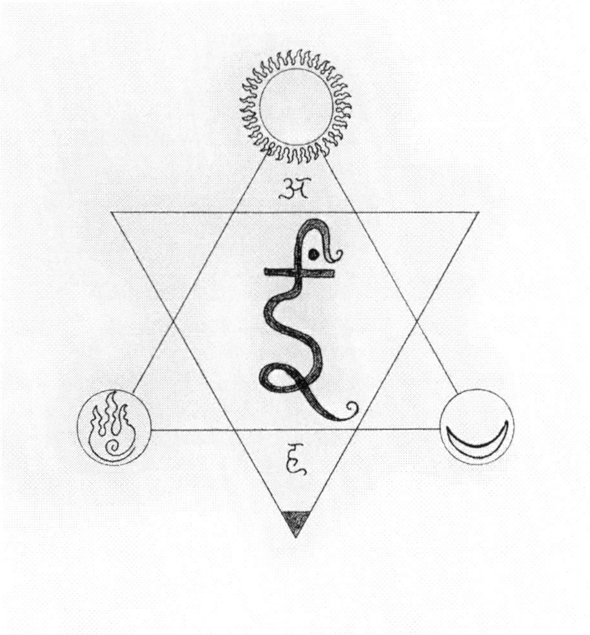

Figure 24. Kāmakalā

contraction and expansion between A (bindu) and HA (visarga). The blissful, ecstatic union of Śiva-Śakti in the Mahābindu spills out into the universe as the rasa known as śṛṅgāra.

What we need to remember about the Śrīcakra is that all of its aspects are emanations of Devī who resides in the bindu as herself. While the Śrīcakra is depicted in a fairly standard way in texts, its study and worship are highly lineage-dependent. While the goal of every sādhaka is to end up at the bindu with its supreme attainments, the *means* to attain this goal vary widely. The kinds of rituals and practices we engage in depend on the particular ācāra or path of the lineage. In the next chapter, we will examine five of these ācāras.

Devī's implements (below): A: Chapa, B: Pushpabana, C: Pasha, D: Ankusha. See p.76/77

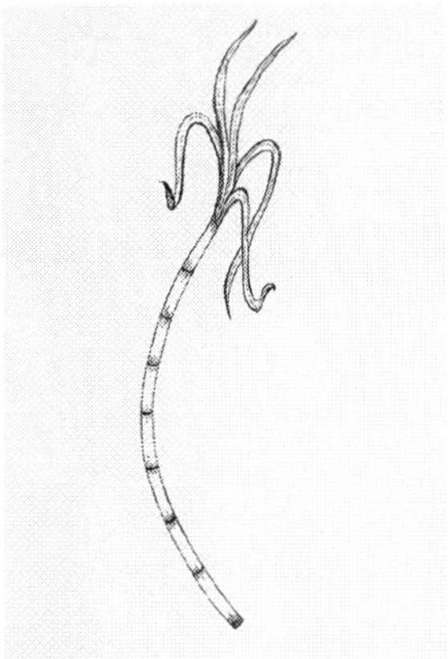

A. Sugarcane Bow

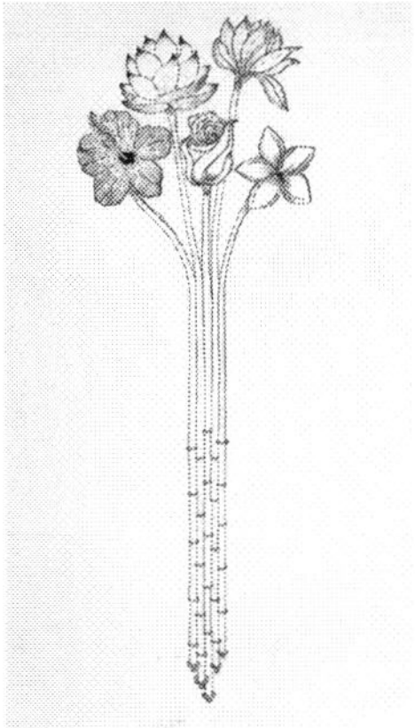

B. Five Flower Arrows

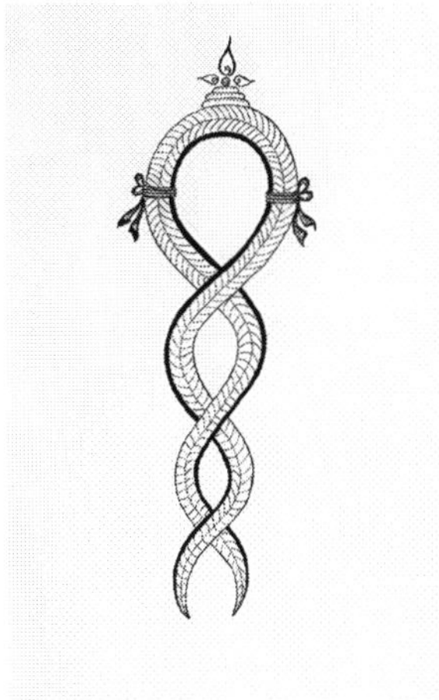

C. Noose

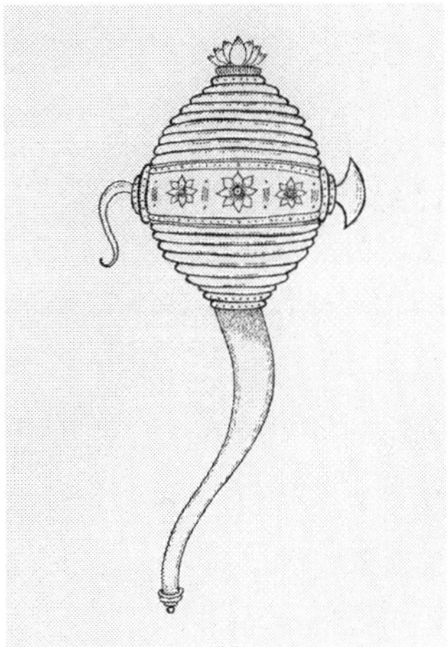

D. Goad

Chapter 11

Ācāras

There are five broad ācāras in Śrīvidyā and to understand them, we must remember the historical context of this path, its birth in the broader tradition of non-dual Śaiva Tantra and eventual incorporation into orthodox Vedik streams. While Śrīvidyā itself is neither entirely Tāntrik nor Vedik, the ācāras carry over the philosophy and view of the particular lineage in which it was propagated. There are many Śrīvidyā lineages that differ in the practice of the central mantra, the worship of the Śrīcakra and associated disciplines.

Samayācāra is a practice that is entirely internalized (see N97-98), being a Vedik form of Śrīvidyā in which all external rituals are disposed of and discouraged. It also excludes antinomian practices—which means the rituals that are not bound by social and moral concepts of right and wrong (described in more detail below). However, elements of this ācāra are adopted in other less strictly Vedik ācārās; visualization of the deity and engaging with the ritual through the understanding of its symbolism would be elements of such a path. In Dakṣiṇācāra, external worship is allowed but not of the "left-handed" variety.

> **Ācāras**
>
> - Means of attainment, or paths.
> - All Śrīvidyā ācāras are centered around Lalitā Mahātripurasundarī, her mantra, and her yantra.
> - Differ in the "flavor" of the approach to Devī.
> - The lineages that are propagated in the context of the orthodox Vedik philosophy tend to be "right-handed," where the practices outside of sanctioned behavior are not allowed.
> - Those that are propagated in certain Tāntrik traditions (such as Kaula) lean toward "left-handed" practices that defy sanctioned behavior.

Kaulacāra is the left-handed Tāntrik path, where practice is centered around Kuṇḍalinī awakening and ascent, and the "kula" (see N90-93, specifically N94). Kula refers to groupings or families of cakras, practitioners, and so on (see previous chapter). This ācāra utilizes transgressive or antinomian practices, including the pañcamakāras, which are five Ms: madya (alcohol), māṃsa (meat), matsya (fish), hand gestures (mudrās)* and ritual sex outside of marriage (maithuna). The purpose of the makāras was to transcend social, cultural and moral norms that added to the sense of being a limited being. These practices were prescribed at a certain level of advancement (see below).

Vāmācāra is also a left-handed path that differs only in the degree of the transgressive practices. The left-handed paths are particularly tricky to navigate without the guidance of a teacher because it is easy to fall into the trap of sense gratification instead of

* Mudrā may also refer to parched grains because they are said to contain aphrodisiac properties.

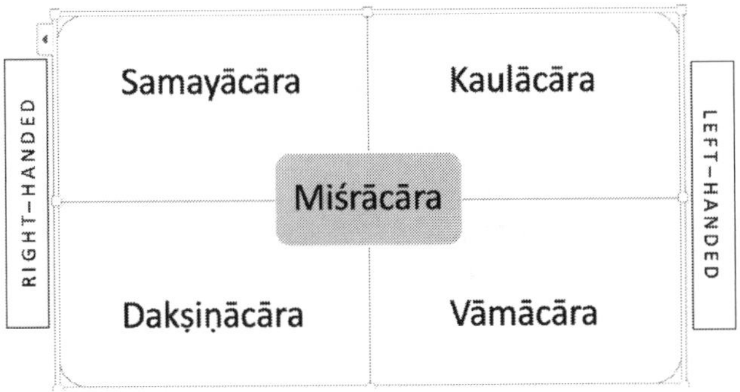

Figure 25. Ācārās

using the makāras to transcend them.

Miśrācāra is the mixed path, where aspects of both the left- and right-handed ācāras exist harmoniously together. Devī is worshiped internally through mantra and externally as the Śrīcakra (right-handed) using nyāsa and mudrā (left-handed). Again, depending on the lineage, alcohol and other makāras may be used in internal worship, with no clear boundaries between the left- and right-handed paths (see Figure 25).

Ācāra Prescription

Tāntrik texts talk about three types of aspirants, based on the aspirant's predominant guṇa:

1. Paśu: When tamas is predominant in our psyche, we are heavily identified as the body-mind, and linearity of thought is our default mode of living and operating in the world. This stage is not conducive to the practice of the makāras or the higher/advanced practices.

2. Vīra: Once we have worked through our attachments, we have a predominantly rajasic mind. In this stage, we have conquered our own passions and have the necessary courage to dig deep so our hidden attachments can surface. In a vīra, the contracted nāḍīs open and blossom into bliss and beauty. Linear thought gives way to circular thought, in which learning, memory, concepts, and beliefs arise and subside in the now. The vīra's stand as awareness is so stable that s/he creates no karma or vāsanās when working with the makāras. The LSN has numerous references to the vīra.

3. Divyā: At this stage of development, sattva is predominant and we have entirely transcended our aversions and attachments. For a divyā, wine is the intoxicating power of Self-knowledge, meat is constant surrender of actions and thoughts to the Divine, fish is unconditional love, parched grain is freedom from bondage, and ritual sex is the eternal inner union of Śiva and Śakti resulting in perpetual bliss and beauty.

The Śrīvidyā ācāras differ in many ways, including the Ṛṣi or sage that is revered as the originator, the manner in which the Śrīcakra is drawn and worshiped, and the particular texts that are studied. Teachers of some lineages are proficient in more than one ācāra, while others adhere to just one. This is one of the many aspects of Śrīvidyā that makes it complex! While many of us may identify as Śrīvidyā upāsakas, that does not mean that we will follow the same practice(s) or philosophy. In the LSN, however, Devī is the embodiment of all ācāras even though the nāmas are often interpreted according to a specific acārā.

Chapter 12

The Sādhanā in Śrīvidyā

In Śrīvidyā, Devī is most often referred to as the Mother Goddess, being the originator of creation. While this approach can work for many, we must remember that the concepts of mother and motherhood are culturally derived. Soul-stirring devotion is easier when the Divine is assigned a revered or treasured relationship. It's possible that the propagation of the worship of the feminine in a patriarchal culture was possible because of the assignment of a relationship that is idealized as pure and sacred. If such a picture of the Divine isn't particularly alluring, perhaps because of challenging relationships with mother figures, we can approach Devī in numerous other ways. In fact, the LSN shows us that she is available to us in a thousand different ways!

There are three primary ways of approaching Devī that correspond to her three main forms—sthūla or the gross/anthropomorphic form, sūkṣma or the subtle form, and parā or the subtlest form. It's far more useful to think of them as stages of sādhanā.

Sthūla

In the first stage, we conceive of the Divine in the human form since this is familiar. We assign attributes to the form, where it is easy to conceptualize abstract thought. Worship of Devī's gross form in

Śrīcakra Pūjā

- Elaborate ritual consisting of making special liquid mixtures and sixty-four types of offerings to the deities the cakra.
- Chanting the LSN follows pūjā, after which the sādhaka settles down for japa.

Śrīvidyā occurs by way of pūjā or ritual worship, which can consist of various numbers of offerings, five or sixteen being common. This form of worship occurs at the vaikharī stage.

Sūkṣma

The second stage of sādhanā utilizes the mantra, the subtle form of the deity. Here, the deity is not seen externally as a mūrti (idol) or picture, but is assigned attributes via the medium of sound. Worship here begins at the madhyamā stage but, with increasing subtlety, evolves into the paśyantī stage to eventually dissolve in parā.

Parā or Vāsanā

With enough practice in the sthūla and sūkṣma stages, our inner apparatus becomes subtle enough for this stage of sādhanā. Here, there is no involvement of the senses. Instead, the deity is visualized and worshiped entirely in the mind because of the subtle vāsanās developed through prolonged practice in the other two stages. By now the vāsanās aren't just impressions but a deep understanding that the deity appearing in our mind's eye is merely a reflection of our own being. We thus realize identity with Devī—her bow, arrows, goad, and noose are seen acting in our own moment-to-moment experience. This transformative process occurs through deep bhāvanā.

> **Vikalpa**
>
> - A vikalpa is a mental construct that is created in the mind with the acquisition of information.
> - Most of our education is based on cultivating mental constructs, not just in the transactional world but also in spirituality.
> - On the path of sādhanā, our elaborate intellectual constructs around spiritual concepts are not only obstacles to growth but become subtle baggage for the ahaṅkāra.

Bhāvanā

Bhāvanā is the contemplative practice of moving from vaikharī to parā, which is a movement from transactional knowledge to Self-knowledge. Ordinarily, we (subject) remain separate from the knowledge (object) in a transactional relationship. Knowledge gained from the outside is used to enhance the sense of "I," and as we have seen earlier, this is a superimposition of objectivity on to the subject.

Transactional knowledge is acquired through information gathering and the cultivation of particular saṃskāras known as *vikalpas*. For example, when we're reading a novel, we create a specific imaginary world in our minds. The characters and settings of the novel have a particular look and feel in our internal landscape. If someone makes a movie based on the same novel, it will consist of characters and props that are products of *their* imagination, which may differ from ours—which is why movies based on books can be disappointing!

However, vikalpas are used in bhāvanā to deconstruct our perception of Reality in a progressive fashion. Vikalpas that seem true and "solid" give way to increasingly more abstract and subtle thought forms, which eventually dissolve into pure awareness. When working with the LSN, for instance, we contemplate a particular nāma or concept by approaching it from various angles and mulling over it in various ways so that it begins to dissolve. Like a sandcastle, it starts to lose its edges and angles, becoming increasingly wordless and formless, to finally dissolve into the clear space of awareness.

Mantra Sādhanā (Japa)

In Śrīvidyā, the mantra is revered as the deity in subtle form. Mantra sādhanā is central to practice in Śrīvidyā and it's important that we look at it carefully.

Japa is the systematic repetition of a mantra. While mantras are central to the Vedik and Tāntrik traditions, it will help our practice if we look at their nuances, especially in the context of the LSN, which as we have seen earlier, straddles both. In the Vedik tradition, there is great emphasis on the correct pronunciation of mantras (and chants), the meter, and the procedure of chanting them aloud (see Introduction). The Vedik rules apply to the loud chanting of the LSN, along with the nyāsa, pronunciation, meter, and so on.

However, the practice of the Śrīvidyā mantras falls under the Tāntrik category, with an emphasis on interiorization through the application of bhāvanā. This means that mental japa without involvement of the vocal apparatus (larynx, lips, and so on) is the recommended method, taking precedence over chanting aloud.

The purpose of japa is to move progressively

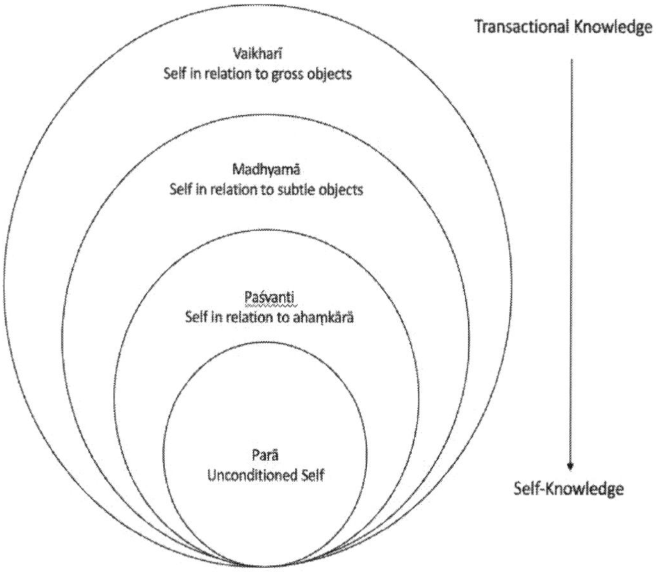

Figure 26. Mantra Sādhanā

inward through our sense of self, which is associated with physical objects (such as house, car, books) and relationships, to subtle objects (such as accomplishment, fame, beauty, age), to the ahaṅkāra or the primordial I-maker, eventually dissolving in the Self, which is devoid of all these attributes. These layers correspond to the levels of vāk (see Figure 26). In other words, the process of japa takes us from transactional knowledge to Self-knowledge.

Another way to look at this is to relate it to the Śrīcakra, where vaikharī and madhyamā relate to the āvaraṇas from the bhūpura to the vasukoṇa, and paśyantī is the trikoṇa. Japa takes us through these levels to the eventual dissolution of the sense of self in the bindu, the abode of parāvāk. The mantra loses its objectivity and is recognized to be non-separate from the Self. Here, the mantra leads to progressive stabilization in the pure path, with dissolution into the various levels of subjectivity and identification with Śiva-Śakti.

As we've seen earlier, the bindu dynamically pulses out as the visarga. In this realization and stabilization of the mantra as Self, the world appears and dissolves in our lived experience of the bindu in ordinary life.

Dissolution into the bindu is the purpose of japa. Accordingly, Tāntrik mantra sādhanā involves a deeper understanding of the mantra through particular modes of practice. The three kūṭas of the Pañcadaśi mantra are first visualized and placed in the cakras of the body. With the progressive interiorization of japa, the bīja mantra *Hrīṃ* of the third kūṭa dissolves into the bindu and returns to its source of Reality. This progressive resorption begins at the bindu and ascends through eight other increasingly subtle stations (ardhacandra, rodhinī, nāda, nādanta, śakti, vyāpika, samanā, and unmanā—see Figure 27). These stages occur within parāvāk, and are a reversal of the process of its descent. With the dissolution into unmanā, our individual awareness melts into Divine awareness. We then engage in bhāvanā of increasing subtlety and complexity, such as contemplation on the five states of consciousness, six void states and seven equinoxes (union of the mind with specific aspects of the mantra*) that correspond with the bīja mantra.**

While the sitting practice of Tāntrik japa in Śrīvidyā is complex and nuanced, we delve further into the *meaning* of the mantra through constant bhāvanā. Various texts delve into the manifold meanings of the Pañcadaśi mantra, which engage our mind in bhāvanā, clarify the buddhi lens and stabilize us in inner silence. In general, the Śrīvidyā mantras have six levels of meanings, which are explored in the LSN in implicit ways (see Table 15). These arthas (meanings) delve into the relationships between the mantra and the deities of the Śrīcakra, the tattvas, prāṇa vāyus, cakras, the pīṭhas (sacred sites corresponding to subtle centers in the body), the guru and the sādhaka. In these *arthas*, the mantra is explored for its power to lead the sādhaka from the impure to the pure path, progressive stabilization in the pure path, and dissolution into ultimate Reality.

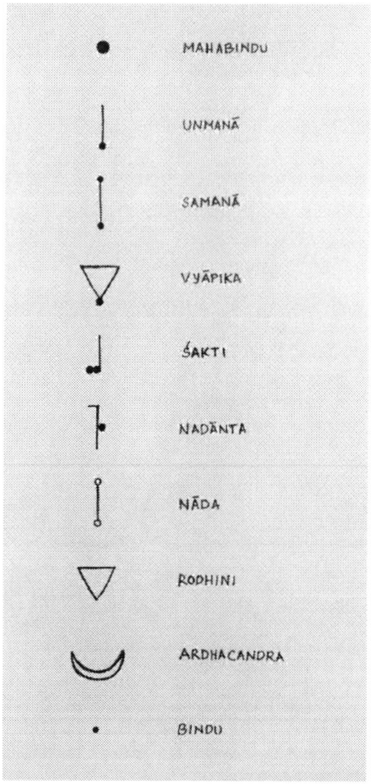

Fig. 27: Stations in Japa

Dīkṣa (Initiation)

As we see here, the practice of japa in Śrīvidyā is complex and subtle, and sādhakas require help and guidance. Since it is quite easy to become stuck in any one particular level, give up, or worse, claim

* Timalsina S. *Meditating Mantras. Theory and Practice of Yoga.* Koninklinjke Brill NV Knut A Jacobson (Ed), 2005.

** Padoux A. *The Heart of the Yoginī:* The Yoginihrdaya, a Sanskrit Tantric Treatise, Oxford University Press, 2013.

Table 15

Six Types of Meanings Assigned to Mantra*

Type	Meaning of the mantra.
Bhāvārtha	Relating to the relationship between letters of the mantra and the deities.
Sampradāyārtha	Relating to the lineage and held in secret by its adepts.
Nigarbhārtha	Relating to the identity of the deity, guru, and sādhaka.
Kaulikārtha	Relating to the identity of the deity, guru, and sādhaka with the Śrīcakra.
Sarvarahasyārtha	Relating to the identity of the mantra with Kuṇḍalinī.
Mahātattvārtha	Relating to the identity of the sādhaka with the ultimate Reality .

* Padoux A. The Heart of the Yoginī: The Yoginihrdaya, a Sanskrit Tantric Treatise, Oxford University Press, 2013.

premature attainment, this is a path that is guru-centric. Even though we say "guru-centric" this requires the guru to be very much focused on the specific requirements of each sādhaka, so it is also a sādhaka-centric practice.

Although the Pañcadaśi is central to Śrīvidyā, most lineages consist of a core group of mantras (Gaṇapatī, Bālā Tripurasundarī, Pañcadaśi, Mātaṅgī, and Vārāhī) that a sādhaka is given in dīkṣa. There tends to be a lineage-specific reasoning for the order in which the mantras are disclosed to the aspirant. The guru is said to have the power to discern the most appropriate mantra for the disciple at the time of initiation. The appropriateness of a mantra for a given disciple is based on balancing comfort and challenge. A given mantra must do its work (for instance, of clearing particular nāḍīs) *and* challenge the sādhaka to grow beyond the confines of his or her conditioning.

A mantra beyond the comfort level of a sādhaka is of little use since it can result in deeper entrapment in the drama of the discomfort (and occasionally, mental, psychological, and emotional imbalance). On the other hand, a mantra that doesn't challenge the sādhaka enough will result in stagnation. This is where the guru comes in—having "walked the walk," and by his or her intuitive reading of a particular sādhaka (usually also combined with extensive experience), the guru is able to mete out the best prescription. Ideally, the guru is available for the sādhaka, answering questions and determining the timing of subsequent initiations, and doesn't anticipate things in return (loyalty, material goods, or emotional dependency). Importantly, in the absence of a well-honed, clear and discerning buddhi on the part of the sādhaka, the guru helps make the all-important decisions such as the choice of mantra and the mode of japa, ancillary practices, level-appropriate study, and so on.

In Śrīvidyā, the guru is non-separate from both Devī and the sādhaka. Realizing the oneness of the three is an important milestone in sādhanā. Traditionally, there are 32 levels of initiation in Śrīvidyā, and at a certain stage, the sādhaka is given a new name and is incorporated permanently into the lineage. The guru maṇḍala, which is a vital aspect of Śrīvidyā, is deeply revered and commands a high level of devotion.* In fact, the guru-disciple relationship is the lifeblood of Śrīvidyā.

Bhakti (Devotion)

You've probably heard it said that devotion is the key to approaching the deity. While this is true, bhakti can't be forced or feigned to the degree that it is often described. Instead, whatever we already love can become the springboard for bhakti.

* The guru maṇḍala is the "network" of the gurus of the lineage.

Bhakti

- Bhakti is the fuel for sādhanā, springing up as the yearning that inspires sitting for japa, meditation, ritual, chanting, and learning.
- It is the un-named something that brings us to the path, often not looking like anything in particular, which is the āṇava mala seeking wholeness.
- It can be the inexpressible sense of wanting to align with something greater than ourselves.
- It takes on the form of love for our children, partners, teachers, parents, friends, pets, nature, art, music, and the work we do.
- It contains the spark of icchā, where we long to love and create.

Cynicism is the biggest obstacle to the cultivation of bhakti. This is tricky because, at least initially, it requires a belief in something that is intangible and inferred, or at very least a provisional commitment to a belief. Especially if we come to it with a sense of striking a bargain with Devī, it becomes an issue—she is under no obligation to keep up her side of it! If we approach the Divine as a give-and-take relationship, we are bound to be disappointed when things don't go our way despite our adherence to the practice. For bhakti to be appropriately cultivated and refined, it's very useful to hang out with like-minded people, so that we keep our attention turned toward the yearning that brought us to the path in the first place.

Saṅghas (communities or associations) often begin with noble intentions. Subject to human behavior that quite naturally centers around ourselves, our individual self-interests can usurp the original intent of the saṅgha. Driven by the āṇava mala, our longing for wholeness can become displaced from wanting material objects to wanting to be accepted in a particular group or to appear to others in a certain way. In this dynamic, we can mistake subservience and obedience to the saṅgha or leader for bhakti. In many religious traditions, devotion takes the form of faith (or blind faith), where a teaching is taken at face value and without question. We then fall into the trap where bhakti, which is the primary fuel for adhering to the tradition, becomes a hindrance to progress.

On the other hand, it helps to have a role model or mentor who walks the talk; it's much easier when the goal becomes tangible through living examples. However, in the process of assigning divinity to a person (any person), we must remember that the *ideal* of the mentor or teacher is a goal for our own sādhanā. Putting anyone on a pedestal comes at the risk of them not meeting our expectations of divinity. The good news is that bhakti becomes increasingly purified in the fire of authentic sādhanā, where the longing for truth takes center stage and subsumes other motives such as wanting to belong to a tradition or group, or gain approval of the teacher or saṅgha. With further refinement, longing is replaced with gratitude and astonishment at the bounty of life that is Devī's infinite and unconditioned grace.

As we have seen in the earlier chapters, unclouding the buddhi is the goal of sādhanā. With this unclouding aided by bhakti, we begin to see perfection in people and situations, not because they are meeting our expectations of divinity but because our concepts of divinity are being cleared of the debris of conditioning.

Discernment

Discernment is the ability to know the difference between related concepts and issues. We are constantly choosing and judging as we go about our lives. Is this the right thing to do? Is this helpful? Ordinarily, discernment arises from our past experiences. We have been there, done that, and that becomes the basis for our choices in a given moment.

As we have seen in Chapter 8, thought is a form of vāk and, in terms of modern science, it can be viewed as arising from two different networks in the brain. Thoughts related to specific tasks arise from the *task-positive network*, referring to those related to planning and organizing, and are purposeful. When not engaged in a task, the brain defaults to the *default-mode network* with self-referential thoughts, as in those revolving around "me." They involve constant rumination, a replay of past events and projection into the future with worry and anxiety, what we or others should have done or should do, and what the outcome of any action should be or should have been. They are the what-ifs and hope-nots that have no relevance to the present moment. These thoughts have no purpose and instead create more and more vāsanās that cloud the buddhi.

Meditation is the process of silencing the self-referential thoughts and mode of being, so that the buddhi is gradually unclouded—not only because we aren't creating more debris but because we are also clearing the previously accumulated stuff. Cultivation of inner silence is the foundation for sādhanā, which is otherwise ineffective. Only with the silencing of self-referential thoughts are we granted access into the progressive āvaraṇas of the Śrīcakra. Discernment is the basis for tarka, which is perfected reasoning.

Tarka

Ordinarily, our choices arise from the buddhi reflecting our vāsanās. Tarka is clear reasoning not influenced by our likes and dislikes and past experiences, but the ability to draw conclusions about Reality based on the ability to see things as they are. We arrive at such conclusions through subtle discernment that has been refined through ever-deepening sādhanā.

Tarka is the subtle discernment that enables us to know the difference between, say, thought and the space in which thought arises. It is the ability to discern between the subject and the object, and to know an object as it is without the coloring of past learning. For example, what is the nature of seeing? When I look at a flower, what is the nature of my direct experience? Ordinarily, our reasoning allows us to know it as a flower, or a specific flower, belonging to this family of plants that grows in this region and under these conditions, and with a particular name and attributes. Tarka goes deeper. Looking at a flower engages the sense of seeing. What is the nature of seeing? What is the entity that sees? Where is the boundary between the seer and the seen? When looking "back" to look at the subject, we see that the sense of seeing is never separate from our awareness of it. There is no boundary between the flower and seeing, and seeing and awareness. What I am is awareness, and there is no separation between me and the flower. I *am* the flower. This is direct experience of a flower.

> **Tarka**
>
> ➢ Tarka (or sat-tarka) is perfected reasoning, which is the result of unclouding of the buddhi and is the blend of inference and direct experience.
>
> ➢ Tarka is cultivated through sādhanā against the backdrop of inner silence that quells self-referential thinking.

Inference plays into applying the knowledge of the View to ordinary life circumstances. While we have spent all this time looking at various maps of the darśana, we realize that most of those aspects are inferred—except for the lowest tattvas and our own bodies, we don't actually experience them through our senses. Even though we have explored the various stages of progression in sādhanā, there are no clear demarcations between them. In short, most of the aspects that make up the path are inferred. In the LSN, inference is symbolized by Devī's tiny waist (see N35) and provides the framework for sound deduction and logic, removed from self-interest and emotional coloring.

Tarka allows for ever-deepening inquiry and unclouding of the buddhi in everything we do. We stop doing things in certain ways because justifications and validations fall away. In the process, we uncover the secrets of the universe and its workings. We fall in love with Reality. This is the dawn of true bhakti. At this point, there is no need to look for Devī in specific relationships or in particular ways. She is all there is! The LSN begins to make more sense because the thousand names (and more) are Devī's presence as Reality. The result of this understanding is the experience of *rasa.*

Rasa

Rasa is the flavor or juice arising from the delight or ānanda of unity of the experiencer with the experience. There are many classifications of rasa depending on the context. It is most commonly studied and depicted in classical Indian arts, where the artist is entrusted with the task of portraying a particular emotion through music or dance. Rasa specifically refers to the transformation of an ordinary emotion such as anger into its aesthetic counterpart. It is often the case that this transmutation is most easily available when engaged with art, because it incites a certain level of equanimity and detachment.

Rasa

- ➢ The nine rasas are śṛṅgāra (erotic love), vīrya (heroism), bībhatsa (disgust), raudra (anger), hāsya (mirth), bhayānaka (terror), kāruṇya (compassion), adbhuta (amazement), and śānta (tranquility).
- ➢ The practice of rasa is less about the particular emotion, and more about constant and quiet restfulness (śānta) in the subtle vibration of awareness.
- ➢ When a particular emotion arises against this backdrop of tranquility, its vibration can be savored as it pulses in and out of awareness.

When watching a movie, even when we are absorbed in it, there is a degree of detachment, where we know that it isn't really happening to us. We are thus able to witness the spectrum of emotions as if "from a distance." Since such detachment isn't available when things are happening to us in real life, we are unable to tap into the essence of the emotion. An emotion like anger brings up great conflict between the biological and vāsanā-driven expression of anger and internal critique of anger. When we attach labels of "good" and "bad" to a given emotion, the labeling takes up vital energy, leaving little for the experience of the emotion.

The transformation of emotion into its aesthetic counterpart is the result of tapping into the arising experience without the involvement of the condi-

Śṛṅgāra

- The juice of life, prāṇa, the functioning of the body-mind, the ascent and interiorization of sādhanā and the outward explosion of the senses.
- The basis for the tattvas, and the five functions of the Divine.
- Although this rasa manifests as all emotions, it is most prominently experienced in joy, connection, sexual union, sweetness, enthusiasm, and lightness.

tioned mind. This requires a high level of sattva, where the default position of the mind is that of open, expansive curiosity. This equanimity becomes the backdrop for moment-to-moment experience, where the pure essence of the emotion is experienced without dualistic modifications. For example, if lust or anger is the arising experience and if we can be calmly aware of it, we can enjoy its essence or its flavor. However, this is impossible to do if we are also trying to fight it with moralistic justifications or seeking to satisfy the emotion by engaging with it.

In other words, rasa is the spanda or pulse of an experience expanding as the particular emotion and contracting back upon itself. It is another expression of Kāmakalā, the pulse of the bindu and visarga. Since the very basis of experience is the union of Śiva-Śakti in the bindu represented by Lalitā Mahātripurasundarī, the fundamental rasa of the cosmos is *śṛṅgāra*. It is ojas,* the subtle essence of life, and the warm and juicy moistness of cells, tissues, and organs that differentiates life from death. This is the juiciness that Bhaṇḍāsura steals from the devas, whereupon they become dry and depleted.

The practice of bhāvanā results in the arising of rasa through progressive stabilization in awareness. Śṛṅgāra rasa is the outpouring of ānanda that occurs with the transmutation of desire.

Transmutation of Desire

With a steady and committed practice that unclouds the buddhi, we begin to see the beauty of the LSN in our day-to-day experience. Unlike other paths where quelling desire is the means to peace, here we are given the tools to *transmute* rāga to icchā.

As Kuṇḍalinī makes her way up the slender stalk of the suṣumnā, we work our way up the āvaraṇas of the Śrīcakra so that the buddhi becomes increasingly clear. With a shift in identity from the limited body-mind (ahaṅkāra) to witnessing awareness (Puruṣa), a significant shift occurs in our way of being. With further sādhanā, the buddhi continues to become clarified with an increasing sense of freedom as the kārma and māyīya malas are relinquished in the first six āvaraṇas of the Śrīcakra. With the direct seeing of the word-object association, another level of

* Ojas is the final end-product of a balanced digestion in Ayurveda and is responsible for immunity and longevity. Known as the bliss molecule, its abundance is associated with contentment, sweetness and groundedness. All preventive measures are geared toward increasing ojas.

freedom is attained and we make a leap towards the trikoṇa. Here, we finally encounter the āṇava mala, and in the direct knowing of the fundamental triad of experience, the bindu reveals itself. However, the journey doesn't end here; it has just begun.

The sādhanā continues in the reverse direction, where the bindu is found in all the structures and sub-structures of the Śrīcakra. Desire which began as rāga has become transmuted to icchā, Devī's will. We stop asking for things and revel in the abundance of life. The movements of life are seen as her implements—the noose of our attractions, the goad of our aversions, and the sugary bow of desire that is constantly hooked to the flowery arrows of the senses. We come to see in our direct experience that Devī is indeed seated on the throne of the five powers of creation, sustenance, dissolution, concealment and revelation that are in play from moment-to-moment. We see her exquisite beauty in ordinary experience and in all states of consciousness.

Our breath, body, speech and actions become refined as Devī becomes our lived experience, pulsing out of the bindu, the stateless state that is the origin of us, our lives, and the world. We lose the ability to see in parts and develop a broader vision that includes the sun, the moon, and the fire that animates them both. These are her three eyes, after all. We become lost in her compassionate gaze when we look around and see grace saturating everything—a blade of grass, the smell of our baby's head, and the chaos of rush-hour traffic. All of our energy is poured into this grace as we realize that she has always been fighting the war against Bhaṇḍāsura on our behalf. We come to revel in freedom from our dead pasts and imagined futures, having accessed the previously closed off nāḍīs. We find that liberation was always available—we just needed to look in the right place.

In the living of the LSN, we come to see that Devī is the supreme force of the universe, not in a mystical out-of-reach way that is at the level of fantasy and myth, but in the very mundane moments that are woven together as our lives.

With this exploration of the most important aspects of the Śrīvidyā philosophy, let's turn our attention to the thousand names of Devī in Part II, which will enable us to walk this exquisite path of svatantra.

Part II

Living the Lalitā Sahasranāma

ŚRĪṂ MEDITATION

Hidden within first three nāmas of the LSN is the bīja mantra of auspiciousness—Śrīṃ. Here, we will explore a meditation on the central channel (suṣumnā nāḍī) with this mantra, which facilitates a gentle and yet powerful opening of the nāḍīs while simultaneously instilling sweetness and wholeness in them.

- ➢ Sit comfortably, ensuring that the spine is erect. If sitting on a chair, have your feet on the floor. If sitting on the floor, place a small cushion if needed under your buttocks to help support the spine.
- ➢ Close your eyes and take a few deep breaths, relaxing your face, shoulders and the rest of your body.
- ➢ Visualize three spheres of light—at the perineum (between the anus and genital organs), heart (center of the chest), and between the eyebrows.
- ➢ Place your attention at the spine, imagining a vertical thread of light connecting the three spheres.
- ➢ Bring your attention to the sphere at the perineum. Silently chant Śrīṃ once, prolonging the sounds Ś---ṛ---ī---ṃ. Trace the thread upward to the heart with the ṃṃṃ of the Ś---ṛ---ī---ṃ (See Figure 28).
- ➢ Silently chant Śrīṃ once at the heart, prolonging the sounds Ś---ṛ---ī---ṃ. Trace the thread upward to the eyebrow center with the ṃṃṃ of the Ś---ṛ---ī---ṃ.
- ➢ Silently chant Śrīṃ once at the eyebrow center, prolonging the sounds Ś---ṛ---ī---ṃ. Trace the thread upward to the crown with the ṃṃṃ of the Ś---ṛ---ī---ṃ.
- ➢ Bring your attention back to the perineum.
- ➢ Repeat this cycle for 10-15 minutes.
- ➢ End the practice by lying down on the floor and resting for a few minutes.

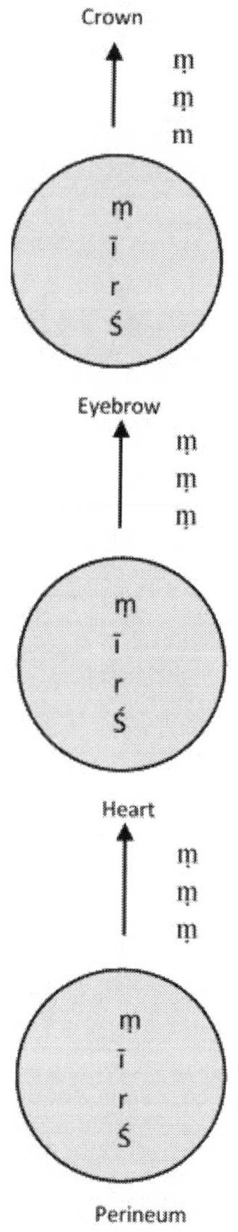

Fig. 28: Śrīṃ Meditation

DHYĀNA MANTRAS OF DEVĪ

Dhyāna is meditation, where an object of concentration takes us from the superficial level of the mind to inner repose, to eventually facilitate the "turning upon itself" of attention. Dhyāna mantras describe the form of the deity to aid visualization. This subtle inner form of the deity becomes the object of meditation, dragging the mind to its Source, which the deity represents.

The Lalitā Sahasranāma contains four dhyāna mantras, which are thought to have been added by different authors over time. The most frequently chanted first dhyāna mantra is credited to the Vāgdevatās, the composers of the LSN (see Chapter 1). Devī's body is the color of vermilion and the rosy hue of dawn (D1). She is three-eyed (D2) and wears a ruby-studded crown (D3) topped by the crescent moon that shines as if it is the leader of the stars (D4). She has a smiling face (D5) and her full breasts (D6) nourish the universe. In one hand, she holds (D7) a jewelled cup brimming with honeyed mead (D8), and in the other, she twirls a red lotus (D9). An epitome of beauty (D10), she rests her radiant red feet on a pot decorated with rubies (D11). We meditate on this supreme form of the goddess, who is Parā and Ambikā (D12) (see Chapter 8).

The second dhyāna mantra is attributed to Dattātreya, the incarnation of the combination of Brahmā, Viṣṇu and Śiva. In this verse, Devī is of the color of the rising sun (D1), compassion emanating from her eyes (D2), supported by a noose, goad, flower arrows and a bow (D3) in her four hands. She is surrounded by Aṇimā and other siddhis (D4, see Deities of the Śrīcakra in Chapter 10) and is radiant like a ray of light (D5). In this way, we meditate on Bhavānī (D6, see N112).

Dhyāna Mantra 1

D1:1 **sindūrāruṇa-vigrahāṃ** body the color of vermilion and the rising sun

D1:2 **tri-nayanāṃ** three-eyed

D1:3 **māṇikya mauli sphurat** wearing a ruby-studded crown

D1:4 **tārānāyaka-śekharāṃ** moon, the leader of the stars

D1:5 **smitamukhīṃ** smiling face

D1:6 **āpīna vakṣoruhām** full breasts

D1:7 **pāṇibhyāṃ** holding in hand

D1:8 **alipūrṇa-ratna-caṣakam** jewelled cup brimming with mead

D1:9 **raktotpalam bibhratīṃ** twirling a red lotus

D1:10 **saumyāṃ** beauty

D1:11 **ratna-ghaṭastha-rakta-caraṇāṃ** red feet resting on gem-studded pot

D1:12 **dhyāyetparāmambikām** meditate on Devī, who is Parā and Ambikā

Dhyāna Mantra 2

D2:1 **aruṇāṃ** color of the rising sun

D2:2 **karuṇā taraṃgitākṣīṃ** eyes emanating waves of compassion

D2:3 **dhṛta-pāśāṅkuśa-puṣpa-bāṇa-cāpām** supported by noose, goad, flower arrows and bow

D2:4 **aṇimādibhir āvṛtām** attended by Aṇimā and the other siddhis

D2:5 **mayūkhai** ray of light

D2:6 **ahamityeva vibhāvaye bhavānīm** like this, I meditate on Bhavānī

The authorship of the third verse is unknown. Here, Devī is meditated upon (D1) as seated on a lotus (D2). She has a beautiful, moon-like face (D3) with eyes like lotus petals (D4). She is of a golden complexion (D5), is clothed in gold-colored garments (D6) and holds in her hand a brilliant, golden (D7) lotus (D8). Her perfect-limbed body (D9) is adorned with all types of ornaments (D10). She bestows unending protection upon her humble devotees (D11). We meditate upon Bhavānī (D12), who as Śrīvidyā (D13) is the embodiment of tranquillity (D14) and is worshiped by all other celestial beings (D15) as the bestower of all riches (D16).

Dhyāna Mantra 3

D3:1 **dhyāyet** meditated upon

D3:2 **padmāsanasthāṃ** seated on a lotus

D3:3 **vikasita-vadanāṃ** beautiful face

D3:4 **padma-patrāyatākṣīṃ** eyes like lotus petals

D3:5 **hemābhāṃ** gold-complexioned

D3:6 **pītavastrāṃ** gold-colored garments

D3:7 **kara-kalita-lasaddhema** holding a gold-colored

D3:8 **padmām** lotus

D3:9 **varāngīm** perfect limbed body

D3:10 **sarvālaṃkāra-yuktāṃ** adorned with all ornaments

D3:11 **satatamabhayadāṃ bhakta-namrām** bestowing unending protection on humble devotees

D3:12 **bhavānīm** Bhavānī

D3:13 **śrividyāṃ** Śrīvidyā

D3:14 **śānta-mūrtim** embodiment of tranquility

D3:15 **sakala-sura-nutāṃ** worshiped by all gods

D3:16 **sarva saṃpat pradātrīm** bestower of all riches

The fourth dhyāna mantra is attributed to Ādi Śaṅkarācārya, and here again, Devī is visualized with a red complexion, anointed with kuṅkuma* (D1) and bee-attracting musk (D2). With her sweet smile, benign glance (D3) and the noose, goad, bow and arrows that she holds in her four hands (D4), she attracts all creatures without exception (D5). She wears a garland of red sandalwood and all types of ornaments (D6), shining like a China

* A red powder made by mixing turmeric and slake lime.

Dhyāna Mantra 4

D4:1 **sakuṅkuma-vilepanāṃ** anointed with kumkum

D4:2 **alika-cumbi-kastūrikāṃ** attracting bees with musk

D4:3 **samanda-hasitekṣaṇām** sweet smile and glance

D4:4 **saśara-cāpa-pāśāṅkuśa** bearing flower arrows, bow, noose and goad,

D4:5 **aśeṣa-jana-mohinīṃ** deluding all

D4:6 **aruṇa-mālya-bhūṣāṃbarāṃ** wearing a garland of sandalwood and other ornaments

D4:7 **japā-kusuma-bhāsurāṃ** shining like a China rose

D4:8 **japavidhau** method of japa

D4:9 **smaredaṃbikām** meditate on Ambikā

rose (hibiscus) (D7). We practice japa according to the prescribed method (D8, see Mantra Sādhanā in Chapter 12), meditating upon Devī as Ambikā (D9).

Section 1

DEVĪ'S STHŪLA (GROSS) FORM

Every great text follows a particular pattern, where the essence of the entire text is declared right up front. If this opening declaration is understood and actualized in our own experience, the text has accomplished its purpose. So it is with the LSN—if we actualize this first nāma, the remaining 999 nāmas become embellishments that refine our understanding of this one.

Devī's Sthūla (Gross) Form

N1 Śrīmātā Auspicious Mother

The LSN begins by declaring that Devī is the Auspicious Mother (N1). This is the most obvious meaning of this nāma, and yet it encapsulates the entire darśana of Śrīvidyā. The root Mā means "to measure." Let's refer back to the Tattva Map (see Chapter 4), where we see that Śiva and Śakti are prakāśa and vimarśa (see Prakāśa and Vimarśa in Chapter 3). The infinite and immeasurable Prakāśa becomes measurable as vimarśa. The spaceless and timeless Reality becomes measurable in space and time.

Everything in manifestation is quantifiable, including our body-mind, which can be measured by the number of heart beats and breaths across a given lifespan, as well as the amount of joy, peace, and suffering that makes up the story of our life. Everything that defines us is measurable in time and space.

Devī as vimarśa differs from what we ordinarily think of as a mother who becomes separate from the child she births. Even though the relationship is cemented by emotional and psychological phenomena, the mother doesn't become the child's body, brain, mind, or biological processes. In contrast, Devī not only births the universe but *becomes* it. In becoming us, the ray of immeasurable prakāśa becomes measurable as vimarśa, making up all aspects of our identity. As vimarśa (*see N548*), Devī *is* our body-mind, the way we think, feel, and behave, our sādhanā and the goal of sādhanā. This nāma alludes to the contemplation upon the bindu and trikoṇa of the Śrīcakra, where we realize the unity of the measurer and the measured. As this great Mā (measurer), Devī inspires devotion and longing for deep bhāvanā into the nature of Reality that results in the collapse of the trikoṇa into the bindu.

Śrī in N1 also refers to the universe, which is a manifestation of auspiciousness. As we see in Chapter 12, there is an inherent perfection in all of creation, even with its apparent messiness. Mātā refers to the mother of Śrī—Devī in the bindu becomes the trikoṇa as the triad of the knower, known, and process of knowing—the basis of manifestation.

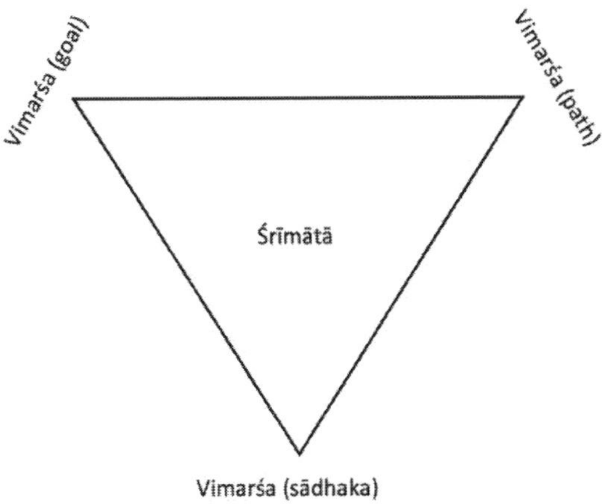

Figure 29. Vimarśa Triad

Mātā is thus the auspiciousness, the knower of auspiciousness, and the process of knowing it.

What is critical to understand with N1 is that auspiciousness is not the property of objects or events. It is the beauty of seeing the non-separation between I, the subject and That, the objects/events. This first nāma has the power to stir us into asking, "How can I realize this non-separation?" The answer is deep contemplation of the darśana of the path along with a committed practice of the Śrīvidyā mantra. Śrīmātā then is the triad of the path, the goal of the path, and the one walking the path (see Figure 29).

> **Devī's Sthūla (Gross) Form**
>
> **N2 Śrīmahārājñī** Auspicious Ruler

As the one that makes the immeasurable measurable, Devī assumes the first Divine function of creation (Srṣṭi). However, it's not enough to create something—whatever is created must be maintained. She assumes this function of maintenance (sthiti) as the auspicious ruler (N2). Rājñī is the feminine equivalent of Rāja or king.

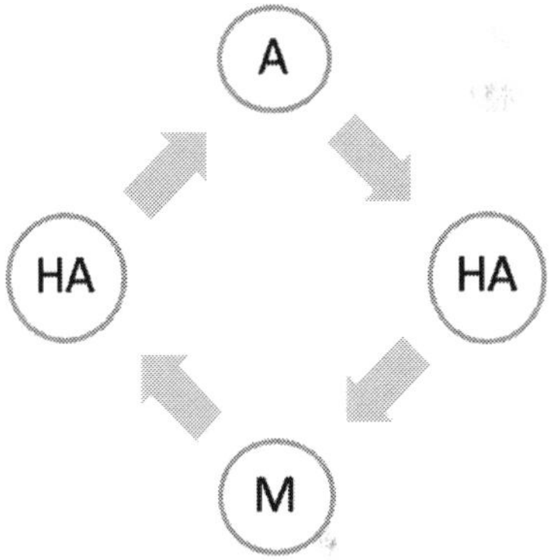

Figure 30. AHAM-MAHA

The addition of Śrī and mahā elevate this nāma to mean Auspicious Great Queen, or Auspicious Empress. A ruler's primary function is to maintain order and prosperity of the kingdom. In this case, Devī's kingdom is all of creation as the tattvas and its preservation requires constant dissolution of the old and creation of the new.

A mantra is hidden in the word MAHĀ, which is the mirror image of AHAM. As we've seen in Chapters 8 and 12, Ahaṃ is the bindu, the concentration of the entire alphabet from AṂ to HA, with the movement toward manifestation. The reverse movement of resorption is represented by its mirror image, MAHA (see Figure 30). This constant movement between the two poles of emission and withdrawal is spanda, the sacred tremor of manifestation. This ecstatic flow between bindu and visarga provides the appearance of continuity and preservation.

Preservation requires the constant dissolution of the old so that the new can be ushered in. Devī assumes this function of dissolution as the supreme ruler of the auspicious throne (N3). We must pause here to consider this—what is the fundamental unit of creation? Time, of course. Creation is defined by linear time, which is a sequence of events. The previous moment has to dissolve so that the next one can arise. Contemplation on time reveals the utter instability of what is created. And yet, the *illusion* of stability keeps time's destructive power hidden. Age creeps up on us. Our parents grow old and pass away even though we don't feel very different than when we were children. Importantly, we can notice change only in the context of what is unchanging. For example, we can tell that a train is moving only in the context of the unmoving platform. And so it is for time. There must be something unchanging that is the yardstick for the change that time brings. Devī's throne is that unchanging entity that determines dissolution. By remaining the eternal and unchanged ruler of the throne, she enables change through the third function of dissolution (saṃhāra).*

Devī's Sthūla (Gross) Form

N3 Śrīmatsiṃhāsaneśvarī Ruler of the auspicious lion-throne

N4 Cidagni kuṇḍasambhūtā born in the fire-pit of consciousness

N5 Devakāryasamudyatā facilitator of the devas' work

Devī is constantly born in the fire-pit of our consciousness (N4) and is projected as the world we behold. At first glance, this nāma seems to refer to Devī rising out of the devas' fire-pit in the Lalitopākhyāna (see Devī's Conquest of Bhaṇḍāsura in Chapter 1) to help them destroy Bhaṇḍāsura (N5). Upon deeper contemplation, we see that it is a description of her power of concealment (tirodhāna) and revelation (anugraha).

When Śakti is turned away from Śiva (see Kuṇḍalinī in Chapter 7), the world appears and Śiva is concealed. When she turns toward him, the world disappears and he is revealed (anugraha). Devī conceals herself in Māyā and the kañcukas so that the One appears as many. Even though the world around us is arising from our own consciousness, we don't see it because of our clouded buddhi. Śiva is concealed because our attention is turned out-

* Hidden within these first three nāmas is Śrīṃ, the bīja mantra of auspiciousness (see Meditation at the beginning of Part II).

ward. When, like the devas, we begin to immolate ourselves in the fire-pit of consciousness, Devī rises out of it to destroy the limitations that keep us in ignorance. Her grace forces attention to turn upon itself, where Śiva as our true nature is revealed.

With the establishment of her powers in the first five nāmas, we will now explore the modes by which they are exercised. As the illuminating power of the universe, she is brilliant as thousands of rising suns (N6). We long to leave a legacy, to contribute somehow, so that our lives have some meaning. What we *really* want is to infuse the world with our consciousness. In fact, everything we do is infused with the light of our consciousness. What to say then about Devī's light that illuminates her handiwork, which is the universe? It surpasses that of countless suns, which are mere reflections of her light.

Devī's Sthūla (Gross) Form

N6 udyadbhānu sahasrābhā brilliant as thousands of rising suns

N7 caturbāhu samanvitā four-armed

N8 rāgasvarūpa pāśāḍhyā bearing the noose of desire

N9 krodhakārāṅkuśojjvalā bearing the goad of wrath

N10 manorūpekṣukodaṇḍā bearing the mind bow

As we see in the Tattva Map (see Chapter 4), icchā, jñāna and kriyā śakti are the three modes of operation. For anything to manifest, we need to have the *intention* to create it and the *knowledge* of how to accomplish it, before we *act* on it. Devī's four arms (N7) represent these modes of action. In her left upper hand, she bears the noose of will or icchā (N8), the first mode of Divine will. With the veiling of Māyā and the effect of the kañcukas, icchā becomes rāga, where desire is centered around the ahaṅkāra. Devī is both icchā and rāga! As icchā, she is the binding force of the macrocosm, and as rāga, she is the binding force of the microcosm. If none of us had self-centered desires, what would be the point of creation? Since our desires create our personalities and sense of separation, rāga is the primary mode through which the One can experience itself as the many.

Devī's aṅkuśa (N9), the goad of wrath in her upper right hand, is symbolic of her second mode of operation—Divine knowledge or jñāna śakti. If will is the seed for action, knowledge is its expansive energy. When we know *how* to go about manifesting something, the seed of wanting it is watered and nourished by the knowledge. Her goad is symbolic of the expansion of the universe, pushed out by the knowledge of how it must unfold in space and time. Her goad moves at an astonishing pace, as if fuelled by krodha or wrath. At the microcosmic level, jñāna śakti becomes limited as vidyā. When our desires are thwarted and we don't get what we want, vidyā becomes tainted by anger and resentment, which

Devī's Sthūla (Gross) Form

N11 pañcatanmātra sāyakā bearing the tanmātras as arrows

N12 nijāruṇa prabhāpūra majjad-brahmāṇḍamaṇḍalā bathing the universe with her rosy effulgence

N13 campakāśoka punnāga saugandhika lasatkacā flowers adorning her hair

leads to greater "expansion" of the ahaṅkāra. The ahaṅkāra takes up the episode of not having gotten a specific outcome and attaches it to the "me story."

In her left lower hand, Devī bears the bow (N10) that represents the mind. The mind is Devī's bow, made of sugarcane to represent the sweet allure of objects. At the cosmic level, the forces of nature submit to Devī's sweet bow of attraction—galaxies are driven together by gravity, life forms come together to mate and thrive, flowers turn to the sun and open up for the bees. At the microcosmic level, our minds are turned outward in the sweet seduction of objects. In all these patterns, we see that, at every level, creation seeks wholeness and to return to the Source that is Śiva-Śakti. This great seeking is the product of Devī's bow, which engages with the five arrows in her right lower hand representing the tanmātras (N11). As we've seen in Chapter 4, the tanmātras are the bridge between the world and the experience of the world through the senses. While Devī's bow is a stalk of sugarcane, her five flower arrows cause five types of agitations—excitement, maddening, confusion, stimulation, and fading.

While her noose and goad represent icchā and jñāna, her bow and arrows are symbolic of her third mode of action, kriyā śakti. Even though our actions also arise from the coming together of intention and knowledge, the crucial difference between Devī's mode of action and ours is that *nothing lies outside of her.* The universe is her body and there is no other—her arrows find their mark within her own being. When veiled by Māyā, kriyā śakti becomes constricted as kalā. We feel that we are "in here" in this body interacting with the world "out there." Māyā prevents us from seeing that nothing exists outside of us and, instead, the arrows of our senses are directed out into the world with the intent of bringing fulfilment *in from the outside.* Sādhanā involves disengaging the arrows from the bow by deeply understanding the nature of Reality.

Devī bathes the entire universe with her own rosy effulgence (N12). As we have seen in the dhyāna mantras, she is characterized by her red complexion, which is the color of blood and life—she is the life-blood of the universe. Red is also the color of desire, and the purpose of this sādhanā is its transmutation (see Transmutation of Desire in Chapter 12).

With the preceding nāmas, we see that Devī has manifested *as* the universe. Now we can begin to see her sthūla form beginning with her head. Not only are the flowers adorning her hair (Campaka, Aśoka, Puṃnāga and Saugandhika) (N13) beautiful, but each has a unique fragrance that is derived from her hair, emphasizing the One Source of all diversity in creation. Her crown is adorned with rows of Kuruvinda (N14), a precious ruby that is said to confer stability and devotion.* It is also a variety of rice that is highly medicinal and stabilizing for all the tissues. Beneath this ruby-studded crown, her forehead shines like the crescent moon of the eighth night of the lunar half-month (N15). The uniqueness of the eighth night of the moon cycle (aṣṭami) is that the moon (candra) is exactly "half" of itself in both the waxing or waning phases. Devī wears this moon on her crown to denote her cyclical nature as time while being simultaneously timeless (*see N3*). On her radiant forehead, she wears a dot of musk that shines like the spot in the moon (N16).

Her eyebrows form the archways of the path leading to Kāma's palace (N17). Throughout the LSN, we will see references to Devī's sensual and erotic nature—there's nothing dry and austere about her! Her face is the epitome of sensuality, which is likened to the palace of Kāma, the God of Love (see The Rise of Bhaṇḍāsura in Chapter 1). If Devī's face can be compared to a beautiful body of water, her eyes are like fish that are constantly moving about in it (N18). The pond is still and serene, while the moving fish are dynamic. Devī's constantly moving eyes denote spanda, the dynamic expansion and contraction of the bindu as the universe (see Kuṇḍalinī in Chapter 7).

Devī's Sthūla (Gross) Form

N14 **kuruvinda maṇiśreṇī kanatkoṭīra maṇḍitā**
Crown adorned with rows of Kuruvinda

N15 **aṣṭamī candra vibhrāja daḷikasthala śobhitā**
Forehead shining like the crescent moon of the eighth night of the lunar half-month

N16 **mukhacandra kaḷaṅkābha mṛganābhi viśeṣakā** wearing a musk mark on her forehead which shines like the spot in the moon

N17 **vadanasmara māṅgalya gṛhatoraṇa cillikā**
eyebrow-arch leading to Kāma's palace

N18 **vaktralakṣmī parīvāha calanmīnābha locanā**
eyes like fish moving in calm waters

N19 **navacampaka puṣpābha nāsādaṇḍa virājitā**
nose like a newly blossoming campaka flower

Aside from a description of Devī's exquisite beauty, these nāmas are prompts for bhāvanā. For instance, we contemplate her nose, which is like the newly blossoming campaka flower (N19). Campaka is a beautiful and highly fragrant flower. If we pause to wonder why this particular flower is used as a metaphor for Devī's nose, we see that it is to point at the essential non-separation between a sense organ (nose) and its sense (smell). When I say I smell this flower, two different unnoticed phenomena are occurring. Firstly, the nose is implied in the sense of smell—I don't have to specify that it is my nose that is smelling. Secondly, awareness is implied—I don't have to specify that, when I say "I" smell the flower, I mean

* Lalitā Sahasranāma with Bhāskararāya's Commentary translated into English by R. Ananthakrishna Sastry (The Adyar Library and Research Center, 2010), page 50.

that there is awareness of the sense of smell. When we inquire into this, we see that there is no separation between the flower and the sense of smell, or the sense of smell and the awareness of it. Where would the boundary be between the nose and smell, and smell and awareness? In this kind of bhāvanā, the triad of experience—the smell, the one who smells, and the process of smelling—collapse into the bindu. This is why Devī's nose is likened to a fragrant flower!

The stars derive their light and brilliance from her sparkling nose-stud (N20), and her face is framed by bunches of Kadamba flowers peeking out above her ears (N21). Although we get the sense that Devī loves flowers in many nāmas, we must remember that they symbolize our saṃskāras (see The Magic of the Lalitā Sahasranāma in Chapter 1), the subtle emotional impressions of past experiences that color our way of being. In offering flowers in worship, we demonstrate a willingness to offer our saṃskāras. Flowers also represent the five great elements—they blossom outward in space, they're carried as seed by the wind, their vibrancy is fire-like, they're moist because of their water content, and they rise from the earth. Devī wears flowers to denote her dominion over the great elements and also over our saṃskāras.

Her earrings are the sun and moon (N22), both deriving their light from her. In another analogy, the sun and moon are her two eyes, and agni or the fire principle is her third eye (see N352). In yet another analogy, they are two breasts, signifying their nourishing and life-giving functions.

Devī's Sthūla (Gross) Form

N20 tārākānti tiraskāri nāsābharaṇa bhāsurā nose-stud of the stars' brilliance

N21 kadamba mañjarīklupta karṇapūra manoharā wearing bunches of Kadambas over the ears

N22 tāṭaṅka yugalībhūta tapanoḍupa maṇḍalā wearing the sun and moon as earrings

N23 padmarāga śilādarśa paribhāvi kapolabhūḥ cheeks surpassing the brilliance of pagmarāga

N24 navavidruma bimbaśrīḥ nyakkāri radanacchadā lips the color of coral and bimba

N25 śuddha vidyāṅkurākāra dvijapaṅkti dvayojjvalā twin rows of teeth of pure knowledge

Devī's cheeks surpass the brilliance of the gemstone known as padmarāga (N23), a sapphire that is orangish and reddish in color, and her lips put to shame the color of freshly cut coral and the intensely red bimba fruit (N24).*

Her two rows of radiant teeth are the buds of pure knowledge or Śuddha Vidyā (N25). The contemplation here is on Devī's 32 teeth. Recall that vāk has four stages (see Chapter 8). Parā (see N366) is the Reality prior to the tattvas, the One without a split into subject and object, or the word and the object to which it refers. At the level of paśyantī (see N368), there is a split into subject and object and word and object, which carries over to madhyamā (see N370) and vaikharī (see N371). This nāma refers

* Here again, we see a reference to red, the color of desire (see Dhyāna Mantras and N12).

to the 16-syllabled ṣodaśi mantra.* We can think of this mantra as a seed at the parā level, beginning as one and splitting as two (the mantra and the knower of the mantra) at the paśyantī and madhyamā. At the vaikharī level, or the most manifest form, it is as if the twin aspects (dvija) of the mantra (16 each as the subject and object) have blossomed into 32 buds. Śuddha Vidyā at the parā level is the sole purpose of the ṣodaśi mantra, where the subject-object differentiation collapses (see The Pure Path in Chapter 5). The mantra therefore takes us in the reverse fashion from vaikharī to parā.** With Śuddha Vidyā, we are as if twice-born (dvija)—born again into Reality.

Devī chews on a camphor-laden betel roll that attracts the universe (N26). Her betel roll (betel leaves*** filled with saffron, areca nuts, camphor, a bit of slaked lime, and other herbs) is like the glue that keeps the universe together. The fragrance of camphor draws every one of us to seek wholeness in Devī, whether we are aware of her presence or not (see N559).

Her speech surpasses the melody of Sarasvatī's vīṇa**** known as Kacchapi (N27), which is the primordial source of sound and language. Its sweet

Devī's Sthūla (Gross) Form

N26 **karpūravīṭi kāmoda samākarṣa digantarā** universe-attracting fragrant camphor-laden betel roll

N27 **nijasallāpa mādhurya vinirbhartsita kacchapī** speech excelling Sarasvatī's vīṇa

melody is the allure of language that keeps us bound in duality. Devī's speech is the source of the vīṇa's melody, and her smile is so seductive that even the great Kāmeśa, who rules over desire,***** is unable to resist it (N28). While this nāma establishes Devī's supremacy over Śiva, it reiterates the fundamental premise of this path, which is the transmutation of desire (see Transmutation of Desire in Chapter 12), unlike other paths that suppress it. In many mythological stories, sages who achieve great attainments through subjugation of the senses eventually succumb to desire, since what is suppressed is bound to resurface sooner or later!

Devī's incomparable chin adds to her unsurpassed beauty (N29), being the point of the bindu into which the universe converges. Her neck is adorned with the thread signifying her auspicious marriage to Kāmeśa (N30).****** Her arms are adorned with golden armlets (N31), and she wears a necklace made of gold, gems, and a dangling pearl

* This is derived by the addition of another bīja mantra to the Pañcadaśi mantra.

** This nāma could mean to refer to a very secret 32-syllable mantra of the tradition known as guhya ṣodaśi, the exclusive purpose of which is Śuddha Vidyā. It could also mean to refer to the 32 types of initiations in the Śrīvidyā tradition that are necessary for Śuddha Vidyā.

*** Leaves of a vine belonging to the piperaceae family; they are considered auspicious and offered in pūjā, and consumed along with areca nuts and other herbs.

**** Stringed Indian instrument.

***** Kāmeśa is Śiva, the ruler (īśa) of desire (kāma).

****** Throughout the LSN, we will see repeated references to the essential oneness of Śiva-Śakti as prakāśa-vimarśa forever bound by the invisible thread of auspiciousness (saubhāgya).

Devī's Sthūla (Gross) Form

N28 **mandasmita prabhāpūra majjat-kāmeśa mānasā** smile seducing Kāmeśvara

N29 **anākalita sādṛśya cibuka śrī virājitā** chin of incomparable beauty

N30 **kāmeśabaddha māṅgalya sūtraśobhita kandharā** wearing the thread of marriage to Kāmeśvara

N31 **kanakāṅgada keyūra kamanīya bhujānvitā** arms adorned with golden armlets

N32 **ratnagraiveya cintāka lolamuktā phalānvitā** necklace made of gold, gems, and dangling pearl

(N32). Here, we pause again to consider the non-separation between gold and ornaments made of gold (*see N19*). In this nāma, we also see that Devī is exacting in her measurements and that our sādhanā is rewarded according to our capacity. The gold, gems, and the pearl of her necklace denote stages of sādhanā.

Initially, we are at the stage of *lola* (unsteady), where our sādhanā is centered around our desires and we approach Devī in a give-and-take relationship. We offer worship so that she will give us something in return. When we move to the next stage, we become *graiveyacintāka*, which means to contemplate on the neck. Esoterically, this nāma refers to the viśuddha cakra or the vaikharī stage of vāk, which, as we know, is the fully manifested state of the Divine. At this stage of sādhanā, we can recognize Devī only in her sthūla form and are yet to cultivate the discernment to know her as the formless Reality. We rely on external worship such as rituals and chants. The next stage of sādhanā is that of a *muktā* (free), where we don't need any external props to recognize Devī in everything and everywhere. Even when engaged in external ritual, we are immersed in the knowledge that Devī is both form and formless.

Our sādhanā is rewarded according to the stage. At the lola stage, we are yet to see that whatever we can possibly ask of Devī in terms of material gains is limited. Devī's icchā does not work in parts or fragments; the whole universe is affected by the minutest change in the course of things. This is why we get what we want only sometimes—what we want specifically may not be harmonious for the universe! We ask for particular outcomes because we are not aligned with Devī's icchā and are driven by rāga. In our passionate wanting of a specific result, we close ourselves off to all other (usually much better) outcomes. Think about all the times when you looked back at an incident that seemed hopeless at the time but in retrospect was the best thing that could have happened. Since we are unable to see into the future or beyond our limited space quantum, we ask for things to be different. The results we get are in accordance with this limited mindset.

At the graiveyacintāka stage, we have matured and are slightly more aligned with Devī's icchā. We stop asking for things to be different, but Devī still appears very strongly in particular roles (such as mother). We are unable to see her in everything and

Devī's Sthūla (Gross) Form

N33 **kāmeśvara premaratna maṇi pratipaṇastanī** offers her breasts to Kāmeśvara in return for his love

N34 **nābhyālavāla romālī latāphala kucadvayī** Breasts growing like fruit on the creeper of the fine hairline

N35 **lakṣyaromalatā dhāratā samunneya madhyamā** waist known only by inference by the creeper-like hair springing from it

everyone, and depend strongly on rituals, teachers, and teachings to maintain devotion and sādhanā. At the muktā stage, we have traversed the āvaraṇas of the Śrīcakra to arrive at the bindu and know in direct experience that Devī is the sādhaka, the sādhanā, the object of sādhanā, and the fruit of sādhanā. The gold of her necklace symbolizes the lola, gemstones the graiveyacintāka, and the dangling pearl the muktā.

In exchange for Kāmeśvara's love, she offers her breasts to him as gifts (N33). Here, it is worthwhile to contemplate love. Love (prema) is identification. We love those with whom we identify, where the boundary between "me" and "not me" is blurred or erased. To love Kāmeśvara is to become one with him. As we've seen earlier (see Kuṇḍalinī in Chapter 7), the universe is manifested when Śakti turns away from Śiva, becoming the "other." She nourishes this otherness with her breasts, maintaining the sense of separation. In turning toward him, she readily stops nourishing the world—this is the extent of her devotion to Śiva! On the other hand, we nourish our sense of separateness by remaining enamored with the world. This nāma gives us much to reflect on. What would *we* give for Śiva's love? Would we be willing to give away all that we create and nourish, especially the "me story"?

Devī's breasts—our current focus of bhāvanā—are like fruits growing on a creeper, which is the fine hairline rising from the depths of her navel (N34). The fine hairline here refers to the suṣumnā nāḍī. Kuṇḍalinī, which lies dormant at the "depths of the navel" rises up this fine creeper-like nāḍī to the heart area, expanding like ripe fruit, when more and more of the universe is included in "me" until boundaries between "me" and "not me" cease to exist (see Pure Path in Chapter 5).

Devī's waist is so slender that it is known only by inference from the creeper-like hair springing from the depths of her navel (N35). When we come to the spiritual journey, we realize that esoteric knowledge is about inference. The concepts we have been studying—Reality, tattvas, inner maps, śuddha vidyā and so on—are known only through inference and the cultivation of tarka (see Tarka in Chapter 12) and not as discrete objects. Devī's waist is similarly inferred, being the conduit for the ascent of Kuṇḍalinī from the depths of the navel to the heart. Burdened by her breasts, her small waist is supported by the girdle made of three folds of skin (N36), referring to the three granthīs that are unravelled by the ascending Kuṇḍalinī (see N84, N99-104, see also Granthis in Chapter 7).

Devī's Sthūla (Gross) Form

N36 **stanabhāra dalan-madhya paṭṭabandha vali-trayā** breast-burdened waist supported by the girdle of the three skin folds

N37 **aruṇāruṇa kausumbha vastra bhās-vat-kaṭītaṭī** hips wrapped in red garment

N38 **ratnakiṅkiṇi kāramya raśanādāma bhūṣitā** golden girdle decorated with gem-studded bells

N39 **kāmeśajñāta saubhāgya mārdavorudvayān-vitā** thighs known only by the fortunate Kāmeśvara

Devī's hips are wrapped in a garment dyed red with an extract from safflower (kusumbha) blossoms (N37). Her golden girdle is decorated with many gem-studded bells (N38), referring to the many internal sounds (including tinkling of bells) that we can experience when Kuṇḍalinī begins her ascent. Only the fortunate Kāmeśvara knows Devī's beautiful thighs (N39), referring to the third kūṭa of the Pañcadaśi. Each of the three kūṭas corresponds to a particular part of Devī's body (*see N85-87*), becoming progressively more esoteric and unavailable without sufficient clarity of the buddhi. The first kūṭa is her face, the second her torso, and the third is her lower body. Only Śiva knows the third kūṭa, referring to the absolute intimacy of the subject-object relationship in the bindu.

Devī's knees are like crowns made of rubies (N40), and her calves gleam like Kāma's jewel-covered quiver (N41), which holds his arrows of desire.

Devī's Sthūla (Gross) Form

N40 **māṇikya makuṭākāra jānudvaya virājitā** knees like crowns made of rubies

N41 **indragopa parikṣipta smara tūṇābha jaṅghikā** calves like the jewel-covered quiver of Kāma

N42 **gūḍhagulphā** hidden ankles

N43 **kūrmapṛṣṭha jayiṣṇu prapadānvitā** feet with arches like the tortoise's back

N44 **nakhadīdhiti saṃchanna namajjana tamo-guṇā** toenails that dispel tamas

N45 **padadvaya prabhājāla parākṛta saroruhā** feet are the source of beauty for the lotus

N46 **śiñjāna maṇimañjīra maṇḍita śrī padāmbujā** feet adorned with gem-studded golden anklets

N47 **marālī mandagamanā** gait of a swan

N48 **mahālāvaṇya śevadhiḥ** treasure house of beauty

N49 **sarvāruṇā** emanating a red hue

N50 **navadyāṅgī** flawless limbs

N51 **sarvābharaṇa bhūṣitā** resplendent ornamentation

Her ankles are concealed (N42), just like the elusive ānava mala, which is the unseen support of the reservoir (the quiver) of our self-serving desires. We seek wholeness in the constant act of shooting sense-arrows out into the world. When we seek refuge at Devī's feet, we cultivate the ability to withdraw our senses, like a tortoise that withdraws its limbs (N43), symbolically returning the arrows of self-centered desire to the quiver.

Devī's toenails are the subject of several myths because they dispel the darkness of ignorance and inertia with their brilliance (N44). In one myth, when devās and asurās prostrate before Devī, the jewels in their crowns are reflected back in the brilliance of her toenails, dispelling their darkness and inertia (tamas). Her feet are the source of beauty for the lotus flower (N45), which is unique in that its seeds germinate in mud and the slender stalk rises through marshy water to bloom on the surface. Despite its humble origins in the mud, the lotus remains unsullied and pure and is thus a symbol for discernment and equanimity—the qualities we acquire when we surrender at Devī's feet. We can sometimes hear her gem-studded golden anklets (N46) in meditation when Devī as Kuṇḍalinī moves playfully like a swan (N47) up the suṣumnā stalk (see also N38).

From head to toe, Devī is the treasure house of beauty (N48), emanating a red hue (N49), with flawless limbs (N50) and resplendent with ornamentation (N51).

Her faultless limbs and perfect symmetry allow for easy absorption in the practice of visualization, which is a delightful path to Śuddha Vidyā. This visualization gives us the tools to cultivate concentration and single-pointedness as we meditate on her physical form with the progressive addition of details. Keeping our attention focused for prolonged periods of time on the many details of an image necessarily involves a comprehensive housecleaning of the subtle and causal bodies (see Śarīrās in Chapter 6).

With this nāma, we come to an end of the description of Devī's sthūla form. In nāmas 52-63, we encounter a description of Devī's abode. As we've seen earlier, Reality's first split is into Śiva-Śakti, or prakāśa-vimarśa. Another way to look at this split is in terms of being endowed with attributes (saguṇa) or being attributeless (nirguṇa). Śiva is nirguṇa and Śakti is saguṇa. And yet, they remain inseparable, each unable to be expressed without the other. As the saguṇa aspect, Devī is visualized as sitting in the lap of the nirguṇa Kāmeśvara (N52). She is known as Śivā (N53) because she is the bestower of Śiva-ness to Śiva! In being every quality that we attribute to Śiva, she wins over him (N54). United with him, she dwells in the middle of Mount Sumeru (N55), the mystical mountain range that is the figurative center of the universe as well as the bindu of the Śrīcakra (see Chapter 1). She rules over the universe from Śrī Nagara, the auspicious city (N56), where she resides in her palace made of Cintāmaṇi (N57), a wish-fulfilling gem that is also the source of all mantras.

Devī's Sthūla (Gross) Form

N52 **śivakāmeśvarāṅkasthā** sitting in Kāmeśvara's lap

N53 **śivā** auspiciousness

N54 **svādhīna vallabhā** won over Śiva

N55 **sumeru madhyaśṛṅgasthā** dwelling in the middle of Mount Meru

Devī's Sthūla (Gross) Form

N56 **śrīmannagara nāyikā** ruling over the auspicious city

N57 **cintāmaṇi gṛhāntasthā** palace made of Cintāmaṇi

N58 **pañcabrahmāsanasthitā** seated on the throne made of five Brahmas

N59 **mahāpadmāṭavī saṃsthā** amidst the lotus forest

Here in this palace, she is seated on a throne made of the five Brahmas (N58). Brahma, Viṣṇu, Rudra, and Íśāna are the four legs of the throne, and Sadāśiva its seat.* Brahma is the creator, Viṣṇu the sustainer, Rudra the destroyer, Íśāna the concealer, and Sadāśiva the revealer (*see N249 and N947*).

Devī's palace is in the midst of the great lotus forest (N59)—the subtle body of the cakras, each of which is a lotus (see Chapter 7). The thousand-petaled sahasrāra is also known as the Padmatavi or the lotus garden, since it is the culmination of all the other cakras. The lotus forest is located within a bigger forest of the quick-growing Kadamba (N60) trees with large leaves and small, fragrant flowers.

This great city is situated on an island in the middle of the mythical ocean of nectar or sudhā (N61),** referring to a phenomenon that occurs at

Devī's Sthūla (Gross) Form

N60 **kadamba vanavāsinī** forest of Kadamba trees

N61 **sudhāsāgara madhyasthā** ocean of nectar

N62 **kāmākṣī** eyes filled with desire

N63 **kāmadāyinī** granting desire

a certain stage in sādhanā. Just before Kuṇḍalinī arrives at the sahasrāra cakra, there is an opening of new neurohormonal pathways with the release of certain chemicals and hormones that drips down through the higher brain centers into the back of the throat with a sweet and minty taste. This fluid known as aṃṛta or sudhā descends into the nāḍīs to transform our behavior, perception, and thoughts.

Devī's divine will as icchā pours from her eyes (N62), granting all desires (N63). While this may superficially mean that Devī grants all our self-serving wishes, the esoteric meaning of this verse lies in the transmutation of desire (see Transmutation of Desire in Chapter 12). She is the bestower of Kāma, which is another name for Śiva. "Bestowing Kāma" is a misnomer, since Śiva is not an object that can be conferred. From the standpoint of sādhanā, Devī grants us the vision to see that who we are *is* Śiva. This has always been the case—she enables this knowledge through the unclouding of the buddhi. By resolving the āṇava mala which is at the root of all self-serving desires, we discover the source of wholeness and our wishes are fulfilled (*see N42*).

* Rudra, Sadāśiva and Īśāna are three of Śiva's many forms.

** One of many types of oceans; the others are of milk, honey, and so on.

Bhāvanā on Devī's Sthūla (Gross) Form

- Begin with the Śrīṃ meditation.
- Contemplate Devī's form as if she's in front of you. Visualize her reddish skin, beautiful, smiling face, jewelry and garments, her throne and her implements.
- Contemplate her five functions (creating, sustaining, destroying, concealing, and revealing) as they apply to you.
- Think of a project you were involved in, where you had to help create something. It can be as mundane as cooking a meal or writing a report. How did the idea originate? What resources were needed to finish the task? How did it end? Were there aspects of it that were concealed at the beginning but were revealed along the way?
- Now contemplate Devī within you. Your skin has her luster, and your face and smile are hers. Contemplate the implements in her (your) hands. Can you see how they've manifested your whole world? What sense objects do your arrows seek? On what desire does your noose land, and how does your goad push away what you dislike? How have your desires, likes and dislikes concealed aspects of reality? Can you recall the sense of relief and freedom resulting from those aspects being revealed?

- **Open-eyed Practice**

  As you go about your day, pause to notice that Devī is within you, functioning as you, every part of her sthūla form scintillating as yours!

Section 2

DEVĪ AND BHAṆḌĀSURA

In this section, we see a description of Devī's war against Bhaṇḍāsura, which is much more than an entertaining story. It is a profound allegory of the process of awakening to the presence of Devī, who is lauded by gods and sages (N64) and is endowed with the army of śaktis capable of slaying Bhaṇḍāsura (N65).

> **Devī And Bhaṇḍāsura**
>
> N64 **devarṣi gaṇasaṅghāta stūyamānātma vaibhavā** lauded by gods and sages
>
> N65 **bhaṇḍāsura vadhodyukta śaktisenā samanvitā** endowed with the army of śaktis capable of slaying Bhaṇḍāsura
>
> N66 **sampatkarī samārūḍha sindhura vrajasevitā** herds of elephants tended by Sampatkarī
>
> N67 **aśvārūḍhādhiṣṭhitāśva koṭikoṭi bhirāvṛtā** crores (millions) of horses commanded by Aśvārūḍha

Let's get reacquainted with Bhaṇḍāsura. He is the distorted form of Kāma, the personification of not only sexual drive but also the spurt of creative energy that drives all our endeavors, be it as mundane as preparing a meal or as extraordinary as an inspired piece of art or poetry that wins the highest accolades. Without this energy, we wouldn't have the motivation to get out of bed in the morning! Distorted as Bhaṇḍāsura, this juicy energy turns into the āṇava mala (see Bhaṇḍāsura and the Āṇava mala, Chapter 4), which is the darkness of being stuck in our deep grooves of conditioning. When we respond to life in patterns based upon fear and pain arising from the āṇava mala, we become paralyzed, losing our ability to respond in creative, ever-fresh ways that are untainted by past experience or future expectations. Devī comes to our rescue to fight off the inertia that Bhaṇḍāsura inflicts upon us. He's not just mighty but also exceedingly cunning, and devises innumerable ways to keep us stuck within our limitations. When we invoke Devī in the fire-pit of our consciousness (*see N4*), she comes to our aid with her entire battalion of powers or śaktis.*

Sampatkarī is the goddess that emanates from Devī's goad (see Chapter 1) and takes command of Devī's war elephants (N66), representing the sum of the knower, known, and knowing in the trikoṇa. In sādhanā, when we arrive at the trikoṇa of the Śrīcakra, we realize that objects that previously seemed to exist outside of us are in reality projections of our own mind. Sampatkarī bestows this insight upon the sādhaka, resulting in fearlessness (see Chapter 10).

Aśvārūḍha emanates from Devī's noose to command her cavalry of horses (N67) that signify the mind and the senses. Aśva is horse and ārūḍha

* We must remember that all the śaktis are forms of Devī; she is the One appearing as many.

Devī And Bhaṇḍāsura

N68 **cakrarāja rathārūḍha sarvāyudha pariṣkṛtā**
seated in the chariot known as Cakrarāja

N69 **geyacakra rathārūḍha mantriṇī parisevitā**
attended by Mantriṇī riding the Geyacakra

N70 **kiricakra rathārūḍha daṇḍanāthā puraskṛtā**
escorted by Daṇḍanāthā riding the Kiricakra

is its rider, which is the mind. Ordinarily, our state of mind is driven by the senses, resulting in endless mental modifications or vṛittis. The senses control the mind, resulting in internal (and external) chaos, confusion, and entanglement in saṃsāra (see Karma in Chapter 4). When Aśvārūḍha takes command of the senses, the mind takes charge of the senses, without which the buddhi remains clouded and Bhaṇḍāsura continues to wreak havoc. Devī herself is seated in the chariot known as cakrarāja, the King of Cakras equipped with all kinds of weapons (N68)—the Śrīcakra.

We must remember that the death of the ego is not the goal of Tāntrik sādhanā. In the Lalitopākhyāna, Devī restores the distorted Bhaṇḍāsura to his original wholeness as Kāma, which is the transmutation of rāga to icchā (see Transmutation of Desire in Chapter 12). This can occur when we realize that who we are is Devī's own essence. Śuddha Vidyā dawns when all phenomena are known to occur in "me" with no separation between Ahaṃ (I) and Idam (That). The dualities of wanting this and not wanting that come to a rest because of a shift of identification from desire to awareness, the ground of desire. The Śrīcakra, with its āvaraṇas, represents all the possible means of arriving here at this shift of identity (see Chapters 9 and 10).

Among Devī's attendants is Mantriṇī, who is also known as Mātaṅgī or Śyāmalā. She is Devī's prime minister (see Devī's Conquest of Bhaṇḍāsura in Chapter 1) as the power of language. We've seen in Chapter 8 that understanding the association between language and experience is a crucial and significant step in sādhanā. In Śrīvidyā, all attainments are the result of mantra sādhanā, where the mantra clarifies the buddhi and facilitates the awakening and ascent of Kuṇḍalinī through the āvaraṇas. Sādhanā takes us on the reverse path of vāk from vaikharī to parā with gradual and progressive refinement of the mantra (see Mantra Sādhanā in Chapter 12) by the grace of Mātaṅgī who is also known as Mantriṇī. She unravels the Viṣṇu granthi at the heart center, directing the power of mantra from her chariot known as Geyacakra (N69).

Devī is also accompanied by Daṇḍanāthā riding her chariot of light known as Kiricakra (N70). Daṇḍanāthā is Vārāhī, the boar-headed goddess who unravels the Rudra granthi at the ājña to bestow the boon of transcending the continuous cycles of saṃsāra. When our sādhanā reaches this level, we are directly contemplating the trikoṇa that leads to its collapse into the bindu with the end of suffering.

Both Mātaṅgī's wisdom and Vārāhī's strength are

Devī And Bhaṇḍāsura

N71 **jvālāmālinī kākṣipta vahniprākāra madhyagā** center of Jvālāmālinī fortress of fire

N72 **bhaṇḍasainya vadhodyukta śakti vikrama-harṣitā** delighting in the valor of the śaktis intent on destroying Bhaṇḍāsura

N73 **nityā parākramāṭopa nirīkṣaṇa samutsukā** rejoicing at the valor of the Nityā Devīs

N74 **bhaṇḍaputra vadhodyukta bālāvikrama nanditā** rejoicing at the valor of Bālā intent on fighting Bhaṇḍāsura's sons

N75 **mantriṇyambā viracita viṣaṅga vadhatoṣitā** celebrating Mantriṇī's conquest of Viṣanga

needed in this great war. While Mātaṅgī deftly dismantles Bhaṇḍāsura's elaborate military formations (think of the many ways in which we use language in thought and deed to justify our old ways), Vārāhī forcefully unearths the saṃskāras that lie hidden beneath the surface.

Devī's entire army marches in the center of a fortress of fire constructed by Jvālāmālinī (N71). Jvālāmālinī is one of the Nityā Devīs who rules over the 14th lunar digit (see Deities of the Śrīcakra in Chapter 9). The five Śakti triangles and the four Śiva triangles of the Śrīcakra (see Table 1 in Chapter 9) form a great wall of fire and Devī resides in the bindu in the middle of it.* When the Kuṇḍalinī fire is lit, it burns away our preoccupations with the drama of our lives and all of our energy is directed toward awakening. It takes over our life as the fire of tapas (*see N359*), the concentrated energy directed toward awakening. It is as if we are surrounded by a wall of fire that keeps distractions out.

Devī rejoices at the valor of her śaktis who are intent on destroying Bhaṇḍāsura (N72). His army is made up of our false ideas and concepts of ourselves and the world that makes the One appear as many, and Devī rejoices as those limiting malas and kañcukas are chipped away by the Nityā Devīs (N73). As the phases of eternity ruling over the fifteen lunar phases, they vanquish fifteen of Bhaṇḍāsura's generals, progressively unveiling the light of Self-knowledge.

Bhaṇḍāsura has many able generals fighting on his side, including thirty of his own sons personifying the thirty tattvas of the impure path (see Chapter 5). Bālā Tripurasundarī is Devī in the form of a young girl,** who descends onto the battlefield to fight Bhaṇḍāsura's sons, delighting Devī with her valor (N74). In Śrīvidyā, initiation usually begins with the Bālā mantra, which clears Bhaṇḍāsura's sons in our nāḍīs and prepares us for the Pañcadaśi. It stabilizes Kuṇḍalinī activation through a systematic resolution of the lower granthīs, preparing us for the transition from the impure to the pure path.

Devī is pleased with Mantriṇī's conquest of

* In Śrīvidyā rituals, Jvālāmālinī is invoked in a ritual known as digbandhah, where an energetic fortress of fire is created around oneself to keep away distractions and burn away the vṛittis (*see N67*) that keep our senses outward-bound.

** Bālā is sometimes known as Devī's daughter.

Devī And Bhaṇḍāsura

N76 **viśukra prāṇaharaṇa vārāhī vīryananditā**
delighting in Vārāhī's conquest of Viśukra

N77 **kāmeśvara mukhāloka kalpita śrī gaṇeśvarā**
birthing Gaṇeśa by glancing at Kāmeśvara

Viṣanga (N75)—he is Bhaṇḍāsura's brother and represents our obsessive attachment to sense objects, which is like blindly consuming poison when we are not even aware that it is toxic. Mantriṇī (*see N69*) turns the poison into nectar by the mantra's power to transmute desire (see Transmutation of Desire in Chapter 12). Viṣanga conceals our ability to delve into the deeper layers of vāk, and keeps us engaged in the superficial world of objects. Mātaṅgī, who is the power of vāk, brings an end to this delusion, much to Devī's great delight.

Our mental, psychological and emotional patterns often remain invisible to us, even after prolonged sādhanā. These patterns are *meant* to remain hidden from our conscious awareness and are formed in early childhood to protect our self-image. Our personhood is made up of all the things we believe about ourselves and the world. If my childhood experience creates the story of unworthiness, that belief becomes my identity and the engine that drives my thoughts and actions in daily life. These deep karmic patterns that drive us tend to be skillfully hidden under the "spiritual" persona, which is Viśukra, Bhaṇḍāsura's other brother. Devī celebrates Vārāhī (N76), who excavates the deep-rooted saṃskāras remaining after the superficial debris is cleaned by Bālā and Mātaṅgī.

Undeterred by the śaktis, Bhaṇḍāsura's army resorts to magic, creating a host of illusory figures that unleash suffering and pain. These magical figures create havoc even amongst Devi's śaktis. Except for Vārāhī and Mātaṅgī, all of them come under the spell of this magic. Overcome with lassitude, they withdraw from the battle with all kinds of justifications. Mātaṅgī and Vārāhī report back to Devī about this new development, and much to their surprise, she begins to laugh and glances at Kāmeśvara. Their cosmic forces coalesce together to become the auspicious, elephant-headed Gaṇeśa (N77). As the union of saguṇa and nirguṇa (*see N52-53*), Gaṇeśa is the leader of the gaṇas (battalions) of subtle microcosmic structures of the impure path. This group is known as puryaṣṭaka or the city of eight, and consists of the jñānendriyās, the karmendriyās, the citta,* the prāṇa vāyus, the mahābhūtas, rāga, karma, and avidyā (*see N356-N362*).**

The puryaṣṭaka's magical and illusory figures give us the appearance of volition and control. Even with advanced sādhanā, we can continue to harbor the kārma and māyīya malas that propagate the sense of separation, where we are unable to see that the unfolding of life is merely the interaction of Prakṛti's three guṇas (see Chapter 4). Our mental and

* Citta is also known as antaḥkaraṇa and made up of the mind, intellect and ahaṅkāra.

** Ajñāna or avidyā: ignorance of our true nature.

psychological faculties, our responses, and our sense of self, which make up the puryaṣṭaka, are merely Prakṛti doing what she always does. However, we continue to harbor the sense of doership and enjoyership, which are obstacles on the path to the bindu. In Śrīvidyā, Gaṇeśa progressively destroys the illusory figures of the puryaṣṭaka (N78).

When we contemplate the puryaṣṭaka, we become aware of the array of justifications, validations and self-sabotaging ways in which the āṇava mala is nourished and maintained (*see N33*). Devī responds to Bhaṇḍāsura's skilful and cunning war moves with a shower of mantras that act as counter-weapons (N79) that pierce through vaikharī, madhyamā and paśyantī to arrive at parāvāk.

While we may get the idea that this is a war occurring at a specific point in time, the āṇava mala is hardy and long-lived. Bhaṇḍāsura possesses a special missile known as the Sarvāsurāstra that creates asurās that live across the yugas,* ten of whom are particular harbingers of darkness and ignorance. Devī's fingernails give birth to the ten incarnations of Nārāyaṇa (Viṣṇu) (N80) to destroy these asuras and re-establish light and knowledge over the yugas.**

With the destruction of Bhaṇḍāsura's army, Devī finally utilizes the ultimate weapon, the Mahāpāśupata that invokes Sadāśiva, the lord of revelation (N81, *see N5*). She incinerates Śūnyakā, Bhaṇḍāsura's capital, with the missile known as Kāmeśvara (N82), which is the light of consciousness (*see N63*). While Bhaṇḍāsura is the absence of rasa (see Chapter 12), his capital is Śūnyakā, which is emptiness or the void. The āṇava mala creates a void that can never be filled—no matter how much we pour into it, it remains the gaping hole that it is.

Devī And Bhaṇḍāsura

N78 **mahāgaṇeśa nirbhinna vighnayantra praharṣitā** delights in Gaṇeśa destroying the obstacle of the illusory figures

N79 **bhaṇḍāsurendra nirmukta śastra pratyastra varṣiṇī** showers missiles in response to Bhaṇḍāsura's weapons

N80 **karāṅguḷi nakhotpanna nārāyaṇa daśākṛtiḥ** ten fingernails giving rise to the ten incarnations of Nārāyaṇa

N81 **mahāpāśupatāstrāgni nirdagdhāsura sainikā** incinerating the asura army with the Mahāpāśupata

N82 **kāmeśvarāstra nirdagdha sabhaṇḍāsura śūnyakā** destroying Bhaṇḍāsura's army with the Kāmeśvara missile

N83 **brahmopendra mahendrādi devasaṃstuta vaibhavā** praised by Brahmā, Viṣṇu and other devas

N84 **haranetrāgni sandagdha kāma sañjīvanauṣadhiḥ** life-giving medicine for Kāma who had been incinerated by Śiva's third eye

* Yuga is a unit of time, occurring cyclically. A Mahā Yuga is an aggregate of 4,320,000 years made up of four yugas: Satya, Tretā, Dvāpara, and Kalī.

** Esoterically, *daśākṛitiḥ* refers to the aggregate of the five states of consciousness (see States of Consciousness in Chapter 8) and the five functions of the Divine (N1-5) that arise from Devī's fingernails.

Now it becomes infused with Kāmeśvara's light, bringing an end to the āṇava mala that had kept us from discovering our true nature. Devī's victory over Bhaṇḍāsura is celebrated by Brahmā, Viṣṇu, Śiva and the other deities (N83). Instead of permanently destroying Bhaṇḍāsura, she restores him to his original glory as Kāma, who had previously been burned to ashes by Śiva's third eye (N84, see Devī's Conquest of Bhaṇḍāsura in Chapter 2). With the dawn of Śuddha Vidyā, we are restored to our original identity, where the sweetness of this knowledge flows out into the world through our body-mind.

Before we move on, it would help us to remember the fundamental difference between Kāma and Bhaṇḍāsura. While Kāma represents the sacred creative desire that honors and cherishes the "other" in its fulfilment, Bhaṇḍāsura is distorted desire and lust that seeks to become fulfilled at the cost of the "other." Devī transforms Bhaṇḍāsura to Kāma, turning distorted desire to sacred creative energy.

Bhāvanā on the Internal War

- Start with the Śrīṃ meditation.
- Contemplate your internal dialogue, and the choices and decisions you make as you go about your day. Often, we know what we must do and, yet, there is an internal conflict because we *want* to be doing something else. Contemplate these wants—where do they come from?
- On the spiritual path, we can easily mistake our wanting for a deeper intuition when it is merely a product of conditioning. We find it easier to justify our choices if we convince ourselves that it comes from a deeper source. It takes discernment to know the source of our longing—Bhaṇḍāsura is exceedingly clever, and our justifications are one way he keeps us entrapped in saṃsāra.
- Contemplate the source of your decisions with absolute honesty.
- We are easily deluded by Bhaṇḍāsura to construct magical figures (vikalpas) in sādhana. We start to experience internal visions, voices and other phenomena that make us feel specially endowed, not realizing that these are merely mental constructs that add to the "me story."

- **Open-eyed Practice**

  Practice being with what is in direct experience without creating vikalpas.

Section 3

DEVĪ IN THE KULAS

Kula refers to groupings of various sorts such as the combination of the knower, known and the process of knowing, the lineage, a group of practitioners of the same tradition, or the same type of practice. In this segment, we will encounter Devī in various kulas, beginning with the Pañcadaśi mantra, which is divided into three kūṭas or divisions corresponding to parts of Devī's body (see Figure 31). Her lotus face is the auspicious Vāgbhava kūṭa (N85). Vāgbhava is both the first kūṭa (*see N39*) of the Pañcadaśi mantra as well as the whole mantra, which bestows auspicious (Srīmat) wisdom to one who attains the mastery over speech (see Vāk in Chapter 8 and Mantra Sādhanā in Chapter 12).

Devī in the Kulas

N85 **śrīmadvāgbhava kūṭaika svarūpa mukhapaṅkajā** face representing the Vāgbhava kūṭa

N86 **kaṇṭhādhaḥ kaṭiparyanta madhyakūṭa svarūpiṇī** from throat to waist representing the Madhyakūta

N87 **śaktikūṭaika tāpanna kaṭyathobhāga dhāriṇī** waist down being the Śakti kūṭa

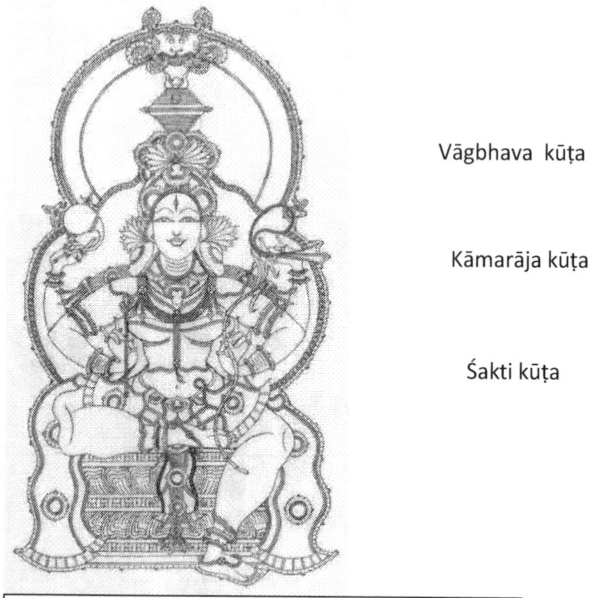

Figure 31. Kūṭas of the Pañcadaśi

Devī's torso from neck to waist is the middle segment of the Pañcadaśi (N86) known as the Kāmarāja kūṭa, referring to her desire to create (icchā śakti) that arises in her heart. From waist down, Devī's form is the Śakti kūṭa or the last segment of the Pañcadaśi (N87). Icchā arising in her heart (Kāmarāja) becomes jñāna at her head (Vāgbhava) and manifests as kriya out of her womb (Śakti kūṭa, N87).

Devī is the embodiment of this root (mūla) mantra (N88) and its three parts (N89) as Kāmakalā (*see N322, N330*, and Chapter 10). The Kāmakalā consisting of three bindus and a triangle are Devī's

Devī in the Kulas

N88 **mūlamantrātmikā** embodiment of the root mantra

N89 **mūlakūṭa traya kalebarā** body composed of the three parts of the root mantra

N90 **kulāmṛtaika rasikā** taste of the nectar of the kula

N91 **kulasaṅketa pālinī** protector of the secrets of the kula

N92 **kulāṅganā** committed to kula

N93 **kulāntaḥsthā** residing in the kula

N94 **kaulinī** of the kula

N95 **kulayoginī** ruling over the yoga of the kula

face, breasts and yonī, which forms the Śakti bīja īm, the esoteric root of the Pañcadaśi.

In her subtlest form, Devī is Kuṇḍalinī, which traverses the kula made up of the granthis* to reach the sahasrāra. Here, the realization of the primordial kula of the experiencer (pramātṛ), experience (prameya), and the process of experiencing (pramāṇa) incites the release of nectar or aṃṛta (*see N61*)—Devī is the taste of this nectar (N90). As this subtlest form of knowledge, she protects the secrets of the kula (N91) by making them impossible to understand until we are ready. Devī guards this knowledge of the trikoṇa by shrouding it in secrecy, where a clarified buddhi** is needed to decipher them.

Not only is Devī the kula and the protector of the kula, but she is singularly committed to it (N92)—we need to be initiated into the kula where she resides (N93) as its seat (N94). At this point, it's important to reiterate that this nāma is not about exclusivity or elitism. Being initiated with a mantra doesn't guarantee instantaneous knowledge of the primordial kula. What we refer to as initiation is the flow of Devī's grace where she grants this great knowledge. This grace flows in unpredictable ways and along mysterious timelines. Obviously, this grace also flows to followers of other paths!

Everything in existence can be seen as a kula, including the tattvas. Devī *is* all kulas and the deity of each of them (N95). Superficially, we may think of this nāma to refer to a specific path or tradition. However, Devī transcends particularities of traditions and kula here refers to the ordinary way of being where we are constantly engaged with the world. Our senses, citta, inner apparatus, energetic and overt interactions are all kulas. All that we hold dear—our breath, thoughts, body, relationships, work, and values—are kulas. In fact, our very sense of self, which is a conglomeration of all these kulas, is a kula. Devī is *all* kulas, including this sense of self.

* Kula refers to various types of groupings (see Deities of the Śrīcakra in Chapter 10, and Kaulācāra in Chapter 11) but, for all intents and purposes, refers to the triad of pramātṛ, prameya and pramāṇa.

** By way of a guru or one's own intuitive abilities honed through bhāvanā.

Whether we are engaged actively in deity worship or not, we constantly worship Devī since this sense of self is the center of all we do. Liberation in this tradition is realization of this essentially divine nature of Reality. In essence then, Devī is the kula that is ignorance as the limited sense of self, the path to freedom from it, as well as its goal. She is *all* kulas.

Kulas (N90-95) refer to Devī in her immanent form (she is everywhere as all forms), while akulā alludes to her transcendence (she is beyond all forms). As we've seen earlier, the Divine is both formless and form, transcendent and immanent (see Chapter 3). We usually think of Śiva as transcendent and Śakti as immanent, but this nāma reminds us of their fundamental non-separation. Devī is both transcendent and immanent, and resides in the internal worship known as samayā (N97, see Ācāra prescription in Chapter 11). Devī is the essence of all kinds of worship, including samayā, where she becomes known as the sama or unity of the worshiper, the worshiped and the act of worshiping, the primordial kula.

When a sādhaka realizes the sameness or non-separation between Śiva and Śakti, kula and akulā, transcendence and immanence (N96), he becomes a samayācārin even while engaged in external rituals. Devī is especially fond of this kind of worship that is the essence of samayā (N98), where the separation between the self and the world dissolves, and the sādhaka comes to experience the nectar of the bindu (*see N61*).

Devī in the Kulas

N96 **akuḷā** devoid of kula

N97 **samayāntaḥsthā** residing in inner worship as samayā

N98 **samayācāra tatparā** devoted to samayācāra

N99 **mūlādhāraika nilayā** principal abode of the mūlādhāra

As Kuṇḍalinī, Devī's principal abode is the mūlādhāra (N99), where she resides in her dormant form, as if asleep (*see N77* and Granthis in Chapter 7). Waking up, she severs the Brahma granthi (N100), emerging at the Maṇipūra cakra (N101).* Here, she severs the Viṣṇu granthi (N102) to make her way up to the Ājña cakra (N103), the center of discernment and perfected reasoning. Here, she dissolves the Rudra granthi (N104) that hinders perfected reasoning. Having severed the three granthis, she ascends to the thousand-petaled Sahasrāra (N105). Opening the nāḍīs that were previously unavailable and activating previously inactive chemical and hormonal pathways, she triggers the release of amṛta also known as sudhā which showers down in streams (N106). As Kuṇḍalinī, she thus flashes forth, brilliant as lightning (N107).

Here, above the six cakras, is Devī's final destination (N108), where she becomes entirely entwined with Śiva in every aspect of creation (N109,

* Maṇipūra = city of gems. When amṛta makes its way down to the gut from the higher centers, it is visualized as a kaleidoscope of colors that look like gems.

Devī in the Kulas

N100 **brahmagranthi vibhedinī** severing the Brahma granthi

N101 **maṇipūrānta ruditā** emerging at the Maṇipūra cakra

N102 **viṣṇugranthi vibhedinī** severing the Viṣṇu granthi

N103 **ājñacakrāntarālasthā** making her way up to the ājña cakra

N104 **rudragranthi vibhedinī** dissolving the Rudra granthi

N105 **sahasrārāmbujā rūḍhā** ascending to the thousand-petaled Sahasrāra

N106 **sudhāsārābhi varṣiṇī** showering sudhā or amṛta

N107 **taṭillatā samaruciḥ** flashing forth, brilliant as lightning

N108 **ṣaṭ-cakropari saṃsthitā** settling above the six cakras

N109 **mahāsaktiḥ** becoming attached

N110 **kuṇḍalinī** the coiled one

N111 **bisatantu tanīyasī** as subtle as the fiber of the lotus stalk

see Kuṇḍalinī in Chapter 7). We must remember here that Śiva and Śakti are *always* entangled and inseparable. The description of Kuṇḍalinī rising to meet Śiva at the sahasrāra specifically means that there is a progressive *awareness* of their essential non-separation.

Kuṇḍalinī, the coiled one (N110), is Devī's embodiment in the microcosm. She is the prāṇaśakti that enlivens every cell, organ and organ system, every thought, emotion, and vāsanā (see Chapter 6). When directed toward the creation and maintenance of the limited sense of self, prāṇaśakti becomes restricted as the ahaṅkāra. When directed toward freedom from limitations, she is Kuṇḍalinī that is like the delicate fiber of the lotus stalk (N111) that rises gracefully from the muddy waters of ignorance and blooms at the sahasrāra as Self-knowledge and the ruler of all kulas.

Bhāvanā on the Kulas

- Begin with the Śrīṃ meditation, noticing the kula made up of the central channel, the three centers, and the movement (felt, seen or visualized) upward.
- Open your eyes and scan your surroundings, contemplating the tattvas. What is the suchness of a coffee cup, a book, a tree, a body of water? What makes a cup a cup? What if you take away the handle or break it into pieces?
- Now shift your attention to your body. Contemplate your bones, muscle, tissues and organs. What is the suchness of each? What tattvas can you identify in them? What do your bones, tissues and organs have in common with the coffee cup, a book, a tree, and a body of water? What do the five great elements have in common?
- Now shift your attention to your mind. Keep your gentle and relaxed attention on your breath (close your eyes if needed), observing thoughts, snippets of images, emotions and memories as they arise and subside. If you get carried away in any of them, simply return to the breath. Contemplate the suchness of the mind. What do thoughts, mind images, emotions, and memories have in common? What does the mind have in common with your external world?
- Contemplate the boundary between internal and external. Where is it? Can you pinpoint the location of the mind inside your body? If not, where does the mind end and the world begin? Can you see the continuity of the suchness of the mind with the body, and the suchness of both with objects of the world?
- Now shift your attention to the sense of "me." Contemplate on its suchness. What makes up the "me"? Notice that anything you can assign to the "me" is a thought, memory, emotion or fragment of an image or sound. They make up the suchness of the mind. What is the suchness of the me without the mind?

- **Open-eyed Practice**

  As you go about your day, pause to recognize the thread of sameness in various groupings (kula), particularly noticing that it freely traverses what we ordinarily think of as being "in here" or "out there."

Section 4

DEVĪ'S AUSPICIOUSNESS

Having seen Devī in her subtle forms traversing the kulas, we'll now look into some of her auspicious attributes, while remembering that everything about her and this path is auspicious. The purpose of Devī sādhanā is to traverse the ocean of saṃsāra, which is supported by Śiva as Bhava. As we know, Śakti is the source of all of Śiva's attributes, and as his quality of support, she is known as Bhavānī (N112). who can only be attained by bhāvanā (meditative contemplation) and is otherwise unattainable (N113). When invoked through bhāvanā, she manifests as Kuṇḍalinī, uprooting the dense overgrowth of our saṃskāras (N114), and turning our attention and energy from saṃsāra to liberation.

Devī delights in the auspiciousness of liberation (N115) since she is its embodiment (N116). She bestows the gift of auspiciousness upon us when we realize our essential non-separateness with her (N117). Bhakti is one of the prerequisites of the path (see Bhakti in Chapter 12). Devī delights in bhakti (N118), which is the fuel for sādhanā. Without bhakti we would have no desire for meditation, japa, chanting the LSN, or learning more. It becomes increasingly refined with sādhanā and the cultivation of discernment, where we fall in love with Reality.

Devī's Auspiciousness

N112 **bhavānī** giver of life to Bhava

N113 **bhāvanāgamyā** attained through bhāvanā

N114 **bhavāraṇya kuṭhārikā** cutting through the jungle of saṃsāra

N115 **bhadrapriyā** delighting in the auspiciousness of liberation

N116 **bhadramūrtiḥ** embodiment of auspiciousness

N117 **bhaktasaubhāgya dāyinī** bestowing the gift of auspiciousness

N118 **bhaktipriyā** delighting in bhakti

N119 **bhaktigamyā** attained through bhakti

N120 **bhaktivaśyā** won over by devotion

N121 **bhayāpahā** dispelling fear

N122 **śāmbhavī** wife of Śambhu

While bhakti was previously directed to a specific form of Devī, we are now devoted to her as the essence of the world. She is attained (N119), and won over (N120) through this all-consuming love and devotion. The love of unity with Devī replaces fear (N121), which was the consequence of separation. It becomes the basis for seeing Devī's oneness with Śambhu as Śāmbhavī (N122),* where objects of the world are recognized to be within us.

* Śiva. All references in the LSN to Devī being the wife of Śiva in his many forms are pointers to their oneness as prakāśa-vimarśa.

Devī's Auspiciousness

N123 **śāradārādhyā** worshiped by Śārada

N124 **śarvāṇī** wife of Śarva

N125 **śarmadāyinī** confers happiness

N126 **śāṅkarī** confers auspiciousness

N127 **śrīkarī** confers abundance

N128 **sādhvī** exclusively devoted to Śiva

N129 **śaraccandranibhānanā** face like the full moon on a clear autumn night

N130 **śātodarī** slender-waisted

N131 **śāntimatī** peaceful

The oneness of Śiva-Śakti transcends language, which is personified by the goddess Śāradā. Śāradā creates language to worship Devī (N123) and to describe in words the Reality that cannot be described.

Devī is the wife of Śarva (N124),* and bestows oneness with herself, thereby ensuring permanent happiness (N125) auspiciousness (N126),** and abundance (N127). However, these wishes are by-products of liberation. Devī remains devoted to Śiva only (N128), and she cannot be desired for anything other than liberation. Ordinarily, we seek wealth and transactional knowledge, both of which add to the "me story" (see Bhāvanā in Chapter 12). By claiming ownership over the goddesses Lakṣmī (wealth) and Sarasvatī (knowledge) as objects, we remain ensnared in the impure path. Devī, however, cannot be attained to add to the "me story." To attain her in the bindu, we have to discard the "me story." In this lack of compromise, she remains steadfastly chaste and faithful to Śiva.

As the bestower of auspiciousness, Devī is the beautiful and benign face of Reality that is like the full moon on a clear autumn night (N129). The moon here is not only a metaphor for beauty but also for wholeness and respite from restless seeking. Slender-waisted (N130) as Kuṇḍalinī (*see N35*), Devī leads us to lasting peace (N131) that is the result of knowing that we have always been whole; nothing needs to be gained and nothing has ever been missing.

* Another name for Śiva.

** Śaṃkara is another name for Śiva, and is translated as the doer (kara) of auspiciousness (Śam), and Devī is this attribute of Śiva.

Bhāvanā on Auspiciousness

- Begin with the Śrīṃ meditation.
- Settle into a gentle, relaxed awareness of the breath.
- Contemplate Devī's gifts of auspiciousness and abundance. How have these manifested in your life? Begin with your breath, the ability of your body to digest what you eat, circulate your blood, and manage the countless cellular reactions that maintain your body—all without your permission, involvement, or interference!
- Contemplate the auspicious and abundant gifts of nature. Everything that sustains and nourishes you had to sprout through the intricate manifestation of the tattvas. *You* are an intricate design of Divine thought.
- Contemplate the concept of inauspiciousness. Even the experience of pain is auspicious in the mere ability to experience it! While pain is a natural consequence of living and playing in the world, suffering is the result of not wanting the pain or wanting something else instead. In this process, the auspiciousness of the ability to experience becomes inauspicious through the mind's interference.

- **Open-eyed Practice**

  As you go about your day, contemplate the facets of auspiciousness: of being able to experience the world, your body and mind with its infinite colors and vibrations. Attempt to keep the focus on this *ability* rather than on the *content* of experience.

  Contemplate Devī's nāmas denoting her auspiciousness in this space of freedom.

Section 5

DEVĪ AS NIRGUṆA (FORMLESS)

In the previous section, we discovered Devī's love for her bhaktas and her generosity in granting unity with her in return for devotion. Now, we will meet Devī as the attributeless (nirguṇa) Brahman, which is the basis for attributes (saguṇa) just as silence is required for sound and paper for words. Being the support of creation, she is herself without support (N132). The theme of this nāma is continued in the sequence of the following nāmas, where Devī is devoid of the very attribute that she supports.

Devoid of duality, she is stainless (N133) without the impurity of the malas (N134, see Chapter 4) that result in fragmentation of the One as the many. She is spotless (N135), without the limitation of the āṇava mala, which is the root of ignorance keeping us trapped in the cycle of saṃsāra. The āṇava mala is based in linear time, created through the cycles of karma (see Karma in Chapter 4). Devī is eternal and timeless (N136) since she is the ground of linear time. She is formless (N137) because she is the basis for all forms. As we've seen earlier, creation occurs through agitation in the perfectly balanced bindu (see Kuṇḍalinī in Chapter 7). Devī as the attributeless principle is herself without agitation (N138).

The three guṇas (sattva, rajas, and tamas) are the fundamental basis of the material world (Prakṛti). Like the screen upon which a movie is projected, Devī is herself devoid of the guṇas (N139) while being their source. She cannot be divided into parts (N140), and remains whole and indivisible.

Devī As Nirguṇa (Formless)

N132 **nirādhārā** without support

N133 **nirañjanā** stainless

N134 **nirlepā** without impurity of the malas

N135 **nirmalā** spotless

N136 **nityā** timeless

N137 **nirākārā** formless

N138 **nirākulā** without agitation

N139 **nirguṇā** without guṇas

N140 **niṣkalā** indivisible

N141 **śāntā** tranquil

N142 **niṣkāmā** desireless

N143 **nirupaplavā** indestructible

N144 **nityamuktā** ever-free

Devī, however, remains tranquil (N141) as the unmoving basis for the dynamism of creation. Once manifestation begins, the desire to return to wholeness becomes the impulse that keeps it in continuity. Since Devī is always whole (N140), she is herself without desire (N142). As the principle of destruc-

Devī As Nirguṇa (Formless)

N145 **nirvikārā** changeless

N146 **niṣprapañcā** without extensions

N147 **nirāśrayā** independent

N148 **nityaśuddhā** ever-pure

N149 **nityabuddhā** ever-wise

N150 **niravadyā** blameless

N151 **nirantarā** uninterrupted

N152 **niṣkāraṇā** causeless

N153 **niṣkalaṅkā** faultless

N154 **nirupādhiḥ** free of limitations

N155 **nirīśvarā** with no superior

tion, Devī is herself indestructible (N143).

She creates and destroys in complete freedom (N144), unfettered by bonds of karma. She is the principle of changelessness (N145) that supports change. Ordinarily, we notice change in our bodies, minds, families, and communities, which we see becoming extensions to ourselves. In contrast, being the nature of everything in existence, Devī needs no extensions (N146). She is absolutely independent (N147), while all tattvas are dependent on her. Being free from time-based phenomena, she is eternally pure (N148) and wise (N149).

Although Devī is the Source of the world, our suffering and misgivings are related to our own actions, the impressions of which carry over as the seeds for how we act in the future (see Karma in Chapter 4). Devī is herself blameless (N150), and is present everywhere without any interruption (N151). Although karma is an endless cycle of cause-and-effect, Devī herself is causeless (N152) and faultless, being untouched by such consequences (N153).

All limitations in creation are the result of Māyā and the five kañcukas (see Kañcukas and Malas in Chapter 4). Although Devī is the support for these limitations, she is herself free of them (N154). Since she is the supreme sovereign (see Śuddha Vidyā and the Bindu in Chapter 5), there is none superior to her (N155).

Devī As Nirguṇa (Formless)

N156 **nīrāgā** devoid of passion

N157 **rāgamathanī** destroyer of passion

In the nāmas that follow, we see Devī as the destroyer of particular attributes because she is herself devoid of them. This goes along with the understanding that we cannot cure someone else of an unwholesome behavior if we harbor it ourselves. If we want to teach love by destroying hatred in someone, we have to be loving. If we want to teach tolerance, we have to be tolerant, and so on.

Devoid of rāga (N156), Devī destroys it (N157). When we function under the influence of the kārma mala, we tend to have a tendency to become conceit-

Devī As Nirguṇa (Formless)

N158 **nirmadā** devoid of conceit

N159 **madanāśinī** destroyer of conceit

ed by taking credit for our talents, achievements, and gifts (see Kañcukas and Malas in Chapter 4). Herself without conceit or mada (N158), Devī destroys it (N159) in us. Without worry (N160) ahaṅkāra (N161) that results in delusion (N162), she destroys delusion (N163). Devoid of self-interest (N164), she destroys it (N165).

Self-interest arises from the sense of separation, the māyīya mala, which is the basis of what we might think of as sin. Taking ourselves to be the limited body-mind is the greatest sin, and the root cause of all other sins. Devī is sinless (N166) and, being free of sin, she destroys it (N167). Being free of anger (N168), she destroys anger (N169). Free of greed herself (N170), she destroys the sense of lack that is its basis (N171). Being the source of all knowledge, she is without doubt (N172) and destroys ignorance, the source of doubt (N173).

Being beginningless (N174), Devī destroys saṃsāra (N175) that originates in her as vikalpas (see Chapter 12). Being free of vikalpas (N176), undisturbed (N177) and devoid of distinctions (N178), she destroys the differentiations (N179) that lead to vikalpas and the perception of the One as many. Being eternal and imperishable (N180), she is the destroyer of death (N181).

Devī As Nirguṇa (Formless)

N160 **niścintā** devoid of anxiety

N161 **nirahaṅkārā** devoid of ahaṅkāra

N162 **nirmohā** devoid of delusion

N163 **mohanāśinī** destroyer of delusion

N164 **nirmamā** devoid of self-interest

N165 **mamatāhantrī** destroyer of self-interest

N166 **niṣpāpā** sinless

N167 **pāpanāśinī** destroying sin

N168 **niṣkrodha** free of anger

N169 **krodhaśamanī** destroying anger

N170 **nirlobhā** free of greed

N171 **lobhanāśinī** destroying greed

N172 **niḥsaṃśayā** free of doubt

N173 **saṃśayaghnī** destroying doubt

N174 **nirbhavā** without origin

N175 **bhavanāśinī** destroying saṃsāra

N176 **nirvikalpā** free of vikalpas

N177 **nirābādhā** undisturbed

N178 **nirbhedā** free of distinctions

N179 **bhedanāśinī** destroys distinctions

N180 **nirnāśā** indestructible

N181 **mṛtyumathanī** destroys death

N182 **niṣkriyā** free of action

Devī As Nirguṇa (Formless)

N183 **niṣparigrahā** free of possessiveness

N184 **nistulā** incomparable

N185 **nīlacikurā** of bluish-black hair

N186 **nirapāyā** imperishable

N187 **niratyayā** impossible to transgress

N188 **durlabhā** difficult to attain

N189 **durgamā** difficult to approach

N190 **durgā** facilitating the journey across the saṃsāra ocean

N191 **duḥkhahantrī** destroying sorrow

N192 **sukhapradā** bestower of happiness

N193 **duṣṭadūrā** unattainable in ignorance

N194 **durācāra śamanī** ending the sin of separation

N195 **doṣavarjitā** free of flaws

Devī, who is devoid of ahaṅkāra, is actionless (N182). Ordinarily, actions arising from our saṃskāras are driven by a longing for wholeness. We are driven to possess objects that are distinctly separate from us. Whether they are material objects or subtle ones like fame or power, they are sought from the outside. Devī, being everything in existence, is without possessions (N183). Such a comparison doesn't even make sense since at least two separate things are needed to compare and contrast. Since there is none other than Devī, she is incomparable (N184).

If all of creation is Devī's own body, her dark hair is the blackness of the void (N185) that is imperishable (N186). As the void, there is no part of her that can be transgressed against (N187)—the Divine doesn't keep score of our misbehavior and mete out punishment accordingly. Devī is not just the good and the just, but is also the misbehaving person and the behavior in question—everything is her. Transgressions are only possible if there is an "other." As far as Devī is concerned, there isn't another.

As the attributeless Divine, Devī is exceedingly difficult to attain (N188) and approached with the great effort of sādhanā that leads to the Śuddha Vidyā (N189, see Pure and Impure Paths in Chapter 5). When approached through right effort, Devī showers her grace, carries us across the ocean of saṃsāra (N190), destroys our sorrow (N191) and bestows ever-lasting happiness (N192). On the other hand, she is unapproachable in paths that keep us entrapped in ignorance (N193). When we surrender to her will, she destroys the sense of separation (N194) that keep us in saṃsāra. In every possible way, Devī is absolutely flawless (N195).

Bhāvanā on Nirguṇa and Saguṇa*

- Begin with the Śrīṃ meditation.
- Contemplate your own death. Visualize yourself lying on a funeral pyre. Under you, there is a pile of dried wood, arranged in a loose pattern to allow for the flames to be fanned when lit. Notice the clothes you're wearing, the posture of your body and the coloring of your lifeless skin.
- Visualize your body being dried up by the blowing wind. Your skin darkens and shrinks, muscles and organs dry and shrivel, and the marrow dries up. Your face is unrecognizable. Your body is no different than the logs of dried wood bearing your weight. *Feel this sensation of dryness.*
- The extreme dryness of the body and the wood creates the perfect environment for a wayward spark of fire. Suddenly, the pyre and the body are in flames. Visualize the fury of the fire as it consumes your body, sparks flying, wood and bones crackling, smoke spreading with the wind. *Feel this sensation of heat.*
- Flames consume the skin and dried flesh, easily reaching the core of the marrow, turning the once vibrant body to ash. Sated at last from consuming everything it can touch, the fire begins to subside. Visualize the shrinking height of the flames that are slowly and eventually extinguished, leaving behind a pile of grey ash. All your attributes – malas, karma, vikalpas, limitations and insecurities are gone. What remains in their place? Contemplate the nothingness of the void of death. *Feel this void.*
- Clouds gather in the sky, bearing nectarine rain. A gentle drizzle begins, wetting the pile of ash. *Feel this sensation of wetness.*
- The pile of ash organizes and molds itself into a form that is gradually infused with rasa and a reddish hue. Clothing and ornaments appear. The shrivelled face turns into the exquisite visage of Devī. *Feel this sensation of juiciness.*
- She opens her eyes and sits up. Contemplate the attributes of Devī arising from the void and replacing your limited body-mind. *Feel this sensation of benevolence and auspiciousness.*

- **Open-eyed Practice**

  Notice the limitations that come up as anger, greed, envy and doubt. Can you put this mass of limitations to rest on the funeral pyre so that Devī can arise in its place?

**This practice is a variation of a traditional Śrīvidyā practice known as Virajā Homā.*

Section 6

DEVĪ'S POWERS

If a description of Devī as nirguṇa makes us think of the Divine as a vacuum, the nāmas in this section dispel that misconception by describing her many powers. The attributeless Divine pulses with inherent consciousness and ānanda. Infinite possibilities exist in that unconditioned awareness which is the basis for svatantra. As soon as we assign a particular form to Devī, she becomes limited. In contrast, when she remains formless, she has infinite powers!

Devī's Powers

N196 **sarvajñā** omniscient

N197 **sāndrakaruṇā** intensely compassionate

N198 **samānādhikavarjitā** with no superior or equal

N199 **sarvaśaktimayī** endowed with all powers

N200 **sarvamaṅgalā** source of good fortune

N201 **sadgatipradā** leading to the right path

N202 **sarveśvarī** ruling over all

N203 **sarvamayī** being all

N204 **sarvamantra svarūpiṇī** essence of all mantras

N205 **sarvayantrātmikā** soul of all yantras

N206 **sarvatantrarūpā** form of all tantras

N207 **manonmanī** eighth plane of consciousness

N208 **māheśvarī** wife of Maheśvara

Devī is omniscient (N196) and, as attributeless non-localized witnessing awareness, she is like a movie screen that welcomes good *and* bad storylines. In allowing all aspects of creation to arise as they are, she is intensely compassionate (N197). All tattvas are welcomed equally into the loving arms of Devī's presence, who has no superior or equal (N198). Being endowed with all powers (N199) and as the source of all good fortune (N200), she leads us to the right path (N201). As the all-powerful Reality, Devī rules over creation (N202), and is the entirety of creation (N203).

She is the essence of all mantras (N204), yantras (N205), and tantras (N206), and coaxes awareness to rise to the stateless plane where she exists as manonmanī (N207). Between the ājña and sahasrāra cakras are eight stations or planes of consciousness (see Mantra Sādhanā in Chapter 12). The last one before the sahasrāra is called unmanī or manonmanī, where time and space cease to exist, resulting in the collapse of the trikoṇa into the bindu of the sahasrāra. Here, Devī becomes known as Māheśvarī (N208), the wife of Maheśvara.* At the unmanī, we arrive at the level where the objective world (That or Idam) is barely separated from pure subjectivity (I or Aham,

* Maheśvara is another name for Śiva who is beyond the three guṇas and exists only as the liṅga, the pillar of light.

see Pure Path in Chapter 5). As this subjective light of awareness, Devī is immeasurable (N209) as the source of abundance and beauty (N210) and is the beloved of Mṛḍa (N211).*

As the all-pervading essence of creation, Devī's great form (N212) is the highest object of worship (N213). In fact, all of creation is engaged in constant worship of Devī simply by virtue of existing! With even the slightest effort of attention, she destroys ignorance, the greatest sin (N214). Yet, by being the one who measures (N1), she is also the source of ignorance and illusion (N215). As with mātā (N1), māyā contains the root "mā," which is to measure. Devī's descent as the tattvas creates the *illusion* of separation and of objects existing independently. Māyā is the reason why we don't perceive ourselves, others, and the objects of the world as Devī, who is the ultimate Reality (N216) of great power (N217) who boundlessly delights in her own essence (N218). In fact, she is the sole enjoyer of creation, delighting in the entire spectrum of experiences (N219) as the individual "I" in every being. As the essence of the "I," she is the seat of supreme sovereignty (N220).

As the power that creates, sustains and destroys (*see N1-3*), Devī is unmatched in valor (N221), strength (N222), and intellect (N223). As the one who manifests everything out of nothing, she is the source of the highest attainments (N224). We think of siddhis as superhuman powers, such as the ability to walk on water or teleport, but Devī's greatest siddhi is her love. Her love makes her become the entire universe, demonstrating her supreme mastery of yoga. She is therefore the object of worship by the greatest of yogis and siddhas (N225). She is the greatest tantra (N226), mantra (N227), and yantra (N228), and is the great seat (N229) of the tattvas, being worshiped in the esoteric sequence known as

Devī's Powers

N209 **mahādevī** the great Devī

N210 **mahālakṣmīḥ** the great Lakṣmī

N211 **mṛḍapriyā** beloved of Mṛḍa

N212 **mahārūpā** great form

N213 **mahāpūjyā** mighty object of worship

N214 **mahāpātaka nāśinī** destroying great sin

N215 **mahāmāyā** the great illusion

N216 **mahāsattvā** great reality

N217 **mahālakṣmīḥ** great power

N218 **mahāratiḥ** great delight

N219 **mahābhogā** great spectrum

N220 **mahaiśvaryā** great sovereignity

N221 **mahāvīryā** great valor

N222 **mahābalā** great strength

N223 **mahābuddhiḥ** great intellect

N224 **mahāsiddhiḥ** great attainment

* Mṛḍa is happiness or contentment and another name for Śiva.

Devī's Powers

N225 **mahāyogeśvareśvarī** ruler of the great yogis

N226 **mahātantrā** great tantra

N227 **mahāmantrā** great mantra

N228 **mahāyantrā** great yantra

N229 **mahāsanā** great seat

N230 **mahāyāga kramārādhyā** worshiped as Mahāyāga

N231 **mahābhairava pūjitā** worshiped by the great Bhairava

N232 **maheśvara mahākalpa mahātāṇḍava sākṣiṇī** witness of Maheśvara's great dance of time

N233 **mahākāmeśa mahiṣī** wife of Mahākāmeśvara

N234 **mahātripura sundarī** great beauty of the triads

N235 **catuṣṣaṣṭyupacārādhyā** worshiped by sixty-four offerings

N236 **catuṣṣaṣṭi kalāmayī** embodiment of the sixty-four arts

N237 **mahācatuṣṣaṣṭikoṭi yoginī gaṇasevitā** attended by 64 crores of yoginīs

Mahāyāga, an internal ritual of invoking the deities of the Śrīcakra within one's own body (N230).*

Devī is worshiped even by the great Bhairava (N231).** The word Bhairava is made up of three roots: bha (meaning creation or Srṣṭi), ra (meaning preservation or sthiti), and va (meaning dissolution or saṃhāra); these three functions are in play in every moment as the basis for linear time. We ordinarily perceive time as a sequence of events that become memories of the past or projections into the future (see Chapter 6). In reality however, every moment arises and subsides in witnessing awareness (see Turya in Chapter 8), free of past or future. Bhairava worships Devī with his dance, where every moment arises and dissolves into her as the great witnessing awareness (N232). In this unity, she is the wife of the great Kāmeśvara (N233) and the great beauty of all triads (N234), who is worshiped by sixty-four offerings (N235).*** She embodies the sixty-four types of arts (N236), and is attended by 640 million yoginis (N237) who are her own emanations.

* Described in the Bhavanopanishad.

** Bhairava is another name for Śiva.

*** In the Śrīcakra pūjā.

Bhāvanā on Time

- Begin with the Śrīṃ meditation.
- Contemplate the stages of your life, beginning with your earliest memory.
- Sift through the memory to the sense of being.
- Recall this sense of being.
- Feel it.
- Fast forward to about age 10, once again resting with the sense of being at that time.
- Feel it.
- Recall the sense of being at various ages all the way up to this moment.
- Take the time to feel the sense of being underneath feelings and thoughts at every stage.

  You have aged and things have changed in the world and in your life.

  Have any of your gains and losses affected this fundamental sense of being?
- Return to the sense of being here and now.
- Notice the breath rising from it and subsiding back into it.
- Notice that your thoughts, sensations, feelings and perceptions arise and subside in this sense of being.

  Everything you think you are arises and subsides in this primordial sense of being. Notice this, the dance of Bhairava in your current experience.

- **Open-eyed Practice**

  Notice when your mind wanders off into the past or the future, and gently redirect it to the current task. If you're not actively engaged in a task, simply become aware of the rhythm of your breath.

Section 7

DEVĪ'S OMNIPRESENCE

Having encountered some of Devī's great powers, we will now explore her presence—her omnipresence—in the macrocosm and microcosm, beginning with the Pañcadaśi mantra with its many variations that are precepted by different deities and sages (see Chapter 3).* Devī is the embodiment of all variations of the Pañcadaśi, including the one of Manu** (N238) and Candra*** (N239). She is the goal of all the Pañcadaśi variations, residing at the center of the moon-like sahasrāra (N240) in communion with Śiva. Unlike the moon, however, her exquisite beauty (N241) doesn't wax or wane and her smile (N242) is reminiscent of the lovely crescent moon that she wears in her crown (N243).

Devī's Omnipresence

N238 **manuvidyā** mantra variation of Manu

N239 **candravidyā** mantra variation of Candra

N240 **candramaṇḍalamadhyagā** residing in the center of the moon disc

N241 **cārurūpā** of exquisite beauty

N242 **cāruhāsā** of beautiful smile

N243 **cārucandrakalādharā** wearing the crescent moon

N244 **carācara jagannāthā** ruling over the animate and inanimate

N245 **cakrarāja niketanā** abiding in the Śrīcakra

N246 **pārvatī** the daughter of the Himālaya

N247 **padmanayanā** eyes shaped like lotus petals

N248 **padmarāga samaprabhā** complexion of rubies

N249 **pañcapretāsanāsīnā** seated on the five-corpse throne

Devī rules over the animate and inanimate aspects of creation (N244) from her seat in the bindu of the Śrīcakra (N245). In the natural world, the peaks of the Himālaya represent the bindu. Although she is the ruler of the universe, she takes birth as Pārvatī (N246), the daughter of the Himālaya, with eyes shaped like lotus petals (N247) and the complexion of rubies (N248). Endowed with exquisite beauty, she sits on a throne supported by five corpses (N249)—Brahma the creator, Viṣṇu the sustainer, Rudra, the destroyer, Íśāna the concealer and Sadāśiva the revealer (*See N1-5*, and Chapter 3). Without Devī's

* Manu, Candra, Kubera, Lopāmudrā, Kāma, Agastya, Agni, Sūrya, Indra, Skanda, Śiva, and Durvāsa vidyās are some variations of the Pañcadaśi.
** Manu is the primordial man (or being). Brahma's day is divided into fourteen parts known as Manvantarās. At the start of every Manvantarā, Brahma creates a Manu, the progenitor of all creatures. The Manu's rule ends with the end a Manvantarā, and a new one is created with the next Manvantarā. The current Manvantarā is known as Vaivasvata.
*** Candra is the personification of the moon.

Devī's Omnipresence

N250 **pañcabrahma svarūpiṇī** form of the five Brahmās

N251 **cinmayī** consciousness

N252 **paramānandā** supreme bliss

N253 **vijñāna ghanarūpiṇī** permanent wisdom

N254 **dhyānadhyātṛ dhyeyarūpā** form of meditation, meditator and object of meditation

N255 **dharmādharma vivarjitā** devoid of virtue and vice

N256 **viśvarūpā** form of the universe

N257 **jāgariṇī** waking state

N258 **svapantī** dream state

N259 **taijasātmikā** subtle dream objects

N260 **suptā** deep sleep state

N261 **prājñātmikā** collective form of the universe

N262 **turyā** witnessing consciousness

N263 **sarvāvasthā vivarjitā** transcending all states

N264 **sṛṣṭikartrī** creator

N265 **brahmarūpā** form of Brahmā

N266 **goptrī** sustainer

N267 **govindarūpiṇī** as Govinda

power, these five beings are corpse-like, but in reality are her form as the five Brahmas (N250) when infused with her consciousness (N251), bliss (N252) and wisdom (N253).

Devī is meditation, the meditator and the object of meditation (N254), devoid of dualities such as virtue and vice (N255) that enables her to become the whole universe (N256). As the waking state (N257), she takes the form of the gross objects in the material world and, as the dream state (N258), she becomes its subtle objects (N259). She is the experience of deep sleep (N260) as well as the collective states and forms of the universe (N261). She is turya (N262) that spans and transcends the three states of consciousness (N263, see States of Consciousness in Chapter 8).

From her seat on the throne of the five Brahmas in the bindu that pervades all states of consciousness, she is the creator (N264) as Brahmā (N265), the sustainer (N266) as Govinda or Viṣṇu (N267), and the destroyer (N268) as Rudra (N269). She conceals herself in Māyā (N270) as the śakti of Īśāna (N271) and becomes Sadāśiva (N272) who confers the grace (N273) of liberation. Devī is constantly engaged in these five functions (N274), seated in the center of the sun-disc of the bindu (N275) as the wife of Bhairava (N276).

All states of consciousness are illuminated by her garland of a million suns (N277). Seated on a lotus (N278) here in the center of the sun's orb, she is the refuge for all of creation (N279). In the microcosm, she is at the lotus of the navel, the maṇipūra (N280), which in its brilliance is like the sister of the sun.*

* Commonly, this nāma is taken to mean "sister of Viṣṇu." According to Bhāskararāya, this nāma secretly

Devī's Omnipresence

N268 **saṃhāriṇī** destroyer

N269 **rudrarūpā** as Rudra

N270 **tirodhānakarī** concealer

N271 **īśvarī** wife of Īśāna

N272 **sadāśiva** as Sadāśiva

N273 **ānugrahadā** revealer

N274 **pañcakṛtya parāyaṇā** performing the five functions

N275 **bhānumaṇḍala madhyasthā** seated in the sun disc

N276 **bhairavī** wife of Bhairava

N277 **bhagamālinī** wearing the garland of suns

N278 **padmāsanā** seated on a lotus

From her seat in the bindu, Devī causes a series of worlds to arise and disappear with the opening and closing of her eyes (N281, see Kuṇḍalinī in Chapter 7). She closes her eyes and the universe dissolves; she opens her eyes and the universe comes into being as her own body with countless heads and faces (N282), countless eyes (N283), and countless feet (N284).

Being the creator of everything in existence, from the great Brahmā to the tiniest insect (N285), she is the order of social divisions known as varṇas and

refers to the bīja Hrīṃ that crowns the three kūṭas of the Pañcadaśi.

Devī's Omnipresence

N279 **bhagavatī** refuge of all

N280 **padmanābha sahodarī** residing at the lotus of the navel, which is like the sister of the sun

N281 **unmeṣa nimiṣotpanna vipanna bhuvanāvaliḥ** blinking causing worlds to appear and disappear

N282 **sahasraśīrṣavadanā** thousand heads and faces

N283 **sahasrākṣī** thousand eyes

N284 **sahasrapāt** thousand feet

N285 **ābrahma kīṭajananī** mother of all from Brahmā to insect

N286 **varṇāśrama vidhāyinī** establishing social orders

N287 **nijājñārūpa nigamā** commanding the Vedas into manifestation

N288 **puṇyāpuṇya phalapradā** giver of good and bad outcomes

āśramas* (N286). She is the source of manifestation of the Vedas (N287) that describe the laws of karma. As karma, she is the giver of the fruit of both selfless and selfish deeds (N288). The Vedas are subservient to her will, and take the form of goddesses that

* Varṇas are the four social classifications of society that are based on guṇas and aptitudes (Brāhmaṇa, Kśatrīya, Vaiśya, and Śūdra). Āśramas are the four stages of life (Brahmacaryā, Gṛhastā, Vānaprastha, and Saṇyāsa). See *Shakti Rising*, Chinnamasta, pages 132-134.

wear the dust of Devī's feet in the parting of their hair (N289).* If the aggregate of scriptures could be imagined as a shell, Devī is its enclosed pearl (N290) as the highest knowledge and goal.

Devī not only bestows the highest knowledge but she also confers all four Puruṣārthas (*see N291*, and Puruṣārthas in Chapter 7). This is because Devī herself is whole (N292), and the path to her excludes nothing. She is the sole enjoyer of all the Puruṣārthas (N293) as Bhuvaneśvarī (N294), the ruler of the universe. In the bindu, she resides as Ambikā (N295, see Chapter 8), the mother of the universe, with neither beginning nor end (N296) and attended by Viṣṇu, Brahmā, and Indra (N297).

Devī's Omnipresence

N289 **śruti sīmanta sindhūrī kṛta pādābjadhūlikā** dust of her feet becoming the sacred vermilion for the Vedas

N290 **sakalāgama sandoha śuktisampuṭa mauktikā** pearl of the aggregate of all scriptures

N291 **puruṣārthapradā** conferring the Puruśārthas

N292 **pūrṇā** whole

N293 **bhoginī** enjoyer

N294 **bhuvaneśvarī** ruler of the universe

N295 **ambikā** mother of the universe

N296 **anāḍī nidhanā** having no beginning or end

N297 **haribrahmendra sevitā** attended by Viṣṇu, Brahmā and Indra

* At this point, it will help us to remember that the purpose of a chant like the LSN is to establish the supremacy of the deity extolled in it over all others, and in the context of the prevailing traditions of the time in which it was composed. Accordingly, we see the reference to Devī's primacy over the Vedas.

Bhāvanā on Devī's Presence

- Begin with the Śrīṃ meditation.
- Contemplate Devī's omnipresence.
- Sit quietly and become aware of your surroundings – the objects you see, the sounds you hear, the taste in your mouth, the feel of air or clothing on your skin, and the smell of the surroundings.
- Open deeply.

  Devī is every sensation. She is all the objects you can experience. She is the one that is experiencing them all through you. She is also the process of seeing, hearing, smelling, tasting, and feeling.
- Now contemplate memories, people and events you treasure.

  She is all that.
- Now contemplate memories, people and events you despise.

  She is all that too.
- Contemplate your own consciousness.

  This is Devī.

  Everything you do, think, feel, and experience is Devī.
- Now try to find one thing that doesn't have her presence.

  Your very attempt and act of finding is Devī!

  Where can you find something that isn't She?

- **Open-eyed Practice**

  As you go about your day, open to every experience, sensation and thought as the presence of Devī.

Section 8

DEVĪ AS THE BĪJA MANTRA

We have seen Devī's powers and her omnipresence in the previous two sections. In this segment, we will see her subtle form as the mantra. Even though creation and dissolution occur constantly, Māyā gives it the appearance of continuity. Creation is therefore compared to an ocean. Although individual waves continually come and go, the ocean maintains the appearance of being unchanged. Viṣṇu or Nārāyaṇa is the deity who maintains this appearance of continuity. Devī is Nārāyaṇī (N298), his śakti.

As the form of the primordial sound or nāda (N299, see Mātṛkā and Mālinī in Chapter 8), she transcends the specifics of name and form (N300). She is the personification of the syllable Hrīṃ (N301), which is known as the śākta praṇava or the bīja (seed) of Śakti. This auspicious syllable is made up of three parts: ha is manifestation, ra is involution, ī is perfection and ṃ controls the three.* As the bearer of this syllable (N302), Devī abides in the heart (N303), where she cannot be won over by objects of the material world (N304). As this great syllable, she is worshiped by Śiva, the king of kings

* *Lalitā Sahasranāma* with Bhāskararāya's Commentary, translated into English by R. Ananthakrishna Sastry (The Adyar Library and Research Center, 2010), page 164.

Devī As The Bīja Mantra

N298 **nārāyaṇī** śakti of Nārāyaṇa

N299 **nādarūpā** form of sound

N300 **nāmarūpa vivarjitā** transcending name and form

N301 **hrīṅkārī** form of the bīja Hrīṃ

N302 **hrīṃatī** possessor of hrī

N303 **hṛdyā** abiding in the heart

N304 **heyopādeya varjitā** accepting and rejecting nothing

N305 **rājarājārcitā** worshiped by Śiva, the king of kings

N306 **rājñī** supreme sovereign

N307 **ramyā** beautiful

N308 **rājīvalocanā** with the eyes of a benevolent ruler

N309 **rañjanī** delightful

N310 **ramaṇī** bestower of joy

N311 **rasyā** of the nature of rasa

N312 **raṇatkiṅkiṇi mekhalā** girdle of tinkling bells

N313 **ramā** form of Lakṣmī

N314 **rākenduvadanā** face like the full moon

N315 **ratirūpā** embodiment of pleasure

N316 **ratipriyā** lover of pleasure

Devī As The Bīja Mantra

N317 **rakṣākarī** protector

N318 **rākṣasaghnī** slayer of demons

N319 **rāmā** of the nature of delight

N320 **ramaṇalampaṭā** devoted to Śiva

N321 **kāmyā** desirable

N322 **kāmakalārūpā** form of Kāmakalā

N323 **kadamba kusumapriyā** fond of Kadamba flowers

N324 **kalyāṇī** bestowing good fortune

N325 **jagatīkandā** root of the world

N326 **karuṇārasa sāgarā** ocean of compassion

N327 **kalāvatī** embodiment of all arts

N328 **kalālāpa** of refined expression

N329 **kāntā** pleasing

(N305) as the supreme sovereign (N306) and the source of all beauty (N307).

When we engage with her mantra, she looks upon us with the benevolent eyes of the ruler (N308). She is delightful (N309) and bestows joy (N310) upon us. As this mantra, she is of the nature of rasa (N311, see Rasa in Chapter 12), and appears in sādhanā as the sound of tinkling bells (N312, *see N36 and N48*). As this praṇava, she is abundance as Lakṣmī (N313), her wholeness symbolized by her face that is like the full moon (N314). As this syllable, Devī

Devī As The Bīja Mantra

N330 **kādambarīpriyā** fond of intoxicants

N331 **varadā** granting wishes

N332 **vāmanayanā** beautiful-eyed

is the embodiment of pleasure (N315). Since she is a lover of pleasure (N316), her sādhanā is not dry or removed from the world, but one that opens to sweetness and an increasing ability to enjoy our moment-to-moment experience.

As the mantra, Devī protects us (N317, see Chapter 10) against the demons of ignorance (N318) and infuses us with delight (N319). Devī as mantra is steadfastly devoted to Śiva as liberation (N320, *see N128*), which becomes our sole desire (N321) as all other desires fall away or are transmuted into her will or icchā. At this stage in sādhanā, Devī reveals herself as Kāmakalā (N322, *see N128* and Kāmakalā in Chapter 10). As this subtle sonic form, she is fond of Kadamba flowers (N323, *see N60*) that bestow good fortune (N324). She is the very root of manifestation (N325) and the ocean of compassion (N326). As the embodiment of all arts (N327), she manifests through us as refined expression (N328) that becomes increasingly more pleasing (N329).

Devī is so intoxicated (N330) with her union with Śiva in the Kāmakalā that she generously grants all our wishes (N331) that seem to flow from her beautiful eyes (N332). It's not that all our trivial desires are magically fulfilled, but that with deepening sādhanā and the discovery of the orgasmic bliss of the bindu, rāga becomes transmuted to icchā (see Transmutation of Desire in Chapter 12). Our focus becomes centered on the sweetness of the nectar itself and we feel drunk on it (N333).

With transmutation of desire, we realize that this intimacy of enjoyment is Devī's own bhoga (*see N293*) resulting from transcending the tattvas (N334). Devī, who is known through the Vedas (N335) and Tantras, is also the dweller of the Vindhyā mountains (N336).* In fact, she is the supporter of the universe (N337) who gives birth to the Vedas (N338), and becomes Viṣṇu's Māyā (N339, *see N298*). Although everything in manifestation is being dynamically created and destroyed, there remains an illusion of continuity—this is Devī being playful (N340) as Viṣṇu's Māyā.

Devī As The Bīja Mantra

N333 **vāruṇīmadavihvalā** intoxicated

N334 **viśvādhikā** transcending the world

N335 **vedavedyā** known through the Vedas

N336 **vindhyācala nivāsinī** residing in the Vindhyā

N337 **vidhātrī** supporter

N338 **vedajananī** mother of the Vedas

N339 **viṣṇumāyā** Māyā of Viṣṇu

N340 **vilāsinī** playful

* Historically, the Vindhya mountains demarcated the boundary between the northern and southern parts of India. The mountain range appears in many mythological stories, including the Lalitopākhyana (Chapter 1), and is thought to be the eternal residence of one of Śakti's many forms.

Bhāvanā on Beauty

- Begin with the Śrīṃ meditation.
- Contemplate an object or person that you find beautiful. Rather than thinking about the particular attributes, focus on the concept of beauty. It helps to do this inquiry from the vastness and generosity of the heart space.
- Notice the sensation of conferring beauty upon an object or person—how does it feel? Where is it? Stay with the sensations rather than the mental story. Allow it to subside.
- Now shift your attention to an object or person you find unattractive, repulsive, or can't stand. What happens in your internal landscape? Allow it to subside.
- Return to the original beautiful object and sensations of open-heartedness. Stay here while thinking of the repulsive object. What happens to the sensations?
- What is beautiful in your direct experience? Your own warmth and sweetness of open-heartedness, or the external object?
- Contemplate beauty, which has nothing to do with external objects and everything to do with our own stance.

- **Open-eyed Practice**

  As you go about your day, redirect your attention to your own warmth and sweetness in the experience of external objects and your own mind.

Section 9

DEVĪ AS KṢETRA AND KṢETRAJÑA

Having discovered Devī as the bīja mantra in our heart, we come now to see her body as all of creation. Kṣetra is a region or field, and Devī's body is this field (N341) for the manifestation of matter —seen and unseen, known and unknown, gross and subtle. The 36 tattvas make up her body, which is reflected (vimarśa) by the light of consciousness (prakāśa) (see Prakāśa and Vimarśa in Chapter 3). If you look at the Tattva Map (see Chapter 4), you see that matter exists as a modification of prakāśa, the first principle. Śiva as prakāśa is the "container" (Kṣetreśa) for creation, which cannot be known without Śakti as vimarśa. As the inseparable wife of Śiva, Devī is known as Kṣetreśi (N342).

At the microcosmic level, our body, thoughts, emotions, and sense perceptions make up the field or kṣetra and the "I" that knows the kṣetra (kṣetrajña) is known as the *jīva*. As consciousness, Devī is this "I" or jīva—the knower of kṣetra. Consciousness or jīva is inherently protective as the impulse to live. Devī is both the knower and the protector of the kṣetra (N343). While kṣetra is subject to growth and decay, Devī as the knower of kṣetra remains unchanged (N344). This is why she is depicted as the ever-youthful goddess!

Devī As Kṣetra And Kṣetrajña

N341 **kṣetrasvarūpā** form of the field of matter

N342 **kṣetreśī** wife of Kṣetreśī

N343 **kṣetra kṣetrajña pālinī** knower and protector of Kṣetra

N344 **kṣayavṛddhi vinirmuktā** free of growth and decay

N345 **kṣetrapāla samarcitā** worshiped by kṣetrapālas

N346 **vijayā** ever-victorious

N347 **vimalā** without impurity

N348 **vandyā** worthy of worship

Everything in nature is made up of the five great elements, and they are governed by particular devas. As the rulers over particular aspects of kṣetra, they are known as kṣetrapālas who derive their consciousness from Devī and worship her (N345). As the primordial principle of consciousness, she is ever victorious (N346) and cannot be touched by impurity (N347). We must remember here that the limitations of the malas and kañcukas don't apply to the primordial consciousness within us. As this pure principle, Devī is worthy of worship and adoration (N348). So, how should we worship her as this principle?

Consciousness rewards attention with the gift of freedom. Ordinarily, our attention is focused on the kṣetra that is the body-mind. Turning our attention

Devī As Kṣetra And Kṣetrajña

N349 **vandāru janavatsalā** fond of those who worship

N350 **vāgvādinī** power of expression

N351 **vāmakeśī** dark-haired

N352 **vahnimaṇḍala vāsinī** residing in the fire disc

N353 **bhaktimat-kalpalatikā** wish-fulfilling creeper of the devotee

N354 **paśupāśa vimocanī** releasing ignorance

from the kṣetra to the ksetrajña is true worship, which is like shifting attention from a kitchen appliance to the electricity that makes it work. Devī is particularly fond of those who worship her with this exquisite shift of attention (N349).

As the primordial consciousness, Devī enables the power of expression (N350) that brings about the diversity of the tattvas (see Chapter 8). The tattvas are known distinctly as "thatness" because of this power of expression, which gives rise to infinite possibilities in the universe-kṣetra. Stars are stars and insects are insects—although both are made up of the same tattvas, they express themselves uniquely as stars or insects. Devī's dark hair is the unseen ground of being (N351) for manifestation of this expressive power (*see N185*).

Devī, as the ksetrajña, resides in the disc of fire (N352). Previously, we have seen that she resides in the moon disc of the sahasrāra (*see N240*) and in the sun disc of the maṇipūra (*see N280*). Fire is the primordial source of light for both the sun and the moon. Here, we must understand the fundamental principle of fire, which is that of transformation. Unlike the sun and the moon, there isn't a specific location for fire in the macrocosm and it exists invisibly as this principle of transformation.

Fire is the principle that transforms one thing to another—fall turning into winter, food turning into the cells of the body, the progressive process of aging, experiences becoming memories and vāsanās, the disintegration of the body at death into the elements, evolution, the movement of the planets around the sun to bring about day and night, and so on. Any change we can think of is the function of fire, also known as vahni or agni. While we may associate fire with heat, agni is also the principle of water becoming ice, and vice versa! In other words, creation (necessarily bound in time and space) cannot exist without agni. And yet, this fire lies in the realm of kṣetra while Devī is the ksetrajña. In the body, this fire disc is at the mūlādhāra, where Kuṇḍalinī resides as the source of the jīva (*see N110* and Chapter 7).

From her residence in the fire-disc of the mūlādhāra, Devī as Kuṇḍalinī rises like a wish-fulfilling creeper (N353), releasing the ignorance (N354) that keeps us bound in cycles of samsara. Paśu refers to total identification with the body-mind, where our way of living and being leads

Devī As Kṣetra And Ksetrajña

N355 **saṃhṛtāśeṣa pāṣaṇḍā** destroyer of heretics

N356 **sadācāra pravartikā** inspiring right behavior

N357 **tāpatrayāgni santapta samāhlādana candrikā** cooling the fire of afflictions

N358 **taruṇī** ever-youthful

N359 **tāpasārādhyā** worshiped by ascetics

N360 **tanumadhyā** slender-waisted

N361 **tamopahā** removing tamas

N362 **cittiḥ** wisdom

N363 **tatpadalakṣyārthā** That, the supreme and transcendent Reality

N364 **cideka rasarūpiṇī** rasa of wisdom

N365 **svātmānandalavībhūta brahmadyānanda santatiḥ** minute portion of her bliss is the combined bliss of Brahma and other deities

to internal and external conflict arising from the sense of existing as separate beings. It is as if we are bound in the noose (pāśa) of saṃsāra (see Ācāra prescription in Chapter 11). As paśus, we are heretics totally devoted to our body-mind, the kṣetra, with no interest in the kṣetrajña. Devī destroys this heresy (N355), and inspires right behavior (N356) by making us aware of her presence as the kṣetrajña.

As the Kuṇḍalinī creeper makes her way to the moon of the sahasrāra, the many afflictions (kleśas) that bind us in the noose of suffering are dissolved (see Figure 32).

Avidya or ignorance of our true divine nature is the fundamental kleśa. As we've seen earlier, this is the result of a clouded buddhi. We take ourselves to be the limited body-mind and are driven by our passions (rāga)—we want specific outcomes that pacify this sense of "me". It's not merely a matter of not wanting some things, but we also *don't* want other things because we are averse to them (dveṣa). Our attractions and aversions make us feel unique and individuated (asmitā) and we cultivate a fear of losing this uniqueness through death (abhiniveśa). Avidya grows through this cycle.

These kleśas are like intense fires that create unrest and a general sense of dissatisfaction. With her ascent along the suṣumnā, Devī cools these fires (N357) by breaking the cycle of afflictions. As nirguṇa or consciousness without form, Devī is ever youthful (N358) and is sought by those who engage in tapas (N359), the heat of single-pointed sādhanā. In this fire of tapas, Devī rises as the slender-waisted (N360)* Kuṇḍalinī and removes the inertia and darkness of tamas (N361, see Kuṇḍalinī in Chapter 7). The raging fires of the kleśas are extinguished by the fire of tapas, and the light of Self-knowledge (N362) replaces avidya.

Being both the embodied and transcendent Supreme (N363), Devī is the rasa of wisdom (N364) and ānanda. In fact, the combined bliss of Brahmā

---

* Devī's slender waist the esoteric equivalent of Kuṇḍalinī (see N35 and N130).

and the multitude of deities is but a drop of Devī's ānanda (N365).

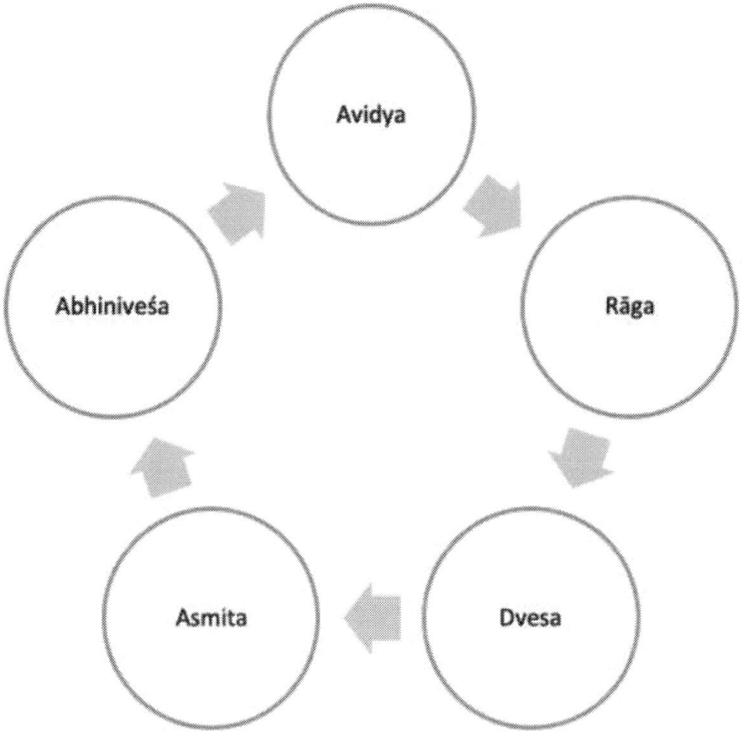

Figure 32. Kleśa

Bhāvanā on Kleśas

- Begin with the Śrīṃ meditation.
- Contemplate the kleśas beginning with abhiniveśa. Do you fear death? If no, skip to the next one. If yes, journal about the causes for the fear. Do you feel that "you" will come to an end with death? What makes up this unique "I"? Where do your specific memories, dreams and aspirations come from? Make a list of all the things that you love and aspire to, and all the things you dread and prefer not to have. Contemplate your list and mark them off as rāga and dveṣa as appropriate.
- Now contemplate on where the rāga and dveṣa come from. See that they are products of learning and conditioning by caregivers, peers, society and past experiences. Who are you without all that?

- **Open-eyed Practice**

  Become aware of the kleśas as you go about your day. Notice if this awareness changes how you interact with the world. Is there a softness and growing tolerance when you see that we are all bound by our kleśas?

Note: This path is not about not having preferences. It is about seeing that even our preferences are emanations of Devī, but this seeing ideally arises from clarity of the buddhi and not as blind faith or belief.

Section 10

DEVĪ AS VĀK

Devī As Vāk

N366 **parā** parāvāk

N367 **pratyakcitī rūpā** form of consciousness

N368 **paśyantī** paśyantī vāk

N369 **paradevatā** perceiving self as Supreme deity

N370 **madhyamā** madhyamā vāk

N371 **vaikharīrūpā** vaikharī vāk

N372 **bhaktamānasa haṃsika** swan of discernment in the devotee's mind

N373 **kāmeśvara prāṇanāḍī** prāṇa of Kāmeśvara

Having encountered Devī as both the kṣetra and the kṣetrajña, we now arrive at the segment where she is described as vāk, the power of expression (see Chapter 8). As the blissful One, Devī is Parā (N366), the undifferentiated Reality that is the innermost core of manifestation (N367). Moving toward manifestation, she becomes paśyantī (N368) where she perceives herself as the supreme deity (N369). Moving further into differentiation, she becomes madhyamā (N370) as the subtle structures of creation. Condensing herself even more, she becomes vaikharī (N371).

Parā is the undifferentiated vāk within which all differentiations arise. Yet, differentiation doesn't divide up parāvāk—it's not like a cake which loses its wholeness when cut up into pieces. Even with differentiation, Parā remains whole and uninterrupted (*see N151*). The other three levels always remain in Parā as potential. All possible types and modes of expression are possible at this level—even those that are yet to be expressed a thousand years from now. At the level of paśyantī, madhyamā and vaikharī lie as potential and Parā is the Source. At the level of madhyamā, vaikharī rests as potential, while Parā is the absolute Source and paśyantī is the immediate precursor. At the level of vaikharī, madhyamā is the immediate precursor, which in turn arises from paśyantī, and the Source of all is Parā. In other words, the four levels of vāk exist together.

We pursue objects at the vaikharī level because we are driven by longing (kāma). The lord of kāma or longing is Kāmeśvara, and so we worship him in all our pursuits, which ordinarily lie in the realm of differentiated objects (vaikharī and madhyamā) because this is all we can see. As we proceed with our sādhanā, Devī bestows the gift of discernment upon us. This discernment is often described as the mythical swan that can separate milk from water when the two are mixed. Devī then arises as this swan of discernment within us (N372) that enables us to see that she is the very life-force of Kāmeśvara (N373). As this prāṇa of longing, she knows our intentions

Devī As Vāk

N374 **kṛtajñā** knower of actions

N375 **kāmapūjitā** worshiped by Kāma

N376 **śṛṅgārarasasampūrṇā** brimming with śṛṅgāra rasa

N377 **jayā** victorious

and actions (N374) even before they occur.

Our saṃskāras and vāsanās direct our desires toward objects, where we hope to attain wholeness through their acquisition. What we fail to see is that in all our pursuits, we are really seeking Devī—she is the object of worship for Kāma, the god of desire (N375). He worships her at the mūlādhāra, where she resides as parāvāk. The mūlādhāra is thus known as the Kāmagiri pīṭha* (Kāma is desire, giri is peak and pīṭha is seat), where Parā's ecstatic union with Śiva results in an overflow of the śṛṅgāra rasa (N376, see Rasa in Chapter 12).

Śṛṅgāra is the rasa or essence of erotic love, where the boundaries between "me" and "other" dissolve. Although this is commonly referred to as the union of Śiva and Śakti, this is not entirely correct, since they are never separate. In sādhanā, śṛṅgāra is the realization of oneness of experience, where the dissolution of the boundaries between the subject and object as well as the word and object gives way to seeing that we are not who we thought we were, the world is not what we thought it was, and there is no real separation between us and the world!** Śṛṅgāra is also the juice of the urge to live that keeps us going even when we are suffering. It is the juice that Bhaṇḍāsura drains from the devas, where they lose their luster and will to live. Bhaṇḍāsura is the epitome of the lack of śṛṅgāra, whereas Devī personifies it. Every bit of her iconography drips with this rasa, which is why we can't help falling in love with her!

Like Bhaṇḍāsura, at the start of this journey our preoccupations at the vaikharī level keep us from experiencing the juice of śṛṅgāra. Devī sādhanā takes us on the reverse path of vāk (see Mantra Sādhanā in Chapter 12) from vaikharī, the world of fully differentiated objects, to parāvāk, the depths of their source at the mūlādhāra.

Now there is a second movement back to vaikharī from parāvāk, where the śṛṅgāra rasa discovered at the mūlādhāra first flows to the anāhata, which is known as the pūrṇagiri pīṭha (pūrṇa is fullness and giri is peak). The anāhata is where our intentions arise. Since it is now the seat of fullness because of the overflowing śṛṅgāra rasa, we are no longer driven by a sense of lack. And because our intentions are flowing directly from the Source, our actions are bound to succeed (N377).

The anāhata brims over with our joyful, rasa-filled intentions that flow into the jālandhara pīṭha

* The pīṭhas mentioned here are four of the well-known Śakti pīṭhas or sacred spots where parts of Sati's body fell (Chapter 1).

** See also Mātaṅgī in *Shakti Rising*, page 181.

Devī As Vāk

N378 **jālandharasthitā** residing at the Jālandhara pīṭha

N379 **oḍyāṇa pīṭhanilaya** residing at the odyāṇa pīṭha

N380 **bindumaṇḍala vāsinī** residing at the bindu

N381 **rahoyāga kramārādhyā** worshiped in secret by sacrificial fires

N382 **rahastarpaṇa tarpitā** gratified by secret oblations

N383 **sadyaḥ prasādinī** bestowing grace

N384 **viśvasākṣiṇī** witness of the universe

N385 **sākṣivarjitā** unwitnessed

(N378) at the viśuddha. From here, we engage with the world of differentiated objects. Externally, we are still acting as before, but nothing is the same. Our actions and intentions have been cleansed, transformed and imbued with the juice of the Oneness of Śiva-Śakti! This transformation has occurred in the three seats of vāk that became the sacred sites of pilgrimage (pīṭhas). We are granted the grace to see that, although these pīṭhas seemed discrete and localized at the mūlādhāra, anāhata and viśuddha, they derive their juice from the most sacred pīṭha of all—the oḍyāṇa pīṭha (N379), which is the non-localized bindu (N380) that pervades and animates all the tattvas.

This great transformation is made possible by the cultivation and refinement of perfected reasoning or tarka by propitiating Devī in the fire of sādhanā (N381, see Tarka in Chapter 12). Devī demands the sacrifice and surrender of transactional knowledge in this fire, and in return, she grants the sweet rasa of Self-knowledge.

However, this is a secret and intimate worship, where we follow the breadcrumbs along the reverse path of Vāk through mantra sādhanā until we dip into its Source. Devī is gratified in these secret oblations (N382) and bestows her grace (N383). When we return to outward expression, the path is brilliantly lit and infused with śṛṅgāra rasa because we have steadfastly sacrificed our self-serving desires to become aligned with her icchā. In this secret worship, we come to see that she is the sole witness of the whole universe (N384) and is herself unwitnessed (N385).

Bhāvanā on Vāk

- This bhāvanā examines raw experience in two stages. The first stage is to separate experience from labeling. The second stage is to separate the experience from its Source. In both stages, insight involves the paradoxical seeing of non-separation of experience and its label, and both with the Source.
- Begin with the Śrīṃ meditation.
- You can work with any experience – a thought, an interaction, a sense perception, a bodily sensation or an emotion.

  Whatever the experience is, meet it with an open-hearted, innocent curiosity without labeling.

  What is sadness without the label of "sadness"?

  What is hunger, irritation, an object, a sound, a taste, an interaction without stories and labels learned from books and texts?
- If we can slow down enough, and resist the urge to manipulate the arising experience with our past learning that is based in language, we can open to its beauty and wonder.

  This is a process of surrender. In every experience, the knowledge is surrendered without a goal to get anywhere or acquire anything, including spiritual insight.
- To meet every experience and interaction this way is to relinquish judgments, justifications and validations, which are all based in memory, which in turn is based in language. Every experience then becomes fresh, new.
- When you're able to differentiate between experience and language, sit again with the experience to examine where it arises and subsides.
- Shift your attention to the "space" in which the sensations, thoughts and emotions arise.

  Notice that the experience comes and goes but the space is always pure and cannot be touched by the temporary arisings, which are all forms of expression.
- Abiding as this space, notice the experience become subtler and subtler as it dissolves.

  At the moment of dissolution, Parā Devī shines as the undifferentiated One that is the Source of both experience and its expression.

- **Open-eyed Practice**

  As you go about your day, notice the role of language in how you interpret the world, your own mind, life experiences and interactions with others. In every situation, ask yourself what would happen without the availability of language.

Section 11

DEVĪ IN THE BINDU

> **Devī In The Bindu**
>
> N386 **ṣaḍaṅgadevatā yuktā** accompanied by the ṣaḍaṅga devatas
>
> N387 **ṣāḍguṇya paripūritā** brimming with six auspicious qualities
>
> N388 **nityaklinnā** ever-moist
>
> N389 **nirupamā** incomparable
>
> N390 **nirvāṇa sukhadāyinī** bliss of liberation
>
> N391 **nityā ṣoḍaśikārūpā** form of Nityā Devīs
>
> N392 **śrīkaṇṭhārdha śarīriṇī** half the body of Śrikaṇṭha
>
> N393 **prabhāvatī** luminous
>
> N394 **prabhārūpā** embodiment of brilliance

Having discovered Devī in the Oḍyāṇa pīṭha, the bindu, we will now meet her here, seated on Śiva's lap in ecstatic loving embrace. In this union, nothing exists for either of them except the other. When we refer to Devī, Śiva is implied because of this boundary-less blending.

Here in the bindu, Devī is accompanied by the deities of the six aṅgas, which are the six areas of the body where a mantra is situated before and after the seated practice of japa (see Introduction). The main deity invoked by a mantra has six ancillary parts, each governed by a subordinate form of the deity and known as an aṅga devata. The ṣaḍaṅga devatas correspond to the heart, head, topmost part of the cranium, arms, eyes and weapons. Before japa, these deities are invoked and installed in the corresponding areas of our own body in the procedure known as nyāsa; the deity is thus installed into our own being in this profound ritual of identification with the deity. The japa that follows is directed at the deity that is non-separate from us. At the end of the japa, these aṅga devatas are released in a complementary procedure. Devī in the bindu is accompanied by the ṣaḍaṅga devatas (N386) and brims with the six auspicious qualities (N387)—omniscience, bliss, wisdom, absolute freedom, absolute power, and eternality.

Devī is ever moist (N388) with the orgasmic energy of her coupling with Śiva, which gives birth to the universe (see Bindu, The Stateless State in Chapter 8). In returning us to the bindu, she is incomparable (N389) because it is her grace that confers the bliss of liberation (N390). In her orgasmic state, she takes the form of the sixteen Nityā Devīs* (N391, see Deities of the Śrīcakra in Chapter 9). As half of the body of Śrīkaṇṭha (Śiva) (N392), she is luminous (N393) and the very form of brilliance (N394). She is the essence of creation and is celebrated as the indi-

* This nāma also refers to the 16-syllabled mantra known as Śodaśi, where Devī takes the form of each syllable.

Devī In The Bindu

N395 **prasiddhā** celebrated

N396 **parameśvarī** supreme ruler

N397 **mūlaprakṛtih** primordial cause

N398 **avyaktā** indistinct

N399 **vyaktāvyakta svarūpiṇī** manifest and unmanifest

N400 **vyāpinī** all-pervading

N401 **vividhākārā** multitude of forms

N402 **vidyāvidyā svarūpiṇī** form of knowledge and ignorance

N403 **mahākāmeśa nayana kumudāhlāda kaumudī** moonlight that gladdens the lotus-eyed Kāmeśvara

N404 **bhaktahārda tamobheda bhānumad-bhānusantatiḥ** ray of sunlight dispelling the darkness of ignorance

N405 **śivadūtī** making Śiva the messenger

N406 **śivārādhyā** worshiped by Śiva

N407 **śivamūrti** form of Śiva

viduality in every form (N395)—she is the very act of celebration. She is the supreme sovereign (N396) and the primordial cause (N397) of creation.

As the bindu, Devī is the indistinct seed of creation (N398), becoming both the manifest and unmanifest forms (N399). She pervades all the tattvas (N400) represented in the Śrīcakra and takes

Devī In The Bindu

N408 **śivaṅkarī** conferring Śivahood

N409 **śivapriyā** beloved of Śiva

N410 **śivaparā** beyond Śiva

N411 **śiṣṭeṣṭā** sought by the wise

a multitude of forms (N401), including those of knowledge and ignorance (N402).

While her wholeness is like cooling moonlight that moves even the great lotus-eyed Kāmeśvara (N403), she shines brightly like sunlight that dispels the darkness of ignorance in the heart of the sādhaka (N404). Devī in her infinite love for Śiva makes him her messenger, commanding him to carry the light of knowledge to the ignorant (N405).* In return, Śiva worships her (N406) because she is his own self (N407). Not only is she the form of Śiva, but she confers Śivahood on her devotees (N408). She is the beloved of Śiva (N409), of course, but being the source of all his attributes, she transcends him too (N410, *see N128*).

Even though Devī is all objects of the universe, she is specifically sought in the bindu by those who have learned the futility of seeking fullfilment in external objects (N411). Wise beings worship her

* In the third episode of the Devī Mahatmyam, Śivaduti is one of the Mātṛkās who emanates from Devī's body to fight off the asuras Śumbha and Niśumbha. She commands Śiva to carry a message to Śumbha to surrender. Śumbha refuses. Devī eventually defeats them both.

Devī In The Bindu

N412 **śiṣṭapūjitā** worshiped by the wise

N413 **aprameyā** immeasurable

N414 **svaprakāśā** self-luminous

N415 **manovācāma gocarā** unattainable through mind and speech

N416 **cicchaktiḥ** power of consciousness

N417 **cetanārūpā** form of consciousness

N418 **jaḍaśaktiḥ** power of Māyā

N419 **jaḍātmikā** objective (inanimate) world

N420 **gāyatrī** mother of mantras

N421 **vyāhṛti** utterance of mantras

N422 **sandhyā** junction of mantra, its practice and its grace

N423 **dvijabṛnda niṣevitā** revered by the twice-born

N424 **tattvāsanā** seat of all tattvas

N425 **tat** suchness or That

N426 **tvam** Thou

N427 **ayī** mother of all

N428 **pañcakośāntarasthitā** residing in the pañca-koṣas

Devī In The Bindu

N429 **niḥsīmamahimā** gloriously unlimited

N430 **nityayauvanā** ever youthful

N431 **madaśālinī** rapturously radiant

here in the bindu (N412) as the immeasurable (N413) and self-luminous (N414) because she is unattainable through mind and ordinary speech (N415). In sādhanā, she is known as the power of consciousness (N416) as well as its form (N417).

When we see through the illusion of separation, we recognize her as the power of Māyā (N418) that is the basis for the inanimate world (N419).

Being the consciousness that is seeded in all mantras (*see N204, N227*), Devī is the revered meter known as Gāyatrī (N420) as well as its utterance (N421). She is non-separation between the mantra, its utterance and its grace (N422).

As the union of prakāśa-vimarśa in the bindu, she is revered by the wise who are re-born in Self-knowledge (N423, *see N25*), who discover her seat in all the tattvas (N424). In direct experience, the "suchness" of every tattva (N425) is known to be Devī as its "I" (N426) when she is evoked as the mother of all (N427). She resides in the five kośas (N428, see kośas in Chapter 7) even though she is gloriously unlimited (N429) and although the kośas decay, she, as awareness soaked in śṛṅgāra, is ever youthful (N430, *see N358*).

How might Devī appear in the bindu as awareness soaked in śṛṅgāra? How might we see her as such? Imagine her being intoxicated with the śṛṅgāra rasa and radiant with rapture (N431). Her reddened

Devī In The Bindu

N432 **madaghūrṇita raktākṣī** reddened eyes rolling inward

N433 **madapāṭala gaṇḍabhūḥ** blushing cheeks

N434 **candana drava-dighdhāṅgī** smelling of sandalwood

N435 **cāmpeya kusuma priyā** fond of Campaka flowers

N436 **kuśalā** skillful

N437 **komalākārā** graceful

N438 **kurukullā** Kurukullā

N439 **kuleśvarī** ruler of the kula

N440 **kulakuṇḍālaya** abiding in the Kulakunda (mūlādhāra)

N441 **kaula mārgatatpara sevitā** worshiped by Kaulas

N442 **kumāra gaṇanāthāmbā** mother of Skanda and Gaṇeśa

N443 **tuṣṭiḥ** contentment

N444 **puṣṭiḥ** nourishment

N445 **matiḥ** intelligence

N446 **dhṛtiḥ** fortitude

eyes roll inward to revel in her own bliss (N432), her cheeks are flushed (N433) and her body emits the fragrance of sandalwood (N434). She is adorned with the Campaka flowers that she loves (N435, *see N13*), which are infused with the fragrance of śṛṅgāra.

Devī is most skilful (N436) and graceful (N437) as Kurukullā (N438), the goddess who fuses ahaṅkāra with the consciousness and bliss of the bindu.* Here, we are reminded that the ahaṅkāra is also powered by consciousness and bliss! Devī rules over the kula of the trikoṇa (pramāṇa, prameya, pramātṛ) (N439, *see N90-96*) and abides in the bindu of the mūlādhāra (N440) as the object of worship among the Kaulas (N441, see Ācārās in Chapter 11). From her seat in the mūlādhāra, she gives birth to Kumāra (Skanda)** and Gaṇapatī (N442), who preside over the hosts of influences (gaṇas) that keep us bound to saṃsāra (*see N77*).

Devī as the bindu is the source of contentment (N443), nourishment (N444), intelligence (N445), fortitude (N446), tranquility (N447), eternal truth (N448), effulgence (N449), and delight (N450), attained when she destroys the darkness of obstacles (N451) with her splendor (N452).

The sun, moon and fire are her three eyes (N453) that roll in the ecstasy that transforms her into desire (N454). She is the sequence of syllables known as Mālinī (N455, see Mātṛkā and Mālinī in Chapter 8) and the attainment of yogins who are established in the haṃsa mantra (N456).***

---

* In Śrīvidyā, Kurukullā is the mother principle and Vārāhī is the father principle, each becoming particular body tissues.

** Who destroys Tārakāsura, Chapter 2.

*** Haṃ-sa is the sound of the breath and because it is uttered naturally without effort, it is known as the ajapā

Devī In The Bindu

N447 **śāntiḥ** tranquility

N448 **svastimatī** eternal truth

N449 **kāntiḥ** effulgence

N450 **nandinī** delight

N451 **vighnanāśinī** destroying obstacles

N452 **tejovatī** splendorous

N453 **trinayanā** three-eyed

N454 **lolākṣī kāmarūpiṇī** rolling eyes

N455 **mālinī** Mālinī

N456 **haṃsinī** haṃsa mantra

N457 **mātā** measure

N458 **malayācala vāsinī** residing in the Malaya mountains

N459 **sumukhī** of a lovely face

N460 **nalinī** body of the softness of lotus petals

N461 **subhrūḥ** of beautiful eyebrows

N462 **śobhanā** shining

N463 **suranāyikā** leader of the devas

N464 **kālakaṇṭhī** united with Śiva

N465 **kāntimatī** radiant

N466 **kṣobhiṇī** causing upheaval

mantra. Becoming established in the continuous awareness of haṃ-sa results in the understanding of the unity of Ahaṃ and IDAM of the pure path.

Devī In The Bindu

N467 **sūkṣmarūpiṇī** subtle form

N468 **vajreśvarī** of the brilliance of diamonds

N469 **vāmadevī** wife of Śiva

Devī in the bindu is the mother of the universe, being the measurer of prakāśa as vimarśa (N457, *see N1*), similar to the measure of the region bordered by the Malaya mountain range where she is said to reside (N458). *

We visualize Devī with a lovely face (N459), a body that is as soft and delicate as lotus petals (N460) and with beautiful eyebrows (N461). She shines brilliantly (N462) as the leader of the Devās (N463).

It is her eternal unity with Śiva** (N464) that makes her beautiful and radiant (N465). Even while being perfectly balanced with him in the bindu, she creates the upheaval (N466) that is the impulse for creation. Playfully she remains concealed in the material world in her subtle form (N467), like a precious diamond (N468)*** hidden in plain sight. As the inseparable left side of Śiva (N469)**** that is the source of time, she is herself exempt from aging

* The Malaya mountains made up an alternative southern border in some Purāṇās.

** Śiva is known as Kālakaṇṭha because in one myth, he consumes a poison known as kālahāla that is generated when the Devās and Asuras churn the milky ocean for nectar of immortality using Vāsuki, the king of snakes, as a rope. Vāsuki spews up the poison that Śiva consumes to protect creation. The Devās eventually procure the nectar.

*** Vajreśvarī is also one of the Nityā Devīs.

**** Vāmadeva is another name of Śiva.

Devī In The Bindu

N470 **vayovasthā vivarjitā** exempt from states

N471 **siddheśvarī** worshiped by siddhās

N472 **siddhavidyā** Pañcadaśi mantra

N473 **siddhamātā** mother of the siddhās

N474 **yaśasvinī** of unparalleled renown

(N470). In every era, she is worshiped by adepts (N471) with the 15-syllable Pañcadaśi mantra that is also known as Siddhavidyā (N472). In this worship, she is extolled as the mother of the siddhas (N473) who is of unequalled renown (N474).

Bhāvanā on Śṛṅgāra

- Begin with the Śrīṃ meditation.
- Place an object in front of you, such as a flower or a rock.
- Close your eyes.
- Open your eyes and look at the object.

  There is a tiny gap between the sense of seeing and the object being recognized. There is another tiny gap between the object being recognized and being labeled as a flower or rock.
- This gap is the bindu.

  If we notice very carefully, at the first contact with the object, there is an ecstatic thrill of recognition, but it is not of us recognizing the object as a flower or a rock. It is the simple recognition of seeing, and of being, where "I" and the object become one at the point of contact. We don't see this because it is fleeting and is immediately followed by labeling or storytelling about the object.
- This ecstatic contact is the union of Śiva and Śakti.

  If this union can be accessed, there is a sweetness that is felt immediately that is orgasmic and uplifting, and includes the whole universe in it. We are in love, but not with anything or anyone in particular.
- This non-localized, welcoming, blissful love is śṛṅgāra.

  The bindu can be discovered in the gap between thoughts, the tiny gap between thought and reflex, and that between memory and emotion. With slowing down, cultivation of discernment and equanimity, and the right view, this practice becomes a moment-to-moment living of life from the vantage of orgasmic bliss. When we surrender into the bindu, the pulse of ecstatic bliss colors our perception, even when outer circumstances are challenging.
- The very act of perception becomes ecstatic, in the pulse of the bindu. The circumstance becomes secondary.

  In this practice, the Śrīcakra becomes a lived experience.

- **Open-eyed Practice**

  Slow down periodically to engage with your senses to access the sweetness of perception. Pause when you open your eyes in the morning, take your first bite of food, hear the hum of traffic, smell your toothpaste, feel the air on your skin. Can you drop into the bindu?

Section 12

DEVĪ IN THE CAKRAS

The bindu, which is the seat of Devī's union with Śiva, is the non-localized center and ground of every experience and all aspects of manifestation. In the microcosm, Devī manifests from the bindu as a multitude of deities that rule over the cakras (see Table 1 in Chapter 7). They are described according to the number of faces they have, beginning with the one-faced Dākinī at the viśuddha and moving down to Sākinī at the root with five faces and back up again to the six-faced Hākinī at the Ājña, finally ending with Yākinī at the sahasrāra with countless faces. Each deity rules over a particular body tissue, and is fond of a specific type of food. We must remember that they are all emanations of Devī.

Residing at the Viśuddha (N475), she has a reddish complexion (N476) and three eyes (N477), and bears a club and other weapons (N478). We can recognize her easily because she has one face (N479) and is fond of pāyasa* (N480). Governing the skin, which is associated with the sense of touch (N481), she is the cause of fear to paśus (N482, *see N354* and Ācāra prescription in Chapter 11). Surrounded by Amṛta and other śaktis (N483)**, she is known as Ḍākinī (N484).

Devī In The Cakras

N475 **viśuddhi cakranilayā** residing at the Viśuddha cakra

N476 **raktavarṇā** of a reddish complexion

N477 **trilocanā** three-eyed

N478 **khaṭvāṅgādi praharaṇā** bearing a club and other weapons

N479 **vadanaika samanvitā** one-faced

N480 **pāyasānnapriyā** fond of pāyasa

N481 **tvaksthā** governing over skin tissue

N482 **paśuloka bhayaṅkarī** inciting fear in paśus

N483 **amṛtādi mahāśakti saṃvṛtā** attended by Amṛta and other śaktis

N484 **ḍākinīśvarī** known as Dākinī

At the Anāhata (N485), she is the one with the black skin (N486) and two faces (N487), each with shining tusks (N488). She wears garlands of rudrākśa beads and assorted objects (N489). Presiding over blood (N490), she is surrounded by Kālarātrī and other śaktis (N491). Fond of offerings cooked in oil or fats (N492) and bestowing grace on vīras (N493, see Ācāra Prescription in Chapter 11), she is known as Rākiṇī (N494).

At the Maṇipūra (N495), she is the three-faced deity (N496) who wields the lightning bolt and other weapons (N497). Surrounded by Ḍāmarī and other

* Pāyasa is rice cooked in milk with a sweetener.

** Each cakra is a lotus with a specific number of petals. Each petal is ruled by an even more minor emanation of Devī. The 50 petals of all the cakras represent the letters of the Sanskrit alphabet; the names of the petal śaktis begin with the corresponding alphabet.

Devī In The Cakras

N485 **anāhatābja nilayā** residing at the Anāhatā

N486 **śyāmābhā** black-complexioned

N487 **vadanadvayā** two-faced

N488 **daṃṣṭrojjvalā** with shining tusks

N489 **akṣamālādhidharā** wearing garlands of beads

N490 **rudhira saṃsthitā** presiding over blood

N491 **kālarātryādi śaktyoghavṛtā** attended by Kālarātri and other śaktis

N492 **snigdhaudanapriyā** fond of greasy offerings

N493 **mahāvīrendra varadā** bestowing grace on vīras

N494 **rākiṇyambā svarūpiṇī** form of Rākiṇi

N495 **maṇipūrābja nilayā** residing at the Maṇipūra

N496 **vadanatraya saṃyutā** three-faced

N497 **vajrādikāyudhopetā** bearing lightning bolt and other weapons

N498 **ḍāmaryādibhir āvṛtā** attended by Ḍāmarī and other śaktis

N499 **raktavarṇā** red-skinned

N500 **māṃsaniṣṭhā** ruling over muscle

N501 **guḍānna prītamānasā** fond of sweet rice with jaggery

N502 **samasta bhakta sukhadā** conferring contentment on all devotees

Devī In The Cakras

N503 **lākinyambā svarūpiṇī** as Lākinī

N504 **svādhiṣṭānāmbujagatā** at the svādhiṣṭāna

N505 **caturvaktra manoharā** four-faced beauty

N506 **śūlādyāyudha sampannā** bearing a trident and other weapons

N507 **pītavarṇā** yellow-complexioned

N508 **atigarvitā** very proud

N509 **medoniṣṭhā** presiding over fat

N510 **madhuprītā** favoring honey

N511 **bandhinyādi samanvitā** attended by Bandhinī and other śaktis

N512 **dadhyannāsakta hṛdayā** fond of yogurt-containing offerings

N513 **kākinī rūpa dhāriṇī** assuming the form of Kākinī

śaktis (N498), she has red skin (N499) and rules over the muscle tissue of the body (N500). Fond of sweet rice made with jaggery (unrefined sugar) (N501), she confers contentment on the sādhaka (N502) and is known as Lākinī (N503).

At the Svādhiṣṭāna (N504), she is the beautiful four-faced one (N505) bearing a trident and other weapons (N506). She has a yellow complexion (N507) and governs with pride (N508) over the body's fat tissue (N509). Favoring honey mead (N510), she is attended by Bandhinī and other śaktis (N511). Particularly fond of offerings containing yogurt (N512), she is Kākinī (N513).

Devī In The Cakras

N514 **mūlādhārāmbujārūḍhā** at the mūlādhāra

N515 **pañcavaktrā** five-faced

N516 **asthisaṃsthitā** presiding over bone

N517 **aṅkuśādi praharaṇā** bearing a goad and other weapons

N518 **varadādi niṣevitā** attended by Varadā and other śaktis

N519 **mudgaudanāsakta cittā** fond of mudga beans

N520 **sākinyambāsvarūpiṇī** she is Sākinī

At the Mūlādhāra (N514), she is five-faced (N515) and presides over the bony parts of the body (N516). Bearing a goad and other weapons (N517), she is attended by Varadā and other śaktis (N518) Particularly fond of mudga (N519),* she is Sākinī (N520).

Residing at the Ājña cakra (N521), she is white-complexioned (N522) with six faces (N523). Presiding over bone marrow (N524) and accompanied by Haṃsavatī (and Kśamatī) (N525), she favors food with saffron (N526) and is known as Hākinī (N527).

At the thousand-petaled Sahasrāra (N528) she is radiant with a multi-hued complexion (N529). Bearing countless weapons of all kinds (N530), she presides over reproductive tissue (N531) and simultaneously faces all directions (N532). Fond of all kinds of offerings (N533), she is Yākinī (N534). She

Devī In The Cakras

N521 **ājñā cakrābjanilayā** residing at the ājña

N522 **śuklavarṇā** white-complexioned

N523 **ṣaḍānanā** six-faced

N524 **majjāsaṃsthā** presiding over bone marrow

N525 **haṃsavatī mukhyaśakti samanvitā** attended by Hamsavatī as the main śakti

N526 **haridrānnaika rasikā** favoring food with saffron

N527 **hākinī rūpadhāriṇī** she is Hākinī

N528 **sahasradaḷa padmasthā** residing at the sahasrāra

N529 **sarvavarnopaśobhitā** complexion of all colors

N530 **sarvāyudhadharā** bearing all weapons

N531 **śukla saṃsthitā** presiding over reproductive tissue

N532 **sarvatomukhī** faces turned in all directions

N533 **sarvadana prītacittā** fond of all offerings

N534 **yākinyambā svarūpiṇī** she is Yākinī

N535 **svāhā** invoked by svāhā

N536 **svadhā** invoked by svadhā

is called upon by invocations of svāhā (N535) and svadhā (N536) in the fire ritual known as homa.**

* Mudga = whole mung beans.

** Svāhā and svadhā are added at the end of mantras in specific rituals; they are said to be the two wives of Agni,

Sādhanā is like the homa, where we invoke agni (*see N352*) as the heat of tapas. Into this fire, we pour all our limitations with a "svāhā!" as we would in a homa. The process of transformation involves moderation in our diet, exercise and other lifestyle elements that invoke agni in the tissues. In Ayurveda, metabolism is a sequential process that moves from one tissue to another, catalyzed by the agni of each. Reproductive fluid is the last step, representing the most refined physical end-product of digestion, containing the genetic material for procreation. The cakra deities are invoked at each step of this transformation, not merely for the maintenance of the physical body but to keep up with the rigorous housecleaning of Kuṇḍalinī awakening and ascent. As the energy "rises," Devī as the cakra deities facilitates the release of saṃskāras at levels of the body-mind that keep us bound in ignorance.

At the level of the sahasrāra, we come to see that Devī herself is both ignorance (N537) and wisdom (N538). As the Vedas (N539) and the smṛtis or derived scriptures (N540), she is unexcelled (N541) as the bestower of good fortune (N542). Now that we have traversed all the cakras, we realize that it is by her grace that we attain her (N543). It is by her grace that we contemplate her, want her and engage in sādhanā. It is by her grace, too, that we even hear of her and are drawn to praise her (N544), just as Indra's wife Pulomajā once did (N545).*

Devī In The Cakras

N537 **amatiḥ** form of ignorance

N538 **medhā** form of wisdom

N539 **śrutiḥ** form of the Vedas

N540 **smṛtiḥ** form of the derived scriptures

N541 **anuttamā** unexcelled

N542 **puṇyakīrtiḥ** bestower of good fortune

N543 **puṇyalabhyā** attained by grace

N544 **puṇyaśravaṇa kīrtanā** listening to her praise is sacred

N545 **pulomajārcitā** worshiped by Pulomajā

N546 **bandhamocanī** freeing from the bond of ignorance

Here in the sahasrāra, Devī releases us from the bonds of ignorance (N546). Yet, this freedom from bondage does not mean the path of renunciation, with a shaved head and a begging-bowl. Devī frees us from bondage but leaves us fully engaged in the world, enjoying every experience but without leaving the traces of vāsanās. In contrast to the renunciatory

---

the god of fire.

* In one legend, Indra is cursed and hides himself in a lotus stalk. Nahuṣa, an asura, takes Indra's place as the leader of the Devās, and is enamored with Pulomajā. With Devī's grace, she locates Indra and they devise a plan to usurp Nahuṣa, asking him to come to her in a palanquin carried by the great sages including Agastya. Nahuṣa disrespects Agastya by placing his foot on his head. The furious sage curses him to forever be a snake. Indra returns to his place.

paths of those with shaved heads, this life-embracing path is denoted by her luxuriant hair (N547).

In the sahasrāra, Devī resides as vimarśa, the reflection of illumination (N548, see Prakāśa and Vimarśa in Chapter 3) and knowledge (N549). As the creator of the universe, which is the aggregate of the five elements starting with space (N550), she is also the only one that can alleviate all disease (N551, see Chapter 10) and free us from death (N552). Ignorance is the greatest disease, and death is the resulting sorrow that arises from loss or not getting what we want. At the sahasrāra, disease and death are conquered when we encounter Devī, who is the foremost principle (N553) beyond the elements.

Being beyond the realm of the mind (which is also subject to the elements), disease and death (N554), she is destroyer of the sin of ignorance that is especially rampant in the Kalī yuga (N555, *see N80* and footnote).

Devī In The Cakras

N547 **bandhurālakā** of luxurious hair

N548 **vimarśarūpiṇī** form of vimarśa

N549 **vidyā** form of knowledge

N550 **viyadādi jagatprasūḥ** creator of the universe of space and other elements

N551 **sarvavyādhi praśamanī** alleviating all disease

N552 **sarvamṛtyu nivāriṇī** dispelling all death

N553 **agragaṇyā** the first

N554 **acintyarūpā** unthinkable

N555 **kalikalmaṣa nāśinī** destroyer of sin in the Kalī yuga

Bhāvanā on Tapas

- Begin with the Śrīṃ meditation.
- Contemplate tapas, which is perseverance.

  While tapas refers specifically to sādhana, it is actually a redirection of attention. In one sense, all of us are tapasvins, since we persevere in maintaining the "me story."
- How do you persevere in maintaining your "me story"? Catch your thoughts throughout the day – what are they mostly about? What sense of "me-ness" do they fuel?
- Become aware of your interactions with others, how you respond and react in word or deed.
- How are you a tapasvin of the "me story"?

  When the light of awareness begins to infiltrate into our modes of tapas toward the "me story," our attention shifts to it. We become increasingly more aware of awareness.
- Every time we favor awareness rather than the "me story," we demonstrate our skill in tapas!

- **Open-eyed Practice**

  Practice the tapas of favoring attention to awareness rather than the "me story" as you go about your day.

Section 13

DEVĪ AT THE SAHASRĀRA

Devī At The Sahasrāra

N556 **kātyāyinī** radiance of the aggregate of deities

N557 **kālahantrī** destroyer of time

N558 **kamalākṣa niṣevitā** worshiped by the lotus-eyed (Viṣṇu)

In the previous section, we encountered Devī in the cakras to arrive at her supreme form in the sahasrāra. Here in this segment, we will meditate on her many attributes as the supreme deity of the sahasrāra. We have to remember that to arrive at the sahasrāra, the buddhi has to become significantly unclouded so that Reality is being perceived increasingly "as is" (see Chapter 5). Accordingly, the reference to Devī's particular attributes implies perception at a very fine level of separation. If she is still being perceived as an entity "out there" or as an imaginary/mystical/mythological being, our sādhanā has not yet ripened to this stage. When we say Devī has such-and-such attribute, we are finding this to be true in our own experience—*we* are endowed with that attribute.

By now, we know that Devī is the vimarśa or reflection of the primordial illumination (*see N548* and Prakāśa and Vimarśa in Chapter 3). This was always the case, even before we took up sādhanā, but with the progressive clearing of the buddhi, we see this more clearly—Devī is now known in direct experience as the radiance of all deities (N556). The deities we are talking about here are those that we were previously worshiping through our senses, when we were driven by rāga. Devī is the illuminator of the senses, sense objects, and the kañcukas including rāga (*see N537*), which are pale reflections of her effulgence. Now that we have turned to the eternal Source of their allure, we realize that we had been chasing after these weak emanations of her glorious radiance that were limited in space and time.

Now, we come to know her as the destroyer of time (N557). Our previous mode of being, driven by attractions and aversions, was based in linear time (*see N231*) and our lives had revolved around past experiences (that no longer exist except as memory) and future projections (that don't exist except as imagination). This linearity, which is the basis for regret, anxiety and fear, made up our default paradigm.* Now, we transcend linear time and see that all experiences arise and subside in the eternal now. It is as if Viṣṇu, who maintains the illusion of linearity and constancy (*see Section 8 and N339*) takes refuge in Devī (N558).

Transcending time and space, we can now experience the fragrance of Devī's betel leaves (N559, *see N26*) that attracts everything in manifestation.

* See Kali in *Shakti Rising*, page 27.

Devī At The Sahasrāra

N559 **tāmbūla pūrita mukhī** mouth full of betel

N560 **dāḍimī kusumaprabhā** red like the pomegranate flower

N561 **mṛgākṣī** doe-eyed

N562 **mohinī** enchantress

N563 **mukhyā** first

N564 **mṛḍānī** wife of Mṛḍa

N565 **mitrarūpiṇī** form of the sun

N566 **nityatṛptā** eternally content

N567 **bhaktanidhiḥ** treasure of the devotee

N568 **niyantrī** guide

N569 **nikhileśvarī** ruler of all

N570 **maitryādi vāsanālabhyā** attained by virtues like friendliness

N571 **mahāpraḷaya sākṣiṇī** witness of the great dissolution

Surrendering rāga, we experience life as a flow of her icchā, which shines like the red pomegranate flower (N560). We begin to see Reality through her beautiful eyes that are like those of a doe (N561). We see her play as the enchantress (N562), as Māyā, but we don't get ensnared by it because we only seek her as the first principle (N563)—the wife of Mṛḍa (N564).*

* Mṛḍa is Śiva, the bestower of happiness.

While we previously approached her in fear, we come to now know her as our very essence, like the life-giving sun (N565). We discover her within ourselves as the one that is eternally content (N566) and the very treasure we had been seeking (N567). All along, she was guiding us on this path (N568) and ruling over all aspects of it (N569), bringing the teachers, the teachings and the life circumstances to facilitate our sādhanā.

We realize that although the path entailed meditation, japa, and other esoteric practices, we could not realize Devī until we had cultivated the four virtuous qualities beginning with friendliness (N570).** We had to develop friendliness without envy toward those who were happy, compassion without disgust or pity for those in pain, delight for those advanced in sādhanā, and dispassion without hatred for the wicked.***

It becomes evident why Devī is known as the witness of the great dissolution (N571). As the principle that is beyond the level of the tattvas, she alone remains as the ultimate Reality at the end of a cycle of yugas (see N80). Importantly, she is the principle that remains when the trikoṇa (pramāṇa, prameya, pramātṛ) that is the basis for creation collapses into the bindu where it remains as potential until it is called forth again by her icchā. As the one that wills creation into being, she is the supreme power (N572).

** From the Yoga Sutras, 1:33.

*** These qualities arise from cultivation of discernment that allows us to see that all of creation is entrapped in Māyā. We are all deluded; it's just a matter of degree!

Devī At The Sahasrāra

N572 **parāśaktiḥ** supreme power

N573 **parāniṣṭhā** supreme end

N574 **prajñāna ghanarūpiṇī** concentrated wisdom

N575 **mādhvīpānālasā** languid

N576 **mattā** intoxicated

N577 **mātṛkā varṇa rūpiṇī** form of Mātṛkā

N578 **mahākailāsa nilayā** residing in the great Kailāsa

N579 **mṛṇāla mṛdudorlatā** with arms like soft lotus stems

N580 **mahanīyā** illustrious

N581 **dayāmūrtiḥ** embodiment of mercy

N582 **mahāsāmrājyaśālinī** empress of all worlds

N583 **ātmavidyā** Self-knowledge

N584 **mahāvidyā** great knowledge

N585 **śrīvidyā** auspicious knowledge

N586 **kāmasevitā** worshiped by Kāma

N587 **śrīṣoḍaśākṣarī vidyā** sixteen-syllabled mantra

N588 **trikūṭā** of the three kūṭas

As the ultimate goal and the one that brings to rest the endless cycles of saṃsāra, she is the Supreme End (N573). As the concentrated wisdom (N574), she puts to rest the other kinds of transactional knowledge (see Chapter 12) that perpetuate our sense of separation.* As this wisdom, she is languid (N575), and intoxicated (N576) with the śṛṅgāra rasa—this wisdom isn't dry or detached, but drips with love and sweetness!

While language previously bound us in saṃsāra (see Language in Sādhanā in Chapter 8), we now see that it is Devī who shines as Mātṛkā (N577, see Mātṛkā and Mālinī in Chapter 8) in the great Kailāsa (N578)** that is the sahasrāra.

Enveloping us in her love with her arms that are soft and soothing as lotus stems (N579), Devī is illustrious (N580) in her mercy (N581). She is the resplendent empress of all the worlds (N582) and the embodiment of Self-knowledge (N583). She is the exalted science (N584) that frees us from sorrow and bestows auspicious wisdom (N585). Worshiped by Kāma (N586), she is the personification of the auspicious sixteen-syllabled Ṣodaśi mantra (N587) as well as the three kūṭas of the Pañcadaśi mantra (N588), both of which are of the nature of Śiva (N589).

She is attended by millions of subservient deities of abundance (N590)—while we had previously pursued abundance in external objects, we now realize Devī as Source of abundance at the sahasrāra (N591) where she is whole and beautiful like the full moon (N592).

Having seen her splendor at the sahasrāra, we can now recognize Devī at the ājña (N593) in her

* See Bhuvaneshwari in *Shakti Rising,* page 87.

** Mahakailāsa is the abode of Śiva and is beyond the material world.

Devī At The Sahasrāra

N589 **kāmakoṭikā** nature of Śiva

N590 **kaṭākṣakiṅkarī bhūta kamalā koṭisevitā** attended by millions of Lakṣmīs

N591 **śiraḥsthitā** at the sahasrāra

N592 **candranibhā** moon-like

N593 **phālasthā** at the ājña

N594 **indradhanuḥprabhā** rainbow-like

N595 **hṛdayasthā** at the anāhatā

N596 **raviprakhyā** sun-like

N597 **trikoṇāntara dīpikā** light of the triangle

N598 **dākṣāyaṇī** daughter of Dakśa (Sati)

N599 **daityahantrī** slayer of asuras

N600 **dakṣayajña vināśinī** destroyer of Dakśa's fire ritual

rainbow-like (N594) form, at the anāhata (N595) where she is brilliant like the sun (N596), and at the mūlādhāra (N597) as the illumination of the trikoṇa. As Sati* (N598), she slays the asuras (N599) that had been performing the misguided fire sacrifice (N600)—those asuras were our own saṃskāra-driven ways of continually pouring our life energies into our senses to gratify the āṇava mala.

* Sati is Dākśāyaṇī, the daughter of Dakśa who immolates herself in her father's sacrificial fire (see Chapter 1).

Bhāvanā on Equanimity

- Begin with the Śrīṃ meditation.
- Contemplate how you interact with others.
- What goes on in your internal landscape when you see friends and acquaintances having fun and being happy?
- Do envy and resentment arise?
- How do you feel about people who are suffering?
- Are you driven by pity, which is different from compassion?
  (Pity is based on hierarchy and compassion is based on equality.)
- What feelings come up when you see other sādhakas who seem to be more advanced?
- How do you feel when you hear news of crimes, injustice, and wars?
  The purpose of this bhāvanā, like anything else in the LSN, is svatantra or absolute freedom. When we contemplate our reactions, we see that they arise from comparison and judgment. While it may seem noble to be self-righteous about wickedness, it doesn't lead to freedom. Instead, when we become acutely aware of the ānava mala, our lens of perception becomes significantly clearer—we can see not only why we do what we do but why anyone does what they do.
  Open-heartedness is the natural result of this clarity, where we can be friendly toward those who are happy, compassionate toward those who are in pain, delighted for advanced sādhakas, and dispassionate without self-righteous hatred for those who are wicked. With this open-heartedness, our stand for justice is devoid of our own limitations and is tinged with the sweetness of freedom.

- **Open-Eyed Practice**

  As you go about your life, become acutely aware of your own reactions to people and events. Note that your reaction to them is entirely dependent on your own internal landscape.

Section 14

DEVĪ IN YOGA

Having encountered Devī at the sahasrāra, we will now see how she directs our lives and propels us on the path to svatantra. In this segment of nāmas, we encounter her in sādhanā that leads to yoga or union with her.

Devī's large, all-seeing eyes (N601) destroy fear that is born of the āṇava mala. With her radiant smile (N602), she assumes the form of the guru (N603), bestowing grace as a treasure-house of virtue (N604) and leading us to the root of our desires that fulfills all our wishes like Kāmadhenu (N605).*

As Māyā, Devī hides our true nature in ignorance so that it remains a secret (N606). This creates the ongoing conflict between the asuras (forces of ignorance) that keep us entrapped in saṃsāra and the devas (forces that propel us toward knowledge). Devī as the śakti of the devas (N607) metes out exacting justice (N608) in this great conflict. We go through the cycles of saṃsāra, enduring the consequences of our own past actions (see Karma in Chapter 4) until we realize her as the one who dwells in the subtle space of the heart (N609).

Even though Devī is all there is, she conceals herself as time in the phases of the moon. She is worshiped in the lunar half-month as the various Nityā Devīs (N610, see Deities of the Śrīcakra in Chapter 9), where we find her as the underlying Source (N611) and ruler (N612) of all measures of time.** While these measures signify the passage of time, Devī remains unchanged as the overarching principle in which linear time unfolds. The purpose of the worship of the kalās is to realize the non-lin-

Devī In Yoga

N601 **darāndolita dīrghākṣī** all-seeing large eyes

N602 **darahāsojjvalanmukhī** of radiant smile

N603 **gurumūrtiḥ** form of the guru

N604 **guṇanidhiḥ** treasure-house of virtue

N605 **gomātā** Kāmadhenu

N606 **guhajanmabhūḥ** keeping the secret of the divine birth of the universe

N607 **deveśī** śakti of the devas

N608 **daṇḍanītisthā** exacting justice

N609 **daharākāśa rūpiṇī** indweller of the space of the heart

N610 **pratipanmukhya rākānta tithimaṇḍala pūjitā** worshiped as digits of the lunar half-months

N611 **kalātmikā** source of the kalās

N612 **kalānāthā** ruler of the kalās

* Wish-fulfilling cow.

** Kalā is a digit of an entity. The moon has sixteen kalās, the sun has twelve kalās and agni (fire) has ten kalās.

Devī In Yoga

N613 **kāvyālāpa vinodinī** delighting in poetry

N614 **sacāmara ramāvāṇī savyadakṣiṇa sevitā** attended by Lakṣmī and Sarasvatī

N615 **ādiśakti** primordial power

N616 **ameyā** immeasurable

N617 **ātmā** Self in all

N618 **paramā** supreme

N619 **pāvanākṛtiḥ** pure

N620 **anekakoṭi brahmāṇḍa jananī** creator of countless universes

N621 **divyavigrahā** divine body

N622 **klīṅkārī** of the bīja Klīṃ

N623 **kevalā** attributeless

N624 **guhyā** secret

N625 **kaivalya pada dāyinī** bestowing liberation

N626 **tripurā** triad

N627 **trijagadvandyā** worshiped by the three worlds

ear nature of existence (*see N231, N558*). As long as we are stationed in linear time, we are subject to the internal war and the consequences of karma (*see N608*).

Devī delights in how we express ourselves in language, which becomes refined and poetry-like (N613) when we transcend time. With the discovery of Devī in our own heart, we stop asking for abundance or mere transactional knowledge, and see that both Ramā[*] (Lakṣmī) and Vāṇī (Sarasvatī) are at her service, attending to her with ceremonial fans (N614). We realize that she is the primordial Source (N615) of all the deities we had previously worshiped.

Devī is the immeasurable (N616) Self in all (N617), the supreme (N618) and unconditioned (N619) creator of countless universes (N620) *within* and *as* her own divine body (N621). Across these universes, she resounds as the bīja Klīṃ[**] (N622), which arises as the vibration of Śiva-Śakti in union as prakāśa-vimarśa (see Chapter 4). When the syllables k and l dissolve, she is what remains as the Śakti praṇava Īm, which is the absolute, independent and attributeless (N623) Reality (see Kāmakalā in Chapter 10). She is this secret (N624) knowledge that bestows liberation (N625).

Devī is the primordial principle (*see N615*) that precedes all triads as the trikoṇa of pramāṇa-prameya-pramātṛ (N626).[***] As all the triads that make up the universe, she is adored by inhabitants of all the three worlds (N627) representing the three states of consciousness (see States of Consciousness in Chapter 8). In each of these three states, Devī

* Not to be confused with Rāma, the hero-avatar of the epic Rāmāyaṇa

** Klīṃ is said to be the bīja of desire and beauty.

*** See Tripura Sundari in *Shakti Rising,* starting at page 67.

Devī In Yoga

N628 **trimurtiḥ** form of triads

N629 **tridaśeśvarī** ruler of triads

N630 **tryakṣarī** three-syllabled

N631 **divyagandhāḍhyā** of divine fragrance

N632 **sindūra tilakāñcitā** with the mark of auspiciousness

N633 **umā** Umā

N634 **śailendratanayā** daughter of the Himālaya

N635 **gaurī** of golden complexion

N636 **gandharva sevitā** attended by celestial singers

N637 **viśvagarbhā** womb carrying the universe

N638 **svarṇagarbhā** golden womb

N639 **avaradā** sacred

N640 **vāgadhīśvarī** presiding over speech

N641 **dhyānagamyā** attained by meditation

N642 **aparicchedyā** unlimited

N643 **jñānadā** giver of knowledge

N644 **jñānavigrahā** embodiment of knowledge

N645 **sarvavedānta saṃvedyā** subject of Vedanta

N646 **satyānanda svarūpiṇī** embodiment of existence and bliss

is the subject *and* the object. She is adored in the interaction between them in all states as the sum of the triad (N628). If the sense perceptions in the three states are devas, she is their ruler (N629)* as the three kūṭas of the Pañcadaśi (N630).**

All triads are pervaded by Devī's divine fragrance (N631) and the auspiciousness emanating from the red vermilion mark on her forehead (N632). She resides as radiance in all creatures and as the desire in yogins that drives them to commune with Śiva (N633).***

She is also known as the daughter of the Himālaya (N634, see Chapter 2) with a golden complexion (N635) who is attended by celestial singers (N636). She holds the entire universe in her womb (N637), enclosed in the golden light (N638) that renders it sacred (N639).

Presiding over expression represented by speech (N640), she is attained through deep meditation (N641) where the limitations of the body-mind are transcended (N642). She is the giver of Self-knowledge (N643) as its embodiment (N644) in the Vedāntas (N645)**** where she is known as existence and bliss (N646).

Worshiped by Lopāmudrā***** (N647, see Chapter

* Devī is the ruler of the thirty-three groups of gods.

** The Pañcadaśi mantra with the three kūṭas is thought to contain all of creation (see Varivasya Rahasya by Bhāskararāya).

*** Umā is also another name for Pārvatī.

**** Vedāntas are the end portions of the Vedas, also known as the Upaniṣads, dealing with Self-knowledge (see Chapter 2).

* Lopāmudrā is the wife of the sage Agastya (see Chapter 1), a philosopher in her own right and the preceptor of the

Devī In Yoga

N647 **lopāmudrārcitā** worshiped by Lopāmudrā

N648 **līlākḷpta brahmāṇḍa maṇḍala** creating the universe for sport

N649 **adṛśyā** invisible

N650 **dṛśyarahitā** transcending the visible

N651 **vijñātrī** sole perceiver

N652 **vedyavarjitā** transcending the knowable

N653 **yoginī** united with Śiva

N654 **yogadā** bestower of yoga

N655 **yogyā** object of all yoga

N656 **yogānandā** bliss of yoga

N657 **yugandharā** bearer of the ages

N658 **icchāśakti jñānaśakti kriyāśakti svarūpiṇī** form of icchā, jñāna and kriya śakti

N659 **sarvādhārā** support of all

N660 **supratiṣṭhā** firmly established

N661 **sadasadrūpa-dhāriṇī** foundation of being and non-being

N662 **aṣṭamūrtiḥ** eight-formed

N663 **ajājaitrī** conquering ignorance

N664 **lokayātrā vidhāyinī** directing the course of the worlds

hādi vidyā (Pañcadaśi beginning with "ha").

2), Devī creates and maintains the universe purely for sport (N648). Although she is the power of the senses, she herself cannot be perceived by the sense organs (N649) and transcends ordinary visibility (N650). She cannot be perceived because she is the sole perceiver (N651) that transcends the knowable (N652).

As the one who is perpetually united with Śiva (N653), she is the bestower of yoga (N654), the object of all yoga (N655), and the bliss attained through yoga (N656). In fact, she is the bearer of the yugas (N657) or ages through which yoga is perpetuated.*

In her triple form as icchā, jñāna and kriyā (N658), Devī is the support of all (N659), firmly established (N660) in transcendence as the foundation of being and non-being (N661). She is eightfold (N662) as the Aṣṭa Mātṛkā (see Deities of the Śrīcakra in Chapter 10), who heal afflictions such as anger, envy, and conceit that lead to ignorance.** Devī, as the Aṣṭa Mātṛkā, conquers ignorance (N663), directing the journey of embodied jīvas toward liberation (N664).

Even though there is the appearance of the many, Devī is the only One that there is (N665) as the sum of all of creation (N666). Devoid of duality (N667), she transcends it (N668) while being its source of nourishment (N669) and abundance (N670). As the most ancient (N671), fundamental principle, she is

* Yuga also means "to yoke" and "a pair"—in this case, Śakti paired with or yoked to Śiva to become the support of the universe.

** The eightfold forms of Devī also correspond to eight forms of Śiva, as his Śakti in each.

Devī In Yoga

N665 **ekākinī** one without a second

N666 **bhūmarūpā** aggregate of all existing things

N667 **nirdvaitā** devoid of duality

N668 **dvaitavarjitā** transcending duality

N669 **annadā** source of nourishment

N670 **vasudā** source of abundance

N671 **vṛddhā** ancient

N672 **brahmātmaikya svarūpiṇī** union of Brahman and atman (jīva)

the oneness of Reality as Brahman* and the individual ātma as jīva (N672, *see N173*), known through the haṃsa mantra (*see N456 and footnote*).

* Brahman is another name for the ultimate Reality that is beyond the tattvas (see Chapter 4).

Bhāvanā on Karma

- Begin with the Śrīṃ meditation.
- Contemplate how you create karma.
- Think about an interaction that is weighing on your mind and the source of your suffering.

  Usually, our suffering comes from thinking that the other person should not have done/said what s/he did, or that we should not have done/said what we did. We have countless scenarios around what we and s/he should have done instead.
- Contemplate why anyone does what they do, including you.

  Each of us speaks, thinks and acts according to our specific "me" stories. What I do has nothing whatsoever to do with you, and everything to do with myself. What you do has nothing whatsoever to do with anyone else except yourself. Even though we are interacting, each of us is responding to our own "me" stories.
- As soon as we place the blame for our response on to someone else, we have created karma with them.

  We act the way we do because that is how the ānava mala specifically finds its home in us. Every person acts the way they do for this same reason. It is the case of Bhaṇḍāsura creating havoc as ongoing karma.
- The fact that a situation is weighing on you is proof of having created the invisible bond of karma with that situation. Although it is long gone, its impression is like a puppet string that will push and pull you in all your present and future interactions.

  The rub is that although I may feel justified at being angry or hurt by someone else, I am the one that suffers and becomes entangled in saṃsāra.
- On the other hand, if I realize in every situation that everybody is merely responding to their own conditioning, my interaction ends right then with no lasting impression. I have stopped creating karma.

- **Open-Eyed Practice**

  As you go about your day, become aware of how you create karma with situations and people. Notice that you are creating vāsanās that will come up sooner or later in how you think and act. If you can become aware of your own inner landscape and approach the situation or person with humor or compassion, there's no vāsanā created – it won't even figure in how you think or act.

Section 15

DEVĪ'S ESOTERIC FORMS

Having encountered Devī in our own sādhanā, we can see her innumerable esoteric forms—they now make so much more sense! At the outset, we see that she is the immeasurable and great (N673) Brahman (N674). As the Word of Brahman (N675), she is eternally immersed in her own bliss (N676) and particularly fond of vīras (see Ācāra prescription in Chapter 11) who are willing to sacrifice their limitations (N677) to realize her.

> **Devī's Esoteric Forms**
>
> N673 **bṛhatī** great
>
> N674 **brāhmaṇī** wife of Śiva
>
> N675 **brāhmī** Brahman as the Word
>
> N676 **brahmānandā** bliss of Brahman
>
> N677 **balipriyā** fond of sacrifice
>
> N678 **bhāṣārūpā** form of language
>
> N679 **bṛhatsenā** vast army
>
> N680 **bhāvābhāva vivarjitā** devoid of existence and non-existence
>
> N681 **sukhārādhyā** easily worshiped
>
> N682 **śubhakarī** bestows good fortune
>
> N683 **śobhanā sulabhāgatiḥ** easy path
>
> N684 **rājarājeśvarī** empress of emperors
>
> N685 **rājyadāyinī** giver of dominion

As language (N678), she commands a vast army (N679), and yet she remains devoid both of existence and non-existence (N680). How would we discern existence and non-existence if it were not for language? It's impossible to conceive of non-existence in thought, feeling, or word because the very fact that it can be conceived makes it existent—and if it is conceived, it is in the realm of language! Non-existence necessarily requires the collapse of the triad of pramāṇa-prameya-pramātṛ, since all three are within the realm of language. Non-existence refers to the state of Śiva-Śakti prior to language, but even this is not a void because of Devī's presence in it! While certain states *seem* to be non-existent because of the absence of language, Devī exists in both the existent and the non-existent, and yet is beyond both as the ultimate Reality.

Because of language, Devī is easily worshiped (N681) in any form of expression (in fact, she is constantly worshiped even in ordinary experience because of her presence in every experience! *See N556*). There is no wrong way to worship Devī, and she bestows her grace easily (N682) on this easy path to her (N683).

As the commander of the army of language, Devī rules supreme over kings and emperors (N684), and is the source of their power and dominion (N685). Each of us is the ruler of the kingdom that is our

Devī's Esoteric Forms

N686 **rājyavallabhā** delights in all dominions

N687 **rājatkṛpā** giver of compassion in all dominions

N688 **rājapīṭha niveśita nijāśritā** establishing devotees on thrones

N689 **rājyalakṣmīḥ** royal wealth

N690 **kośanāthā** ruler of the kośas

N691 **caturaṅga baleśvarī** commander of the four armies

N692 **sāmrājyadāyinī** bestower of the supreme dominion

N693 **satyasandhā** devoted to truth

N694 **sāgaramekhalā** girdle of oceans

N695 **dīkṣitā** giver of dīkṣa

N696 **daityaśamanī** destroyer of demons

N697 **sarvaloka vaśaṅkarī** subjugating all the worlds

N698 **sarvārthadātrī** granting all desires

body-mind and our sphere of influence in the world, and we constantly either create karma through our rāga and dveṣa, or dissolve it through sādhanā. The "dominion" we are granted depends on the way we rule our kingdom. Creating more karma entrenches us in saṃsāra, taking us through cycles of heaven and hell. We are constantly dying and being reborn to repeat some variation on the seemingly endless theme (see Karma in Chapter 4) until we are guided to the path of liberation.* Devī is the source of all these karma-directed dominions and she delights in them (N686). In every dominion, she is the source of compassion (N687), goading us toward liberation.

When we take up sādhanā, Devī establishes us on the thrones (N688) of the various kingdoms of limitations we conquer along the way (see Chapter 10). We acquire access to the royal wealth (N689) of these kingdoms in the form of progressive freedom in the five kośas (see kośas in Chapter 6). As we become aligned with Devī's icchā, we surrender to her as the mistress of the kośa treasury (N690) and the commander of four types of armies (N691) that are needed to conquer the senses, mind, buddhi and ahaṅkāra. When we ascend through the limitations of the kingdoms represented by the āvaraṇas of the Śrīcakra, she bestows us with the supreme dominion (N692) in the bindu where she remains devoted to the highest truth (N693) without modifications.

Devī is the ground of all, including the turbulent oceans, which she wears as a girdle (N694). She is the support of oceans with their endless arising and subsiding waves. As this support of all, she is the true giver of dīkṣa or initiation (N695, see Dīkṣa in Chapter 12) that destroys our inner demons (N696). As the subjugator of all worlds (N697), she is one that grants all desires (N698). Here, we must remember that dīkṣa and sādhanā don't ensure that all our

* To be clear, this doesn't mean any "one" path—any path that dissolves our limitations is the path to liberation.

Devī's Esoteric Forms

N699 **sāvitrī** creator of the universe

N700 **saccidānanda rūpiṇī** of the nature of existence, consciousness, and bliss

N701 **deśakālā paricchinnā** unlimited by time and space

N702 **sarvagā** omnipresent

N703 **sarvamohinī** deluder of all

N704 **sarasvatī** embodiment of knowledge

N705 **śāstramayī** form of scriptures

N706 **guhāmbā** dweller of the cave of the heart

N707 **guhyarūpiṇī** of secret form

N708 **sarvopādhi vinirmuktā** free of limitations

N709 **sadāśiva pativratā** exclusively devoted to Śiva

N710 **sampradāyeśvarī** guardian of sacred traditions

N711 **sādhu** inherent quality of doing well

N712 **Kāmakalā** ecstatic union of Śiva-Śakti

N713 **gurumaṇḍala rūpiṇī** form of guru lineages

petty or self-serving desires are fulfilled. Instead, they purify our desires so that they become aligned with Devī's icchā (see Transmutation of Desire in Chapter 12).

Devī is the creator of the universe (N699), whose nature is Existence, Consciousness, and Bliss (N700). Not limited by time and space (N701), she is omnipresent (N702). She is both the deluder (N703) and the embodiment of knowledge (N704) as scripture (N705).

Dwelling in the cave of the heart (N706, *see N609*) in a secret form (N707) that is free of all limitations (N708), she is devoted only to Śiva (N709). Unmodified by Māyā, she is the guardian of sacred traditions (N710). This devotion to Śiva is her inherent quality (N711) that manifests as the Śakti praṇava, Īm, in her form as Kāmakalā (*see p.78 and figure 24).* As this praṇava, she is established in the lineage of gurus in every tradition (N713).

Bhāvanā on Space

- Begin with the Śrīṃ meditation.
- Notice the inner spaciousness for a few moments.
- Now, silently enunciate the mantra Śrīṃ once.
- Allow it to fill this inner space.
- Let it subside.
- When the last vibrations of the mantra come to rest, notice the inner spaciousness.
- Repeat the mantra while now turning your attention to the *space* in which the sound arises.
- Notice the feeling of space compared to the sound of the mantra that arises in it.

  Does the space feel constricting or freeing?
- Now think of a label or role that is part of your "me story".

  Such as good parent, hard-working employee or proud American.
- Allow the image or thought to arise fully.

  Does this thought or image feel constricting or freeing?
- Shift your attention from the image or thought to the space in which it arises.

  Does the space feel constricting or freeing?
- Go back and forth between the image and the space, focusing on the feeling each evokes.

  The image or thought of being someone is accompanied by a sense of constriction, whereas shifting your attention to the space in which it arises evokes expansiveness.
- Notice that the image or identity comes and goes, but the space in which it arises is always present.

  Clearly, you are not the image that comes and goes because you are still here when the it goes!
- Who are you then?

- **Open-Eyed Practice**

  Practice shifting your attention to the space in which your thoughts, emotions, sensations, memories and anxieties arise. Notice what comes and goes and what remains. Who are you? The stuff that comes and goes or that which remains?

Section 16

DEVĪ AS TRANSFORMATION

Devī As Transformation

N714 **kulottīrṇā** transcending kula

N715 **bhagārādhyā** worshiped in the sun

N716 **māyā** Māyā

N717 **madhumatī** sweet as honey

N718 **mahī** great form

N719 **gaṇāmbā** mother of gaṇas

N720 **guhyakārādhyā** worshiped in secret

N721 **komalāṅgī** tender-limbed

N722 **gurupriyā** beloved of gurus

N723 **svatantrā** absolutely free

N724 **sarvatantreśī** embodiment of all tantras

Having seen Devī's many esoteric forms and her presence in the cave of the heart, we will now see her force of transformation as Kuṇḍalinī. She pierces through our limitations and transforms the various groupings known as kulas, although she herself transcends them (N714, *see N90-96*, and Deities of the Śrīcakra in Chapter 10). As we have seen earlier, kulas refer not only to the groupings of the tattvas and various categories of the macrocosm, but also to our ways of thinking and being that are determined by the specific ways in which prāṇa flows in our nāḍīs. All kulas are nourished by the life-giving sun, which is symbolic of prakāśa. Devī as Prāṇakuṇḍalinī is the very source of the sun and is worshiped in its disc (N715, *see N275-277* and Kuṇḍalinī in Chapter 7).

In other words, she is the very source of the kula that entraps us in Māyā (N716), which is also her! Yet, we don't realize her omnipresence because as Māyā, she is alluring and sweet as honey (N717). Our limited stories are juicy and hold our attention, even when they lead to misery and pain—in fact, the whole world of our limitations is her great form (N718) and she is the creator of the hosts of gaṇas or influences that keep us bound to saṃsāra (N719, *see N77*).

Devī is Kuṇḍalinī that binds *and* liberates, and is worshiped in secret (N720) at the mūlādhāra. She is tender-limbed (N721) as she ascents in the suṣumnā to dissolve the binding kulas in the granthis (see Granthis in Chapter 7). As this liberating power, she is the beloved of gurus (N722). Absolutely free from all limitations (N723) she is the embodiment of all the tantras (N724) and takes the form of Dakṣiṇāmūrti (N725).* Revered by the

* Dakṣiṇāmūrti is a form of Śiva. Śiva returns to the Himālaya after Sati's self-immolation (see Chapter 1), sits facing south and becomes absorbed in meditation. He is approached by the four sons of Brahmā for Self-knowledge, and in the process of teaching them in complete silence, he becomes the first guru of yoga. Dakṣiṇāmūrti also refers to the formless, silent Reality that is the real guru.

Devī As Transformation

N725 **dakṣiṇāmūrti rūpiṇī** embodiment of Dakṣiṇāmūrti

N726 **sanakādi samārādhyā** revered by Sanaka and others

N727 **śivajñāna pradāyinī** bestower of knowledge of Śiva

N728 **citkalā** consciousness limited as jīva

N729 **ānandakalikā** bud of bliss

N730 **premarūpā** form of love

N731 **priyaṅkarī** cause of love

N732 **nāmapārāyaṇa prītā** delights in the chanting of nāmas

N733 **nandividyā** knowledge of Nandi

N734 **naṭeśvarī** wife of Natarāja

N735 **mithyā jagadadhiṣṭhānā** source of the illusory universe

four sons of Brahma (Sanaka, Sana, Sanatkumāra, and Sanandana) (N726) she is the bestower of liberation as the knowledge of Śiva (N727).

Devī is the consciousness of Brahman that becomes limited as the jīva (N728), where she resides as a bud of bliss in the ānandamaya kośa (N729, see kośas in Chapter 6). Here, she is the very form of unconditional love (N730) and its root cause (N731).

Devī delights in listening to the chanting of her nāmas (N732)—while we may think that this nāma refers specifically to the LSN, it is much grander in its scope. As we have seen earlier (see Sections 10 and 15 and Chapter 8), Devī takes the form of language at every level. Another way to look at this is to consider the unique vibrational frequencies that make up the countless objects of the universe. We know a flower to be different from a stone because they vibrate at their own unique frequencies. Every object is speaking a unique language as its own unique frequency. Our very beings are made up of the frequency of language, as is every thought and deed. Each frequency is a nāma of Devī. Even when we know nothing about Devī or the LSN, we are constantly chanting her nāmas because she is everything that exists. She delights in the chanting of her countless nāmas because it fulfils her purpose of manifestation—to experience herself in and as every form.

Devī is the embodiment of the Nandi* mantra (N733),** and as the wife of Naṭarāja, the cosmic dancer (N734), she is the source of the illusory universe (N735). Here, we realize that the author of the LSN is differentiating Tantra from other paths, which proclaim that Brahman alone is real and creation is illusory. The argument here is that if Brahman and creation are different, then there is an irresolvable duality. Instead of the One becoming many, the One and the many remain separate. The Tāntrik view is that Reality (or Brahman) *becomes* the world. The

* Nandi—the bull who is the guardian of the sacred Mount Kailasa and the steed of Śiva.

** Also refers to a variation of the Pañcadaśi mantra.

Devī As Transformation

N736 **muktidā** bestower of liberation

N737 **muktirūpiṇī** embodiment of liberation

N738 **lāsyapriyā** fond of the dance form known as lāsya

N739 **layakarī** causing absorption

N740 **lajjā** modesty

N741 **rambhādi vanditā** adored by Rambhā and others

N742 **bhavadāva sudhāvṛṣṭiḥ** nectar extinguishing the fire of saṃsāra

Devī As Transformation

N743 **pāpāraṇya davānalā** burning the forest of sin (of ignorance)

N744 **daurbhāgyatūla vātūlā** undoing the knot of misfortune

N745 **jarādhvānta raviprabhā** ray of light dispelling darkness and decay

N746 **bhāgyābdhicandrikā** bringing about good fortune

illusion or Māyā is merely the inability to recognize Reality in creation—they *appear* to be separate. Liberation is the knowledge of non-separation between them—Devī is not only the bestower of liberation (N736); she *is* liberation (N737).

While Naṭarāja's dance is the powerful cosmic cycle of creation and destruction, Devī is particularly fond of the deliberate dance of Māyā known as lāsya (N738) that results in the absorption (N739) of the Divine in creation. This is also the dance of prāṇa undulating in the īḍa and piṇgala, where we are entrapped in duality. In contrast to this undulating snake-like movement, she becomes straight and staff-like as Kuṇḍalinī when she enters the suṣumnā.

Despite her immeasurable splendor, she remains shy (N740), hidden in creation under the veil of Māyā. When invoked by Hrīṃ and the other bījas of the Pañcadaśi (N741),* she becomes the nectar that soothes the fire of worldly existence brought about by Māyā (N742) (*see N61*).

The Pañcadaśi invokes her grace as the ascent of Kuṇḍalinī, which burns through the forest of ignorance like a wildfire (N743). Like a gust of wind that blows away wisps of cotton, Kuṇḍalinī unties the tight balls of karma (N744) in the granthis that keep us trapped in Māyā (see Granthis in Chapter 7). Like the sunlight that dispels darkness, she dispels the decay (N745) that occurs when we are stuck in linear time (*see N612*). Like the full moon that soothes and rejuvenates, she brings about great good fortune (N746) in her ascent. If our heart is like a peacock, she is the dark cloud that makes it dance with joy (N747). Like a thunderbolt that can shake a mountain loose, she shatters the mountain of disease

* Rambhā also refers to one of the celestial dancers in Indra's court, who are known for their beauty and mastery of arts such as music and dance.

Devī As Transformation

N747 **bhaktacittakeki ghanāghanā** rousing joy in the devotee's heart, like clouds that incite a peacock's dance

N748 **rogaparvata dambholī** shattering the mountain of disease

N749 **mṛtyudāru kuṭhārikā** cutting down the tree of death

(N748) that is ignorance of our true nature. Like an axe, she cuts down the tree that is death (N749).

Bhāvanā on Entrapment and Freedom

- Begin with the Śrīṃ meditation.
- Contemplate the stories you tell about yourself.

  How do you resolve the feelings of not being good enough?

  Remember that this is pervasive and fundamental

  Even feelings of superiority over others comes from the ānava mala.
- Think about a situation where you reacted in your "usual" way—be it withdrawal, anxiety, irritation, or annoyance.
- Return to the situation as vividly as possible, taking the time to notice your "usual" reaction as it arises.
- *This is the movement of limitation.*
- Pause and breathe in a relaxed way.
- Deliberately find another way to respond that is the opposite of your "usual" way.

  Notice the freedom in your ability to choose!

- **Open-eyed Practice**

  Practice this in real-life situations, pausing before responding and searching your internal landscape for another way.

  Avoid placing blame on parents, caregivers, peers, politics, and others for your behaviour.

  They are as much under Bhaṇḍāsura's influence as you are!

  Stay entirely in your own sphere of thinking, feeling, and behaving

Section 17

DEVĪ'S GREAT FORMS

Devī's Great Forms

N750 **maheśvarī** supreme ruler

N751 **mahākālī** great Kālī

N752 **mahāgrāsā** great devourer

N753 **mahāśanā** great eater

N754 **aparṇā** annihilating ṛṇa

N755 **caṇḍikā** wrathful

N756 **caṇḍamuṇḍāsura niṣūdinī** destroyer of Caṇḍa and Muṇḍa

N757 **kṣarākṣarātmikā** being perishable and imperishable

Now that we have been graced by Devī as Kuṇḍalinī, the force of transformation, we have the eyes to see her great forms. As the supreme goddess (N750), she is the great Kālī (N751) who, as time, devours creation (N752).* Let's revisit karma, which is based in linear time and where events are linked in a cause-and-effect model. In our self-centered dealings, we knowingly or unknowingly create karmic debt, which is known as ṛṇa (not to be confused with RNA—ribonucleic acid). For example, in any given relationship, we operate in circles of give and take, each leaving behind vāsanās. These vāsanās carry the relationship forward in harmony or discord. The debt we owe in karmic relationships is ṛṇa as the impressions of past interactions that have not been fully processed. These impressions are not processed because we operate from the sense of separation that is the product of the three malas (see Kañcukas and Malas in Chapter 4). Not only are these transactions unprocessed but they become more vāsanās that add to the sense of separation. We simply can't forgive or forget.

As the great one that devours (N753) time and space, Devī annihilates karmic debt or ṛṇa (N754) that keeps us limited in time and space. In her great wrath (N755), she destroys Caṇḍa, Muṇḍa (N756),** and the other asuras that are the limitations that keep us entrapped in ṛṇa. When we contemplate mythological stories of Devī destroying asuras, we must remember that she is the many *and* the One. Just as language in the form of syllables (kṣara) and the alphabet (akṣara) (N757) arises from the same Source (parāvāk, *see N366* and Chapter 8), all beings including the asuras are emanations of Devī.*** In

* See Kali in *Shakti Rising*, starting at page 27.

** In the Devī Mahātmyam, Kālī arises from Devī's body during the war with Śumbha and Niśumbha and beheads Caṇḍa and Muṇḍa, two of the asura generals, and is conferred with the name Cāmuṇḍā.

*** In the same episode of the Devī Mahātmyam, the Mātṛkās army destroys all the asura leaders and Śumbha alone remains. He challenges her to face him alone instead of depending on her śaktis. She absorbs them and says, "I

Devī's Great Forms

N758 **sarvalokeśī** supreme ruler of the worlds

N759 **viśvadhāriṇī** supporter of the universe

N760 **trivargadātrī** granting the three goals of life

N761 **subhagā** good fortune

N762 **tryambakā** three-eyed

N763 **triguṇātmikā** source of the three guṇas

N764 **svargāpavargadā** bestower of heaven and liberation

N765 **śuddhā** unconditioned

N766 **ajapāpuṣpa nibhākṛtiḥ** body blooming as the universe from ajapa

N767 **ojovatī** of ojas

N768 **dyutidharā** brilliance

N769 **yajñarūpā** form of yajña

being everything everywhere, she is the supreme ruler of all worlds and planes (N758), supporting them all (N759).

Although we can intellectually understand that Devī transcends time and space, the only way for us to actually experience this seemingly magical truth is through the unclouding of the buddhi. Clarity of the buddhi reveals the nature of the trikoṇa that is the fundamental basis of separation. Even though this is the path of mokṣa, we are granted the other three Puruṣārthas as well (N760, see Puruṣārthas in Chapter 7). We must pause here to understand that attainment of dharma, artha and kāma don't occur via the fulfilment of our self-serving, saṃskāra-driven desires. On the contrary, they are attained as a result of aligning with Devī's icchā by walking the path of mokṣa.

Devī, who is the seat of prosperity (N761), has for her three eyes (N762) the sun, moon, and fire. As the source of the three guṇas (N763), she is the bestower of heaven and liberation (N764). Heaven and hell are dominions created by our own karmas driven by rāga and dveṣa, or attractions and aversions (*see N686*). In fact, the cycles of saṃsāra can be viewed as the constant commute between the two dominions, where heaven and hell are the states of joy and pain. Apavarga is liberation, which is freedom from cycles of saṃsāra. The result of this freedom is svarga, which is the state of contentment or ānanda. As the one that grants heaven and liberation, Devi is the unconditioned (N765) Reality prior to thought or mantra (ajapa), from whom the universe blossoms (N766) like a flower. She is the ojas or vitality of creation (N767), manifesting as the perpetual juiciness of śṛṅgāra in every tattva.* As this ojas, she is the brilliance (N768) in creation who takes the form of yajña, the fire sacrifice (N769, *see N535-536*). At this yajña, Devī worships herself constantly, delighting in the countless ways in which

am all that exists. What exists other than me?"

* Ojas is the subtle end product of digestion in Ayurveda responsible for longevity, immunity, and contentment. It is the "bliss molecule" of wellness and vitality.

Devī's Great Forms

N770 **priyavratā** fond of vows

N771 **durārādhyā** difficult to worship

N772 **durādharṣā** impossible to subjugate

N773 **pāṭalī kusumapriyā** fond of the Pāṭalī flowers

N774 **mahatī** great

N775 **merunilayā** residing on Mount Meru

N776 **mandāra kusumapriyā** fond of Mandāra flowers

she can experience herself. It is as if she pours herself into the fire, emerging as the world in every moment. She is the sacrifice, the one who performs the sacrifice, the procedure of the sacrifice, as well as its end result.

Being the only one (*see N665*) that exists, Devī is fond of the rigor (N770) of sādhanā directed toward any deity and any path. She is extremely difficult to understand or worship (N771) as the nondual Reality, and certainly cannot be controlled, subdued or attacked (N772). She can only be approached in worship, which is the expression of śṛṅgāra and the desire for union with her. Devī is particularly fond of worship with the red trumpet-like flower known as pāṭalī (N773).

She is the great mahat (N774), the first principle of Puruṣa and Prakṛti that differentiates into the tattvas of manifestation (see Tattva Map in Chapter 4). As this great principle, she resides on Mount

Devī's Great Forms

N777 **vīrārādhyā** worshiped by vīras

N778 **virāḍrūpā** form of the cosmos

N779 **virajā** without passion

N780 **viśvatomukhī** facing every way

N781 **pratyagrūpā** interior

N782 **parākāśā** supreme ether

N783 **prāṇadā** source of prāṇa

N784 **prāṇarūpiṇī** prāṇa

N785 **mārtāṇḍa bhairavārādhyā** worshiped by Mārtāṇḍa Bhairava

N786 **mantriṇī nyastarājyadhūḥ** entrusting dominion to Mantriṇī

N787 **tripureśī** Tripureśī

N788 **jayatsenā** ever-victorious army

N789 **nistraiguṇyā** devoid of the guṇas

N790 **parāparā** subject and object, the process of knowing

Meru (N775) where she is worshiped with mandāra* flowers that she loves (N776).

Devī is worshiped by vīras (N777) as the form of the cosmos (N778) that exists without the agitation of passion (N779). She is omniscient, as if facing every way (N780). She is the indwelling Self of all (N781) as well as the transcendent space (N782) in which the world arises. She is the source of prāṇa (N783)

* Indian coral.

and the prāṇa itself (N784), and is worshiped by the vīra who merges with Śiva to become Mārtāṇḍa Bhairava (N785).*

When we dive deep into the Source through mantra sādhanā. (see Mantra Sādhanā in Chapter 12), we encounter Mantriṇī or Mātaṅgī (*see N69*), to whom Devī entrusts the responsibilities of the various dominions (N786). As the power of language, Mantriṇī rules over all the dominions in manifestation (*see N678-680*). As the power of the mantra, Mantriṇī helps us win the grace of Tripureśī (N787) in the āvaraṇa of the Śrīcakra known as Sarvāśāparipūraka (see Deities of the Śrīcakra in Chapter 10) of the sixteen attractions.** Mantriṇī enables us to march through the other āvaraṇas accompanied by Devī's ever-victorious army (N788) to finally become free of the conditioning of the three guṇas (N789) at the bindu.

At the trikoṇa, we can now see that Devī is both Parā, the subject, Aparā, the object (N790), as well as the relationship between the subject and object, Parāparā. To arrive at this stage of sādhanā is an immense gift of grace. Previously, we had divided the world (and ourselves) into the good and bad, the desirable and undesirable, the beautiful and the ugly. Now, we see that Devī is everything!

---

* Mārtāṇḍa Bhairava is one of 64 forms of Bhairava (Śiva).

** Buddhi, kāma, ahaṅkāra, sense perceptions, cittā, courage, memory, language, seed (procreation), ātma, amṛta or nectar, and the body.

Bhāvanā on Prāṇa

- Begin with the Śrīṃ meditation.
- Over the course of several breaths, notice the five prāṇa vāyus.

  Allow the breath to be natural, without changing its depth or duration.

  To become aware of prāṇa and apāna simply notice the direction of the breath as you inhale and exhale. With inhalation, there is a subtle upward movement from the belly to above the crown, which reverses with exhalation.

  Samāna is where they "meet" in the belly.

  Vyāna is a subtle, non-localized, diffuse movement at the end of inhalation and exhalation.

  To become aware of udāna, hum softly to feel the vibration in your throat.
- Once you're comfortable with this practice, delve deeper.

  Observe the impulse to breathe before the breath begins.

  It is also the subtle vibratory movement prior to thought or speech.
- Become curious about the "thing" that makes the breath, heartbeat, and mind arise.
- Subtle and non-localized, this is prāṇa.

- **Open-eyed Practice**

  Dip into the tiny gaps between thoughts and breaths to discover the Source of prāṇa. Notice that it is the Source of you – your body, mind, story, hopes and aspirations, and pain and disappointment. Notice them arising from, and subsiding into, the great void of the Source.

Section 18

DEVĪ AS TRANSCENDENCE AND IMMANENCE

Thus far, we have seen Devī in her transcendent and immanent forms separately. In this segment, we encounter a description of Devī simultaneously in both her transcendent and immanent forms. Even when concealed in Māyā, she is truth, knowledge and bliss (N791) at every level of manifestation and is immersed in the rasa of oneness (N792) with Kaparda (N793).*

In her immanent form, we see Devī wearing the garland of the sixty-four forms of art (N794) and granting all our wishes like Kāmadhenu (N795). However, when we tear our attention away from the objects of our desire, we see Devī as the very essence of longing (N796), the sciences (N797), and poetry (N798). She is the experiencer of rasa (N799) in every experience as well as the rasa (N800) that nourishes (N801) experience. She is the ancient (N802) Source of nourishment (N804) for the universe that emits from her lotus eyes (N805).

As the transcendent principle, she is the Supreme light (N806) of the stateless state that resides in the bindu, the abode (N807) that is beyond perception. She is the subtlest of the subtle (N808) and the

* Śiva with matted hair.

Devī As Transcendence And Immanence

N791 **satyajñānānandarūpā** truth, knowledge, and bliss

N792 **sāmarasya parāyaṇā** rasa of oneness

N793 **kapardinī** wife of Kaparda

N794 **kalāmālā** garland of arts

N795 **kāmadhuk** Kāmadhenu

N796 **kāmarūpiṇī** essence of desire

N797 **kalānidhiḥ** reservoir of sciences

N798 **kāvyakalā** poetry

N799 **rasajñā** knower of rasa

N800 **rasaśevadhiḥ** reservoir of rasa

N801 **puṣṭā** nourished

N802 **purātanā** ancient

N803 **pūjyā** revered

N804 **puṣkarā** nourishment

N805 **puṣkarekṣaṇā** lotus-eyed

N806 **parañjyotiḥ** supreme light

N807 **parandhāmā** supreme abode

N808 **paramāṇuḥ** subtlest

N809 **parātparā** most supreme

N810 **pāśahastā** bearing the noose

N811 **pāśahantrī** destroyer of the noose

Devī As Transcendence And Immanence

N812 **paramantra vibhedinī** destroyer of the illusion of language

N813 **mūrtā** form

N814 **amūrtā** formless

N815 **anityatṛptā** perishable

N816 **muni mānasa haṃsikā** swan of discernment in the minds of the wise

N817 **satyavratā** abiding in truth

N818 **satyarūpā** truth

N819 **sarvāntaryāminī** indweller of all

N820 **Satī** Sati

N821 **brahmāṇī** śakti of Brahman

N822 **brahma** Brahman

N823 **jananī** mother

N824 **bahurūpā** of many forms

N825 **budhārcitā** worshiped by the wise

N826 **prasavitrī** creator

N827 **pracaṇḍā** fierce

N828 **ājñā** commander

N829 **pratiṣṭhā** foundation

N830 **prakaṭākṛtiḥ** manifested

N831 **prāṇeśvarī** ruler of prāṇa

N832 **prāṇadātrī** nourisher of prāṇa

Supreme among the supreme (N809). She is the bearer of the noose (N810) that entraps us in Māyā, as well as its destroyer (N811). She breaks the spell of the mantras (language) that keep us bound in ignorance (N812). While it previously seemed like our suffering was caused by others' words and deeds (para mantra), we now come to see through the illusion of the other.

From our vantage point in the bindu, we now see that Devī is both form (N813) and formless (N814), immanent and transcendent. Although she is also the perishable (N815), she is the swan of discernment in the minds of the wise (N816) that firmly abide in eternal truth (N817). In fact, the discerning sādhaka knows her as the highest truth (N818) that is the indweller of all (N819) as Sati (N820), the eternal being. She is both the śakti of Brahman (N821) *and* Brahman (N822), and the mother of the universe (N823) who becomes its many forms (N824).

Worshiped by the wise (N825) as the creator (N826), Devī is the fierce (N827) commander (N828) that brings order to the universe. Being the foundation (N829) of manifestation (N830), she rules over prāṇa and the senses (N831, *see N783-784* and Chapter 6) and nourishes them (N832) with her own essence.

For a sādhaka, one of the most significant leaps in sādhanā is to realize the power of language (see Language in Sādhanā in Chapter 8) in determining how we see the world and ourselves. This realization changes the relationship with the mantra and Devī,

Devī As Transcendence And Immanence

N833 **pañcāśat-pīṭharūpiṇī** fifty seats

N834 **viśṛṅkhalā** unfettered

N835 **viviktasthā** abiding in seclusion

N836 **vīramātā** mother of vīras

N837 **viyatprasūḥ** mother of space

N838 **mukundā** bestower of salvation

N839 **mukti nilayā** abode of liberation

N840 **mūlavigraha rūpiṇī** body being the root

N841 **bhāvajñā** knower of thought

N842 **bhavarogaghnī** destroyer of saṃsāra

N843 **bhavacakra pravartinī** turning the wheel of earthly existence

with an immense release of pent up energy that was previously caught up in word-object association. In her immanent form, Devī is then seen to reside in the subtle body in the fifty pīṭhas of the cakra petals as the Sanskrit alphabet (N833, see Mātṛkā and Mālinī in Chapter 8). In seeing the relationship between language and experience, we come to see Devī in her transcendence being entirely unfettered (N834), and abiding in the secluded plane (N835) of absolute freedom.

The vīras recognize her as their mother (N836) who is also the Source of space (N837) in which the universe arises. As transcendence, she is the bestower of liberation (N838), residing in the bindu that is the abode of liberation (N839). As immanence, her body is the root of form (N840), and as transcendence, she is knower of thought (N841). She is the eradicator of saṃsāra (N842) as transcendence, and its maintainer (N843) as immanence.

Bhāvanā on Offering the Perishable

- Begin with the Śrīṃ meditation.
- Visualize Devī in front of you – see Bhāvanā in Section 1.

  You have invoked her in a great fire ritual, and now she demands sacrifice of perishables.
- Contemplate the perishables that make up your identity.

  Everything that fades, disintegrates, collapses or is forgotten is a perishable.

  Are you willing to pour the perishables into the fire?
- Start with the most obvious—your body.

  Sooner or later, this body will perish and will be absorbed back into the five elements. How about your history that will eventually be lost and forgotten, or your ideas you have about yourself? Ideas and impressions will die too. Can you throw them all in the fire?
- How about your inner vision of Devī?

  Isn't that perishable? Can you pour it into the fire?
- Keep pouring all perishables into the great fire

  Until there is no trace of them.
- What remains?

  You've sacrificed your ability to behold Devī in front of you (because that is perishable).

  What is her true essence?

  What is <u>your</u> true essence?

- **Open-eyed Practice**

  Make it a habit to throw perishables into the fire ritual that invokes Devī. In every situation, ask yourself, "What is perishable here?" and discard into the fire with a mental "Svāhā!"

Section 19

DEVĪ'S OMNIPRESENCE

Since Devī is both transcendent and immanent, she is omnipresent, the aspect we'll explore in this section. She is the essence of meter (chandas) and of the Vedas (N844),* scriptures and texts (N845) and of all mantras (N846). However, she remains subtle and hidden like her slim waist (N847) in all of creation.** As the content of all scriptures, she is of exalted fame (N848) and glory (N849) in her form as the letters of the alphabet (N850).

Devī bestows peace as a respite from the constant cycles of birth and death (N851, *see N764 and N843*, and Karma in Chapter 4) and is celebrated in all the Upaniṣads (N852) as the Reality that transcends peace (N853). She is unfathomable (N854) as space (N855), and becomes the proud (N856) embodiment of Reality.

She delights in the music (N857) of creation with its drama, while herself remaining free of vikalpa or imagination (N858). She is the highest goal (N859) that puts an end to the sin (N860) of ignorance. In the form of one-half of Śiva*** (N861, see Chapter 4) and free from the bonds of cause-and-effect (N862),

* See N289, N338, N339, N538.

** All nāmas referring to Devī's waist imply her form as Kuṇḍalinī.

*** Kānta is a form of Śiva.

Devī's Omnipresence

N844 **chandahsārā** essence of meter

N845 **śāstrasārā** essence of scripture

N846 **mantrasārā** essence of mantras

N847 **talodarī** slim-waisted

N848 **udārakīrtiḥ** of exalted fame

N849 **uddāmavaibhavā** glorious

N850 **varṇarūpiṇī** letters of the alphabet

N851 **janmamṛtyu jarātapta jana viśrānti dāyinī** repose for the constant cycles of saṃsāra

N852 **sarvopaniṣad udghuṣṭā** celebrated in all Upaniṣads

N853 **śāntyatīta kalātmikā** transcending peace

N854 **gambhīrā** unfathomable

N855 **gaganāntaḥsthā** residing in ether

N856 **garvitā** proud

N857 **gānalolupā** delighting in music

N858 **kalpanārahitā** free of imaginary attributes

N859 **kāṣṭhā** goal

N860 **akāntā** end of sin

N861 **kāntārdha vigrahā** half body of Śiva

N862 **kāryakāraṇa nirmuktā** free of karma

N863 **kāmakeli taraṅgitā** overflowing with desire and pleasure she overflows with the rasa of pleasure (N863, see Rasa in Chapter 12).

She is transcendent like gold and immanent like the earrings made of gold (N864, *see N31*), she takes on temporary forms for the sake of sport (N865) even though she is herself unborn (N866) and free from decay (N867). Captivatingly beautiful (N868), Devī is easily pleased (N869) with internal worship (N870) and the steady cultivation of bhakti and tarka in every experience. On the other hand, she is difficult to attain when attention is directed outward (N871). With the right approach, Devī is experienced as the revelation in the three Vedas* (N872), the form of the three material goals of life** (N873, see Puruṣārthas in Chapter 7) and the seat of all triads (N874).

She is Tripuramālinī (N875, see Deities of the Śrīcakra), the presiding deity of the āvaraṇa of the Śrīcakra known as Antardaśāra. A sādhaka that traverses this āvaraṇa becomes free of the disease of ignorance (N876) and revels in independence (N877).

Being the only One there is, Devī constantly rejoices in her own self (N878), and in the sweetness of her nectar (N879). She's adept at rescuing us from the depths of saṃsāra (N880), especially pleased when we pour our limitations into the fire of sādhanā (N881, *see N769* and Bhāvanā in Section 18), where we come to see that she is both the sacrificer (N882) as well as the organizer of the sacrifice (N883).

* Ṛg, Yajur, and Sāma.

** Dharma, artha, and kāma.

Devī's Omnipresence

N864 **kanatkanakatāṭaṅkā** wearing shining gold earrings

N865 **līlāvigraha dhāriṇī** having a body merely for sport

N866 **ajā** unborn

N867 **kṣaya vinirmuktā** free from decay

N868 **mugdhā** beautiful

N869 **kṣipraprasādinī** easily pleased

N870 **antarmukha samārādhyā** internally worshiped

N871 **bahirmukha sudurlabhā** difficult to attain when devoted to external objects

N872 **trayī** revelation of three

N873 **trivarga nilayā** three-fold goals

N874 **tristhā** seated in triads

N875 **tripuramālinī** Tripuramālinī

N876 **nirāmayā** free of disease

N877 **nirālambā** independent

N878 **svātmārāmā** rejoicing in self

N879 **sudhāsṛtiḥ** stream of nectar

N880 **saṃsārapaṅka nirmagna samuddharaṇa paṇḍitā** skillfully raising those sinking in saṃsāra

N881 **yajñapriyā** fond of sacrifice

N882 **yajñakartrī** doer of sacrifice

N883 **yajamāna svarūpiṇī** sacrificer

Devī is the support of dharma (N884, see Puruṣārthas in Chapter 7), and as the ruler of wealth (N885), she bestows abundance and harvests (N886). She is fond of the sādhaka who attains liberation (N887) because the vipras (the learned) know themselves as her forms (N888), having realized that it is she who turns the wheel of the universe (N889) and devours it (N890) at the end of time.

Her coral-like reddish hue (N891) is the allure of objects that maintains the illusion of the wheel of the universe (*see N298*, *N558*). In this, she is the śakti (N892) and the embodiment (N893) of Viṣṇu (*see Section 8*). Being herself without origin (N894), she is the origin (N895) of the universe who veils her own nature (N896) in Māyā.

As the beloved deity of the Kaulas (N897, see Chapter 11), Devī delights in the assembly of valorous vīras (N898) because she is the epitome of valor (N899) herself. Devoid of action (N900), she is the transcendent Reality and the primordial vibration (N901)* that is the cause of perception (N902). A vīra is one who recognizes Devī as the skilful (N903), artful (N904) Reality whose seat is in the bindu (N905) of the Śrīcakra.

Devī's Omnipresence

N884 **dharmādhārā** support of dharma

N885 **dhanādhyakṣā** ruler of wealth

N886 **dhanadhānya vivardhinī** bestowing wealth and harvests

N887 **viprapriyā** fond of those with Self-knowledge

N888 **viprarūpā** taking the form of vipras

N889 **viśvabhramaṇa kāriṇī** turning the universe

N890 **viśvagrāsā** devouring the universe

N891 **vidrumābhā** of the color of coral

N892 **vaiṣṇavī śakti** of Viṣṇu

N893 **viṣṇurūpiṇī** Viṣṇu

N894 **ayoniḥ** without origin

N895 **yoninilayā** place of origin

N896 **kūṭasthā** veiling own nature

N897 **kularūpiṇī** kula

N898 **vīragoṣṭhīpriyā** fond of assembly of viras

N899 **vīrā** valorous

N900 **naiṣkarmyā** devoid of action

N901 **nādarūpiṇī** primordial vibraion

N902 **vijñāna kalanā** cause of perception

N903 **kalyā** skilful

N904 **vidagdhā** artful

N905 **baindavāsanā** seated at the bindu

* See Tara in *Shakti Rising*, starting at page 47.

Bhāvanā on Dhana (Wealth)

- Begin with the Śrīṃ meditation.
- Use the following prompts to journal. Allow the answers to come up from the depths of silence that follows the meditation. You can practice this bhāvanā over several days.
- What does wealth mean to you?

  Be very honest with yourself, writing clearly from your own experience and thoughts and not based upon what wealth "should" mean.

  How do you feel about people that have more wealth than you? How do you feel about those that have less? When you have answered these questions, return to the first question. How did you define their wealth?
- If needed, meditate for a few minutes to re-center yourself. Favor the spaciousness that the meditation opens up within you.

  Now contemplate a current situation that requires resources. Perhaps it is something you or your loved ones need or want. What happens in your internal landscape? Do you experience a contraction arising from anxiety or fear about not having enough?
- Return to the sense of spaciousness.

  Contemplate the promise of the LSN that Devī provides. Offer up the contraction to her, trusting her to provide as she sees fit.
- What happens in your internal landscape when you offer up your contraction of not having enough?

  It is somewhat difficult for most of us to trust that Devī will provide, especially when we are in financial difficulties or resource-depleted. However, cultivating this trust is one of the biggest aspects of Devī sādhanā. To cultivate an unshakeable faith is to remain unwavering in challenging times. One important way to cultivate unwavering faith is to see that nothing belongs to us – all material and subtle objects are Devī's. The more we operate from this paradigm, the more we see that she does indeed provide. This is one of the many paradoxes of this path.

- **Open-eyed Practice**

Notice contractions in your inner landscape arising from a sense of lack as you go about your day. They result from feelings of wanting something, not having enough, anxiety about the future, envy when witnessing others who have more, and so on. To the best of your ability, offer up these contractions to Devī. Allow her to provide.

Section 20

DEVĪ'S SUPREMACY IN THE BINDU

Devī's Supremacy In The Bindu

N906 **tattvādhikā** transcending tattvas

N907 **tattvamayī** tattvas

N908 **tattvamartha svarūpiṇī** meaning of That and Thou

N909 **sāmagānapriyā** fond of the Sāmaveda

N910 **saumyā** benign

N911 **sadāśiva kuṭumbinī** wife of Sadāśiva

N912 **savyāpasavya mārgasthā** of the right- and left-handed paths

N913 **sarvāpadvinivāriṇī** remover of misfortune

N914 **svasthā** free

N915 **svabhāvamadhurā** of sweet nature

N916 **dhīrā** wise

N917 **dhīra samarcitā** adored by the wise

N918 **caitanyārghya samārādhyā** consciousness as oblation

N919 **caitanya kusumapriyā** fond of the flower of consciousness

N920 **sadoditā** perpetually sublime

N921 **sadātuṣṭā** ever-content

N922 **taruṇāditya pāṭalā** rosy like the dawn

Having met Devī in her many manifestations representing the many aspects of the Śrīcakra, we will now see her reigning supreme in the bindu where she transcends the tattvas (N906) while simultaneously becoming them (N907). She is the very essence and meaning of the Mahāvākya, "Tat tvam asi!" (N908). Fond of the Sāmaveda (N909), she is the beatific (N910) spouse of Sadāśiva (N911), referring to the third tattva and the first movement toward manifestation (see Tattva Map in Chapter 4).

Devī in the bindu is worshiped in both the left- and right-handed paths (N912), putting to rest the debate of which is superior or better (see Chapter 11). In every path, she eliminates the dangers and misfortunes that a sādhaka encounters (N913) since she is always free (N914) of all such afflictions and abides in her own bliss that is inherently sweet (N915) and welcoming.

In the bindu, Devī is the bestower of the wisdom of nonduality (N916), and is thus adored by the wise (N917), who pour their very consciousness into the bindu as oblation (N918). Devī delights in this flower of consciousness (N919) that is offered up in worship.

Being perfectly balanced in the bindu, she is perpetually sublime (N920), content (N921), and rosy-hued like the sun at dawn (N922). Adored by sādhakas of both the right- and left-handed paths (N923, *see N912*, and Ācāra Prescription in

Devī's Supremacy In The Bindu

N923 **dakṣiṇādakṣinārādhyā** adored by sādhaka of the right- and left-handed paths

N924 **darasmera mukhāmbujā** lotus face beaming with smile

N925 **kaulinī kevalā** worshiped by Kaulas as the pure

N926 **anarghyā kaivalya padadāyinī** conferring priceless liberation

N927 **stotrapriyā** fond of praise

N928 **stutimatī** recipient of praise

N929 **śrutisaṃstuta vaibhavā** celebrated in scriptures

N930 **manasvinī** intelligence

Chapter 11), the beautiful smile of her lotus-like face (N924) is equally available to all. For a Kaula, she is the pure knowledge (N925) that confers the priceless gift of liberation (N926).

Fond of praise (N927), Devī is the true recipient of all praises (N928) in every situation! She is celebrated in all scriptures (N929), being the source of intelligence (N930). Worshiped by those that are free of pettiness and are high-minded (N931), she is the śakti of Maheśa (N932), the supreme ruler. Not only is she is the auspicious (N933) mother of the universe (N934) and its sole support (N935), but is all-seeing (N936), dispassionate (N937), resolute (N938), supremely generous (N939), and delightful

Devī's Supremacy In The Bindu

N931 **māṇavatī** of high mind

N932 **maheśī** wife of Maheśa

N933 **maṅgalākṛtiḥ** good fortune

N934 **viśvamātā** mother of the universe

N935 **jagaddhātrī** support of the world

N936 **viśālākṣī** large-eyed

N937 **virāgiṇī** dispassionate

N938 **pragalbhā** resolute

N939 **paramodārā** supremely generous

N940 **parāmodā** supremely delightful

N941 **manomayī** mind

N942 **vyomakeśī** whose hair is space

N943 **vimānasthā** residing in celestial chariot

N944 **vajriṇī** lightning

N945 **vāmakeśvarī** worshiped by the Vāmācārins

N946 **pañcayajñapriyā** fond of the five sacrifices

(N940). She is the universal mind (N941) and wears space as her hair (N942, *see N351*).

Seated in her celestial chariot, the Śrīcakra (N943, *see N68*), Devī is the lightning-like Source of Brahman (N944) that is worshiped by the Vāmācārins (N945, see Chapter 11). She delights in the five types of sacrifices (N946)

Devī's Supremacy In The Bindu

N947 **pañcapreta mañcādhiśāyinī** reclining on the five-corpse throne

N948 **pañcamī** fifth (wife of Sadāśiva)

N949 **pañcabhūteśī** ruler of the five elements

N950 **pañca saṅkhyopacāriṇī** worshiped by the five objects

N951 **śāśvatī** eternal

N952 **śāśvataiśvaryā** possessing eternal sovereignity

N953 **śarmadā** bestower of happiness

N954 **śambhumohinī** deluding Śiva

N955 **dharā** earth

N956 **dharasutā** daughter of the Himālaya

N957 **dhanyā** auspicious

N958 **dharmiṇī** virtuous

N959 **dharmavardhinī** promoting dharma

we perform in the five sense perceptions. We take in sense objects into the fire of consciousness through the five sense organs, which transforms the objects into perceptions through the tanmātras. In this great fire of consciousness, the elements that make up both the sense objects as well as the sense organs are transformed into perception

Reclining on the five-corpse throne (N947, *see N249-250*), Devī is the spouse of the Sadāśiva, the fifth (N948, *see N911*) who is the great revealer.

Devī's Supremacy In The Bindu

N960 **lokātītā** transcending the worlds

N961 **guṇātītā** transcending the guṇas

N962 **sarvātītā** transcending all

N963 **śamātmikā** tranquil

N964 **bandhūka kusuma prakhyā** resembling the bandhūka flower

N965 **bālā** girl (child-like)

N966 **līlāvinodinī** taking pleasure in sport

As the essence of the five elements (N949), she is worshiped through the five senses (N950, *see N946*). As the eternal (N951) Reality, Devī possesses perpetual sovereignty (N952).

She is the bestower of happiness (N953), having the power to delude even Śiva (N954). As the support of the earth (N955), she is known as the daughter of the Himālaya (N956) who in endowed with auspiciousness (N957) and inherent virtue (N958) that promotes dharma (N959).

As the bindu, Devī transcends all the worlds (N960), the guṇas (N961) and everything (N962) in manifestation as tranquility (N963). She is the personification of śṛṅgāra, appearing as red as the flower known as bandhūka (N964). Delightful in her child-like (N965) innocence, she relishes her sport (N966) of creation.

She is the ever-auspicious (N967) bestower of

contentment (N968) that is decked in auspiciousness (N969). Forever in union with Śiva (N970), she is particularly fond of sādhakas who are similarly united with Śiva (N971) through their abidance in the bindu. In Śrīvidyā, the purpose of practice is to discover the bindu, the shimmering stateless state that underlies all experience. Ordinarily, this experience is discovered most easily in the sexual act. At the moment of orgasm, there is a concentration of energy into a seemingly single point which explodes out with a temporary collapse of "otherness" with the beloved and the three (subject/me-object/beloved-experience/union) become one. In orgasm, there is just *this*, which transcends time and space. For a brief timeless and spaceless moment, we experience the core of our being, the bindu, where the distinction between "me" and "the other" ceases to exist. However, this experience is so temporary and brief that even before we recognize it, the veil of conditioning promptly obscures our perception.

The experience of orgasm is so primally ecstatic that we long for it again, mistaking the ānanda of the bindu for the specific person, the sexual act, or both. The bindu need not be accessed only in sexual contact. It is accessible in *every* experience, throbbing and pulsing immediately prior to the split of the one into three. We just need to slow down enough to "catch" it as it pulses up. Accessing it does not mean that we can have it or harness it or own it or control it. Accessing it means to *become* it. Orgasm in sexual encounter is an act of surrender. Similarly, the practice of accessing the bindu from moment to moment requires effortlessness and surrender, rather than efforting or grasping for it. With this practice, we become the suvasinīs "married" to Śiva that Devī particularly loves!

Devī's Supremacy In The Bindu

N967 **sumaṅgalī** very auspicious

N968 **sukhakarī** giving happiness

N969 **suveṣāḍhyā** decked in auspiciousness

N970 **suvāsinī** ever the wife of Śiva

N971 **suvāsinyarcanaprītā** delighting in adoration by suvāsinīs

N972 **āśobhanā** ever beautiful

N973 **śuddha mānasā** pure minded

N974 **bindu tarpaṇa santuṣṭā** pleased by oblations to the bindu

N975 **pūrvajā** first-born

N976 **tripurāmbikā** Tripurāmbikā

N977 **daśamudrā samārādhyā** worshiped by the ten mudrās

N978 **tripurā śrīvaśaṅkarī** ruler of Tripurā

N979 **jñānamudrā** mudrā of knowledge

N980 **jñānagamyā** attained by knowledge

N981 **jñānajñeya svarūpiṇī** knowledge and knowing

Ever-radiant (N972) and pure of conditioning

Devī's Supremacy In The Bindu

N982 **yonimudrā** yonimudrā

N983 **trikhaṇḍeśī** ruler of Trikhaṇḍā

N984 **triguṇā** endowed with the three guṇas

N985 **ambā** mother

N986 **trikoṇagā** residing in the trikoṇa

N987 **anaghā** sinless

N988 **adbhuta cāritrā** of astonishing deeds

N989 **vāñchitārtha pradāyinī** bestowing all desires

N990 **abhyāsātiśayajñātā** known through constant devotion

N991 **ṣaḍadhvātīta rūpiṇī** transcending the six methods

N992 **avyāja karuṇāmūrtiḥ** unconditioned compassion

of the mind (N973), Devī is particularly pleased by oblations to the bindu (N974), the first (N975) emanation of Reality. As this first emanation, she is Tripurāmbikā, the presiding deity of the trikoṇa (N976). While we ordinarily think that this nāma refers to the oblations to the bindu in the Śrīcakra pūjā, the esoteric meaning is that, in every experience, we can oblate the bindu with such exquisite attention that it leads to the collapse of the trikoṇa, so that we know Devī as our own essence.

With this supreme knowledge, we honor Devī with the ten mudrās or hand gestures (N977, see Deities of the Śrīcakra in Chapter 10). With every mudrā, we perceive the unique flow of prāṇa in the internal Śrīcakra and become the master of the fifth āvaraṇa by the grace of Devī as Tripurāśrī (N978). With this, mastery over the prāṇa vāyus, we become worthy of the mudrā of supreme knowledge (N979).

Devī can only be attained by knowledge (N980) through the cultivation of discernment and higher reasoning. She is both the knowledge and the knowing (N981) as the supreme yonimudrā (N982) and is adored in the bindu by the trikhaṇḍā mudrā that transcends and pervades all the āvaraṇas of the Śrīcakra (N983).

Although Devī transcends the guṇas (*see N961*), she is endowed with them in the bindu (N984) where they remain in perfect balance. Manifestation of the material world begins when the three guṇas go out of balance, emanating out of Devī's womb. She is the great mother (N985), who, unlike mortal mothers not only gives birth to but also *becomes* the universe.

Residing in the primordial triad (N986), Devī is sinless (N987) and her emanation is an astonishing feat (N988). She fulfills all our desires (N989) but is intimately known only through arduous sādhanā and constant devotion (N990), when she reveals herself as the very Source of desire.

Devī sādhanā can involve any of the six methods, since Devī transcends them all (N991). She is the very form of unconditioned compassion (N992), which is like the lamp that dispels the darkness of

Devī's Supremacy In The Bindu

N993 **ajñānadhvānta dīpikā** lamp that dispels the darkness of ignorance

N994 **ābālagopa viditā** accessible to children and cowherds

N995 **sarvānullaṅghya śāsanā** whose commands are never disobeyed

N996 **śrī cakrarājanilayā** residing in the king of cakras, the Śrīcakra

N997 **śrīmat tripurasundarī** the auspicious Tripurasundarī

N998 **śrī śivā** auspicious Śiva

N999 **śivaśaktyaikya rūpiṇī** union of Śiva-Śakti

N1000 **Lalitāmbikā** Mother Lalitā

ignorance (N993). Devī is impartial and everyone is equally welcome into her loving embrace. She is easily accessible to all, including children and those who may not be literate in the complex philosophy of the path, such as cowherds (N994). Here, we recall that this was Agastya's original intent—to discover a method to salvation that is easy for anyone!

As the commander whose wishes are never disobeyed (N995), Devī's will drives the universe as well as the lives of each of us. She works through us in our thought and deed, residing in the king of cakras, the Śrīcakra (N996).

Devī is the supreme beauty of the triads of creation (N997), which she pervades as the auspicious Śivā (N998), and the auspicious union of Śiva-Śakti (N999). As this Supreme auspiciousness, she is known as the great mother Lalitā (N1000).

Bhāvanā on Śṛṅgāra

- Begin with the Śrīṃ meditation.
- Place an object in front of you, such as a flower or a rock.
- Close your eyes.
- Open your eyes and look at the object.

  There is a tiny gap between the sense of seeing and the object being recognized. There is another tiny gap between the object being recognized and being labeled as a flower or rock.
- This gap is the bindu.

  If we notice very carefully, at the first contact with the object, there is an ecstatic thrill of recognition, but it is not of us recognizing the object as a flower or a rock. It is the simple recognition of seeing, and of being, where "I" and the object become one at the point of contact. We don't see this because it is fleeting and is immediately followed by labeling or storytelling about the object.

  This ecstatic contact is the union of Śiva and Śakti.
- If this union can be accessed, there is a sweetness that is felt immediately that is orgasmic and uplifting, and includes the whole universe in it.

  We are in love, but not with anything or anyone in particular.

  This non-localized, welcoming, blissful love is śṛṅgāra.
- The bindu can be discovered in the gap between thoughts, the tiny gap between thought and reflex, and that between memory and emotion. With slowing down, cultivation of discernment and equanimity, and the right view, this practice becomes a moment-to-moment living of life from the vantage of orgasmic bliss. When we surrender into the bindu, the pulse of ecstatic bliss colors our perception, even when outer circumstances are challenging. The very act of perception becomes ecstatic, in the pulse of the bindu; the circumstance becomes secondary.

- **In this practice, the Śrīcakra becomes a lived experience.**

Part III

The Lalitā Sahasranāma

N1 **Śrīmātā** Auspicious Mother

N2 **Śrīmahārājñī** Auspicious Ruler

N3 **Śrīmatsiṃhāsaneśvarī** Ruler of the auspicious lion-throne

N4 **cidagni kuṇḍasambhūtā** born in the fire-pit of consciousness

N5 **devakāryasamudyatā** facilitator of the devas' work

N6 **udyadbhānu sahasrābhā** brilliant as thousands of rising suns

N7 **caturbāhu samanvitā** four-armed

N8 **rāgasvarūpa pāśāḍhyā** bearing the noose of desire

N9 **krodhakārāṅkuśojjvalā** bearing the goad of wrath

N10 **manorūpekṣukodaṇḍā** bearing the mind bow

N11 **pañcatanmātra sāyakā** bearing the tanmātras as arrows

N12 **nijāruṇa prabhāpūra majjad-brahmāṇḍamaṇḍalā** bathing the universe with her rosy effulgence

N13 **campakāśoka punnāga saugandhika lasatkacā** flowers adorning her hair

N14 **kuruvinda maṇiśreṇī kanatkoṭīra maṇḍitā** crown adorned with rows of Kuruvinda

N15 **aṣṭamī candra vibhrāja daḷikasthala śobhitā** forehead shining like the crescent moon of the eighth night of the lunar half-month

N16 **mukhacandra kaḷaṅkābha mṛganābhi viśeṣakā** wearing a musk mark on her forehead which shines like the spot in the moon

N17 **vadanasmara māṅgalya gṛhatoraṇa cillikā** eyebrow-arch leading to Kāma's palace

N18 **vaktralakṣmī parīvāha calanmīnābha locanā** eyes like fish moving in calm waters

N19 **navacampaka puṣpābha nāsādaṇḍa virājitā** nose like a newly blossoming campaka flower

N20 **tārākānti tiraskāri nāsābharaṇa bhāsurā** nose-stud of the stars' brilliance

N21 **kadamba mañjarīklupta karṇapūra manoharā** wearing bunches of Kadambas over the ears

N22 **tāṭaṅka yugalībhūta tapanoḍupa maṇḍalā** wearing the sun and moon as earrings

N23 **padmarāga śilādarśa paribhāvi kapolabhūḥ** cheeks surpassing the brilliance of pagmarāga

N24 **navavidruma bimbaśrīḥ nyakkāri radanacchadā** lips the color of coral and bimba

N25 **śuddha vidyāṅkurākāra dvijapaṅkti dvayojjvalā** twin rows of teeth of pure knowledge

N26 **karpūravīṭi kāmoda samākarṣa digantarā** universe-attracting fragrant camphor-laden betel roll

N27 **nijasallāpa mādhurya vinirbhartsita kacchapī** speech excelling Sarasvatī's vīṇa

N28 **mandasmita prabhāpūra majjat-kāmeśa mānasā** smile seducing Kāmeśvara

N29 **anākalita sādṛśya cibuka śrī virājitā** chin of incomparable beauty

N30 **kāmeśabaddha māṅgalya sūtraśobhita kandharā** wearing the thread of marriage to Kāmeśvara

N31 **kanakāṅgada keyūra kamanīya bhujānvitā** arms adorned with golden armlets

N32 **ratnagraiveya cintāka lolamuktā phalānvitā** necklace made of gold, gems, and dangling pearl

N33 **kāmeśvara premaratna maṇi pratipaṇastanī** offers her breasts to Kāmeśvara in return for his love

N34 **nābhyālavāla romālī latāphala kucadvayī** breasts growing like fruit on the creeper of the fine hairline

N35 **lakṣyaromalatā dhāratā samunneya madhyamā** waist known only by inference by the creeper-like hair springing from it

N36 **stanabhāra dalan-madhya paṭṭabandha valitraya** breast-burdened waist supported by the girdle of the three skin folds

N37 **aruṇāruṇa kausumbha vastra bhāsvat-kaṭītaṭī** hips wrapped in red garment

N38 **ratnakiṅkiṇi kāramya raśanādāma bhūṣitā** golden girdle decorated with gem-studded bells

N39 **kāmeśajñāta saubhāgya mārdavorudvayānvitā** thighs known only by the fortunate Kāmeśvara

N40 **māṇikya makuṭākāra jānudvaya virājitā** knees like crowns made of rubies

N41 **indragopa parikṣipta smara tūṇābha jaṅghikā** calves like the jewel-covered quiver of Kāma

N42 **gūḍhagulphā** hidden ankles

N43 **kūrmapṛṣṭha jayiṣṇu prapadānvitā** feet with arches like the tortoise's back

N44 **nakhadīdhiti saṃchanna namajjana tamoguṇā** toenails that dispel tamas

N45 **padadvaya prabhājāla parākṛta saroruhā** feet are the source of beauty for the lotus

N46 **śiñjāna maṇimañjīra maṇḍita śrī padāmbujā** feet adorned with gem-studded golden anklets

N47 **marālī mandagamanā** gait of a swan

N48 **mahālāvaṇya śevadhiḥ** treasure house of beauty

N49 **sarvāruṇā** emanating a red hue

N50 **navadyāṅgī** flawless limbs

N51 **sarvābharaṇa bhūṣitā** resplendent ornamentation

N52 **śivakāmeśvarāṅkasthā** sitting in Kāmeśvara's lap

N53 **śivā** auspiciousness

N54 **svādhīna vallabhā** won over Śiva

N55 **sumeru madhyaśṛṅgasthā** dwelling in the middle of Mount Meru

N56 **śrīmannagara nāyikā** ruling over the auspicious city

N57 **cintāmaṇi gṛhāntasthā** palace made of Cintāmaṇi

N58 **pañcabrahmāsanasthitā** seated on the throne made of five Brahmas

N59 **mahāpadmāṭavī saṃsthā** amidst the lotus forest

N60 **kadamba vanavāsinī** forest of Kadamba trees

N61 **sudhāsāgara madhyasthā** ocean of nectar

N62 **kāmākṣī** eyes filled with desire

N63 **kāmadāyinī** granting desire

N64 **devarṣi gaṇasaṅghāta stūyamānātma vaibhavā** lauded by gods and sages

N65 **bhaṇḍāsura vadhodyukta śaktisenā samanvitā** endowed with the army of śaktis capable of slaying Bhaṇḍāsura

N66 **sampatkarī samārūḍha sindhura vrajasevitā** herds of elephants tended by Sampatkarī

N67 **aśvārūḍhādhiṣṭhitāśva koṭikoṭi bhirāvṛtā** crores (millions) of horses commanded by Aśvārūḍha

N68 **cakrarāja rathārūḍha sarvāyudha pariṣkṛtā** seated in the chariot known as Cakrarāja

N69 **geyacakra rathārūḍha mantriṇī parisevitā** attended by Mantriṇī riding the Geyacakra

N70 **kiricakra rathārūḍha daṇḍanāthā puraskṛtā** escorted by Daṇḍanāthā riding the Kiricakra

N71 **jvālāmālinī kākṣipta vahniprākāra madhyagā** center of Jvālāmālinī fortress of fire

N72 **bhaṇḍasainya vadhodyukta śakti vikramaharṣitā** delighting in the valor of the śaktis intent on destroying Bhaṇḍāsura

N73 **nityā parākramāṭopa nirīkṣaṇa samutsukā** rejoicing at the valor of the Nityā Devīs

N74 **bhaṇḍaputra vadhodyukta bālāvikrama nanditā** rejoicing at the valor of Bālā intent on fighting Bhaṇḍāsura's sons

N75 **mantriṇyambā viracita viṣaṅga vadhatoṣitā** celebrating Mantriṇī's conquest of Viṣanga

N76 **viśukra prāṇaharaṇa vārāhī vīryananditā** delighting in Vārāhī's conquest of Viśukra

N77 **kāmeśvara mukhāloka kalpita śrī gaṇeśvarā** birthing Gaṇeśa by glancing at Kāmeśvara

N78 **mahāgaṇeśa nirbhinna vighnayantra praharṣitā** delights in Gaṇeśa destroying the obstacle of the illusory figures

N79 **bhaṇḍāsurendra nirmukta śastra pratyastra varṣiṇī** showers missiles in response to Bhaṇḍāsura's weapons

N80. **karāṅguḷi nakhotpanna nārāyaṇa daśākṛtiḥ** ten fingernails giving rise to the ten incarnations of Nārāyaṇa

N81 **mahāpāśupatāstrāgni nirdagdhāsura sainikā**

incinerating the asura army with the Mahāpāśupata

N82 **kāmeśvarāstra nirdagdha sabhaṇḍāsura śūnyakā** destroying Bhaṇḍāsura's army with the Kāmeśvara missile

N83 **brahmopendra mahendrādi devasaṃstuta vaibhavā** praised by Brahmā, Viṣṇu and other devas

N84 **haranetrāgni sandagdha kāma sañjīvanauṣadhiḥ** life-giving medicine for Kāma who had been incinerated by Śiva's third eye

N85 **śrīmadvāgbhava kūṭaika svarūpa mukhapaṅkajā** face representing the Vāgbhava kūṭa

N86 **kaṇṭhādhaḥ kaṭiparyanta madhyakūṭa svarūpiṇī** from throat to waist representing the Madhyakūta

N87 **śaktikūṭaika tāpanna kaṭyathobhāga dhāriṇī** waist down being the Śaktikūta

N88 **mūlamantrātmikā** embodiment of the root mantra

N89 **mūlakūṭa traya kalebarā** body composed of the three parts of the root mantra

N90 **kulāmṛtaika rasikā** taste of the nectar of the kula

N91 **kulasaṅketa pālinī** protector of the secrets of the kula

N92 **kulāṅganā** committed to kula

N93 **kulāntaḥsthā** residing in the kula

N94 **kaulinī** of the kula

N95 **kulayoginī** ruling over the yoga of the kula

N96 **akulā** devoid of kula

N97 **samayāntaḥsthā** residing in inner worship as samayā

N98 **samayācāra tatparā** devoted to samayācāra

N99 **mūlādhāraika nilayā** principal abode of the mūlādhāra

N100 **brahmagranthi vibhedinī** severing the Brahma granthi

N101 **maṇipūrānta ruditā** emerging at the Maṇipūra cakra

N102 **viṣṇugranthi vibhedinī** severing the Viṣṇu granthi

N103 **ājñacakrantarālasthā** making her way up to the ājña cakra

N104 **rudragranthi vibhedinī** dissolving the Rudra granthi

N105 **sahasrārāmbujā rūḍhā** ascending to the thousand-petaled Sahasrāra

N106 **sudhāsārābhi varṣiṇī** showering sudhā or amṛta

N107 **taṭillatā samarucih** flashing forth, brilliant as lightning

N108 **ṣaṭ-cakropari saṃsthitā** settling above the six cakras

N109 **mahāśaktiḥ** becoming attached

N110 **kuṇḍalinī** the coiled one

N111 **bisatantu tanīyasī** as subtle as the fiber of the lotus stalk

N112 **bhavānī** giver of life to Bhava

N113 **bhāvanāgamyā** attained through bhāvanā

N114 **bhavāraṇya kuṭhārikā** cutting through the jungle of saṃsāra

N115 **bhadrapriyā** delighting in the auspiciousness of liberation

N116 **bhadramūrtih** embodiment of auspiciousness

N117 **bhaktasaubhāgya dāyinī** bestowing the gift of auspiciousness

N118 **bhaktipriyā** delighting in bhakti

N119 **bhaktigamyā** attained through bhakti

N120 **bhaktivaśyā** won over by devotion

N121 **bhayāpahā** dispelling fear

N122 **śāmbhavī** wife of Śambhu

N123 **śāradarādhyā** worshiped by Śārada

N124 **śarvāṇī** wife of Śarva

N125 **śarmadāyinī** confers happiness

N126 **śāṅkarī** confers auspiciousness

N127 **śrīkarī** confers abundance

N128 **sādhvī** exclusively devoted to Śiva

N129 **śaraccandranibhānanā** face like the full moon on a clear autumn night

N130 **śātodarī** slender-waisted

N131 **śāntimatī** peaceful

N132 **nirādhārā** without support

N133 **nirañjanā** stainless

N134 **nirlepā** without impurity of the malas

N135 **nirmalā** spotless

N136 **nityā** timeless

N137 **nirākārā** formless

N138 **nirākulā** without agitation

N139 **nirguṇā** without guṇas

N140 **niṣkalā** indivisible

N141 **śāntā** tranquil

N142 **niṣkāmā** desireless

N143 **nirupaplavā** indestructible

N144 **nityamuktā** ever-free

N145 **nirvikārā** changeless

N146 **niṣprapañcā** without extensions

N147 **nirāśrayā** independent

N148 **nityaśuddhā** ever-pure

N149 **nityabuddhā** ever-wise

N150 **niravadyā** blameless

N151 **nirantarā** uninterrupted

N152 **niṣkāraṇā** causeless

N153 **niṣkalaṅkā** faultless

N154 **nirupādhih** free of limitations

N155 **nirīśvarā** with no superior

N156 **nīrāgā** devoid of passion

N157 **rāgamathanī** destroyer of passion

N158 **nirmadā** devoid of conceit

N159 **madanāśinī** destroyer of conceit

N160 **niścintā** devoid of anxiety

N161 **nirahaṅkārā** devoid of ahaṅkāra

N162 **nirmohā** devoid of delusion

N163 **mohanāśinī** destroyer of delusion

N164 **nirmamā** devoid of self-interest

N165 **mamatāhantrī** destroyer of self-interest

N166 **niṣpāpā** sinless

N167 **pāpanāśinī** destroying sin

N168 **niṣkrodha** free of anger

N169 **krodhaśamanī** destroying anger

N170 **nirlobhā** free of greed

N171 **lobhanāśinī** destroying greed

N172 **niḥsaṃśayā** free of doubt

N173 **saṃśayaghnī** destroying doubt

N174 **nirbhavā** without origin

N175 **bhavanāśinī** destroying saṃsāra

N176 **nirvikalpā** free of vikalpas

N177 **nirābādhā** undisturbed

N178 **nirbhedā** free of distinctions

N179 **bhedanāśinī** destroys distinctions

N180 **nirnāśā** indestructible

N181 **mṛtyumathanī** destroys death

N182 **niṣkriyā** free of action

N183 **niṣparigrahā** free of possessiveness

N184 **nistulā** incomparable

N185 **nīlacikurā** of bluish-black hair

N186 **nirapāyā** imperishable

N187 **niratyayā** impossible to transgress

N188 **durlabhā** difficult to attain

N189 **durgamā** difficult to approach

N190 **durgā** facilitating the journey across the saṃsāra ocean

N191 **duḥkhahantrī** destroying sorrow

N192 **sukhapradā** bestower of happiness

N193 **duṣṭadūrā** unattainable in ignorance

N194 **durācāra śamanī** ending the sin of separation

N195 **doṣavarjitā** free of flaws

N196 **sarvajñā** omniscient

N197 **sāndrakaruṇā** intensely compassionate

N198 **samānādhikavarjitā** with no superior or equal

N199 **sarvaśaktimayī** endowed with all powers

N200 **sarvamaṅgalā** source of good fortune

N201 **sadgatipradā** leading to the right path

N202 **sarveśvarī** ruling over all

N203 **sarvamayī** being all

N204 **sarvamantra svarūpiṇī** essence of all mantras

N205 **sarvayantrātmikā** soul of all yantras

N206 **sarvatantrarūpā** form of all tantras

N207 **manonmanī** eighth plane of consciousness

N208 **māheśvarī** wife of Maheśvara

N209 **mahādevī** the great Devī

N210 **mahālakṣmīh** the great Lakṣmī

N211 **mṛḍapriyā** beloved of Mṛḍa

N212 **mahārūpā** great form

N213 **mahāpūjyā** mighty object of worship

N214 **mahāpātaka nāśinī** destroying great sin

N215 **mahāmāyā** the great illusion

N216 **mahāsattvā** great reality

N217 **mahāśaktih** great power

N218 **mahāratiḥ** great delight

N219 **mahābhogā** great spectrum

N220 **mahaiśvaryā** great sovereignity

N221 **mahāvīryā** great valor

N222 **mahābalā** great strength

N223 **mahābuddhih** great intellect

N224 **mahāsiddhih** great attainment

N225 **mahāyogeśvareśvarī** ruler of the great yogis

N226 **mahātantrā** great tantra

N227 **mahāmantrā** great mantra

N228 **mahāyantrā** great yantra

N229 **mahāsanā** great seat

N230 **mahāyāga kramārādhyā** worshiped as Mahāyāga

N231 **mahābhairava pūjitā** worshiped by the great Bhairava

N232 **maheśvara mahākalpa mahātāṇḍava sākṣiṇī** witness of Maheśvara's great dance of time

N233 **mahākāmeśa mahiṣī** wife of Mahākāmeśvara

N234 **mahātripura sundarī** great beauty of the triads

N235 **catuṣṣaṣṭyupacārādhyā** worshiped by sixty-four offerings

N236 **catuṣṣaṣṭi kalāmayī** embodiment of the sixty-four arts

N237 **mahācatuṣṣaṣṭikoṭi yoginī gaṇasevitā** attended by 64 crores of yoginīs

N238 **manuvidyā** mantra variation of Manu

N239 **candravidyā** mantra variation of Candra

N240 **candramaṇḍalamadhyagā** residing in the center of the moon disc

N241 **cārurūpā** of exquisite beauty

N242 **cāruhāsā** of beautiful smile

N243 **cārucandrakalādharā** wearing the crescent moon

N244 **carācara jagannāthā** ruling over the animate and inanimate

N245 **cakrarāja niketanā** abiding in the Śrīcakra

N246 **pārvatī** the daughter of the Himālaya

N247 **padmanayanā** eyes shaped like lotus petals

N248 **padmarāga samaprabhā** complexion of rubies

N249 **pañcapretāsanāsīnā** seated on the five-corpse throne

N250 **pañcabrahma svarūpiṇī** form of the five Brahmās

N251 **cinmayī** consciousness

N252 **paramānandā** supreme bliss

N253 **vijñāna ghanarūpiṇī** permanent wisdom

N254 **dhyānadhyātṛ dhyeyarūpā** form of meditation, meditator and object of meditation

N255 **dharmādharma vivarjitā** devoid of virtue and vice

N256 **viśvarūpā** form of the universe

N257 **jāgariṇī** waking state

N258 **svapantī** dream state

N259 **taijasātmikā** subtle dream objects

N260 **suptā** deep sleep state

N261 **prājñātmikā** collective form of the universe

N262 **turyā** witnessing consciousness

N263 **sarvāvasthā vivarjitā** transcending all states

N264 **sṛṣṭikartrī** creator

N265 **brahmarūpā** form of Brahmā

N266 **goptrī** sustainer

N267 **govindarūpiṇī** as Govinda

N268 **saṃhāriṇī** destroyer

N269 **rudrarūpā** as Rudra

N270 **tirodhānakarī** concealer

N271 **īśvarī** wife of Īśāna

N272 **sadāśiva** as Sadāśiva

N273 **ānugrahadā** revealer

N274 **pañcakṛtya parāyaṇā** performing the five functions

N275 **bhānumaṇḍala madhyasthā** seated in the sun disc

N276 **bhairavī** wife of Bhairava

N277 **bhagamālinī** wearing the garland of suns

N278 **padmāsanā** seated on a lotus

N279 **bhagavatī** refuge of all

N280 **padmanābha sahodarī** residing at the lotus of the navel, which is like the sister of the sun

N281 **unmeṣa nimiṣotpanna vipanna bhuvanāvaḷiḥ** blinking causing worlds to appear and disappear

N282 **sahasraśīrṣavadanā** thousand heads and faces

N283 **sahasrākṣī** thousand eyes

N284 **sahasrapāt** thousand feet

N285 **ābrahma kīṭajananī** mother of all from Brahmā to insect

N286 **varṇāśrama vidhāyinī** establishing social orders

N287 **nijājñārūpanigamā** commanding the Vedas into manifestation

N288 **puṇyāpuṇya phalapradā** giver of good and bad outcomes

N289 **śruti sīmanta sindhūrīkṛta pādābjadhūlikā** dust of her feet becoming the sacred vermilion for the Vedas

N290 **sakalāgama sandoha śuktisampuṭa mauktikā** pearl of the aggregate of all scriptures

N291 **puruṣārthapradā** conferring the Puruśārthas

N292 **pūrṇā** whole

N293 **bhoginī** enjoyer

N294 **bhuvaneśvarī** ruler of the universe

N295 **ambikā** mother of the universe

N296 **anāḍī nidhanā** having no beginning or end

N297 **haribrahmendra sevitā** attended by Viṣṇu, Brahmā and Indra

N298 **nārāyaṇī** śakti of Nārāyaṇa

N299 **nādarūpā** form of sound

N300 **nāmarūpa vivarjitā** transcending name and form

N301 **hrīṅkārī** form of the bīja Hrīṃ

N302 **hrīṃatī** possessor of hrī

N303 **hṛdyā** abiding in the heart

N304 **heyopādeya varjitā** accepting and rejecting nothing

N305 **rājarājārcitā** worshiped by Śiva, the king of kings

N306 **rājñī** supreme sovereign

N307 **ramyā** beautiful

N308 **rājīvalocanā** with the eyes of a benevolent ruler

N309 **rañjanī** delightful

N310 **ramaṇī** bestower of joy

N311 **rasyā** of the nature of rasa

N312 **raṇatkiṅkiṇi mekhalā** girdle of tinkling bells

N313 **ramā** form of Lakṣmī

N314 **rākenduvadanā** face like the full moon

N315 **ratirūpā** embodiment of pleasure

N316 **ratipriyā** lover of pleasure

N317 **rakṣākarī** protector

N318 **rākṣasaghnī** slayer of demons

N319 **rāmā** of the nature of delight

N320 **ramaṇalampaṭā** devoted to Śiva

N321 **kāmyā** desirable

N322 **kāmakalārūpā** form of Kāmakalā

N323 **kadamba kusumapriyā** fond of Kadamba flowers

N324 **kalyāṇī** bestowing good fortune

N325 **jagatīkandā** root of the world

N326 **karuṇārasa sāgarā** ocean of compassion

N327 **kalāvatī** embodiment of all arts

N328 **kalālāpa** of refined expression

N329 **kāntā** pleasing

N330 **kādambarīpriyā** fond of intoxicants

N331 **varadā** granting wishes

N332 **vāmanayanā** beautiful-eyed

N333 **vāruṇīmadavihvalā** intoxicated

N334 **viśvādhikā** transcending the world

N335 **vedavedyā** known through the Vedas

N336 **vindhyācala nivāsinī** residing in the Vindhyā

N337 **vidhātrī** supporter

N338 **vedajananī** mother of the Vedas

N339 **viṣṇumāyā** Māyā of Viṣṇu

N340 **vilāsinī** playful

N341 **kṣetrasvarūpā** form of the field of matter

N342 **kṣetreśī** wife of Kṣetreśī

N343 **kṣetra kṣetrajña pālinī** knower and protector of Kṣetra

N344 **kṣayavṛddhi vinirmuktā** free of growth and decay

N345 **kṣetrapāla samarcitā** worshiped by kṣetrapālas

N346 **vijayā** ever-victorious

N347 **vimalā** without impurity

N348 **vandyā** worthy of worship

N349 **vandāru janavatsalā** fond of those who worship

N350 **vāgvādinī** power of expression

N351 **vāmakeśī** dark-haired

N352 **vahnimaṇḍala vāsinī** residing in the fire disc

N353 **bhaktimat-kalpalatikā** wish-fulfilling creeper of the devotee

N354 **paśupāśa vimocanī** releasing ignorance

N355 **saṃhṛtāśeṣa pāṣaṇḍā** destroyer of heretics

N356 **sadācāra pravartikā** inspiring right behavior

N357 **tāpatrayāgni santapta samāhlādana candrikā** cooling the fire of afflictions

N358 **taruṇī** ever-youthful

N359 **tāpasārādhyā** worshiped by ascetics

N360 **tanumadhyā** slender-waisted

N361 **tamopahā** removing tamas

N362 **cittiḥ** wisdom

N363 **tatpadaḷakṣyārthā** That, the supreme and transcendent Reality

N364 **cideka rasarūpiṇī** rasa of wisdom

N365 **svātmānandaḷavībhūta brahmādyānanda santatiḥ** minute portion of her bliss is the combined bliss of Brahmā and other deities

N366 **parā** parāvāk

N367 **pratyakcitī rūpā** form of consciousness

N368 **paśyantī** paśyantī vāk

N369 **paradevatā** perceiving self as Supreme deity

N370 **madhyamā** madhyamā vāk

N371 **vaikharīrūpā** vaikharī vāk

N372 **bhaktamānasa haṃsika** swam of discernment in the devotee's mind

N373 **kāmeśvara prāṇanāḍī** prāṇa of Kāmeśvara

N374 **kṛtajñā** knower of actions

N375 **kāmapūjitā** worshiped by Kāma

N376 **śṛṅgārarasasampūrṇā** brimming with śṛṅgāra rasa

N377 **jayā** victorious

N378 **jālandharasthitā** residing at the jālandhara pīṭha

N379 **oḍyāṇa pīṭhanilaya** residing at the odyāṇa pīṭha

N380 **bindumaṇḍala vāsinī** residing at the bindu

N381 **rahoyāga kramārādhyā** worshiped in secret by sacrificial fires

N382 **rahastarpaṇa tarpitā** gratified by secret oblations

N383 **sadyaḥ prasādinī** bestowing grace

N384 **viśvasākṣiṇī** witness of the universe

N385 **sākṣivarjitā** unwitnessed

N386 **ṣaḍaṅgadevatā yuktā** accompanied by the ṣaḍaṅga devatas

N387 **ṣāḍguṇya paripūritā** brimming with six auspicious qualities

N388 **nityaklinnā** ever-moist

N389 **nirupamā** incomparable

N390 **nirvāṇa sukhadāyinī** bliss of liberation

N391 **nityā ṣoḍaśikārūpā** form of Nityā Devīs

N392 **śrīkaṇṭhārdha śarīriṇī** half the body of Śrikaṇṭha

N393 **prabhāvatī** luminous

N394 **prabhārūpā** embodiment of brilliance

N395 **prasiddhā** celebrated

N396 **parameśvarī** supreme ruler

N397 **mūlaprakṛtih** primordial cause

N398 **avyaktā** indistinct

N399 **vyaktāvyakta svarūpiṇī** manifest and unmanifest

N400 **vyāpinī** all-pervading

N401 **vividhākārā** multitude of forms

N402 **vidyāvidyā svarūpiṇī** form of knowledge and ignorance

N403 **mahākāmeśa nayana kumudāhlāda kaumudī** moonlight that gladdens the lotus-eyed Kāmeśvara

N404 **bhaktahārda tamobheda bhānumad-bhānusantatiḥ** ray of sunlight dispelling the darkness of ignorance

N405 **śivadūtī** making Śiva the messenger

N406 **śivārādhyā** worshiped by Śiva

N407 **śivamūrti** form of Śiva

N408 **śivaṅkarī** conferring Śivahood

N409 **śivapriyā** beloved of Śiva

N410 **śivaparā** beyond Śiva

N411 **śiṣṭeṣṭā** sought by the wise

N412 **śiṣṭapūjitā** worshiped by the wise

N413 **aprameyā** immeasurable

N414 **svaprakāśā** self-luminous

N415 **manovācāma gocarā** unattainable through mind and speech

N416 **cicchaktih** power of consciousness

N417 **cetanārūpā** form of consciousness

N418 **jaḍaśaktih** power of Māyā

N419 **jaḍātmikā** objective (inanimate) world

N420 **gāyatrī** mother of mantras

N421 **vyāhṛtih** utterance of mantras

N422 **sandhyā** junction of mantra, its practice and its grace

N423 **dvijabṛnda niṣevitā** revered by the twice-born

N424 **tattvāsanā** seat of all tattvas

N425 **tat** suchness or That

N426 **tvam** Thou

N427 **ayī** mother of all

N428 **pañcakośāntarasthitā** residing in the pañcakoṣas

N429 **niḥsīmamahimā** gloriously unlimited

N430 **nityayauvanā** ever youthful

N431 **madaśālinī** rapturously radiant

N432 **madaghūrṇita raktākṣī** reddened eyes rolling inward

N433 **madapāṭala gaṇḍabhūḥ** blushing cheeks

N434 **candana dravadigdhāṅgī** smelling of sandalwood

N435 **cāmpeya kusuma priyā** fond of Campaka flowers

N436 **kuśalā** skillful

N437 **komalākārā** graceful

N438 **kurukullā** Kurukullā

N439 **kuleśvarī** ruler of the kula

N440 **kulakuṇḍālaya** abiding in the Kulakunda (mūlādhāra)

N441 **kaula mārgatatpara sevitā** worshiped by Kaulas

N442 **kumāra gaṇanāthāmbā** mother of Skanda and Gaṇeśa

N443 **tuṣṭiḥ** contentment

N444 **puṣṭiḥ** nourishment

N445 **matiḥ** intelligence

N446 **dhṛtiḥ** fortitude

N447 **śāntiḥ** tranquility

N448 **svastimatī** eternal truth

N449 **kāntih** effulgence

N450 **nandinī** delight

N451 **vighnanāśinī** destroying obstacles

N452 **tejovatī** splendorous

N453 **trinayanā** three-eyed

N454 **lolākṣī kāmarūpiṇī** rolling eyes

N455 **mālinī** Mālinī

N456 **haṃsinī** hamsa mantra

N457 **mātā** measure

N458 **malayācala vāsinī** residing in the Malaya mountains

N459 **sumukhī** of a lovely face

N460 **nalinī** body of the softness of lotus petals

N461 **subhrūḥ** of beautiful eyebrows

N462 **śobhanā** shining

N463 **suranāyikā** leader of the devas

N464 **kālakaṇṭhī** united with Śiva

N465 **kāntimatī** radiant

N466 **kṣobhiṇī** causing upheaval

N467 **sūkṣmarūpiṇī** subtle form

N468 **vajreśvarī** of the brilliance of diamonds

N469 **vāmadevī** wife of Śiva

N470 **vayovasthā vivarjitā** exempt from states

N471 **siddheśvarī** worshiped by siddhās

N472 **siddhavidyā** Pañcadaśi mantra

N473 **siddhamātā** mother of the siddhās

N474 **yaśasvinī** of unparalleled renown

N475 **viśuddhi cakranilayā** residing at the Viśuddha cakra

N476 **raktavarṇā** of a reddish complexion

N477 **trilocanā** three-eyed

N478 **khaṭvāṅgādi praharaṇā** bearing a club and other weapons

N479 **vadanaika samanvitā** one-faced

N480 **pāyasānnapriyā** fond of pāyasa

N481 **tvaksthā** governing over skin tissue

N482 **paśuloka bhayaṅkarī** inciting fear in paśus

N483 **amṛtādi mahāśakti saṃvṛtā** attended by Amṛta and other śaktis

N484 **ḍākinīśvarī** known as Dākinī

N485 **anāhatabja nilayā** residing at the Anāhata

N486 **śyāmābhā** black-complexioned

N487 **vadanadvayā** two-faced

N488 **daṃṣṭrojjvalā** with shining tusks

N489 **akṣamālādhidharā** wearing garlands of beads

N490 **rudhira saṃsthitā** presiding over blood

N491 **kālarātryād śaktyoghavṛtā** attended by Kālarātri and other śaktis

N492 **snigdhaudanapriyā** fond of greasy offerings

N493 **mahāvīrendra varadā** bestowing grace on vīras

N494 **rākiṇyambā svarūpiṇī** form of Rākiṇi

N495 **maṇipūrābja nilayā** residing at the Maṇipūra

N496 **vadanatraya saṃyutā** three-faced

N497 **vajrādhikāyudhopetā** bearing lightning bolt and other weapons

N498 **ḍāmaryādibhir āvṛtā** attended by Ḍāmarī and other śaktis

N499 **raktavarṇā** red-skinned

N500 **māṃsaniṣṭhā** ruling over muscle

N501 **guḍānna prītamānasā** fond of sweet rice with jaggery

N502 **samasta bhaktasukhadā** conferring contentment on all devotees

N503 **lākinyambā svarūpiṇī** as Lākinī

N504 **svādhiṣṭānāmbujagatā** at the svādhiṣṭāna

N505 **caturvaktra manoharā** four-faced beauty

N506 **śūlādyāyudha sampannā** bearing a trident and other weapons

N507 **pītavarṇā** yellow-complexioned

N508 **atigarvitā** very proud

N509 **medoniṣṭhā** presiding over fat

N510 **madhuprītā** favoring honey

N511 **bandhinyādi samanvitā** attended by Bandhinī and other śaktis

N512 **dadhyannāsakta hṛdayā** fond of yogurt-containing offerings

N513 **kākinī rūpadhāriṇī** assuming the form of Kākinī

N514 **mūlādhārāmbujā rūḍhā** at the mūlādhāra

N515 **pañcavaktrā** five-faced

N516 **asthisaṃsthitā** presiding over bone

N517 **aṅkuśādi praharaṇā** bearing a goad and other weapons

N518 **varadādi niṣevitā** attended by Varadā and other śaktis

N519 **mudgaudanāsakta cittā** fond of mudga beans

N520 **sākinyambāsvarūpiṇī** she is Sākinī

N521 **ājñā cakrābjanilayā** residing at the ājña

N522 **śuklavarṇā** white-complexioned

N523 **ṣaḍānanā** six-faced

N524 **majjāsaṃsthā** presiding over bone marrow

N525 **haṃsavatī mukhyaśakti samanvitā** attended by Hamsavatī as the main śakti

N526 **haridrānnaika rasikā** favoring food with saffron

N527 **hākinī rūpadhāriṇī** she is Hākinī

N528 **sahasradaḷa padmasthā** residing at the sahasrāra

N529 **sarvavarnopaśobhitā** complexion of all colors

N530 **sarvadanadharā** bearing all weapons

N531 **śukla saṃsthitā** presiding over reproductive tissue

N532 **sarvatomukhī** faces turned in all directions

N533 **sarvaudana prītacittā** fond of all offerings

N534 **yākinyambā svarūpiṇī** she is Yākinī

N535 **svāhā** invoked by svāhā

N536 **svadhā** invoked by svadhā

N537 **amatiḥ** form of ignorance

N538 **medhā** form of wisdom

N539 **śrutiḥ** form of the Vedas

N540 **smṛtiḥ** form of the derived scriptures

N541 **anuttamā** unexcelled

N542 **puṇyakīrtiḥ** bestower of good fortune

N543 **puṇyalabhyā** attained by grace

N544 **puṇyaśravaṇa kīrtanā** listening to her praise is sacred

N545 **pulomajārcitā** worshiped by Pulomajā

N546 **bandhamocanī** freeing from the bond of ignorance

N547 **bandhurālakā** of luxurious hair

N548 **vimarśarūpiṇī** form of vimarśa

N549 **vidyā** form of knowledge

N550. **viyadādi jagatprasūḥ** creator of the universe of space and other elements

N551 **sarvavyādhi praśamanī** alleviating all disease

N552 **sarvamṛtyu nivāriṇī** dispelling all death

N553 **agragaṇyā** the first

N554 **acintyarūpā** unthinkable

N555 **kalikalmaṣa nāśinī** destroyer of sin in the Kalī yuga

N556 **kātyāyinī** radiance of the aggregate of deities

N557 **kālahantrī** destroyer of time

N558 **kamalākṣa niṣevitā** worshiped by the lotus-eyed (Viṣṇu)

N559 **tāmbūla pūrita mukhī** mouth full of betel

N560 **dāḍimī kusumaprabhā** red like the pomegranate flower

N561 **mṛgākṣī** doe-eyed

N562 **mohinī** enchantress

N563 **mukhyā** first

N564 **mṛḍānī** wife of Mṛḍa

N565 **mitrarūpiṇī** form of the sun

N566 **nityatṛptā** eternally content

N567 **bhaktanidhiḥ** treasure of the devotee

N568 **niyantrī** guide

N569 **nikhileśvarī** ruler of all

N570 **maitryādi vāsanālabhyā** attained by virtues like friendliness

N571 **mahāpraḷaya sākṣiṇī** witness of the great dissolution

N572 **parāśaktiḥ** supreme power

N573 **parāniṣṭhā** supreme end

N574 **prajñāna ghanarūpiṇī** concentrated wisdom

N575 **mādhvīpānālasā** languid

N576 **mattā** intoxicated

N577 **mātṛkā varṇa rūpiṇī** form of Mātṛkā

N578 **mahākailāsa nilayā** residing in the great Kailāsa

N579 **mṛṇāla mṛdudorlatā** with arms like soft lotus stems

N580 **mahanīyā** illustrious

N581 **dayāmūrtiḥ** embodiment of mercy

N582 **mahāsāmrājyaśālinī** empress of all worlds

N583 **ātmavidyā** Self-knowledge

N584 **mahāvidyā** great knowledge

N585 **śrīvidyā** auspicious knowledge

N586 **kāmasevitā** worshiped by Kāma

N587 **śrīṣoḍaśākṣarī vidyā** sixteen-syllabled mantra

N588 **trikūṭā** of the three kūṭas

N589 **kāmakoṭikā** nature of Śiva

N590 **kaṭākṣakiṅkarī bhūta kamalā koṭisevitā** attended by millions of Lakṣmīs

N591 **śiraḥsthitā** at the sahasrāra

N592 **candranibhā** moon-like

N593 **phālasthā** at the ājña

N594 **indradhanuḥprabhā** rainbow-like

N595 **hṛdayasthā** at the anāhata

N596 **raviprakhyā** sun-like

N597 **trikoṇāntara dīpikā** light of the triangle

N598 **dākṣāyaṇī** daughter of Dakśa (Sati)

N599 **daityahantrī** slayer of asuras

N600 **dakṣayajña vināśinī** destroyer of Dakśa's fire ritual

N601 **darāndolita dīrghākṣī** all-seeing large eyes

N602 **darahāsojjvalanmukhī** of radiant smile

N603 **gurumūrtiḥ** form of the guru

N604 **guṇanidhiḥ** treasure-house of virtue

N605 **gomātā** Kāmadhenu

N606 **guhajanmabhūḥ** keeping the secret of the divine birth of the universe

N607 **deveśī** śakti of the devas

N608 **daṇḍanītisthā** exacting justice

N609 **daharākāśa rūpiṇī** indweller of the space of the heart

N610 **pratipanmukhya rākānta tithimaṇḍala pūjitā** worshiped as digits of the lunar half-months

N611 **kalātmikā** source of the kalās

N612 **kalānāthā** ruler of the kalās

N613 **kāvyālāpa vinodinī** delighting in poetry

N614 **sacāmara ramāvāṇī savyadakṣiṇa sevitā** attended by Lakṣmī and Sarasvatī

N615 **ādiśakti** primordial power

N616 **ameya** immeasurable

N617 **ātmā** Self in all

N618 **paramā** supreme

N619 **pāvanākṛtiḥ** pure

N620 **anekakoṭi brahmāṇḍa jananī** creator of countless universes

N621 **divyavigrahā** divine body

N622 **klīṅkārī** of the bīja Klīṃ

N623 **kevalā** attributeless

N624 **guhyā** secret

N625 **kaivalya padadāyinī** bestowing liberation

N626 **tripurā** triad

N627 **trijagadvandyā** worshiped by the three worlds

N628 **trimūrtih** form of triads

N629 **tridaśeśvarī** ruler of triads

N630 **tryakṣarī** three-syllabled

N631 **divyagandhāḍhyā** of divine fragrance

N632 **sindūra tilakāñcitā** with the mark of auspiciousness

N633 **umā** Umā

N634 **śailendratanayā** daughter of the Himālaya

N635 **gaurī** of golden complexion

N636 **gandharva sevitā** attended by celestial singers

N637 **viśvagarbhā** womb carrying the universe

N638 **svarṇagarbhā** golden womb

N639 **avaradā** sacred

N640 **vāgadhīśvarī** presiding over speech

N641 **dhyānagamyā** attained by meditation

N642 **aparicchedyā** unlimited

N643 **jñānadā** giver of knowledge

N644 **jñānavigrahā** embodiment of knowledge

N645 **sarvavedānta saṃvedyā** subject of Vedanta

N646 **satyānanda svarūpiṇī** embodiment of existence and bliss

N647 **lopāmudrārcitā** worshiped by Lopāmudrā

N648 **līlākḷpta brahmāṇḍamaṇḍalā** creating the universe for sport

N649 **adṛśyā** invisible

N650 **dṛśyarahitā** transcending the visible

N651 **vijñātrī** sole perceiver

N652 **vedyavarjitā** transcending the knowable

N653 **yoginī** united with Śiva

N654 **yogadā** bestower of yoga

N655 **yogyā** object of all yoga

N656 **yogānandā** bliss of yoga

N657 **yugandharā** bearer of ages

N658 **icchāśakti jñānaśakti kriyāśakti svarūpiṇī** form of icchā, jñāna and kriya śakti

N659 **sarvādhārā** support of all

N660 **supratiṣṭhā** firmly established

N661 **sadasadrūpa-dhāriṇī** foundation of being and non-being

N662 **aṣṭamūrtih** eight-formed

N663 **ajājaitrī** conquering ignorance

N664 **lokayātrā vidhāyinī** directing the course of the worlds

N665 **ekākinī** one without a second

N666 **bhūmarūpā** aggregate of all existing things

N667 **nirdvaitā** devoid of duality

N668 **dvaitavarjitā** transcending duality

N669 **annadā** source of nourishment

N670 **vasudā** source of abundance

N671 **vṛddhā** ancient

N672 **brahmātmaikya svarūpiṇī** union of Brahman and atman (jīva)

N673 **bṛhatī** great

N674 **brāhmaṇī** wife of Śiva

N675 **brāhmī** Brahman as the Word

N676 **brahmānandā** bliss of Brahman

N677 **balipriyā** fond of sacrifice

N678 **bhāṣārūpā** form of language

N679 **bṛhatsenā** vast army

N680 **bhāvābhāva vivarjitā** devoid of existence and non-existence

N681 **sukhārādhyā** easily worshiped

N682 **śubhakarī** bestows good fortune

N683 **śobhanā sulabhāgatiḥ** easy path

N684 **rājarājeśvarī** empress of emperors

N685 **rājyadāyinī** giver of dominion

N686 **rājyavallabhā** delights in all dominions

N687 **rājatkṛpā** giver of compassion in all dominions

N688 **rājapīṭha niveśita nijāśritā** establishing devotees on thrones

N689 **rājyalakṣmīḥ** royal wealth

N690 **kośanāthā** ruler of the kośas

N691 **caturaṅga baleśvarī** commander of the four armies

N692 **sāmrājyadāyinī** bestower of the supreme dominion

N693 **satyasandhā** devoted to truth

N694 **sāgaramekhalā** girdle of oceans

N695 **dīkṣitā** giver of dīkṣa

N696 **daityaśamanī** destroyer of demons

N697 **sarvaloka vaśaṅkarī** subjugating all the worlds

N698 **sarvārthadātrī** granting all desires

N699 **sāvitrī** creator of the universe

N700 **saccidānanda rūpiṇī** of the nature of existence, consciousness, and bliss

N701 **deśakālā paricchinnā** unlimited by time and space

N702 **sarvagā** omnipresent

N703 **sarvamohinī** deluder of all

N704 **sarasvatī** embodiment of knowledge

N705 **śāstramayī** form of scriptures

N706 **guhāmbā** dweller of the cave of the heart

N707 **guhyarūpiṇī** of secret form

N708 **sarvopādhi vinirmuktā** free of limitations

N709 **sadāśiva pativratā** exclusively devoted to Śiva

N710 **sampradāyeśvarī** guardian of sacred traditions

N711 **sādhu** inherent quality of doing well

N712 **Ī Kāmakalā**

N713 **gurumaṇḍala rūpiṇī** form of guru lineages

N714 **kulottīrṇā** transcending kula

N715 **bhagārādhyā** worshiped in the sun

N716 **māyā** Māyā

N717 **madhumatī** sweet as honey

N718 **mahī** great form

N719 **gaṇāmbā** mother of gaṇas

N720 **guhyakārādhyā** worshiped in secret

N721 **komalāṅgī** tender-limbed

N722 **gurupriyā** beloved of gurus

N723 **svatantrā** absolutely free

N724 **sarvatantreśī** embodiment of all tantras

N725 **dakṣiṇāmūrti rūpiṇī** embodiment of Dakṣiṇāmūrti

N726 **sanakādi samārādhyā** revered by Sanaka and others

N727 **śivajñāna pradāyinī** bestower of knowledge of Śiva

N728 **citkalā** consciousness limited as jīva

N729 **ānandakalikā** bud of bliss

N730 **premarūpā** form of love

N731 **priyaṅkarī** cause of love

N732 **nāmapārāyaṇa prītā** delights in the chanting of nāmas

N733 **nandividyā** knowledge of Nandi

N734 **naṭeśvarī** wife of Natarāja

N735 **mithyā jagadadhiṣṭhānā** source of the illusory universe

N736 **muktidā** bestower of liberation

N737 **muktirūpiṇī** embodiment of liberation

N738 **lāsyapriyā** fond of the dance form known as lāsya

N739 **layakarī** causing absorption

N740 **lajjā** modesty

N741 **rambhādi vanditā** adored by Rambhā and others

N742 **bhavadāva sudhāvṛṣṭiḥ** nectar extinguishing the fire of saṃsāra

N743 **pāpāraṇya davānalā** burning the forest of sin (of ignorance)

N744 **daurbhāgyatūla vātūlā** undoing the knot of misfortune

N745 **jarādhvānta raviprabhā** ray of light dispelling the darkness and decay

N746 **bhāgyābdhicandrikā** bringing about good fortune

N747 **bhaktacittakeki ghanāghanā** rousing joy in the devotee's heart, like clouds that incite a peacock's dance

N748 **rogaparvata dambholī** shattering the mountain of disease

N749 **mṛtyudāru kuṭhārikā** cutting down the tree of death

N750 **maheśvarī** supreme ruler

N751 **mahākālī** great Kālī

N752 **mahāgrāsā** great devourer

N753 **mahāśanā** great eater

N754 **aparṇā** annihilating ṛṇa

N755 **caṇḍikā** wrathful

N756 **caṇḍamuṇḍāsura niṣūdinī** destroyer of Caṇḍa and Muṇḍa

N757 **kṣarākṣarātmikā** being perishable and imperishable

N758 **sarvalokeśī** supreme ruler of the worlds

N759 **viśvadhāriṇī** supporter of the universe

N760 **trivargadātrī** granting the three goals of life

N761 **subhagā** good fortune

N762 **tryambakā** three-eyed

N763 **triguṇātmikā** source of the three guṇas

N764 **svargāpavargadā** bestower of heaven and liberation

N765 **śuddhā** unconditioned

N766 **ajapāpuṣpa nibhākṛtiḥ** body blooming as the universe from ajapa

N767 **ojovatī** of ojas

N768 **dyutidharā** brilliance

N769 **yajñarūpā** form of yajña

N770 **priyavratā** fond of vows

N771 **durārādhyā** difficult to worship

N772 **durādharṣā** impossible to subjugate

N773 **pāṭalī kusumapriyā** fond of the Pāṭalī flowers

N774 **mahatī** great

N775 **merunilayā** residing on Mount Meru

N776 **mandāra kusumapriyā** fond of Mandāra flowers

N777 **vīrārādhyā** worshiped by vīras

N778 **virāḍrūpā** form of the cosmos

N779 **virajā** without passion

N780 **viśvatomukhī** facing every way

N781 **pratyagrūpā** interior

N782 **parākāśā** supreme ether

N783 **prāṇadā** source of prāṇa

N784 **prāṇarūpiṇī** prāṇa

N785 **mārtāṇḍa bhairavārādhyā** worshiped by Mārtāṇḍa Bhairava

N786 **mantriṇī nyastarājyadhūḥ** entrusting dominion to Mantriṇī

N787 **tripureśī** Tripureśī

N788 **jayatsenā** ever-victorious army

N789 **nistraiguṇyā** devoid of the guṇas

N790 **parāparā** subject and object, the process of knowing

N791 **satyajñānānandarūpā** truth, knowledge, and bliss

N792 **sāmarasya parāyaṇā** rasa of oneness

N793 **kapardinī** wife of Kaparda

N794 **kalāmālā** garland of arts

N795 **kāmadhuk** Kāmadhenu

N796 **kāmarūpiṇī** essence of desire

N797 **kalānidhiḥ** reservoir of sciences

N798 **kāvyakalā** poetry

N799 **rasajñā** knower of rasa

N800 **rasaśevadhiḥ** reservoir of rasa

N801 **puṣṭā** nourished

N802 **purātanā** ancient

N803 **pūjyā** revered

N804 **puṣkarā** nourishment

N805 **puṣkarekṣaṇā** lotus-eyed

N806 **parañjyotiḥ** supreme light

N807 **parandhāma** supreme abode

N808 **paramāṇuḥ** subtlest

N809 **parātparā** most supreme

N810 **pāśahastā** bearing the noose

N811 **pāśahantr**ī destroyer of the noose

N812 **paramantra vibhedinī** destroyer of the illusion of language

N813 **mūrtā** form

N814 **amūrtā** formless

N815 **anityatṛptā** perishable

N816 **muni mānasa haṃsikā** swan of discernment in the minds of the wise

N817 **satyavratā** abiding in truth

N818 **satyarūpā** truth

N819 **sarvāntaryāminī** indweller of all

N820 **satī** Satī

N821 **brahmāṇī** śakti of Brahman

N822 **brahma** Brahman

N823 **jananī** mother

N824 **bahurūpā** of many forms

N825 **budhārcitā** worshiped by the wise

N826 **prasavitrī** creator

N827 **pracaṇḍā** fierce

N828 **āj**ñā commander

N829 **pratiṣṭhā** foundation

N830 **prakaṭākṛtiḥ** manifested

N831 **prāṇeśvarī** ruler of prāṇa

N832 **prāṇadātrī** nourisher of prāṇa

N833 **pañcāśat-pīṭharūpiṇī** fifty seats

N834 **viśṛṅkhalā** unfettered

N835 **viviktasthā** abiding in seclusion

N836 **vīramātā** mother of vīras

N837 **viyatprasūḥ** mother of space

N838 **mukundā** bestower of salvation

N839 **mukti nilayā** abode of liberation

N840 **mūlavigraha rūpiṇī** body being the root

N841 **bhāvajñā** knower of thought

N842 **bhavarogaghnī** destroyer of saṃsāra

N843 **bhavacakra pravartinī** turning the wheel of earthly existence

N844 **chandahsārā** essence of meter

N845 **śāstrasārā** essence of scripture

N846 **mantrasārā** essence of mantras

N847 **talodarī** slim-waisted

N848 **udārakīrtiḥ** of exalted fame

N849 **uddāmavaibhavā** glorious

N850 **varṇarūpiṇī** letters of the alphabet

N851 **janmamṛtyu jarātapta jana viśrānti dāyinī** repose for the constant cycles of saṃsāra

N852 **sarvopaniṣad udghuṣṭā** celebrated in all Upaniṣads

N853 **śāntyatīta kalātmikā** transcending peace

N854 **gambhīrā** unfathomable

N855 **gaganāntaḥsthā** residing in ether

N856 **garvitā** proud

N857 **gānalolupā** delighting in music

N858 **kalpanārahitā** free of imaginary attributes

N859 **kāṣṭhā** goal

N860 **akāntā** end of sin

N861 **kāntārdha vigrahā** half body of Śiva

N862 **kāryakāraṇa nirmuktā** free of karma

N863 **kāmakeli taraṅgitā** overflowing with desire and pleasure

N864 **kanatkanakatāṭaṅkā** wearing shining gold earrings

N865 **līlāvigraha dhāriṇī** having a body merely for sport

N866 **ajā** unborn

N867 **kṣaya vinirmuktā** free from decay

N868 **mugdhā** beautiful

N869 **kṣipraprasādinī** easily pleased

N870 **antarmukha samārādhyā** internally worshiped

N871 **bahirmukha sudurlabhā** difficult to attain when

devoted to external objects

N872 **trayī** revelation of three

N873 **trivarga nilayā** three-fold goals

N874 **tristhā** seated in triads

N875 **tripuramālinī** Tripuramālinī

N876 **nirāmayā** free of disease

N877 **nirālambā** independent

N878 **svātmārāmā** rejoicing in self

N879 **sudhāsṛtiḥ** stream of nectar

N880 **saṃsārapaṅka nirmagna samuddharaṇa paṇḍitā** skillfully raising those sinking in saṃsāra

N881 **yajñapriyā** fond of sacrifice

N882 **yajñakartrī** doer of sacrifice

N883 **yajamāna svarūpiṇī** sacrificer

N884 **dharmādhārā** support of dharma

N885 **dhanādhyakṣā** ruler of wealth

N886 **dhanadhānya vivardhinī** bestowing wealth and harvests

N887 **viprapriyā** fond of those with Self-knowledge

N888 **viprarūpā** taking the form of vipras

N889 **viśvabhramaṇa kāriṇī** turning the universe

N890 **viśvagrāsā** devouring the universe

N891 **vidrumābhā** of the color of coral

N892 **vaiṣṇavī** śakti of Viṣṇu

N893 **viṣṇurūpiṇī** Viṣṇu

N894 **ayonih** without origin

N895 **yoninilayā** place of origin

N896 **kūṭasthā** veiling own nature

N897 **kularūpiṇī** kula

N898 **vīragoṣṭhīpriyā** fond of assembly of viras

N899 **vīrā** valorous

N900 **naiṣkarmyā** devoid of action

N901 **nādarūpiṇī** primordial vibration

N902 **vijñāna kalanā** cause of perception

N903 **kalyā** skilful

N904 **vidagdhā** artful

N905 **baindavāsanā** seated at the bindu

N906 **tattvādhikā** transcending tattvas

N907 **tattvamayī** tattvas

N908 **tattvamartha svarūpiṇī** meaning of That and Thou

N909 **sāmagānapriyā** fond of the Sāmaveda

N910 **saumyā** benign

N911 **sadāśiva kuṭumbinī** wife of Sadāśiva

N912 **savyāpasavya mārgasthā** of the right- and left-handed paths

N913 **sarvāpadvinivāriṇī** remover of misfortune

N914 **svasthā** free

N915 **svabhāvamadhurā** of sweet nature

N916 **dhīrā** wise

N917 **dhīra samarcitā** adored by the wise

N918 **caitanyārghya samārādhyā** consciousness as oblation

N919 **caitanya kusumapriyā** fond of the flower of consciousness

N920 **sadoditā** perpetually sublime

N921 **sadātuṣṭā** ever-content

N922 **taruṇāditya pāṭalā** rosy like the dawn

N923 **dakṣiṇādakṣinārādhyā** adored by sādhaka of the right- and left-handed paths

N924 **darasmera mukhāmbujā** lotus face beaming with smile

N925 **kaulinī kevalā** worshiped by Kaulas as the pure

N926 **anarghyā kaivalya padadāyinī** conferring priceless liberation

N927 **stotrapriyā** fond of praise

N928 **stutimatī** recipient of praise

N929 **śrutisaṃstuta vaibhavā** celebrated in scriptures

N930 **manasvinī** intelligence

N931 **māṇavatī** of high mind

N932 **maheśī** wife of Maheśa

N933 **maṅgalākṛtiḥ** good fortune

N934 **viśvamātā** mother of the universe

N935 **jagaddhātrī** support of the world

N936 **viśālākṣī** large-eyed

N937 **virāgiṇī** dispassionate

N938 **pragalbhā** resolute

N939 **paramodārā** supremely generous

N940 **parāmodā** supremely delightful

N941 **manomayī** mind

N942 **vyomakeśī** whose hair is space

N943 **vimānasthā** residing in celestial chariot

N944 **vajriṇī** lightning

N945 **vāmakeśvarī** worshiped by the Vāmācārins

N946 **pañcayajñapriyā** fond of the five sacrifices

N947 **pañcapreta mañcādhiśāyinī** reclining on the five-corpse throne

N948 **pañcamī** fifth (wife of Sadāśiva)

N949 **pañcabhūteśī** ruler of the five elements

N950 **pañca saṅkhyopacāriṇī** worshiped by the five objects

N951 **śāśvatī** eternal

N952 **śāśvataiśvaryā** possessing eternal sovereignity

N953 **śarmadā** bestower of happiness

N954 **śambhumohinī** deluding Śiva

N955 **dharā** earth

N956 **dharasutā** daughter of the Himālaya

N957 **dhanyā** auspicious

N958 **dharmiṇī** virtuous

N959 **dharmavardhinī** promoting dharma

N960 **lokātītā** transcending the worlds

N961 **guṇātītā** transcending the guṇas

N962 **sarvātītā** transcending all

N963 **śamātmikā** tranquil

N964 **bandhūka kusuma prakhyā** resembling the bandhūka flower

N965 **bālā** girl (child-like)

N966 **līlāvinodinī** taking pleasure in sport

N967 **sumaṅgalī** very auspicious

N968 **sukhakarī** giving happiness

N969 **suveṣāḍyā** decked in auspiciousness

N970 **suvāsinī** ever the wife of Śiva

N971 **suvāsinyarcanaprītā** delighting in adoration by suvāsinīs

N972 **āśobhanā** ever beautiful

N973 **śuddha mānasā** pure minded

N974 **bindu tarpaṇa santuṣṭā** pleased by oblations to the bindu

N975 **pūrvajā** first-born

N976 **tripurāmbikā** Tripurāmbikā

N977 **daśamudrā samārādhyā** worshiped by the ten mudrās

N978 **tripurā śrīvaśaṅkarī** ruler of Tripurā

N979 **Jñānamudrā** mudrā of knowledge

N980 **jñānagamyā** attained by knowledge

N981 **jñānajñeya svarūpiṇī** knowledge and knowing

N982 **yonimudrā** yonimudrā

N983 **trikhaṇḍeśī** ruler of Trikhaṇḍā

N984 **triguṇā** endowed with the three guṇas

N985 **ambā** Mother

N986 **trikoṇagā** residing in the trikoṇa

N987 **anaghā** sinless

N988 **adbhuta cāritrā** of astonishing deeds

N989 **vāñchitārtha pradāyinī** bestowing all desires

N990 **abhyāsāti śayajñātā** known through constant devotion

N991 **ṣaḍadhvātīta rūpiṇī** transcending the six methods

N992 **avyāja karuṇāmūrtih** unconditioned compassion

N993 **ajñānadhvānta dīpikā** lamp that dispels the darkness of ignorance

N994 **ābālagopa viditā** accessible to children and cowherds

N995 **sarvānullaṅghya śāsanā** whose commands are never disobeyed

N996 **śrī cakrarājanilayā** residing in the king of cakras, the Śrīcakra

N997 **śrīmat tripurasundarī** the auspicious Tripurasundarī

N998 **śrī śivā** auspicious Śiva

N999 **śivaśaktyaikya rūpiṇī** union of Śiva-Śakti

N1000 **Lalitāmbikā** Mother Lalitā

THE THOUSAND NAMES OF LALITĀ

Dhyānam

sindhūrāruṇa vigrahāṃ triṇayanāṃ
māṇikya maulisphurattārānāyaka śekharāṃ
smitamukhīmāpīna vakṣoruhām |
pāṇibhyāmalipūrṇa ratna caṣakaṃ
raktotpalaṃ bibhratīṃ
saumyāṃ ratnaghaṭastha rakta caraṇāṃ
dhyāyetparām-ambikām || 1 ||

aruṇāṃ karuṇā taraṅgitākṣīṃ
dhṛtapāśāṅkuśa puṣpabāṇacāpām |
aṇimādibhirāvṛtā mayūkhaiḥ
ahamityeva vibhāvaye bhavānīm || 2 ||

dhyāyet padmāsanasthāṃ vikasitavadanāṃ
padma patrāyatākṣīṃ hemābhāṃ pītavastrāṃ
karakalita
lasamaddhemapadmāṃ varāṅgīm |
sarvālaṅkārayuktāṃ satatamamabhayadāṃ
bhaktanamrāṃ bhavānīṃ śrīvidyāṃ śāntamūrtiṃ
sakala surasutāṃ sarvasampatpradātrīm || 3 ||

sakuṅkuma vilepanāmalikacumbi kastūrikāṃ
samanda hasitekṣaṇāṃ saśaracāpa pāśāṅkuśām |
aśeṣa janamohinīm aruṇamālya bhūṣāmbarām
japākusuma bhāsurāṃ japavidhau smaredambikām
|| 4 ||

Śrī Lalitā Sahasranāma Stotram

śrī mātā śrī mahārāṅñī śrīmat-siṃhāsaneśvarī |
cidagni kuṇḍa sambhūtā devakārya samudyatā || 1 ||

udyadbhānu sahasrābhā caturbāhu samanvitā |
rāgasvarūpa pāśāḍhyā krodhākārāṅkuśojjvalā || 2 ||

manorūpekṣukodaṇḍā pañcatanmātra sāyakā |
nijāruṇa prabhāpūra majjad-brahmāṇḍamaṇḍalā
|| 3 ||

campakāśoka punnāga saugandhika lasatkacā
kuruvinda maṇiśreṇī kanatkoṭīra maṇḍitā || 4 ||

aṣṭamī candra vibhrāja dalikasthala śobhitā |
mukhacandra kalaṅkābha mṛganābhi viśeṣakā || 5 ||

vadanasmara māṅgalya gṛhatoraṇa cillikā |
vaktralakṣmī parīvāha calanmīnābha locanā || 6 ||

navacampaka puṣpābha nāsādaṇḍa virājitā |
tārākānti tiraskāri nāsābharaṇa bhāsurā || 7 ||

kadamba mañjarīklupta karṇapūra manoharā |
tāṭaṅka yugalībhūta tapanoḍupa maṇḍalā || 8 ||

padmarāga śilādarśa paribhāvi kapolabhūḥ |
navavidruma bimbaśrīḥ nyakkāri radanacchadā || 9 ||

śuddha vidyāṅkurākāra dvijapaṅkti dvayojjvalā |
karpūravīṭi kāmoda samākarṣa digantarā || 10 ||

nijasallāpa mādhurya vinirbhartsita kacchapī |
mandasmita prabhāpūra majjat-kāmeśa mānasā || 11 ||

anākalita sādṛśya cibuka śrī virājitā |
kāmeśabaddha māṅgalya sūtraśobhita kantharā || 12 ||

kanakāṅgada keyūra kamanīya bhujānvitā |
ratnagraiveya cintāka lolamuktā phalānvitā || 13 ||

kāmeśvara premaratna maṇi pratipaṇastanī|
nābhyālavāla romālī latāphala kucadvayī || 14 ||

lakṣyaromalatā dhāratā samunneya madhyamā |
stanabhāra dalan-madhya paṭṭabandha valitrayā
|| 15 ||

aruṇāruṇa kausumbha vastra bhāsvat-kaṭītaṭī |
ratnakiṅkiṇi kāramya raśanādāma bhūṣitā || 16 ||

kāmeśa ṅñāta saubhāgya mārdavorudvayānvitā |
māṇikya makuṭākāra jānudvaya virājitā || 17 ||

indragopa parikṣipta smara tūṇābha jaṅghikā |
gūḍhagulphā kūrmapṛṣṭha jayiṣṇu prapadānvitā
|| 18 ||

nakhadīdhiti saṃchanna namajjana tamoguṇā |
padadvaya prabhājāla parākṛta saroruhā || 19 ||

śiñjāna maṇimañjīra maṇḍita śrī padāmbujā |
marālī mandagamanā mahālāvaṇya śevadhiḥ || 20 ||

sarvāruṇā navadyāṅgī sarvābharaṇa bhūṣitā |
śivakāmeśvarāṅkasthā śivā svādhīna vallabhā || 21 ||

sumeru madhyaśṛṅgasthā śrīmannagara nāyikā |
cintāmaṇi gṛhāntasthā pañcabrahmāsanasthitā || 22 ||

mahāpadmāṭavī saṃsthā kadamba vanavāsinī |
sudhāsāgara madhyasthā kāmākṣī kāmadāyinī
|| 23 ||

devarṣi gaṇasaṅghāta stūyamānātma vaibhavā |
bhaṇḍāsura vadhodyukta śaktisenā samanvitā || 24 ||

sampatkarī samārūḍha sindhura vrajasevitā |
aśvārūḍhādhiṣṭhitāśva koṭikoṭi bhirāvṛtā || 25 ||

cakrarāja rathārūḍha sarvāyudha pariṣkṛtā |
geyacakra rathārūḍha mantriṇī parisevitā || 26 ||

kiricakra rathārūḍha daṇḍanāthā puraskṛtā |
jvālāmālini kākṣipta vahniprākāra madhyagā || 27 ||

bhaṇḍasainya vadhodyukta śakti vikramaharṣitā |
nityā parākramāṭopa nirīkṣaṇa samutsukā || 28 ||

bhaṇḍaputra vadhodyukta bālāvikrama nanditā |
mantriṇyambā viracita viṣaṅga vadhatoṣitā || 29 ||

viśukra prāṇaharaṇa vārāhī vīryananditā |
kāmeśvara mukhāloka kalpita śrī gaṇeśvarā || 30 ||

mahāgaṇeśa nirbhinna vighnayantra praharṣitā |
bhaṇḍāsurendra nirmukta śastra pratyastra varṣiṇī || 31 ||

karāṅguli nakhotpanna nārāyaṇa daśākṛtiḥ |
mahāpāśupatāstrāgni nirdagdhāsura sainikā || 32 ||

kāmeśvarāstra nirdagdha sabhaṇḍāsura śūnyakā |
brahmopendra mahendrādi devasaṃstuta vaibhavā || 33 ||

haranetrāgni sandagdha kāma sañjīvanauṣadhiḥ |
śrīmadvāgbhava kūṭaika svarūpa mukhapaṅkajā || 34 ||

kaṇṭhādhaḥ kaṭiparyanta madhyakūṭa svarūpiṇī |
śaktikūṭaika tāpanna kaṭyathobhāga dhāriṇī || 35 ||

mūlamantrātmikā mūlakūṭa traya kalebarā |
kulāmṛtaika rasikā kulasaṅketa pālinī || 36 ||

kulāṅganā kulāntaḥsthā kaulinī kulayoginī |
akulā samayāntaḥsthā samayācāra tatparā || 37 ||

mūlādhāraika nilayā brahmagranthi vibhedinī |
maṇipūrānta ruditā viṣṇugranthi vibhedinī || 38 ||

ājñā cakrāntarālasthā rudragranthi vibhedinī |
sahasrārāmbujā rūḍhā sudhāsārābhi varṣiṇī || 39 ||

taṭillatā samaruciḥ ṣaṭ-cakropari saṃsthitā |
mahāśaktiḥ kuṇḍalinī bisatantu tanīyasī || 40 ||

bhavānī bhāvanāgamyā bhavāraṇya kuṭhārikā |
bhadrapriyā bhadramūrtir bhaktasaubhāgya dāyinī || 41 ||

bhaktipriyā bhaktigamyā bhaktivaśyā bhayāpahā |
śāmbhavī śāradārādhyā śarvāṇī śarmadāyinī || 42 ||

śāṅkarī śrīkarī sādhvī śaraccandranibhānanā |
śātodarī śāntimatī nirādhārā nirañjanā || 43 ||

nirlepā nirmalā nityā nirākārā nirākulā |
nirguṇā niṣkalā śāntā niṣkāmā nirupaplavā || 44 ||

nityamuktā nirvikārā niṣprapañcā nirāśrayā |
nityaśuddhā nityabuddhā niravadyā nirantarā || 45 ||

niṣkāraṇā niṣkalaṅkā nirupādhir nirīśvarā |
nīrāgā rāgamathanī nirmadā madanāśinī || 46 ||

niścintā nirahaṅkārā nirmohā mohanāśinī |
nirmamā mamatāhantrī niṣpāpā pāpanāśinī || 47 ||

niṣkrodhā krodhaśamanī nirlobhā lobhanāśinī |
niḥsaṃśayā saṃśayaghnī nirbhavā bhavanāśinī || 48 ||

nirvikalpā nirābādhā nirbhedā bhedanāśinī |
nirnāśā mṛtyumathanī niṣkriyā niṣparigrahā || 49 ||

nistulā nīlacikurā nirapāyā niratyayā |
durlabhā durgamā durgā duḥkhahantrī sukhapradā || 50 ||

duṣṭadūrā durācāra śamanī doṣavarjitā |
sarvajñā sāndrakaruṇā samānādhikavarjitā || 51 ||

sarvaśaktimayī sarvamaṅgalā sadgatipradā |
sarveśvarī sarvamayī sarvamantra svarūpiṇī || 52 ||

sarvayantrātmikā sarvatantrarūpā manonmanī |
māheśvarī mahādevī mahālakṣmīr mṛḍapriyā || 53 ||

mahārūpā mahāpūjyā mahāpātaka nāśinī |
mahāmāyā mahāsattvā mahāśaktir mahāratiḥ || 54 ||

mahābhogā mahaiśvaryā mahāvīryā mahābalā |
mahābuddhir mahāsiddhir mahāyogeśvareśvarī || 55 ||

mahātantrā mahāmantrā mahāyantrā mahāsanā |
mahāyāga kramārādhyā mahābhairava pūjitā || 56 ||

maheśvara mahākalpa mahātāṇḍava sākṣiṇī |
mahākāmeśa mahiṣī mahātripurasundarī || 57 ||

catuṣṣaṣṭyupacārāḍhyā catuṣṣaṣṭi kalāmayī |
mahācatuṣṣaṣṭikoṭi yoginī gaṇasevitā || 58 ||

manuvidyā candravidyā candramaṇḍalamadhyagā |
cārurūpā cāruhāsā cārucandra kalādharā || 59 ||

carācara jagannāthā cakrarāja niketanā |
pārvatī padmanayanā padmarāga samaprabhā || 60 ||

pañcapretāsanāsīnā pañcabrahma svarūpiṇī |
cinmayī paramānandā vijñāna ghanarūpiṇī || 61 ||

dhyānadhyātṛ dhyeyarūpā dharmādharma vivarjitā |
viśvarūpā jāgariṇī svapantī taijasātmikā || 62 ||

suptā prājñātmikā turyā sarvāvasthā vivarjitā |
sṛṣṭikartrī brahmarūpā goptrī govindarūpiṇī || 63 ||

saṃhāriṇī rudrarūpā tirodhānakarīśvarī |
sadāśivānugrahadā pañcakṛtya parāyaṇā || 64 ||

bhānumaṇḍala madhyasthā bhairavī bhagamālinī |
padmāsanā bhagavatī padmanābha sahodarī || 65 ||

unmeṣa nimiṣotpanna vipanna bhuvanāvaliḥ |
sahasraśīrṣavadanā sahasrākṣī sahasrapāt || 66 ||

ābrahma kīṭajananī varṇāśrama vidhāyinī |
nijājñārūpanigamā puṇyāpuṇya phalapradā || 67 ||

śruti sīmanta sindhūrīkṛta pādābjadhūlikā |
sakalāgama sandoha śuktisampuṭa mauktikā || 68 ||

puruṣārthapradā pūrṇā bhoginī bhuvaneśvarī |
ambikā nādi nidhanā haribrahmendra sevitā || 69 ||

nārāyaṇī nādarūpā nāmarūpa vivarjitā |
hrīṅkārī hrīmatī hṛdyā heyopādeya varjitā || 70 ||

rājarājārcitā rājñī ramyā rājīvalocanā |
rañjanī ramaṇī rasyā raṇatkiṅkiṇi mekhalā || 71 ||

ramā rākenduvadanā ratirūpā ratipriyā |
rakṣākarī rākṣasaghnī rāmā ramaṇalampaṭā || 72 ||

kāmyā kāmakalārūpā kadamba kusumapriyā |
kalyāṇī jagatīkandā karuṇārasa sāgarā || 73 ||

kalāvatī kalālāpā kāntā kādambarīpriyā |
varadā vāmanayanā vāruṇīmadavihvalā || 74 ||

viśvādhikā vedavedyā vindhyācala nivāsinī |
vidhātrī vedajananī viṣṇumāyā vilāsinī || 75 ||

kṣetrasvarūpā kṣetreśī kṣetra kṣetrajña pālinī |
kṣayavṛddhi vinirmuktā kṣetrapāla samarcitā || 76 ||

vijayā vimalā vandyā vandāru janavatsalā |
vāgvādinī vāmakeśī vahnimaṇḍala vāsinī || 77 ||

bhaktimat-kalpalatikā paśupāśa vimocanī |
saṃhṛtāśeṣa pāṣaṇḍā sadācāra pravartikā || 78 ||

tāpatrayāgni santapta samāhlādana candrikā |
taruṇī tāpasārādhyā tanumadhyā tamopahā || 79 ||

citis tatpadalakṣyārthā cideka rasarūpiṇī |
svātmānandalavībhūta brahmādyānanda santatiḥ
|| 80 ||

parā pratyakcitī rūpā paśyantī paradevatā |
madhyamā vaikharīrūpā bhaktamānasa haṃsikā
|| 81 ||

kāmeśvara prāṇanāḍī kṛtajñā kāmapūjitā |
śṛṅgāra rasasampūrṇā jayā jālandharasthitā || 82 ||

oḍyāṇa pīṭhanilayā bindumaṇḍala vāsinī |
rahoyāga kramārādhyā rahastarpaṇa tarpitā || 83 ||

sadyaḥ prasādinī viśvasākṣiṇī sākṣivarjitā |
ṣaḍaṅgadevatā yuktā ṣāḍguṇya paripūritā || 84 ||

nityaklinnā nirupamā nirvāṇa sukhadāyinī |
nityā ṣoḍaśikārūpā śrīkaṇṭhārdha śarīriṇī || 85 ||

prabhāvatī prabhārūpā prasiddhā parameśvarī |
mūlaprakṛti ravyaktā vyaktāvyakta svarūpiṇī || 86 ||

vyāpinī vividhākārā vidyāvidyā svarūpiṇī |
mahākāmeśa nayanā kumudāhlāda kaumudī || 87 ||

bhaktahārda tamobheda bhānumad-bhānusantatiḥ |
śivadūtī śivārādhyā śivamūrtiḥ śivaṅkarī || 88 ||

śivapriyā śivaparā śiṣṭeṣṭā śiṣṭapūjitā |
aprameyā svaprakāśā manovācāma gocarā || 89 ||

cicchaktiś cetanārūpā jaḍaśaktir jaḍātmikā |
gāyatrī vyāhṛtis sandhyā dvijabṛnda niṣevitā || 90 ||

tattvāsanā tattvamayī pañcakośāntarasthitā |
niḥsīmamahimā nityayauvanā madaśālinī || 91 ||

madaghūrṇita raktākṣī madapāṭala gaṇḍabhūḥ |
candana dravadigdhāṅgī cāmpeya kusuma priyā || 92 ||

kuśalā komalākārā kurukullā kuleśvarī |
kulakuṇḍālayā kaula mārgatatpara sevitā || 93 ||

kumāra gaṇanāthāmbā tuṣṭiḥ puṣṭir matir dhṛtiḥ |
śāntiḥ svastimatī kāntir nandinī vighnanāśinī || 94 ||

tejovatī trinayanā lolākṣī kāmarūpiṇī |
mālinī haṃsinī mātā malayācala vāsinī || 95 ||

sumukhī nalinī subhrūḥ śobhanā suranāyikā |
kālakaṇṭhī kāntimatī kṣobhiṇī sūkṣmarūpiṇī || 96 ||

vajreśvarī vāmadevī vayovasthā vivarjitā |
siddheśvarī siddhavidyā siddhamātā yaśasvinī || 97 ||

viśuddhi cakranilayā raktavarṇā trilocanā |
khaṭvāṅgādi praharaṇā vadanaika samanvitā || 98 ||

pāyasānnapriyā tvaksthā paśuloka bhayaṅkarī |
amṛtādi mahāśakti saṃvṛtā ḍākinīśvarī || 99 ||

anāhatābja nilayā śyāmābhā vadanadvayā |
daṃṣṭrojjvalā kṣamālādhidharā rudhira saṃsthitā || 100 ||

kālarātryādi śaktyoghavṛtā snigdhaudanapriyā |
mahāvīrendra varadā rākiṇyambā svarūpiṇī || 101 ||

maṇipūrābja nilayā vadanatraya saṃyutā |
vajrādhikāyudhopetā ḍāmaryādibhir āvṛtā || 102 ||

raktavarṇā māṃsaniṣṭhā guḍānna prītamānasā |
samasta bhaktasukhadā lākinyambā svarūpiṇī || 103 ||

svādhiṣṭhānāmbujagatā caturvaktra manoharā |
śūlādyāyudha sampannā pītavarṇātigarvitā || 104 ||

medoniṣṭhā madhuprītā bandinyādi samanvitā |
dadhyannāsakta hṛdayā kākinī rūpadhāriṇī || 105 ||

mūlā dhārāmbujārūḍhā pañcavaktrāsthisaṃsthitā |
aṅkuśādi praharaṇā varadādi niṣevitā || 106 ||

mudgaudanāsakta cittā sākinyambāsvarūpiṇī |
ājñā cakrābjanilayā śuklavarṇā ṣaḍānanā || 107 ||

majjāsaṃsthā haṃsavatī mukhyaśakti samanvitā |
haridrānnaika rasikā hākinī rūpadhāriṇī || 108 ||

sahasradala padmasthā sarvavarṇopa śobhitā |
sarvāyudhadharā śukla saṃsthitā sarvatomukhī
|| 109 ||

sarvaudana prītacittā yākinyambā svarūpiṇī |
svāhā svadhā matir medhā śrutiḥ smṛtir anuttamā
|| 110 ||

puṇyakīrtiḥ puṇyalabhyā puṇyaśravaṇa kīrtanā |
pulomajārcitā bandhamocanī bandhurālakā || 111 ||

vimarśarūpiṇī vidyā viyadādi jagatprasūḥ |
sarvavyādhi praśamanī sarvamṛtyu nivāriṇī || 112 ||

agragaṇyā cintyarūpā kalikalmaṣa nāśinī |
kātyāyinī kālahantrī kamalākṣa niṣevitā || 113 ||

tāmbūla pūrita mukhī dāḍimī kusumaprabhā |
mṛgākṣī mohinī mukhyā mṛḍānī mitrarūpiṇī || 114 ||

nityatṛptā bhaktanidhir niyantrī nikhileśvarī |
maitryādi vāsanālabhyā mahāpralaya sākṣiṇī || 115 ||

parāśaktiḥ parāniṣṭhā prajñāna ghanarūpiṇī |
mādhvīpānālasāmattā mātṛkā varṇa rūpiṇī || 116 ||

mahākailāsa nilayā mṛṇāla mṛdudorlatā |
mahanīyā dayāmūrtīr mahāsāmrājyaśālinī || 117 ||

ātmavidyā mahāvidyā śrīvidyā kāmasevitā |
śrīṣoḍaśākṣarī vidyā trikūṭā kāmakoṭikā || 118 ||

kaṭākṣakiṅkarī bhūta kamalā koṭisevitā |
śiraḥsthitā candranibhā phālasthendra
dhanuḥprabhā || 119 ||

hṛdayasthā raviprakhyā trikoṇāntara dīpikā |
dākṣāyaṇī daityahantrī dakṣayajña vināśinī || 120 ||

darāndolita dīrghākṣī darahāsojjvalanmukhī |
gurumūrtir guṇanidhir gomātā guhajanmabhūḥ
|| 121 ||

deveśī daṇḍanītisthā daharākāśa rūpiṇī |
pratipanmukhya rākānta tithimaṇḍala pūjitā || 122 ||

kalātmikā kalānāthā kāvyālāpa vinodinī |
sacāmara ramāvāṇī savyadakṣiṇa sevitā || 123 ||

ādiśakti rameyātmā paramā pāvanākṛtiḥ |
anekakoṭi brahmāṇḍa jananī divyavigrahā || 124 ||

klīṅkārī kevalā guhyā kaivalya padadāyinī |
tripurā trijagadvandyā trimūrtistridaśeśvarī || 125 ||

tryakṣarī divyagandhāḍhyā sindhūra tilakāñcitā |
umā śailendratanayā gaurī gandharva sevitā || 126 ||

viśvagarbhā svarṇagarbhā varadā vāgadhīśvarī |
dhyānagamyā paricchedyā jñānadā jñānavigrahā ||
127 ||

sarvavedānta saṃvedyā satyānanda svarūpiṇī |
lopāmudrārcitā līlāklṛpta brahmāṇḍamaṇḍalā || 128 ||

adṛśyā dṛśyarahitā vijñātrī vedyavarjitā |
yoginī yogadā yogyā yogānandā yugandharā || 129 ||

icchāśakti jñānaśakti kriyāśakti svarūpiṇī |
sarvādhārā supratiṣṭhā sadasadrūpa-dhāriṇī || 130 ||

aṣṭamūrtir-ajājaitrī lokayātrā vidhāyinī |
ekākinī bhūmarūpā nirdvaitā dvaitavarjitā || 131 ||

annadā vasudā vṛddhā brahmātmaikya svarūpiṇī |
bṛhatī brāhmaṇī brāhmī brahmānandā balipriyā
|| 132 ||

bhāṣārūpā bṛhatsenā bhāvābhāva vivarjitā |
sukhārādhyā śubhakarī śobhanā sulabhāgatiḥ || 133 ||

rājarājeśvarī rājyadāyinī rājyavallabhā |
rājat-kṛpā rājapīṭha niveśita nijāśritāḥ || 134 ||

rājyalakṣmīḥ kośanāthā caturaṅga baleśvarī |
sāmrājyadāyinī satyasandhā sāgaramekhalā || 135 ||

dīkṣitā daityaśamanī sarvaloka vaśaṅkarī |
sarvārthadātrī sāvitrī saccidānanda rūpiṇī || 136 ||

deśakālā paricchinnā sarvagā sarvamohinī |
sarasvatī śāstramayī guhāmbā guhyarūpiṇī || 137 ||

sarvopādhi vinirmuktā sadāśiva pativratā |
sampradāyeśvarī sādhvī gurumaṇḍala rūpiṇī || 138 ||

kulottīrṇā bhagārādhyā māyā madhumatī mahī |
gaṇāmbā guhyakārādhyā komalāṅgī gurupriyā
|| 139 ||

svatantrā sarvatantreśī dakṣiṇāmūrti rūpiṇī |
sanakādi samārādhyā śivajñāna pradāyinī || 140 ||

citkalā nandakalikā premarūpā priyaṅkarī |
nāmapārāyaṇa prītā nandividyā naṭeśvarī || 141 ||

mithyā jagadadhiṣṭhānā muktidā muktirūpiṇī |
lāsyapriyā layakarī lajjā rambhādi vanditā || 142 ||

bhavadā vasudhāvṛṣṭiḥ pāpāraṇya davānalā |
daurbhāgyatūla vātūlā jarādhvānta raviprabhā || 143 ||

bhāgyābdhicandrikā bhaktacittakeki ghanāghanā |
rogaparvata dambholir mṛtyudāru kuṭhārikā || 144 ||

maheśvarī mahākālī mahāgrāsā mahāśanā |
aparṇā caṇḍikā caṇḍamuṇḍāsura niṣūdinī || 145 ||

kṣarākṣarātmikā sarvalokeśī viśvadhāriṇī |
trivargadātrī subhagā tryambakā triguṇātmikā
|| 146 ||

svargāpavargadā śuddhā japāpuṣpa nibhākṛtiḥ |
ojovatī dyutidharā yajñarūpā priyavratā || 147 ||

durārādhyā durādharṣā pāṭalī kusumapriyā |
mahatī merunilayā mandāra kusumapriyā || 148 ||

vīrārādhyā virāḍrūpā virajā viśvatomukhī |
pratyagrūpā parākāśā prāṇadā prāṇarūpiṇī || 149 ||

mārtāṇḍa bhairavārādhyā mantriṇī nyastarājyadhūḥ |
tripureśī jayatsenā nistraiguṇyā parāparā || 150 ||

satyajñānānandarūpā sāmarasya parāyaṇā |
kapardinī kalāmālā kāmadhuk kāmarūpiṇī || 151 ||

kalānidhiḥ kāvyakalā rasajñā rasaśevadhiḥ |
puṣṭā purātanā pūjyā puṣkarā puṣkarekṣaṇā || 152 ||

parañjyotiḥ parandhāma paramāṇuḥ parātparā |
pāśahastā pāśahantrī paramantra vibhedinī || 153 ||

mūrtāmūrtā nityatṛptā muni mānasa haṃsikā |
satyavratā satyarūpā sarvāntaryāminī satī || 154 ||

brahmāṇī brahmajananī bahurūpā budhārcitā |
prasavitrī pracaṇḍājñā pratiṣṭhā prakaṭākṛtiḥ || 155 ||

prāṇeśvarī prāṇadātrī pañcāśat-pīṭharūpiṇī |
viśṛṅkhalā viviktasthā vīramātā viyatprasūḥ || 156 ||

mukundā mukti nilayā mūlavigraha rūpiṇī |
bhāvajñā bhavarogaghnī bhavacakra pravartinī || 157 ||

chandassārā śāstrasārā mantrasārā talodarī |
udārakīrtir uddāmavaibhavā varṇarūpiṇī || 158 ||

janmamṛtyu jarātapta jana viśrānti dāyinī |
sarvopaniṣa dudghuṣṭā śāntyatīta kalātmikā || 159 ||

gambhīrā gaganāntaḥsthā garvitā gānalolupā |
kalpanārahitā kāṣṭhā kāntā kāntārdha vigrahā || 160 ||

kāryakāraṇa nirmuktā kāmakeli taraṅgitā |
kanat-kanakatāṭaṅkā līlāvigraha dhāriṇī || 161 ||

ajākṣaya vinirmuktā mugdhā kṣipraprasādinī |
antarmukha samārādhyā bahirmukha sudurlabhā || 162 ||

trayī trivarga nilayā tristhā tripuramālinī |
nirāmayā nirālambā svātmārāmā sudhāsṛtiḥ || 163 ||

saṃsārapaṅka nirmagna samuddharaṇa paṇḍitā |
yajñapriyā yajñakartrī yajamāna svarūpiṇī || 164 ||

dharmādhārā dhanādhyakṣā dhanadhānya vivardhinī |
viprapriyā viprarūpā viśvabhramaṇa kāriṇī || 165 ||

viśvagrāsā vidrumābhā vaiṣṇavī viṣṇurūpiṇī |
ayonir yoninilayā kūṭasthā kularūpiṇī || 166 ||

vīragoṣṭhīpriyā vīrā naiṣkarmyā nādarūpiṇī |
vijñāna kalanā kalyā vidagdhā baindavāsanā || 167 ||

tattvādhikā tattvamayī tattvamartha svarūpiṇī |
sāmagānapriyā saumyā sadāśiva kuṭumbinī || 168 ||

savyāpasavya mārgasthā sarvāpadvinivāriṇī |
svasthā svabhāvamadhurā dhīrā dhīra samarcitā
|| 169 ||

caitanyārghya samārādhyā caitanya kusumapriyā |
sadoditā sadātuṣṭā taruṇāditya pāṭalā || 170 ||

dakṣiṇādakṣiṇārādhyā darasmera mukhāmbujā |
kaulinī kevalānarghyā kaivalya padadāyinī || 171 ||

stotrapriyā stutimatī śrutisaṃstuta vaibhavā |
manasvinī mānavatī maheśī maṅgalākṛtiḥ || 172 ||

viśvamātā jagaddhātrī viśālākṣī virāgiṇī|
pragalbhā paramodārā parāmodā manomayī || 173 ||

vyomakeśī vimānasthā vajriṇī vāmakeśvarī |
pañcayajñapriyā pañcapreta mañcādhiśāyinī || 174 ||

pañcamī pañcabhūteśī pañca saṅkhyopacāriṇī |
śāśvatī śāśvataiśvaryā śarmadā śambhumohinī
|| 175 ||

dharā dharasutā dhanyā dharmiṇī dharmavardhinī |
lokātītā guṇātītā sarvātītā śamātmikā || 176 ||

bandhūka kusuma prakhyā bālā līlāvinodinī |
sumaṅgalī sukhakarī suveṣāḍyā suvāsinī || 177 ||

suvāsinyarcanaprītā śobhanā śuddha mānasā |
bindu tarpaṇa santuṣṭā pūrvajā tripurāmbikā || 178 ||

daśamudrā samārādhyā tripurā śrīvaśaṅkarī |
jñānamudrā jñānagamyā jñānajñeya svarūpiṇī || 179 ||

yonimudrā trikhaṇḍeśī triguṇāmbā trikoṇagā |
anaghādbhuta cāritrā vāñchitārtha pradāyinī || 180 ||

abhyāsāti śayajñātā ṣaḍadhvātīta rūpiṇī |
avyāja karuṇāmūrtir ajñānadhvānta dīpikā || 181 ||

ābālagopa viditā sarvānullaṅghya śāsanā |
śrī cakrarājanilayā śrīmat tripurasundarī || 182 ||

śrī śivā śivaśaktyaikya rūpiṇī lalitāmbikā || 183 ||

evaṃ śrīlalitādevyā nāmnāṃ sāhasrakañjaguḥ ||

iti śrī brahmāṇḍapurāṇe uttarakhaṇḍe
śrī hayagrīvāgastya saṃvāde
śrī lalitā sahasranāmastotra kathanaṃ sampūrṇam ||

RESOURCES

Lalitā Sahasranāma

1. Sastry, Ananthakrishna R. *Lalitā Sahasranāma With Bhāskararāyas Commentary Translated Into English*. Madras: Adyar Library and Research Centre (first edition 1899, last edition 2010). This is the most accessible English translation of Bhāskararāya's commentary on the Lalitā Sahasranāma.

2. Tapasyananda, Swami *Śrī Lalitā Sahasranāma: The Text, Transliteration and English Translation*. Mylapore, Chennai: Śrī Ramakrishna Math Printing Press, 2006. This is a text of the Lalitā Sahasranāma with a concise introduction.

Śrīvidyā (by no means an exhaustive list):

3. Avalon, Arthur. *Kāmakalā Vilāsa by Puṇyānanda Nātha with the commentary of Naṭanānanda Nātha*. Madras: Ganesh and Co (Pvt) Ltd, 1961. A comprehensive examination of Kāmakalā in English.

4. Avalon, Arthur, Shastri, Lakshmana *Tantraraja Tantra*. Delhi: Motilal Banarsidass, 2000. Although the text is in Sanskrit, this version has an excellent introduction by Arthur Avalon.

5. Avalon, Arthur. *Tantra of the Great Liberation: Mahanirvana Tantra*. Rockville, MD: Wildside Press, 2009. The most accessible English translation of an essential Tāntrik text.

6. Bhāskararāya, Sastri, Subrahmanya S. *Varivasyā-Rahasya and its commentary*. Chennai: Adyar Library and Research Centre, 2000. This is the most accessible English version of Bhāskararāya's Varivasyā Rahasya, which explains the manifold meanings of the Pañcadaśi mantra.

7. Bowden, Michael M *The Goddess and The Guru*. 45th Parallel Press, 2017. This book details the remarkable journey of Śrī Amritananda Natha Saraswati from his education and work as an eminent scientist to becoming a Śrīvidyā adept and founder of the temple at Devipuram.

8. Bowden, Michael M, ed. *Gifts from the Goddess: Selected Works of Śrī Amritananda Natha Saraswati*. 45th Parallel Press, 2019. This book is a much-anticipated resource of Śrīvidyā traditions and procedures as expounded by Śrī Amritananda Natha Saraswati.

9. Brooks, Douglas R. *Auspicious Wisdom: The Texts and Traditions of Śrīvidyā Śākta Tantrism in South India.* Albany, NY: SUNY Press, 1992. This is an academic exploration of the tradition of Śrīvidyā and a good resource for upāsakas interested in learning more about the context and history of the path.

10. Caitanyānandā. *Śrī Vidyā Śrī Cakra Pūjā Vidhiḥ.* Rush NY: Śrī Vidyā Temple Society, 2013. This is the most comprehensive handbook on the Śrīcakra pūjā, and is highly recommended for upāsakas interested in performing the pūjā as part of their sādhanā.

11. Chinnaiyan, Kavitha M. *Shakti Rising: Embracing Shadow and Light on the Goddess Path to Wholeness.* Oakland, CA: New Harbinger Publications, 2017. A comprehensive exploration of the Daśa Mahāvidyās with extensive practice prompts for sādhanā.

12. Finn, Louise M. *The Kulacūḍāmaṇi Tantra and the Vāmakeśvara Tantra with the Jayaratha Commentary.* Otio Harrassowitz Wiesbaden 1986. A scholarly exploration of two important Tāntrik texts of the Kaula tradition.

13. Kaviraj, Gopinath M. M. *Selected Writings.* Varanasi: Indica Books, 2006. A very handy resource for understanding key concepts of Tantra.

14. Kinsley, D. R. *Tantric Visions of the Divine Feminine: The Ten Mahavidyas.* Berkeley: University of California Press, 1997. Scholarly and thorough, this book describes the Mahavidyas in detail.

15. Lakshmanjoo, Swami. *Shiva Sutras, The Supreme Awakening.* Culver City, CA: Universal Shaiva Fellowship, 2007. A superb commentary on the Śiva Sūtras by one of the last lineage holders of Non-dual Śaiva Tantra.

16. Padoux, André (translated by Jacques Gontier), Vāc. *The Concept of the Word in Selected Hindu Tantras.* Delhi: Sri Satguru Publications, 1992. Thorough and superb work on Vāc (or Vāk) in Tantra; an essential read.

17. Padoux, André, Jeanty, Roger-Orphé. *The Heart of the Yogini: The Yoginihrdaya, A Sanskrit Tantric Treatise.* Oxford, UK: Oxford University Press, 2013. The most accessible English translation of an essential Śrīvidyā text.

18. *Paraśurāmakalpasūtra.* A reliable and easy-to-understand English translation is difficult to find in book form. Here is an excellent online resource to learn about this essential Śrīvidyā text: http://amritananda-natha-saraswati.blogspot.com/p/parashurama-kalpa-sutra.html (last accessed on August 19, 2019).

19. Pandit, M.P. *Bases of Tantra Sādhanā.* Pondicherry: Dipti Publications, 1972. An English commentary on the *Paraśurāmakalpasūtra.*

20. Rao, Ramachandra S.K *Śrīvidyā kośa.* Delhi: Sri Satguru Publications, 2005. An exploration of Śrīvidyā and its many contexts, this is a wonderful resource for practitioners.

21. Rao, Ramachandra S.K. *The Tantra of Sri-Chakra (Bhavanopanishat).* Delhi: Sri Satguru Publications, 2008. Based on the Bhāvanā Upaniṣad, this book examines the Śrīcakra for practice.

22. Sastri, Srikanta S. *Iconography of Śrī Vidyarnava Tantra.* Mysore, 1944.

23. Shankaranarayanan, S. *Sri Chakra.* Chennai: Samata Books, 2013. This is a short and concise explanation of the Śrīcakra.

24. Shankaranarayanan, S. *The Ten Great Cosmic Powers.* Chennai, Tamil Nadu, India: Samata Books, 2013. A concise and yet superb exploration of the Daśa Mahāvidyās.

25. Silburn, Lilian. *Kuṇḍalinī: Energy of the Depths.* Albany, NY: SUNY Press 1988. An excellent work on the concept of Kuṇḍalinī in Tāntrik traditions.

26. Singh, Jaideva (Edited by Bettina Bäumer) *Parā-trīśikā-Vivaraṇa. The Secret of Tantric Mysticism.* Delhi: Motilal Banarsidass, 8th reprint 2017. An accessible English translation and commentary on a very dense and essential Tāntrik text.

27. Tapasyananda, Swami. *Saundarya Lahari of Sri Sankaracarya.* Ramakrishna Math, 1987. An excellent commentary on an essential Śrīvidyā text.

28. Wallis, Christopher D. *The Recognition Sutras: Illuminating a 1,000-Year-Old Spiritual Masterpiece.* Mattamayura Press, 2017. A modern commentary on the Pratyabhijña Hṛdayam, useful for practitioners of Śrīvidyā and Non-dual Śaiva Tantra.

Othr relevant books

1. Amazzone, Laura. *Goddess Durga and Sacred Female Power.* Hamilton Books, 2010.
2. Dyczkowski, Mark S. G. *The Doctrine of Vibration. An Analysis of the Doctrines and Practices of Kashmir Shaivism.* Albany, NY: SUNY Press, 1987. Excellent academic exploration of the principle of spanda in Non-dual Śaiva Tantra.
3. Johari, H. *Tools for Tantra.* Rochester, VT: Destiny Books, 1988. This is a practical handbook for those interested in traditional practices of tantra, including sacred sound and geometry.
4. Kali, Devadatta. *In Praise of the Goddess: The Devīmahātmaya and Its Meaning.* Berwick, ME: Nicolas-Hays, 2003. This is an excellent commentary and analysis of the Devī Mahātmyam, particularly useful for sādhanā.
5. Kempton, S. *Awakening Shakti: The Transformative Power of the Goddesses of Yoga.* Boulder, CO: Sounds True, 2013. This book contains comprehensive descriptions of Shakti in her different forms, including practices to realize them.
6. Kempton, Sally. *Doorways to the Infinite: The Art and Practice of Tantric Meditation.* Boulder, CO: Sounds True, 2014. A modern and accessible exploration of the Vijñāna Bhairava Tantra, an essential text of Non-dual Śākta-Śaiva Tantra
7. Lakshmanjoo, Swami. *Vijnana Bhairava: The Manual for Self- Realization*: New Delhi: Munshiram Manoharlal Publishers Pvt. Ltd., 2011. Well-organized commentary on an essential text of Non-dual Śaiva Tantra.
8. Muller-Ortega, Paul Eduardo. *The Triadic Heart of Śiva. Kaula Tantricism of Abhinavagupta in the Non-dual Shaivisim of Kashmir.* Albany, NY: SUNY Press, 1989. Comprehensive work on Abhinavagupta's teachings on Non-dual Śaiva Tantra.
9. Odier, D. *Tantric Kali: Secret Practices and Rituals.* New York, NY: Inner Traditions, 2016. An exploration of the left-handed path of goddess worship.
10. Rai, Ramkumar, *Mantra Mahodadhih,* 2 volumes. Benaras: Prachya Prakashan, 1992. The most accessible English translation of one of the authoritative texts on mantra sādhanā.
11. Swami, Om. *The Ancient Science of Mantras: Wisdom of the Sages.* Black Lotus, 2017. An excellent resource for understanding the science and practice of mantras.
12. Wallis, Christopher D. *Tantra Illuminated: The Philosophy, History, and Practice of a Timeless Tradition.* Mattamayura Press, 2013. A comprehensive examination of Tantra and its myriad nuances, and much-needed resource for those interested in learning about classical Tantra.

Websites

(last accessed on August 19, 2019)

1. http://amritananda-natha-saraswati.blogspot.com/. A comprehensive blog with articles by Śrī Amritananda Natha Saraswati, my parama guru and founder of the temple at Devipuram in India.
2. https://www.devipuram.com/. The official website of the Devipuram temple in India.
3. https://grdiyers.weebly.com/. An excellent resource for learning chants, pujas and other nuances of Santana Dharma.
4. https://hareesh.org. This site contains excellent articles and blog posts by Hareesh (Christopher) Wallis on Non-dual Śaiva Tantra.
5. https://www.kamakotimandali.com/. A superb resource for Śrīvidyā and related texts, practices and articles.
6. https://kavithamd.com. This is my website where I post frequently about Śrīvidyā, Non-dual Śaiva Tantra and non-duality.
7. https://manblunder.com. An informative website for Śrīvidyā-related articles and practices.
8. http://omswami.com/. An excellent resource for living spirituality, with posts written by Om Swami. Swamiji is a dynamic example of the fruit of Śrīvidyā sādhanā.
9. http://www.shivashakti.com/. An excellent resource for Śrīvidyā-related texts, practices and articles.
10. https://sreenivasaraos.com. An informative website for Śrīvidyā-related articles and practices.
11. https://srividyasadhana.com. An informative website for Śrīvidyā-related articles and practices, dīkṣa information and events.
12. https://srividya.org. The official website of the Rā.

About the Author

Dr. Kavitha Chinnaiyan (Saundaryāmbikā) is a cardiologist and Professor of Medicine at Oakland University William Beaumont School of Medicine in Royal Oak, MI. An initiate in the Tāntrik lineages of Śrī Vidyā and Nondual Saiva Tantra (also known as Kashmir Saivisim), she has studied Advaita Vedānta, Ayurveda, and Yoga with teachers across the globe. Her workshops, courses and writings on meditation, Yoga, Tantra, Ayurveda and non-duality strive to bring these time-honored traditions to modern living in practical ways. She is the author of *The Heart of Wellness* (Llewellyn Publications, January 2018), and *Shakti Rising* (Non-Duality Press, October 2017), which won the Nautilus Gold Award in the category Religion/Spirituality–Eastern Thought, 2017.

Audio files

A valuable resource of Vedic hymns and mantras (including the *Lalitā Sahasranāma* in its entirety) chanted and sung by Kavitha can be found on her website: https://kavithamd.com/chants/ and on Soundcloud: https://soundcloud.com/user-662757549/lalita-sahasranama

A reader describes Kavitha's rendering of the *Lalitā Sahasranāma* as "*Hauntingly beautiful and emotive while being true to the ageless wisdom from which it springs*".

Books in print from New Sarum Press

Real World Nonduality—Reports From The Field;
Various authors

The Ten Thousand Things by Robert Saltzman

Depending on No-Thing by Robert Saltzman

The Joy of True Meditation by Jeff Foster

'What the...' A Conversation About Living by Darryl Bailey

The Freedom to Love—The Life and Vision of Catherine Harding by Karin Visser

Death: The End of Self-Improvement by Joan Tollifson

Coming in Winter 2019/Spring 2020

Collision with the Infinite by Suzanne Segal

Open to the Unknown by Jean Klein

Transmission of the Flame by Jean Klein

Yoga in The Kashmir Tradition (2nd Edition) by Billy Doyle

The Mirage of Separation by Billy Doyle

Conversations on Non-Duality
Twenty-six Awakenings

Interviews by Iain and Renate McNay for conscious.tv

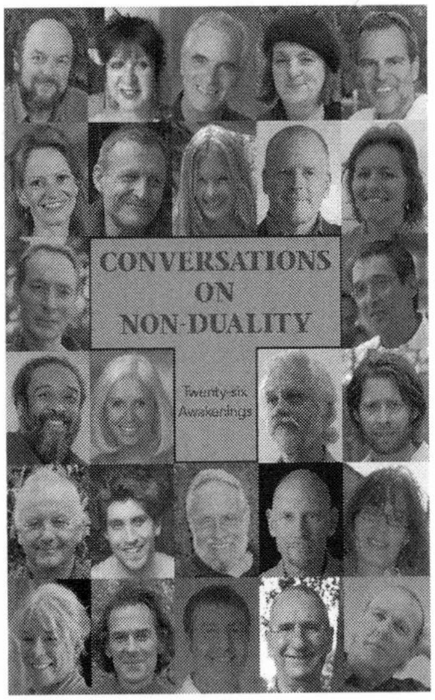

Self-realisation, awakening or enlightenment has been the goal of spiritual seeking since time immemorial. Another way of saying this is that everyone is searching for happiness. What is the nature of this happiness? What is the self that is to be realised? What is meant by 'awakening' or 'enlightenment'? Can it be brought about by effort? To whom does it occur? How is it expressed in life?

Everybody seeks happiness although it is not often noticed that seeking itself is precisely the activity that veils the very happiness that is being sought. When it is seen very clearly that happiness is not to be found in any particular object, state of circumstance, a deep relaxation takes place. This relaxation leaves us at the threshold of another possibility. This possibility is felt as an invitation from an unknown and yet strangely familiar direction. It is a call to return to our true home, the source of happiness.

Conversations on Non-Duality gives twenty-six expressions of liberation which have been shaped by different life experiences, each offering a unique perspective.

David Bingham, Daniel Brown, Sundance Burke, Katie Davis, Peter Fenner, Steve Ford, Jeff Foster, Suzanne Foxton, Gangaji, Richard Lang, Roger Linden, Wayne Liquorman, Francis Lucille, Mooji, Catherine Noyce, Jac O'Keeffe, Tony Parsons, Bernie Prior, Halina Pytlasinska, Genpo Roshi, Florian Schlosser, Mandi Solk, Rupert Spira, James Swartz, Richard Sylvester and Pamela Wilson.

www.conscious.tv

Made in the USA
Middletown, DE
20 March 2021

35907565R00175